LASHON HAKODESH

History, Holiness, & Hebrew

MOSAICA PRESS

LASHON HAKODESH

History, Holiness, & Hebrew

A Linguistic Journey from Eden to Israel

BY RABBI REUVEN CHAIM KLEIN

Anyone who has a copy of the first edition may receive a free PDF of the "Additions and Corrections" section of this edition by sending a request to historyofhebrew@gmail.com

Mosaica Press, Inc.

First edition: 2014
Revised Second edition: 2015

Edited by Shira Yael Klein

Typeset and designed by Daniella Kirsch

ISBN-10: 1937887545 ISBN-13: 978-1-937887-54-4

Published and distributed by:

Mosaica Press, Inc.

www.mosaicapress.com

info@mosaicapress.com

In Honor of our Children and Grandchildren

The Teichman Family

Los Angeles, CA

Sponsored by Max and Judy Steg

הונצח ע"י

הרב מרדכי חיים ורעייתו מרת יטש שטעג הי"ו

in loving memory of their parents
Israel and Feigey Steg

לז"נ ישראל בן מאיר ואלטע פייגע בת מרדכי ז"ל

and

Kalman and Katherine Messinger

לז"נ קלונימוס קלמן בן שמעון וקיילע בת ברוך ז"ל

ת.נ.צ.ב.ה.

Lovingly dedicated by
David Aaron and Edi Boxstein
l'zecher neshamos

Chaim ben Zissel and Rachel bas Chaim Dovid

לז"נ חיים בן זיסל ורחל בת חיים דוד ע"ה

whose enduring memories have inspired generations of maasim tovim and Torah learning.

This work is dedicated to our dear parents
Michael and Edith Klein

לכבוד ר' מרדכי מאיר ומרת ברכה קליין שיח'

for their hard work and commitment in our upbringing and education. They always struggled to give us the very best and we hope that they are enjoying the fruits of their labor. They toiled nonstop for close to a year in helping secure financial support for this book and their efforts cannot go unmentioned. Without their enthusiasm and perseverance, this book would have remained another manuscript.

From the bottom of our hearts and the depths of our souls, we thank you.

Your three sons,
Reuven Chaim, Avi, and Yerucham Shimon Klein

The second printing of this sefer is dedicated
in loving memory

of my dear mother, who was everything to me
Faiga Rivkah bas Mordechai

לז"נ פייגע רבקה בת מרדכי זצ"ל

of my dear father
Leib Hirsch ben Dovid

ל"נ לייב הירש בן דוד זצ"ל

of my beloved younger brother
Eliezer Don ben Leib Hirsch

לז"נ אליעזר דן בן לייב הירש זצ"ל

by
Moshe Dick, of blessed memory
Moshe Gershon ben Leib Hirsch

משה גרשון בן לייב הירש זצ"ל

נלב"ע ערב חג השבועות תשע"ה

Dedicated with great pride
in memory of David Jannol
דוד בן משה
&
in honor of Goldy Jannol
גולדי בת מייקל

In memory of
Charles and Ruth Ash of blessed memory
לז"נ יחזקאל בן דוד שלמה ורבקה בת אברהם הכהן ז"ל

by David and Peggy Ash

The publication of this work is sponsored
in memory of our beloved grandparents

Rozsi and Dezider Messinger
לז"נ חיה רחל בת יחזקאל הכהן ודוד בן ברוך ז"ל
who survived the horrors of the Holocaust and remained true to tradition in Communist Czechoslovakia. While they continued to live there, their love and support crossed the Atlantic to all their children and grandchildren. Their dedication was a source of inspiration to all of us.

Your cousins, Yossi and Naomi Manela

Sponsored by Mr. and Mrs. Barry Weiss
in memory of their dear mother
Mrs. Bessie Weiss
חיה פעסל בת ר' יששכר דוב הכהן
נלב"ע ד' תשרי תשע"ד

This work is partially sponsored by
Uncle Yossi and Aunt Debra (and Atara, Reuven Chaim,
Meira Leah, and Yonina Chagit) Klein
in honor of our dear mother and grandmother
Mrs. Rozsi Klein
לכבוד מרת שפרינצא קליין שתחי'
as a token of our appreciation for her caring and motherly role in our life. Her quiet disposition did not stop her from instilling in us the proper beliefs and values. She and her two sisters survived the Holocaust and rebuilt a beautiful family in America. May she continue seeing nachas from her children, grandchildren, and great-grandchildren for many years to come.

Dedicated to the memory of
Zev ben Nachum Chaim HaKohen
לז"נ זאב בן נחום חיים הכהן ז"ל
by his loving children:
Martin, Bruce, and Arthur Kay and their families

בס"ד

Rabbi Aaron Lopiansky
ROSH YESHIVA

הרב אהרון לאפיאנסקי
ראש ישיבה

ישיבה גדולה דוואשינגטאן
YESHIVA GEDOLAH OF WASHINGTON

Nissan 5774

To Whom it may concern:

Harav Reuvain Chaim Klein has put together an extraordinary compilation about Loshon Hakodesh. It is extraordinary that something that we all are so familiar with, we at the same time so ignorant about the "envelope" information. Did everyone speak Hebrew during Adam's times? When did it change? What was the commonly spoken language in each era? What about the alphabets?

Rabbi Klein has done an extraordinary job in searching all the traditional sources, laying out the different approaches of each opinion. He points out problems in each position, and sometimes offers possible resolutions. He also has a section about the attitude of various gedolim as regards modern day ivrit.

It is an incredible work, giving anyone with a modicum of intellectual curiosity, the sources and structure to know and further research this extraordinarily fascinating topic.

May the author be zocheh to the day when the "pi hamedaber Aleichem" of loshon kodesh, speak to us once again , and bring us the tidings of redemption

אהרן שרגא לופיאנסקי

1216 Arcola Avenue Silver Spring, MD 20902 w Phone: 301.649.7077

בס"ד

Rabbi Zev Leff

הרב זאב לף

Rabbi of Moshav Matityahu
Rosh HaYeshiva—Yeshiva Gedola Matityahu

מרא דאתרא מושב מתתיהו
ראש הישיבה—ישיבה גדולה מתתיהו

D.N. Modiin 71917 Tel: 08-976-1138 טל' Fax: 08-976-5326 פקס' ד.נ. מודיעין 71917

Dear Friends,

I have read the manuscript "Lashon Hakodesh: History, Holiness, and Hebrew" by Rabbi Reuven Chaim Klein. I have found it to be scholarly, comprehensive, and very interesting. The author traces the origins of lashon hakodesh and its development throughout the ages until modern times. He includes many interesting ideas that are well rooted in solid true Torah sources.

I commend the author on this enlightening presentation and recommend this work to all those who want to enrich their understanding of the importance and implications of our holy language.

May Hashem bless the author with the wherewithal to provide for more works to enrich the community with Torah knowledge.

Sincerely,

With Torah blessings

Rabbi Zev Leff

בס"ד

ק"ק אהבת תורה
Woodside Synagogue Ahavas Torah
9001 Georgia Avenue
Silver Spring, MD 20910

Sivan 5775

Rabbi Reuven Chaim Klein has written a truly fascinating book about the sanctity, history, growth, and evolution of Lashon HaKodesh ("the Holy Tongue") and its relationship to other "Jewish" languages such as Aramaic, Yiddish, Ladino, and Modern Hebrew. He elucidates with clarity and comprehensiveness many fundamental issues which are somewhat obscure even to seasoned *talmidei chachamim* and *yodei sefer*.

What language did Adam HaRishon speak? What was the universal world language that was spoken before the Tower of Babel? Was Lashon HaKodesh the ancestral language of Avraham Avinu or was it acquired only when he entered Eretz Yisrael? What is the significance of the older Hebrew alphabet called Ksav Ivri? What does the Talmud mean when it states that the Torah given to Moshe was in Ksav Ivri and only hundreds of years later in the days of Ezra after the Babylonian Exile was the alphabet changed to the Assyrian Script we use today? How can we assume that our holy *aleph bet* is of foreign origin? For each of these issues and many more, Rabbi Klein surveys a wide gamut of authoritative rabbinic literature: Talmud; Midrash; Rishonim, such as Rashi, Rambam, Ramban, Kuzari; and Acharonim, such as Maharal up to the most recent authorities, are cited, explained, and analyzed. As befitting a *talmid chacham* and *ben Torah*, Rabbi Klein's approach to our sacred *mekoros* is respectful but also scholarly, pointing out difficulties and inconsistencies and offering resolutions. When helpful and appropriate, he employs the results of academic historical literature in the spirit of "handmaidens and cooks" (*lerakchos u'letabchos*) (see *Teshuvos HaRambam* no. 49).

Proceeding to the other "Jewish" languages, he explains the origins of Yiddish and why and how it developed in different countries in somewhat different ways. He then proceeds to discuss the "language wars," a number of controversies pertaining to Modern Hebrew. The relationship of modern Ivrit to Lashon HaKodesh is a complicated one. Why, for example, did Ivrit abandon an age-old Ashkenazis pronunciation? Why does it use the term *chashmal*, reserved in Tanach for the Divine light of the Shechinah, and apply it to the lowly incandescent bulb? Is it proper for Hebrew to become the language of the marketplace, the cinema, or the street? What were the motives and goals of those who pushed for the revival of Hebrew? Discussion of these questions is often obscured by polemics and acrimony. To his credit, Rabbi Klein explores this relationship with objectivity, precision, and *derech eretz*, shedding real light on a subject that is rarely understood or even addressed.

In sum, this is a work of both *asifah* (compilation) and *chiddush* (original insight), one that is the product of prodigious research and *ameilus b'Torah*. It deserves an honored place in a Torah library. It will surely enlighten, inform, and inspire every Jew who feels a connection to the language through which the Almighty created Heaven and Earth. This is a *sefer* that is truly hard to put down.

B'virkas HaTorah,
Yitzchak A. Breitowitz
Magid Shiur, Yeshivas Ohr Somayach
Rav, Kehillas Ohr Somayach

TABLE OF CONTENTS

ACKNOWLEDGMENTS

I have long felt that the "acknowledgments" section of a published book is a very important tool in publicly acknowledging and thanking those who helped the author become who he is. Therefore, I would like to take this rare opportunity to do so (in chronological order). Everyone listed below served as a worthy messenger of Hashem in bringing much blessing and success to the world at large and to me in specific.

Firstly, I would like to thank **my dear parents** for bringing me into This World and educating me in the Torah path. Without their warm support and encouragement, none of this would be at all possible. They were the ones who so constantly ensured that I receive a proper Jewish education. They directly made this book possible by taking the time and effort to secure funding, reach out to potential donors, and follow up with them.

Secondly, I would like to thank **Emek Hebrew Academy/Teichman Family Torah Center** for contributing to my formation as a mature human being for over a decade. The school's administration, under the watchful eyes of **Rabbi Yochanan Stephen**, **Rabbi Eliezer Eidlitz**, and **Rabbi Pesach**

Wachsman, helped shape me into a productive member of society. I will never forget Rabbi Stephen visiting me in Children's Hospital when, as a fifth grader, I had emergency surgery to remove my ruptured appendix. I would also like to thank my elementary school teachers who imparted to me the basic knowledge required to advance in Torah study: **Rabbi Meshullam Weiss**, **Rabbi Joseph Schreiber**, **Rabbi Yochanan Mansouri**, **Rabbi Sheleim Furst**, **Rabbi Shmuli Kornfeld**, and, most importantly, **Rabbi Avrohom Berman**. Additionally, **Rabbi Mordechai Shifman,** the current head of Emek, also helped make this work possible.

Rabbi Zvi Block's name also bears significant mention for his role in my religious upbringing from the pulpit of **Aish HaTorah/Beis Midrash Toras Hashem/Young Israel of Valley Village**. May all these figures live long and healthy lives.

Upon graduating Emek, I enrolled in **Yeshiva Gedolah of Los Angeles/Michael Diller High School** (YGLA) under the leadership of the Rosh Yeshiva **Rabbi Eliezer Gross** and its principal **Rabbi Shlomo Zalman Hauer**. As a high school student there, I was exposed to its characteristically intense secular and Judaic programs. With each grade, the studies grew increasingly more concentrated, yet the progression flowed naturally. For their involvement, I thank my high school teachers **Rabbi Moshe Yom Tov Rubnitz**, **Rabbi Dovid Gruman**, and **Rabbi Yitzchok Altusky**. After three years studying in Yeshiva Gedolah's high school, I advanced to their *Beis Midrash* program, spearheaded by the erudite **Rabbi Moshe Yosef Moldaver** (with whom I briefly learned *b'chavrusa*) and supported by **Rabbi Dovid Grossman** and **Rabbi Dovid Revah**. My two-year experience there adequately prepared me for my next step in life.

I merited joining the world-famous **Mir Yeshiva** in Jerusalem where I attended the daily lectures of **Rabbi Asher Arieli** (along with 600 other students). It was there that I began to mature as a self-sufficient person while engaging in advanced Torah study. I owe a great debt of gratitude to the Mir Yeshiva. At its helm was the sagely and venerable **Rabbi Nosson Tzvi Finkel** (1943–2011), the Rosh Yeshiva of what he liked to call *Mishpachas Mir* ("the Mir Family"). Indeed, the Yeshiva functioned much like a family. It was **Rabbi and Rebbetzin Binyamin Carlebach** who, several years later, helped me out in a time of great need. In over two years as a bachelor in the Mir, I had accrued much Torah knowledge in the Mir and it was there that I had developed a personal relationship with the brother of the late Rosh Yeshiva, **Rabbi Gedalia Finkel** (author of *Imrei Gedalia)*, with whom I learned *b'chavrusa*. As part of the extended "Mir Family," I also developed a more personal bond with my blood second cousins **Rabbi and Mrs. Shlomo Kravitz.**

As I approached marriageable age, I decided to return to America to seek a suitable wife. During this period, I studied at **Beth Medrash Govoha of America** (BMG) in Lakewood, NJ. Although my stint there was relatively brief, I very much enjoyed the lectures of **Rabbi Malkiel Kotler** and **Rabbi Yerucham Olshin**. On Shabbos, I was able to attend the *shiurim* of **Rabbi Yitzchok Sorotzkin**, which I also immensely enjoyed. I owe a great debt of gratitude to **Rabbi Aryeh Leib Paretzky** (son-in-law of Rabbi Shmuel Irons of Detroit) and **Rabbi Sruli Newman** (son-in-law of Rabbi Kalman Krohn), under whom I studied, for helping me gain the most possible out of my time in Lakewood. Rabbi Paretzky also supplied me with a few sources which are used in this work. It was in the library of BMG that I began compiling some of the material that eventually evolved into this work.

After my marriage, I quickly returned to the Mir Yeshiva where I learned one more tractate under Rabbi Arieli. Not long after I stopped attending Rabbi Arieli's lectures regularly, tragedy struck the Mir Yeshiva: our beloved Rosh Yeshiva Rabbi Finkel suddenly passed away. His roles and responsibilities were taken over by his eldest son, **Rabbi Eliezer Yehuda Finkel.** I would like to take this opportunity to personally thank him for his hard work and dedication to the preservation of the Mir; I wish him much success in maintaining the Yeshiva. A few weeks later, my firstborn son, **Binyamin Eliezer** (who is tugging at my pants as I type this) was born.

During that period, I was studying part-time in the vicinity of the Mir at **Beis Midrash L'Horaah Toras Shlomo** as a student of the highly-talented **Rabbi Yosef Yitzchok Lerner** (author of *Shemiras HaGuf*

V'HaNefesh and other works). It was there that I received instruction in *Issur V'Heter* and rabbinic ordination from Rabbi Lerner and Rabbi Moshe Sternbuch. I thank Rabbi Lerner for his personal commitment and devotion to his students. His unique style of broad-ranging material and genial humor helped make the massive amounts of information easy to digest.

My early education helped prepare me to embark on this work about the Hebrew language, especially the classes of **Morah Malik** in Emek and **Rabbi Oelbaum** in YGLA who taught *Ivrit*—or *Ivris* as Rabbi Oelbaum called it—in a complete and organized fashion.

◆ ◆ ◆

In preparing this book, there were many individuals who offered invaluable contributions. Among them, I would also like to thank my good friends who have all contributed to this work in varying ways: Rabbis **Yisroel Aryeh Gradmann, Chaim Tzvi Lehrfeld**, **Tzvi Mordechai Libber, Naftali Kassorla, Moshe Silberstein, Zvi Selevan, Yosef Don Snow,** and, of course, the **Schlussel brothers**, Chaim and Shmuel. Special thanks to **Rabbi Dovid Edelstein** and **Levi Ehrman.**

I am also deeply indebted to another member of the "Mir Family," **Rabbi Aharon Lopiansky** (Rosh Yeshiva at Yeshiva Gedolah of Greater Washington), who took the time to review an early version of my manuscript, offering much practical feedback and advice. **Rabbi Sholom Kamenetsky** (Rosh Yeshiva at the Talmudical Yeshiva of Philadelphia) also read some parts of the book and offered kind encouragement.

The capable and experienced team at **Mosaica Press** helped transform this book from an idea to a reality. In particular, **Shui Haber**, an old friend from my early years at the Mir, was the one who encouraged me to get this work published. His father, **Rabbi Yaacov Haber**, toiled tirelessly to make this happen. **Rabbi Doron Kornbluth**, Mosaica's senior editor, patiently worked with me to make this book as awesome as possible. Without the help of Mosaica Press and their professional expertise, this book would not be the same.

◆ ◆ ◆

אחרון אחרון חביב, I would like to thank **my dear wife** (my "in-house editor") for giving me an ally in life. Her unwavering dedication and loyalty has immensely contributed to my continuing success. Undoubtedly, **her parents** (whose sagely advice and input is always appreciated) instilled in her a firm and upright background. It is she who had to "put up" with me constantly wanting to add "just one more small point" to this book instead of going to sleep. It is she who helped me phrase some of the most complicated explanations in this work. It is she who takes upon herself much responsibility for the household so that I can focus on intellectual pursuits. It is she who is the loving and caring mother of our two sons, **Binyamin Eliezer** and **Yisrael Elimelech**. It is she to whom I turn for moral support and encouragement. May it be the will of Hashem that our family shall continue on the path of Torah and mitzvos so that the Torah shall not leave the mouths of my children and my children's children for now and forever: Amen.

As this book went to press, we were saddened by the passing of

RABBI MESHULLAM DOV WEISS (1935-2014)

הרב משולם דב ב"ר יעקב יואל וויס זצ"ל

נלב"ע כ"ה תמוז תשע"ד

His firm but gentle demeanor touched the hearts and souls of many Jews across America from Brooklyn, NY (where he studied in the Mir Yeshiva and developed a close relationship with the Lubavitcher Rebbe) to Miami Beach, FL (where inter alia he ran a kosher bakery and served as a Rabbi at Beth Israel) to Los Angeles, CA (where he was the author's second grade Rebbe at Emek Hebrew Academy) to Postville, IA (where he continued to teach and inspire through retirement); and back to Los Angeles. There he spent his final years with his daughter and her family, touching more lives, including those in the fledging community of Calabasas. May his wife and children be comforted among the mourners of Zion and Jerusalem.

המקום ינחם אתכם בתוך שאר אבלי ציון וירושלים

INTRODUCTION

As someone who dresses in an overtly Jewish manner, I have often been asked by well-meaning Christians: "Do you speak Jewish?"

For some reason, I am always dumbfounded by this question. I think to myself, "How do I answer such a question? What in the world does this guy mean?" A stream of possible answers flows through my head: Maybe he's talking about *Lashon HaKodesh* (lit. "The Holy Tongue"),[1] the language in which the "Old Testament" was originally written. Maybe he's talking about Aramaic, the language spoken by the Jews at the time of Christianity's origins. Maybe he's talking about Modern Hebrew, the official language of the State of Israel. Maybe he's talking about Yiddish, which, after all, literally means "Jewish."

Then, I imagine a less likely explanation. Perhaps he means to ask if I speak in that certain refined and sophisticated way in which Jews speak, without actually meaning to ask if I speak any specific language, as if he were asking, "Do you speak Jewishly?"

Why is this such a loaded a question?

---

1 Technically, the language should be called *Leshon HaKodesh*, not *Lashon HaKodesh*, because the word *Lashon* is attached to the modifier *HaKodesh*. However, since the latter spelling is more popular, I shall use it throughout this work.

As a Jew, several languages are important to me:

- First and foremost is *Lashon HaKodesh*, in which I pray and study.
- Second is Aramaic, the language of the Talmud, the Targumim, and other important works and prayers.
- Third is Modern Hebrew, the language through which I can connect and communicate with my Israeli brethren.
- Fourth is Yiddish, the language historically used by Ashkenazic Jews for hundreds of years and the language that allows me to communicate with elders from the previous generation.

Why are there so many different languages associated with Judaism? Furthermore, who decided which language to use for which purpose?

I am reminded of a witticism supposedly uttered by the Prussian King Frederick the Great: "I speak French to my ambassadors, English to my accountant, Italian to my wife, Latin to my God, and German to my horse." (His disdain for the German language is well-documented.) Similarly, each language that is important to Judaism has its own purpose.

In this work, I shall attempt to summarize and present the traditional Jewish outlook on language in general and our Jewish languages in particular. In order to achieve that aim, I have gathered information from many different sources and compiled them to form a complete picture. To illustrate the appropriate uses for each language, I first delved into the linguistic history of Judaism to find out how and when each language was introduced. Only after understanding the historical background can one truly appreciate the philological, Kabbalistic, and halachic approaches to this topic taken by various rabbinic figures through the ages. To better highlight the historicity of rabbinic tradition, I also compare and contrast that tradition to the consensus views commonly held by modern-day academia, offering proofs and difficulties to both approaches.

Throughout Jewish literature, the Hebrew language is referred to as *Lashon HaKodesh*. This language has been associated with the Jewish nation for tens of centuries. Though its usage has waxed and waned, the Jewish nation has always regarded it as a sacred language.

Rabbinic sources differ in exactly when *Lashon HaKodesh* developed and when its decline began. Some trace the language's origins to Adam, the first man. According to traditional accounts, Aramaic—and perhaps even other languages—are derived from *Lashon HaKodesh*. As these "offspring" languages became more and more prevalent, the "mother tongue" was relegated to near obscurity. Although it was preserved by religious Jews and (oddly enough) Christian Hebraists as a language of study and prayer, and although it strongly influenced Jewish dialects (such as Yiddish and Ladino), *Lashon HaKodesh* itself essentially fizzled out of everyday speech.

In the late nineteenth century, a movement to resurrect *Lashon HaKodesh* as a spoken language sprouted. This movement succeeded in establishing "Hebrew," in its modern form, as the principal language of the nascent State of Israel.

Lashon HaKodesh is called such because it is intrinsically sacred and used for sacred purposes. In this work, we will seek to understand how *Lashon HaKodesh* is holy, and the source of that holiness. We will also focus on the significance of Aramaic and how it relates to *Lashon HaKodesh*. Finally, we will examine the current incarnation of *Lashon HaKodesh*, Modern Hebrew, and its implications from a religious perspective. These three (*Lashon HaKodesh*, Aramaic, and Modern Hebrew) make up the pantheon of Jewish languages.

As the old saying goes, "Two Jews, three opinions." This adage applies to the study of the history of *Lashon HaKodesh* no less than to other areas of scholarship. In fact, we shall see time and again that many details are subject to dispute. In almost every chapter, more than one way of looking at the matter at hand is presented. In some cases, with extra thought, we can harmonize the differing opinions, but ultimately many matters remain subject to dispute amongst the commentators. Instead of trying to decide among the opinions of great figures, the reader is often left with a list of possibilities. Hopefully, the mere knowledge of these sources will satisfy the reader's intellectual curiosity and might arouse him to engage in deeper investigations of the topics discussed.

Now, back to our main question:

Do you speak Jewish?

How to use this book

Here are some important tips for making the most out of this book:

- The author suggests first reading the body text without footnotes, and then reading it again with the footnotes. This will prevent the reader from getting "bogged down" in the minute details discussed in the footnotes until he has a basic understanding of the material.
- A summary appears towards the end of each chapter and appendix which encapsulates all of the major points discussed.
- Gray boxes like this one are scattered throughout the book to provide the reader with interesting, yet somewhat tangential information.
- The Biographical Index provides the reader with details about the people and works mentioned in this book. It is organized by time period, and by alphabetical order within each time period. Bold names within the Biographical Index have their own entry in the Index.
- The "Additions and Corrections" section offers new insights regarding the ideas discussed in the book. The entries are arranged according to the page number where the topic under discussion is located. A separate Biographical Index is appended to that section, which contains information regarding the people cited therein.

CHAPTER 1:
The Language of Adam

Our study of the history of *Lashon HaKodesh* begins with the history of the world itself. The Mishnah teaches that God created the world with ten utterances.[2] The Midrash adds that they were spoken in *Lashon HaKodesh*.[3] On the sixth day of Creation, God brought humankind into existence. Man's first words recorded in the Torah were also in *Lashon HaKodesh*, for upon the creation of Eve, Adam declared:

> "[She is] bone from my bones, flesh from my flesh. This shall be called *isha* (אשה, woman) because this was taken from *ish* (איש, man)."[4]

LASHON HAKODESH AS THE LANGUAGE OF CREATION

By this declaration, Adam named his mate "woman." Only in *Lashon HaKodesh* is the word for "woman" related to the word for "man"; for in

2 *Avos* 5:1.

3 *Bereishis Rabbah* §18:4, §31:8.

4 *Genesis* 2:23.

Lashon HaKodesh, "man" is *ish* (איש) and "woman" is *isha* (אשה)—essentially the same word with one extra letter appended to it.[5] The Midrash points out that in no other ancient language is the word for "woman" related to the word for "man." For example, in Greek, the word for "woman" is *gini (γυναίκα)*, while the word for "man" is *anthro* (άνθρωπος); and in Aramaic, the word for "woman" is *itssa (אתתא)*, while the word for "man" is *gavra (גברא)*.[6]

THE TORAH WAS WRITTEN IN LASHON HAKODESH

From this, the Midrash deduces that the Torah was originally written in *Lashon HaKodesh*. In other words, the current *Lashon HaKodesh* text of the Torah that we read regularly is the original, not merely a translation from some other language.[7] Given that the Torah is the

---

5 Ibn Ezra and Radak (to *Genesis* 2:23) point out that the dot inside the ש of אשה marks the absence of the letter י, because technically אשה should be spelled אישה. They explain that it is spelled without a י in order to avoid confusion with the word אישה ("her husband"). According to their explanation, the relationship between the *Lashon HaKodesh* words for "man" and "woman" is etymological.

Interestingly, Radak writes elsewhere (*Sefer HaShorashim* s.v. אנש) that the Hebrew word for "woman" is related to the root אנש as opposed to איש, and the dot inside the ש marks the absence of the letter נ. According to this explanation (which is preferred by academia), the relationship between "man" and "woman" in *Lashon HaKodesh* is simply phonetic, rather than etymological. See D. Curwin, "ish and isha," *Balashon: Hebrew Language Detective* (October 17, 2008) [http://www.balashon.com/2008/10/ish-and-isha.html].

6 Abarbanel (to *Genesis* 2:23) adds that in the "Roman language" (i.e., Latin), male is *masculus* and female is *foemineus*. See *Eitz Yosef* (*Bereishis Rabbah* §18:4) who notes that the Midrash only felt the need to show that the words for "man" and "woman" are not related in Greek and Aramaic, because those are the most ancient and well-respected of languages. Therefore, the Midrash only sought to disprove the notion that the Torah was originally written in one of those languages and was then translated into *Lashon HaKodesh*.

This answers the obvious question that in English, the words "woman" and "female" seem related to the words "man" and "male." However, since English is clearly a more recent language, one would not seriously think that the Torah was originally written in it. Furthermore, according to linguistics scholars, the word "woman" is not etymologically related to the word "man;" it evolved from the Middle English word *wifmone* (related to the Modern English word "wife"). The same is true of the English word "female," which evolved from *femelle* and is not related to the word "male." See "woman, n.," *Oxford English Dictionary Online* 3rd ed. (Oxford University Press, June 2011), and "female, n. and adj.," *Oxford English Dictionary Online* 3rd ed. (Oxford University Press, March 2012).

7 The Midrash (*Bereishis Rabbah* §31:8) also proves this point from the fact that Moses was commanded to "make a snake" (*Numbers* 21:8), and, without explaining why, the Bible states that

blueprint of the world,[8] the fact that the Torah was written in *Lashon HaKodesh* supports the Midrash's earlier claim that the world was created through *Lashon HaKodesh.*

ADAM SPOKE LASHON HAKODESH

This Midrash also implies that Adam himself spoke *Lashon HaKodesh*, for the starting point of the Midrash's claims is the name that Adam gave his wife.[9] Nonetheless, as we shall soon see, this idea is not universally accepted.

HOW DID ADAM KNOW LASHON HAKODESH?

Indeed, Rabbi Yitzchak ben Moshe HaLevi Duran (1350–1415), also known as Efodi after his *magnum opus*, writes that God ingrained *Lashon HaKodesh* in Adam, making it an innate component of his nature.[10] Rabbi Yitzchak Abarbanel (1437–1508) elaborates on this idea[11] and explains that God did not teach the language itself to Adam. Rather, He imbued Adam with the intellectual ability to deduce the words of

---

he "made a copper snake" (*Numbers* 21:9). The Midrash notes that in several other instances God commanded people to make objects, and each time He told them which material to use, yet God did not tell Moses to make the snake out of copper. If so, then how did Moses know what to do? The Midrash explains that Moses reasoned that the snake should be created out of a material that is similar to snakes, so he decided to make the snake out of copper, because the word for "snake," *nachash* (נחש), in *Lashon HaKodesh* is very similar to the word for "copper," *nechoshes* (נחשת). The Midrash deduces from this that the Torah was originally written in *Lashon HaKodesh*, because in no other language is the word for "snake" related to the word for "copper." (Interestingly, in English there is a connection between snakes and copper because of the "copperhead" snake.)

8 Before something is built, a blueprint is designed to record every detail of the future edifice, and then the blueprint is used to direct its construction. So too, the Torah contained the design of the entire creation. When God created the universe, He followed the plan recorded in the Torah. This is what the *Zohar* (*Exodus* 161a) means when it writes that God looked into the Torah and created the world. Similarly, *Bereishis Rabbah* §1:1 states in regard to the creation of the world that the Torah was the tool of God's craft. Thus, the physical universe is a manifestation of the Torah. Incidentally, this also explains why the Torah is so complex: it parallels the universe's complexity.

9 In fact, *Maharzu* (*Bereishis Rabbah* §18:4) interprets this Midrashic passage's ultimate goal as proving that Adam spoke *Lashon HaKodesh* (as opposed to proving that the world was created through *Lashon HaKodesh*).

10 *Ma'aseh Efod* (Vienna, 1865), pgs. 27, 29–31.

11 In his commentary to *Genesis* 2:19–20.

Lashon HaKodesh through his own capacities. This intellectual potential, coupled with the fact that God spoke to Adam in *Lashon HaKodesh,* allowed Adam to instinctively develop fluency in it. Only after God instilled in Adam this ability to develop *Lashon HaKodesh* on his own was he deemed worthy of naming the animals.[12] This is because, as shall be explained later, only the words of *Lashon HaKodesh* intrinsically reflect their meaning. Therefore, Adam had to know the language in order to give the most fitting names to the various entities.

ADAM SPOKE ARAMAIC

Although the sources above assume that Adam spoke *Lashon HaKodesh*, the Talmud clearly states that Adam's spoken language was actually Aramaic,[13] as if to reject the notion that he spoke *Lashon HaKodesh*. The Talmud proves this from a verse in Psalms ascribed to Adam: "How honorable (*yakar*, יקר) to me are Your thoughts, God."[14] In this verse, the Aramaic word for "honorable," *yakar*, is used instead of the Hebrew word *kavod* (כבוד).[15] If Adam used an Aramaic word, it means that he spoke Aramaic.

The Talmud's statement contradicts the aforementioned Midrash. Furthermore, it begs the question: If *Lashon HaKodesh* was the language with which God created the world, then why did Adam—the pinnacle of creation—not speak *Lashon HaKodesh*? While there are no conclusive answers to this question, several answers have been proposed, each of which bears mention.

THE KUZARI'S BRIEF HISTORY OF LASHON HAKODESH

In his epic work *The Kuzari*, Rabbi Yehuda HaLevi (1075–1141) records a debate over the significance of *Lashon HaKodesh*. The Kuzari king

---

12 See *Genesis* ibid.

13 TB *Sanhedrin* 38b.

14 *Psalms* 139:17.

15 See Maharsha to TB *Bava Basra* 75b who explains the Talmud's assertion thusly. Rabbi Ben-Zion Meir Chai Uziel (in his glosses to TB *Megillah* 9a) points out that the word *yakar* (יקר) also exists in *Lashon HaKodesh*, where it means "precious," see A. Buxbaum (ed.), *Kovetz Moriah*, vol. 337–338 (Jerusalem: Machon Yerushalayim, 2008), pg. 95.

asks the Jewish scholar how *Lashon HaKodesh* can justifiably be held in higher esteem than Arabic, given that Arabic contains a richer and fuller vocabulary. To this, the Jewish scholar counters that Arabic is actually a corruption of *Lashon HaKodesh*, whose history he then proceeds to outline. Throughout this work, we will revisit many of the ideas mentioned in this important passage. He writes:

> It [*Lashon HaKodesh*] is the most important of all languages, as evident both from tradition and through logic.
>
> According to tradition, God spoke to Adam and Eve in this language, and Adam and Eve themselves spoke this language. This is evident from the roots of their names: Adam is derived from the Hebrew word for ground, *adamah* (אדמה), Eve from *chai* (חי, meaning life), Kayin from *kanissi* (קניתי, I acquired), Seth from *shas* (שת, provide), and Noah from *yenachameini* (ינחמיני, He will comfort me).[16] According to the testimony of the Torah, *Lashon HaKodesh* was passed down to Eber from Noah and from Adam. Since it was the language spoken by Eber, who preserved it after the division of languages, it is called "Hebrew."
>
> Even Abraham spoke Aramaic, the local language in his homeland Ur Kasdim, because Aramaic was indeed the language of the Chaldeans there. Nonetheless, Abraham believed *Lashon HaKodesh* to be a special and holy language, while Aramaic was merely a mundane language. Ishmael brought *Lashon HaKodesh* to Arabia.
>
> These three languages, Aramaic, Hebrew, and Arabic, use similar nouns and rules of grammar, but Hebrew is the most esteemed of them. The value of Hebrew is also logically evident from the fact that those who employ the language find that it is amply sufficient for what they need in terms of poetry, prophecies, and songs. One never finds that their leaders, Moses, Joshua, David, and Solomon lacked a poetic expression due to the parity of the language, even

16 See Appendix B "Egyptian Names in the Bible," for a discussion regarding whether or not proper nouns can prove *The Kuzari's* assertion.

> though nowadays much of the language has been lost from us. One never finds that the stories and descriptions in the Torah needed to borrow foreign words. One never finds that the Torah needs to borrow foreign words for the names of people, birds, and stones.[17]

In this passage, *The Kuzari* explains that Abraham spoke Aramaic in his day-to-day communication, and reserved *Lashon HaKodesh* for sacred purposes.[18]

ANSWER #1: ADAM ONLY USED LASHON HAKODESH FOR SPIRITUAL MATTERS

Rabbi Reuven Margolis (1889–1971)[19] and Rabbi Uri Langner (1896–1971)[20] independently suggested extending *The Kuzari's* explanation of Abraham's linguistic practices to Adam, by explaining that while Adam spoke *Lashon HaKodesh*, he did so only when speaking of spiritual matters. For mundane matters, he spoke Aramaic. This is why the Talmud mentions Adam's spoken language as Aramaic, even though he also spoke *Lashon HaKodesh*.[21]

ANSWER #2: ADAM SPOKE SEVENTY LANGUAGES

There is another way in which the Talmud's assertion that Adam spoke Aramaic can be reconciled with the Midrashic understanding that he spoke *Lashon HaKodesh*.

---

17 *The Kuzari, Ma'amar* 2, §67–68.

18 Rabbi Yaakov Emden, in his work *Migdal Oz* (*Beis Middos, Aliyas HaLashon*), questions the *Kuzari's* assertion that Abraham did not use *Lashon HaKodesh* for mundane purposes, because according to Jewish law one is technically allowed to use *Lashon HaKodesh* for mundane purposes, even in a bathroom (see *Magen Avraham, Orach Chaim* §85:2). In light of this, Rabbi Emden asks why Abraham did not use it for mundane matters. Rabbi Emden concludes that while such mundane usage of *Lashon HaKodesh* is technically allowed *post facto*, one should ideally nonetheless attempt to refrain from such usage. Indeed, Rambam (in his commentary to the Mishnah, *Avos* 1:16) writes that it is fitting to use *Lashon HaKodesh* only for exalted purposes. Interestingly, Rabbi Yehuda HaChasid relates (*Sefer Chassidim* §994) that a certain elderly individual attributed his longevity to the fact that he refrained from speaking *Lashon HaKodesh* in the bathroom and bathhouse.

19 *Margolios HaYam* to TB *Sanhedrin* 38b, §16 and *HaMikra V'HaMesorah* (Jerusalem: Mossad HaRav Kook, 1989), pg. 30.

20 M. Amsel (ed.), "*Lashon HaKodesh* and Ivrit," *Kovetz Hamaor* vol. 81 (Brooklyn, 1958), pg. 6.

21 It seems that this differentiation can only apply after Adam had sinned by eating from the Tree of Knowledge, because before his sin, the mundane and the holy were one and the same; see the commentary of Rabbi Ovadiah ben Yaakov Sforno (1475–1550) to *Genesis* 2:25.

In this view, there is actually no contradiction: The Talmud was simply saying that his preferred or most commonly used language was Aramaic, but he was fluent in other languages as well.[22] In fact, several Midrashic sources imply that Adam spoke seventy languages.[23]

For example, this idea is tangentially alluded to in a Midrashic elucidation of a conversation between Moses and God. When God commanded Moses to demand that Pharaoh release the enslaved Jews, Moses responded, "I am not a man of words."[24] The Midrash explains that Moses told God that all the men in Pharaoh's court spoke seventy languages, yet he (Moses) did not know all of those languages. To this, God responded, "Just as Adam did not learn the seventy languages from anyone, yet he was still able to name each creature in all seventy languages,[25] so too, you, Moses, will be fluent in all seventy languages and will be able to converse properly with Pharaoh and the men of his court." God's response to Moses is built on the notion that Adam spoke all seventy languages.[26] (We will discuss this Midrash again in Chapter 4.)

Based on this, it is reasonable to explain that while Adam was in fact fluent in all languages, his preferences changed based on his circumstances. At one time, he preferred to speak *Lashon HaKodesh;* and at another time, Aramaic. When Adam gave names to his surroundings, it was of the utmost importance for him to give those names in *Lashon HaKodesh*; the

---

22 Rabbi Yosef Chaim of Baghdad (*Ben Yehoyada* to TB *Sanhedrin* 38b) writes that while Adam spoke seventy languages, the Talmud specifically pointed out that he spoke Aramaic. He explains that the Talmud did so because one might otherwise think that he only spoke *Lashon HaKodesh*, the language in which the Bible records him speaking.

23 The concept of seventy languages and seventy nations is found throughout rabbinic literature in varying contexts. The languages correspond to the seventy families whose genealogy is traced in *Genesis* 10. Interestingly, the number "seventy" also has a place among the amount of languages in linguistic surveys. One such source writes that there are seventy Semitic languages, as well as seventy Cushitic languages. See Edward Lipiński, *Semitic Languages: Outline of a Comparative Grammar* (Leuven, Belgium: Peeters Publishers & Catholic University of Leuven Department of Oriental Studies, 1997), pgs. 29, 41.

24 *Exodus* 4:10.

25 *Genesis* 2:20 says that Adam named the creations using the phrase, "Adam called them names," with the word "names" in plural, as if to imply that each creature was called by multiple names. Each name was in a different language.

26 S. Buber (ed.), *Old Midrash Tanchuma* on *Deuteronomy* (Vilna, 1885) pg. 2a–b, and *Midrash Sechel Tov* (to *Exodus* 4:11).

world was created in that language, and giving names was the completion of the creation process. Perhaps at other times he gave preferential treatment to Aramaic.[27]

This approach neatly complements the theory presented above that Adam spoke *Lashon HaKodesh* only for holy purposes and reserved Aramaic (and other languages) for other purposes. However, most commentators do not follow this approach and instead understand that Adam spoke either *Lashon HaKodesh* or Aramaic, but not both together, and remain silent about whether or not Adam spoke seventy languages.

How does Sarah dying in Kiryat Arba prove that Adam spoke Aramaic?

The Midrash says (*Midrash Pliyah* §166) that the verse "Sarah died in Kiryat Arba" (*Genesis* 23:2) shows that Adam spoke Aramaic. The commentaries explain (*Niv Sfasaim* to *Midrash Pliyah* §166) that "Kiryat Arba" is an Aramaic name, and since the town was called by an Aramaic name, one deduces that Adam spoke Aramaic. However, this explanation is insufficient, because it fails to explain how one sees that Adam spoke Aramaic from the fact that a town's name is Aramaic.

Rabbi Aharon Lewin of Reische (1879–1941) proves (in *Birkas Aharon* to TB *Brachos*, *Ma'amar* §89 and *HaDrash V'HaIyun*, vol. 1, *Ma'amar* §24:2) from Rabbinic sources that Aramaic is a language especially fitting for one in mourning (e.g., see below Chapter 8 "Development of Aramaic," that Aramaic is the best language for composing elegies). Therefore, he explains that Adam spoke Aramaic after he was exiled from the Garden of Eden, because he spent the rest of his life mourning the effects of his sin.

Based on this understanding, the late Rabbi Shalom Weiss (in *Kesones Tashbetz* to *Midrash Pliyah* there) explains that Abraham eulogized Sarah in Aramaic because that is the language of mourning. Thus, Adam spoke Aramaic for the same reason that Abraham referred to Sarah's burial place (i.e., Kiryat Arba) in Aramaic while eulogizing her. Accordingly, we can explain that even though in general Adam spoke seventy languages, after he sinned and was exiled he chose to speak Aramaic to reflect his sorrow over the ramifications of his sin.

27 See Appendix D "Maharal on Aramaic and *Lashon HaKodesh*" for an explanation as to why Adam would favor Aramaic over any other language.

ANSWER #3: ADAM SPOKE LASHON HAKODESH BEFORE HE SINNED AND ARAMAIC AFTERWARDS

Rabbi Yehonassan Eyebschitz (1690–1764) offers several possible explanations to resolve the ambiguity regarding Adam's language habits. In one instance, he explains that before Adam sinned by eating from the Tree of Knowledge, he spoke *Lashon HaKodesh*, but afterwards, he spoke Aramaic.[28]

Rabbi Eyebschitz explains that by defying God's order not to eat from the Tree of Knowledge, Adam slighted His all-encompassing dominion, thus affronting His Oneness. The word for "one" in *Lashon HaKodesh* is *echad* (אחד), but in Aramaic the word for "one" is *chad* (חד). In other words, in *Lashon HaKodesh*, "one" is spelled with an *aleph* (א) at its beginning, while in Aramaic, the *aleph* is omitted. *Aleph* is the first letter of the Hebrew alphabet and, as such, has a numerical value of one and represents the concept of "one." Therefore, explains Rabbi Eyebschitz, before Adam slighted the Oneness of God he spoke *Lashon HaKodesh*, the language that symbolizes God's uniqueness (by virtue of the fact that its word for "one" starts with an *aleph*). However, after dishonoring His Oneness, Adam was punished by being demoted to speaking only Aramaic, which does not symbolize God's Oneness.[29]

In another context, Rabbi Eyebschitz offers an additional layer of explanation as to why Adam spoke *Lashon HaKodesh* before sinning and Aramaic afterwards. He assumes that Aramaic is a mixture of *Lashon HaKodesh* and other languages. When Adam sinned by eating from the Tree of Knowledge, he introduced evil into the world. This evil intermingled with the good that had originally dominated the world. The result of this amalgamation is the current world condition in which good and bad are mixed together so homogeneously that it is difficult to discern one from the other. Before eating

28 *Tiferes Yehonassan* to *Genesis* 11:1.

29 Interestingly, although in *Lashon HaKodesh* the word for "one" has an *aleph* while in Aramaic it does not, the Aramaic counterparts of many other Hebrew words are the same as (or very similar to) the Hebrew words, with the addition of an *aleph* as their ultimate or penultimate letter. This strengthens the assertion that the fact that the Aramaic word for "one" lacks an *aleph* is not coincidental. Note that the feminine form of the word for "one" in Aramaic, *chada* (חדא), has an *aleph* at the end.

from the Tree of Knowledge, Adam spoke *Lashon HaKodesh*, the purest and most elegant of languages—the linguistic epitome of good. However, after his sin, God punished him accordingly by limiting his speech to Aramaic—a crossbreed of *Lashon HaKodesh* (good) and foreign languages (bad). This punishment is quite apropos to his sin, because his sin exposed the world to the hazy mixture of good and bad.

ANSWER #4: ADAM ONLY SPOKE LASHON HAKODESH IN THE LAND OF ISRAEL

In the same discussion, Rabbi Eyebschitz mentions another possible way of resolving which language Adam spoke. He writes that *Lashon HaKodesh* is the regional language of the Land of Israel,[30] which is the geographic epitome of good.[31] Since Adam did not dwell in the Land of Israel, he was unable to speak *Lashon HaKodesh*.[32] Rabbi Eyebschitz does not elaborate on whether or not according to this explanation Adam spoke *Lashon HaKodesh* before he sinned. It is also unclear whether this explanation connecting *Lashon HaKodesh* to the Land of Israel is separate from the explanation above linking it to good and Aramaic to bad.

THE LINK BETWEEN THE LAND OF ISRAEL AND LASHON HAKODESH

The connection between *Lashon HaKodesh* and the Land of Israel arises in many contexts. For example, this connection sheds light on Rabbi Heschel of Krakow's (1596–1663) otherwise enigmatic interpretation of a biblical verse. The Torah states: "*Arami* (ארמי) destroyed my father and he descended to Egypt."[33] Rabbi Heschel assumes that in this context

30 Perhaps the Garden of Eden, Adam's home before his sin, is also a geographical embodiment of good, like the Land of Israel. According to this, Adam spoke *Lashon HaKodesh* until he sinned, at which point he was expelled from Eden. On the other hand, one could argue to the contrary that Adam did not speak *Lashon HaKodesh* even while he lived in Eden since it is not in the Land of Israel and *Lashon HaKodesh* is specifically tied to the Land of Israel. This point remains unclear.

31 For example, *Numbers* 14:7 says that the land is "very very good"; see also *Deuteronomy* 8:7, 8:10, 11:17, which describe it as "good".

32 *Ya'aros Devash*, vol. 1, *Drush* 1 (elucidation of the blessing *Refa'enu*).

33 *Deuteronomy* 26:5.

Arami means the Aramaic language, even though it is usually translated as "an Aramean."[34]

He explains that since Jacob caused Aramaic to be included in the Torah, he was punished by being exiled to Egypt.[35] To what is he referring?

When Jacob cemented a peace treaty with Laban (his uncle and father-in-law) who was from Aram, they erected a cairn (a mound of stones built as a memorial) as a testimony to their everlasting covenant. Jacob called the site *gal'ed* (גלעד), which means "witness mound" in Hebrew, while Laban called the site *yegar sehaddusa* (יגר שהדותא), which means the same in Aramaic.[36] By authorizing this treaty, Jacob caused Laban's Aramaic words to be included in the Torah. Thus, Jacob was punished in that he and his descendants were exiled to Egypt.[37]

At first, Rabbi Heschel's explanation seems incomplete. He fails to explain why being exiled to Egypt is a fitting punishment for introducing Aramaic into the Torah. However, this explanation can be understood in light of the concept set forth by Rabbi Eyebschitz that *Lashon HaKodesh* is linked to the Land of Israel. By deviating from *Lashon HaKodesh*, or even by granting another language some kind of significance, Jacob distanced himself from the Land of Israel. Thus, his punishment was to be exiled from the Land of Israel to Egypt.[38]

Similarly, the Torah says that when Rachel gave birth to Benjamin

---

34 For a survey and discussion of many other explanations of this verse, see M. First, "Arami Oved Avi: Uncovering the Interpretation Hidden in the Mishnah," printed in the journal *Hakirah*, vol. 13 (2012), pgs. 127–144.

35 *Chanukas HaTorah, Ki Savo* (see also *Lev Aryeh* to *Parashas Shemos*).

36 See *Genesis* 31:47.

37 Interestingly, Sforno (to *Genesis* ibid.) writes that Jacob specifically did not use Laban's Aramaic name for the site, in consonance with the Midrashic notion (see below, Chapter 4, "The Jews in Egypt") that the Jews in Egypt never changed their language. Sforno implies that Jacob acted righteously by rejecting the Aramaic name given by Laban, instead offering his own name for the site in *Lashon HaKodesh*. Nonetheless, Rabbi Heschel seems to criticize Jacob for even agreeing to enter a covenant with Laban in the first place, even though he offered his own name for the site in *Lashon HaKodesh*.

38 Rabbi Shalom Mordechai Schwadron (1835–1911), among others, questions this based on the fact that there are many instances in the Torah of words whose origins are not found in *Lashon HaKodesh*, as we shall see in Chapter 7 (see indices to responsa *Maharsham*, vol. 5, §9). Thus, one cannot say that Jacob had actually *sinned*, per se, in allowing words from another language to be included in the Torah, even if it was enough of a reason for him to deserve punishment.

on her deathbed, she called him Ben Oni (בן אוני), while Jacob called him Benjamin (בנימין).[39] In delineating the difference between these two names, the Midrash[40] remarks that the name that Rachel called him was in Aramaic, while the name that Jacob chose was in *Lashon HaKodesh*. In fact, according to one explanation of the name's meaning, Jacob called him so because he was the only son born in the "Land of the Right (i.e., South[41]—the Land of Israel,— as opposed to Aram in the North)."[42] Thus, Jacob not only named his youngest son in *Lashon HaKodesh*, but he also alluded to his son's connection to the Land of Israel in that name. Based on this idea, one can explain that Rachel did not merit to live in the Land of Israel (she died almost immediately upon entering) because she deviated from *Lashon HaKodesh* and named her child in Aramaic, thereby distancing herself from the Holy Land.

ANSWER #5: BEFORE SINNING, ADAM SPOKE ARAMAIC; AFTERWARDS, LASHON HAKODESH

Rabbi Alexander Sender Schor (1673–1737) explains Adam's linguistic habits differently. He writes that Adam originally spoke Aramaic, but after he sinned by eating from the Tree of Knowledge, he spoke *Lashon HaKodesh*.[43] As the Talmud states, God originally created Adam to be a creation halfway between animals and angels.[44] He made Adam's characteristics resemble both in order to maintain peace and harmony between them.[45] That is, Adam resembled angels in two ways and animals in two ways. He resembled angels because he possessed intelligence and

---

39 *Genesis* 35:17.

40 *Bereishis Rabbah* §82:9.

41 See *Targum Onkelos* and *Targum Jonathan* (to *Genesis* 13:9) and *Targum Jonathan* (to *Genesis* 24:49) who translate the direction "right" as "south." Interestingly, in Arabic, north is *shimal* (شمال) which is related to the Hebrew word *smol* (שמאל, left).

42 *Sefer HaYashar* (Bene Barak: Mishor Publishing, 2005), pg. 129.

43 *Bechor-Schor* to TB *Sanhedrin* 38b.

44 See TB *Chagigah* 16a with Rabbi Yoshiyahu Pinto's commentary *Pirush HaRif* to Rabbi Yaakov ibn Chaviv's *Ein Yaakov*.

45 See Rashi (to *Genesis* 2:7) who writes that God specifically created Adam with elements from the Heavens and elements from the earth in order to avoid causing jealousy between the two realms.

stood upright with his neck erect,[46] while he resembled animals in that he possessed both the digestive and reproductive systems. In order to maintain this neutrality, Adam originally spoke Aramaic, a language that is spoken neither by the angels (as we shall discuss in Chapter 8), nor by the animals. By eating from the forbidden fruit of the Tree of Knowledge, Adam introduced death to humanity, thereby adding an aspect of similarity to animals. In order to maintain the balance, God had Adam change his language to *Lashon HaKodesh*, which the angels spoke. Thereafter he resembled angels in three ways and animals in three ways.

Nonetheless, this explanation is still inconsistent with the above-cited sources, which indicate that Adam already spoke *Lashon HaKodesh* when he named Eve. Note that it is also the exact opposite of Rabbi Eyebschitz's first approach mentioned above.

LANGUAGE DEVELOPED FROM A CRUDER FORM OF SPEECH

Another possible answer to the question of which language Adam spoke has its roots in an idea proposed by certain academic schools of thought.[47] They claim that language began as onomatopoeic sounds that

---

46 Rabbi Shimon Betzalel Neuman (1860–1942) points out in *Pninim Yekarim* (Budapest, 1941), pg. 3, that this explanation is mistaken. Adam's upright posture did not make him dissimilar to animals, because even amongst the animal kingdom, the snake was able to stand upright (see TB *Sotah* 9b). Thus, standing upright is not a trait reserved exclusively for angels. Similarly, one can claim that speaking *Lashon HaKodesh* was not a trait that was more similar to angels than to animals; before the sin, even the snake spoke *Lashon HaKodesh*.
We know that the snake spoke *Lashon HaKodesh* because he enticed Eve to eat from the Tree of Knowledge in that language (see *Pesikta Zutrasa* to *Genesis* 3:1). J. Klugmann (ed.), *Pirush Rabbeinu Efrayim*, vol. 1 (Bene Barak, 1992), pg. 15, goes even further and explains that before the Tower of Babel, all of creation spoke *Lashon HaKodesh*—even the birds and animals. Rabbi David ben Avraham (1125–1198), known as Raavad, mentions in his commentary to TB *Avodah Zarah* 24b that Balaam's donkey, which was created on the sixth day of Creation, spoke *Lashon HaKodesh*. Nonetheless, see Ibn Ezra and Radak (to *Genesis* 3:1), who offer alternate explanations for how Eve was able to understand the snake.

47 Rabbi Aharon Marcus (1843–1916) authored *Barsilai: Sprache als Schrift der Psyche* (1905) in German, which was translated into Modern Hebrew as *Barzilai* (Jerusalem: Mossad HaRav Kook, 1983). In the beginning of this work (*Barzilai*, pgs. 16–18), he discusses various theories about the origins of language, including the notions that language evolved from music, the chirping of birds, and other such natural phenomena. In that work, he discusses the development and significance of language (especially *Lashon HaKodesh)* from psychological and anatomical perspectives and explains the etymology of many words in *Lashon HaKodesh* and how they were adopted by other languages.

referred to various objects and concepts in nature by imitating those sounds of nature. But, in the course of time, as the objects for which designations were required became more and more numerous, the necessity of a nicer distinction and an easier way of pronouncing their sounds gradually led to the development of articulate speech, in which one could simply use an accepted word instead of attempting an actual imitation. As language developed more, other ways of referring to these objects developed, not based on an onomatopoeic imitation of the sounds they made, but as references to other characteristics or perceived characteristics of those objects.[48]

ANSWER #6: ADAM SPOKE PROTO-LASHON HAKODESH

While this approach developed outside of the schools of Jewish thought, Rabbi Yaakov Yehuda Zilberberg/Di Kasif (1914–2003) sought to apply it to Jewish tradition. That is, he explains that Adam heard the sounds of nature and, in attempting to learn from them and imitate them, he developed the first phonemes (the smallest units of speech) from whence speech eventually developed. As mentioned above, God did not teach him *Lashon HaKodesh,* rather He gave Adam the necessary tools to intuit *Lashon HaKodesh* on his own. According to this approach as well, Adam did not develop speech on his own; he required special assistance from God in order to have the intelligence required to learn from his surroundings.[49]

In Rabbi Zilberberg/Di Kasif's view, the original language that Adam spoke was simplistic and undeveloped, but was built on strong foundations. The Adamic language only consisted of short words for the most common things and ideas, but was based on a formula that allowed it to vastly expand its vocabulary. This formula, without any impurities, leads directly to *Lashon HaKodesh*. All other languages that developed from the Adamic language are adulterated with unnatural sounds and their distorted meanings.[50] Thus,

---

48 H. Wedgwood, *On the Origin of Language* (London, 1866), pgs. 19, 22.

49 Y. Y. Zilberberg/Di Kasif, *Leshonenu HaKedoshah* (Tel Aviv, 1963), pgs. 9–10, 15, 17–18, 63–64.

50 See I. E. Mozeson, "Could Pre-Hebrew Be the *Safa Ahat* of Genesis 11:1?" *Jewish Bible Quarterly,* vol. 38:1 (Jerusalem: Jewish Bible Association, 2010), pgs. 55–61, for an explanation of how various language families are derived from this proto-*Lashon HaKodesh* language (which he calls the Edenic language).

Why do some people sound like wailing pigs?

The Greek philosopher Galen of Pergamon (129–216) argued that different peoples have different inclinations in their linguistic tendencies. Therefore, the speech of some groups of people resembles the wailing of pigs or the croaking of frogs or the chirping of birds. He explains that this is directly correlated to their most natural way of producing sound. That is, for some people the natural way of producing sound is through their throat (which produces a snoring sound), while others twist their mouths in a whistling style. Some open their mouths wide and extend their tongue, while others only open their mouths minimally and allow their tongues to remain inside.

The Muslim philosopher Muhammad ibn Zakariya al-Razi (854–925) disagrees with Galen and instead argues that the perceived differences in speech simply stem from unfamiliarity with various spoken languages. In other words, al-Razi understood that all people produce sounds in the same ways, but they are not mutually understandable and sometimes even sound bizarre to non-native speakers of a given language simply because such people are not accustomed to such sounds.

In his medical writings, Rambam discusses this dispute between Galen and al-Razi, and sides with Galen, adding that geographical conditions also contribute to one's natural way of producing sound. However, Rambam does concede that migration could bring one form of speech to another location without geographical conditions affecting it.

Source: *Pirkei Moshe* (Lemberg, 1834), pg. 53a; S. Muntner (ed.), *Pirkei Moshe B'Refuah* (Jerusalem: Mossad HaRav Kook, 1940), pgs. 360–361; and Y. Kapach (ed.), *Iggros HaRambam* (Jerusalem: Mossad HaRav Kook, 1994), pgs. 148–150.

while Adam did not speak *Lashon HaKodesh* as a fully developed language in the sense that we understand it, the language that he spoke was the prototype of *Lashon HaKodesh*. This proto–*Lashon HaKodesh* was a common ancestor of all languages, but was the *direct* ancestor of *Lashon HaKodesh*.[51] In view of this, it is fair to state that on one hand Adam spoke *Lashon HaKodesh*, and on the other hand also spoke Aramaic (and indeed all seventy languages), because he did not literally speak those languages; rather, he spoke in a way that followed a formula from which those languages could develop.

---

51 Y. Y. Zilberberg/Di Kasif, *Leshonenu HaKedoshah* (Tel Aviv, 1963), pgs. 121–125.

CHAPTER SUMMARY

Thus, we conclude our discussion of *Lashon HaKodesh* as it pertains to the life of the first man. We presented what seems to be a contradiction between the Midrashic assumption that Adam spoke *Lashon HaKodesh* and the Talmud's assertion that he spoke Aramaic. Assuming that these two ideas are mutually exclusive, some have sought to explain that Adam did not literally speak either language, rather his speech reflected an earlier form of speaking from which both *Lashon HaKodesh* and Aramaic would later develop. Nonetheless, according to most commentators, Adam certainly did speak *Lashon HaKodesh*.

These commentators offer several ways of reconciling the apparent contradiction between the Midrash and the Talmud:

- Some argue that Adam only used *Lashon HaKodesh* for spiritual matters while he relegated Aramaic for other matters.
- Others understand that there is a difference between before his sin (of eating from the Tree of Knowledge) and afterwards. This approach branches into two sub-explanations:
    - Rabbi Yehonassan Eyebschitz understood that Adam spoke *Lashon HaKodesh* before his sin and Aramaic afterwards.
    - Rabbi Alexander Sender Schor understood that Adam spoke *Lashon HaKodesh* after his sin and Aramaic beforehand.
- Rabbi Yehonassan Eyebschitz also proposes that Adam only spoke *Lashon HaKodesh* in the Land of Israel and not elsewhere. In understanding this approach, we elaborated on the connection between *Lashon HaKodesh* and the Land of Israel, a point that will arise time and again in this work.

Now let us move on to the next historical junction that is of supreme importance in the history of language—the Tower of Babel.

CHAPTER 2:
The Tower of Babel

FROM NOAH UNTIL THE TOWER OF BABEL

The Tower of Babel episode is noteworthy from a linguistic perspective, because God abruptly halted its construction by changing the language of its builders. This change created huge ramifications in the development of language. In order to fully understand the catalyst for the Tower of Babel, a summary of the geopolitical background behind the story, gleaned from the Bible[52] and rabbinic tradition, is required.

The Bible says that several centuries after the creation of Adam, God decided to "restart" humanity by subjecting the world to a massive flood. The only survivors were Noah, his three sons (Shem, Ham, and Japheth), and their wives. The family miraculously survived the Deluge by taking refuge in a large wooden ark. At the flood's end, the family disembarked from the ark, having settled on Mount Ararat (located in present-day Turkey). After an embarrassing incident involving Ham (or Ham's son, Canaan) castrating

52 *Genesis* Ch. 9–11.

him,[53] Noah conferred a curse upon Ham's descendants that they should be "slaves" to the descendants of Shem and Japheth.

NOAH DIVIDES THE WORLD AMONG HIS THREE SONS

After the flood, Noah's sons repopulated the world. Noah divided the ancient world into three portions and granted a region to each of his sons. Shem received the "Eastern" portion, i.e., Asia; Ham received the "Southern" portion, i.e. Africa; and Japheth received the "Northern" portion, i.e., Europe.[54] While the Levant (the eastern seaboard of the Mediterranean, including the Land of Israel and Mesopotamia) actually fell to Shem, Ham's descendants decided to annex it. Thus began a struggle between the two families. Through most of the Levant, Semitic and Hamitic families co-existed, with some cities belonging to one and other cities belonging to the other.[55] In the future Land of Israel, Shem's descendants originally prevailed, but were ultimately conquered by invading Hamitic tribes, most notably the Canaanites.[56]

UNITING HUMANITY TO REBEL AGAINST GOD

After some time, Nimrod of Babylon (a grandson of Ham)[57] emerged as a dominant figure and united much of humanity under his reign. Babylon (in the southern Mesopotamian region of Sumer known in the Bible as

53 Or, doing even worse. See the Midrashim and commentaries to *Genesis* 9:22.

54 Rabbi Eliyahu of Vilna writes (in *Eliyahu Rabbah* to *Negaim* 2:1) that Shem's family moved to the east (i.e., Mesopotamia), Ham's family moved to the south (i.e., Egypt, Africa), and Japheth's family moved to the north (i.e., Greece, Europe).

55 Rabbi Mordechai Yaffe (1530–1612) in his commentary to the Pentateuch (*Levush HaOrah* to *Genesis* 12:6) writes that Noah only divided the undeveloped property of the world (i.e., fields, vineyards, and uninhabited areas), but regarding cities and the like, whoever built it owned the rights to it. His student, Rabbi Yissocher Ber Eilenberg, repeats this assertion in his commentary to the Talmud (*Beer Sheva* to TB *Sanhedrin* 91a), and alludes to it again in his own commentary to the Pentateuch (*Tzeidah L'Darech* to *Genesis* 12:6).

56 Rashi to *Genesis* 12:6. See Chizkuni (to Genesis 12:6 and Deuteronomy 11:10) who discusses whether the Land of Israel originally fell to the lot of Shem or Ham.

57 Some scholars have suggested that Hammurabi, the Babylonian king famous for authoring an ancient legal code, was identical to Nimrod, see D. S. Farkas, "In Search of the Biblical Hammurabi," *Jewish Bible Quarterly*, vol. 39:3 (Jerusalem: Jewish Bible Association, 2011), pgs. 159-165. Interestingly, the name Amraphel (which is another name for Nimrod, as we shall discuss in Chapter 3), bears some similarity to the name Hammurabi.

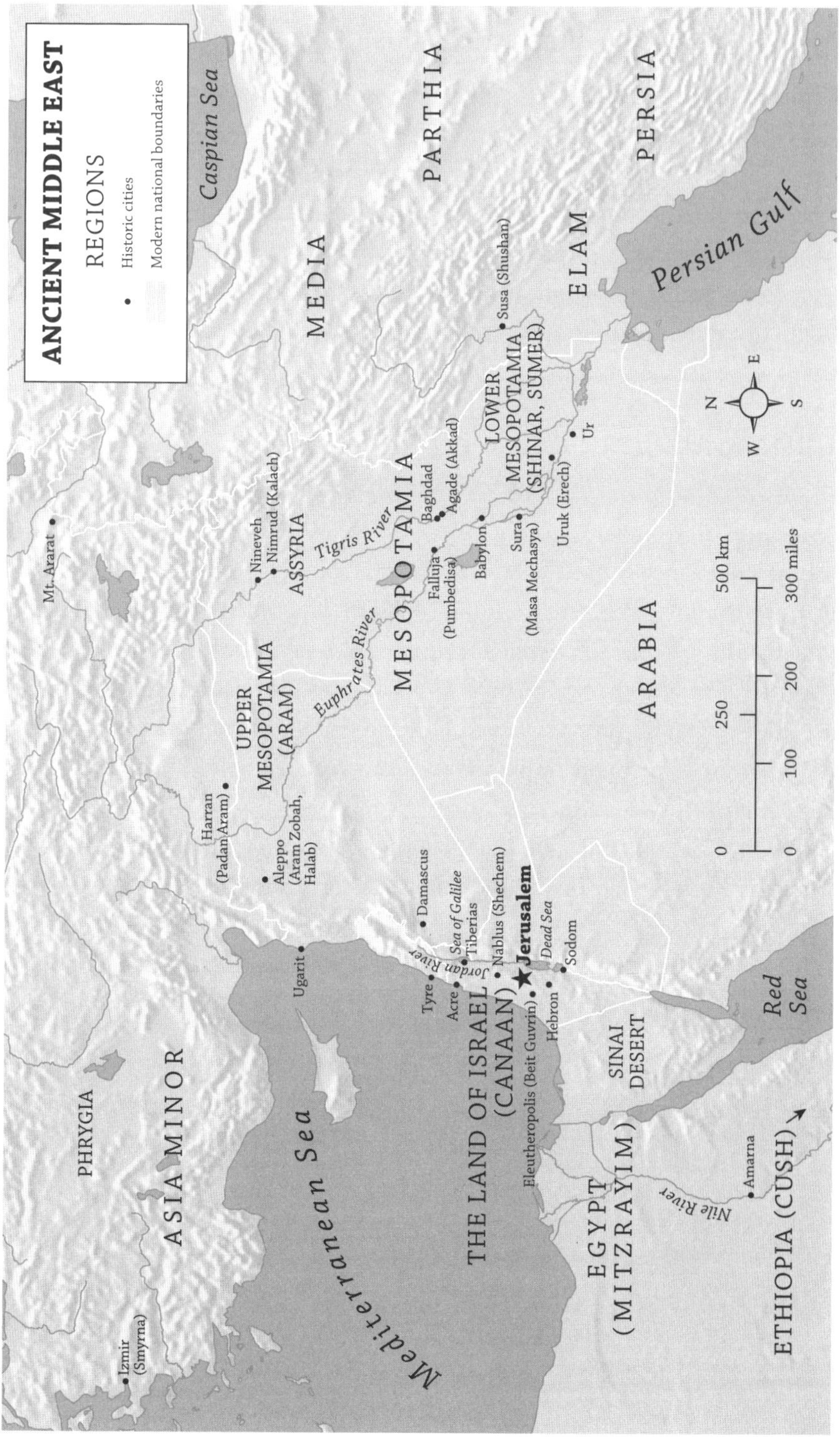
ANCIENT MIDDLE EAST
REGIONS
Historic cities
Modern national boundaries
Caspian Sea
PARTHIA
PERSIA
MEDIA
ELAM
Persian Gulf
Susa (Shushan)
LOWER MESOPOTAMIA (SHINAR, SUMER)
Ur
Uruk (Erech)
Agade (Akkad)
Baghdad
MESOPOTAMIA
Tigris River
Euphrates River
ASSYRIA
Nineveh
Nimrud (Kalach)
Mt. Ararat
Falluja (Pumbedisa)
Babylon
Sura (Masa Mechasya)
ARABIA
UPPER MESOPOTAMIA (ARAM)
Harran (Padan Aram)
Aleppo (Aram Zobah, Halab)
Damascus
Sea of Galilee
Tiberias
Nablus (Shechem)
Jerusalem
Dead Sea
Sodom
Hebron
Eleutheropolis (Beit Guvrin)
Jordan River
Tyre
Acre
Ugarit
THE LAND OF ISRAEL (CANAAN)
SINAI DESERT
Red Sea
EGYPT (MITZRAYIM)
Nile River
Amarna
ETHIOPIA (CUSH)
Mediterranean Sea
ASIA MINOR
PHRYGIA
Izmir (Smyrna)
N
E
S
W
0
250
500 km
0
100
200
300 miles

Shinar), the seat of Nimrod's rule, became the "cradle of civilization." Nimrod also founded three other cities in the region: Erech (Uruk), Akkad (Agade), and Calneh. Employing a technique that was later used throughout history, Nimrod created unity amongst his various subjects by creating a common external enemy—God Himself.[58] He convinced the people of the world to join him in rebelling against their Creator, and coordinated the construction of a giant tower to wage battle against God. Although much of humanity united in this effort to rebel against God, there were notable exceptions.[59]

THOSE WHO DID NOT PARTICIPATE

When Assur, the son of Shem, saw that his descendants heeded Nimrod's call to rebel against God, he left Nimrod's area of influence and established settlements elsewhere.[60] His family migrated northwestward to the Mesopotamian region of Aram, where they built several cities including Rechovos, Kalach (Nimrud), Resen, and their capital city Nineveh. The empire established by Assur and his descendants is known as the Assyrian Empire. However, Nimrod and his minions, bent on world domination, continued to harass and attack those Semites who had fled his domain.[61]

Midrash Yelamdenu says that five pious people did not participate in the rebellion at the Tower of Babel. Assur, as mentioned above, left southern Mesopotamia and thus distanced himself from Nimrod's actions. Shem, Eber, and Abraham,[62] all of whom were Semites, hid themselves in order to avoid joining the rebellion. Noah risked his life at-

---

58 According to *Pirkei D'Rabbi Eliezer* (Ch. 24), Nimrod used the special garments of Adam and Eve in order to miraculously subdue wild animals and birds. This led people to assume that he possessed great powers, so they appointed him as king over them.

59 See TB *Chullin* 89a and Rashi there.

60 Ibn Ezra (to *Genesis* 10:11) writes that this occurred after the division of the languages at the Tower of Babel.

61 Ramban to *Genesis* ibid.

62 Another source for the fact that Abraham did not participate in the building of the Tower of Babel is TB *Avodah Zarah* 19a. However, see Ibn Ezra (to *Genesis* 11:1) who proves from the Bible that Abraham was alive during the time of the Tower of Babel and contributed to its construction.

tempting to rebuke the sinners at the Tower of Babel,[63] but his efforts were rebuffed.[64]

Why did Balaam and the builders at Babel speak *Lashon HaKodesh*?

The *Zohar* (*Noach* 75b), the principal textbook of Kabbalah, also adopts the approach favored by Rashi and *Midrash Tanchuma* that the builders of the Tower of Babel spoke *Lashon HaKodesh*. The *Zohar* writes that because the builders of the Tower of Babel had arranged their sin by using *Lashon HaKodesh* for communication, they were granted supernatural powers to complete their ambitious project. *Lashon HaKodesh* is an especially holy language and when used for good, it can help significantly raise one's spiritual potential. However, the converse is also true: When *Lashon HaKodesh* is used to sin, it enables the sinner to sink deeper into the depths of evil. Thus, explains the *Zohar*, God stopped the builders from finishing their project of rebellion against Him by causing them to forget *Lashon HaKodesh*, thereby cutting off their supernatural support.

Based on this concept, Rabbi Aharon Roth (1893–1946) and Rabbi Yoel Teitelbaum note that a verbal sin (e.g., immoral speech, slander, blasphemy) committed in *Lashon HaKodesh* is a much more serious offense than such a sin committed in any another language.

Source: Rabbi Roth's *Ma'amar Tzahali V'Rini* (chps. 2–4, printed at the end of *Shomrei Emunim*, Jerusalem, 2002), and Rabbi Teitelbaum's *VaYoel Moshe (Ma'amar Lashon HaKodesh* §18–19).

Similarly, the *Old Midrash Tanchuma (Balak* §13) says that Balaam, the infamous prophet of impurity, spoke *Lashon HaKodesh*—as if to imply that it was the source of his evil powers. Interestingly, in 1967 archeologists in Jordan found an ancient inscription that purports to be a transcription of Balaam's prophecies. This text, known as the Deir `Alla Inscription, was written in a distinct dialect of *Lashon HaKodesh*/Canaanite which bears close resemblance to the language of the Bible.

Source: G. Rendsburg, "The Dialect of the Deir `Alla Inscription," *Bibliotheca Orientalis* (Leiden, May–July 1993) pgs. 309–329.

---

63 Although this Midrash seems to imply that Noah was martyred by the sinners at the Tower of Babel because he tried to stop them, this cannot be. A simple calculation reveals that Noah continued to live for several years after the destruction of the Tower of Babel, see *Seder Olam Rabbah* (Ch. 1). Perhaps the sinners fatally wounded him and he died afterwards.

64 S. A. Wertheimer (ed.), *Batei Midrashos*, vol. 1 (Jerusalem: Mossad HaRav Kook, 1954), pg. 149.

THE TORAH RECORDS THE DIVISION OF LANGUAGES

The Torah introduces the narrative of the Tower of Babel by noting its time period in a very unique way: "It was when all the land was of one language [lit. lip or mouth][65] and one word."[66] After the Torah describes the rebellion, it tells of God's response: In order to punish the builders of the Tower, He said, "Let us[67] descend and mix their speech, so that one man cannot hear the speech of his fellow."[68] God caused a loss of communication between the offending rebels, thus halting the rebellion in its tracks.

WHICH LANGUAGE(S) WAS SPOKEN PRE-BABEL? A DISPUTE IN THE JERUSALEM TALMUD

The Jerusalem Talmud records a dispute between two sages concerning which language(s) was spoken before the Tower of Babel.[69] One rabbi says that prior to the destruction of the Tower of Babel, the entire world

---

65 There are two Hebrew words to refer to a language: a "mouth" (שפה, *safa*) and a "tongue" (לשון, *lashon*). Here, regarding the language spoken in pre-Babel civilization, the Bible refers to their language as a "mouth." However, when referring to *Lashon HaKodesh*, we automatically use the latter word, which literally means "tongue."

Rabbi Eliyahu Eliezer Dessler (1892–1953), as quoted by his student Rabbi Aharon Rother (author of the popular *Sha'arei Aharon*), explains the difference between these two terms: One's "mouth" is an external feature of his body, while one's "tongue" is an internal feature. Consequently, one can only refer to a language as a "tongue" when its speakers embody the inner meaning of that language. A language can be called a "mouth" when its speakers only embody the technical, external features of the language. Consequently, the Jews refer to *Lashon HaKodesh* as a "tongue" because they strive to internalize the moral and esteemed values signified by the language. Although the sinners of the generation of Babel may have spoken the same language, they only applied it externally, without incorporating its values. This explanation was printed in an article by Rabbi Rother in *Kovetz Eitz Chaim* (Bobov), vol. 8 (Brooklyn, 2009), pg. 275, and was more recently mentioned by Rabbi Mordechai Shifman of Emek Hebrew Academy/Teichman Family Torah Center in his popular Daf Yomi *shiur* (JT *Shekalim* 9). This concept is already discussed by Rabbi Eliyahu Kramer of Vilna (*Biur HaGra* to *Proverbs* 12:19) and Malbim (to *Song of Songs* 4:11 and *Psalms* 120:2).

66 *Genesis* 11:1.

67 Here, the Torah specifically uses verbs in their plural form. This implies that God did not act alone in mixing the languages of the world. In fact, *Targum Jonathan* (to *Genesis* 11:7) and *Pirkei D'Rabbi Eliezer* (Ch. 24) maintain that God dispatched seventy angels to disseminate the seventy languages throughout the world. However, see Rashi there for another explanation as to why the plural form is used.

68 *Genesis* 11:7.

69 JT *Megillah* 1:9.

civilization spoke seventy languages.[70] The other rabbi says that they only spoke the "one mouth," which is *Lashon HaKodesh*. The reason for this nomenclature is that *Lashon HaKodesh* is the language, or "mouth," of God, who is the Unique One in the world.[71]

RASHI'S VIEW THAT THE PRE-BABEL LANGUAGE WAS LASHON HAKODESH

Rabbi Shlomo ben Yitzchak (1040–1105), better known as Rashi,[72] adopts the latter approach that before the incident of the Tower of Babel, all of the world's civilizations shared a single common language: *Lashon HaKodesh*. Therefore, he explains that when the Torah writes "one mouth," it refers to *Lashon HaKodesh*.[73] In essence, *Midrash Tanchuma* also follows this view, and links the fact that God created the world using *Lashon HaKodesh* to the fact that it was humanity's language until the Tower of Babel.[74] *Midrash Tanchuma* reinforces this picture of events by saying that God diversified the world's languages in order to prevent the collaborators of the Tower of Babel from being able to understand each other. Global communication spontaneously broke down, resulting in utter chaos and confusion.

IBN EZRA EXPLAINS HOW THE LANGUAGES WERE DIVIDED

In his commentary to Genesis, Rabbi Avraham ibn Ezra (1092–1167) offers an interesting description of how the languages were divided. He writes that originally the one spoken language was indeed *Lashon HaKodesh*.[75] However, after the episode of the Tower of Babel, God spread

---

70 Rabbi David Frankel (*Korban HaEidah* to JT *Megillah* 1:9) explains that according to this opinion, everybody was able to understand all seventy languages (see below). *Pnei Moshe* (there) adds that these seventy languages predated the Deluge, and that Noah and his sons taught them to the world after the Deluge.

71 A third sage, Bar Kapara, opined that before the Tower of Babel, they spoke Greek. The significance of Greek within the grouping of Jewish languages is discussed later (Chapters 5 and 7).

72 In his commentary to *Genesis* 11:1.

73 *Baal HaTurim* to *Genesis* 11:1 says that the *gematria* (numerical value) of the Hebrew term "one mouth" (שפה אחת, *safa echas*) equals the numerical value of the term "*Lashon HaKodesh*" (לשון הקדש).

74 See *Midrash Tanchuma, Noach* §19. This Midrash is also quoted in the *Old Tanchuma* (Buber) *Noach*, §28 and *Midrash Aggadah, Noach*.

75 Ibn Ezra writes that he is inclined to explain that "one mouth" (*Genesis* 11:1) means that

the peoples across the world. In their newfound habitats, the varying societies did not remain in contact with each other. Thus, the single language that all of humanity spoke was eventually forgotten and instead various other languages developed based on peoples' locale. Ibn Ezra's approach leans toward a more natural progression than the approach assumed by others that the new languages sprung up miraculously, as we shall discuss below.

ARCHEOLOGICAL SUPPORT FOR THE IBN EZRA'S VIEW

Archeology supports Ibn Ezra's explanation by affirming that people in the areas closer to where the Tower of Babel stood spoke languages that resembled *Lashon HaKodesh* more closely than the languages spoken by people who lived in areas farther away. For example, the languages spoken in Mesopotamia and the Levant include Aramaic, Arabic, Akkadian, and Ugaritic. Of all languages, these are the most similar to *Lashon HaKodesh*. The languages spoken in the Middle East, but farther away from Babylon, such as Ancient Egyptian and Coptic, less resemble *Lashon HaKodesh*. However, both of these language groups bear more of a semblance to *Lashon HaKodesh* than languages that were spoken in areas even farther away from the Tower of Babel, such as the Indo-European languages, which were spoken in Europe.[76]

BECHOR-SCHOR: SEVENTY LANGUAGES WERE SPOKEN PRE-BABEL

Unlike Rashi, Rabbi Yosef Bechor-Schor (a twelfth-century French Tosafist) adopts the first approach mentioned in the Jerusalem Talmud. He writes in his commentary to *Genesis* 11:1 that before the destruction of the Tower of Babel, the entire world spoke all seventy languages. Then, he writes, God punished them by making each person

---

everybody spoke *Lashon HaKodesh* (like Rashi, see also Ralbag there who is so inclined). He proves this from Adam, Eve, Kayin, Seth, and Peleg, whose names are sourced in words found in *Lashon HaKodesh*. This proof, which is similar to what we have mentioned in Chapter 1 from *The Kuzari*, is also quoted in *Akeidas Yitzchak* (Gate 8) and *Tosafos HaShaleim* (*Genesis* 11:1 §6). However, see *Safa Berurah* (Fürth, 1839), pg. 4a, where Ibn Ezra concedes that the words for "life" in Aramaic (חייא) and Arabic (الحياة) are very similar to the word for "life" in Hebrew *chayim* (חיים). Thus, Eve's name does not necessarily prove that they spoke *Lashon HaKodesh*.

76 See Y. Y. Zilberberg/Di Kasif, *Leshonenu HaKedoshah* (Tel Aviv, 1963), pgs. 124–125.

forget sixty-nine languages and remember only one, thus wreaking havoc upon society.[77]

TEXTUAL SUPPORT FOR BECHOR-SCHOR'S VIEW

Like Bechor-Schor, Rabbeinu Chaim Paltiel (a thirteenth-century German Tosafist) also accepts the first approach cited in the Jerusalem Talmud.[78] He supports this position from the fact that the Torah chronicles pre-Tower of Babel civilization "according to their families and according to their *languages*."[79] This implies that multiple languages already existed before the Tower of Babel. However, Rabbi David Kimchi (1160–1235), known as Radak, mentions this proof[80] and refutes it by explaining that this passage is not written in chronological order. It refers to the nations that developed *after* the destruction of the Tower of Babel, each of which had its own language. Before the Tower, only *Lashon HaKodesh* was spoken.

ANOTHER SUPPORT FOR BECHOR-SCHOR'S VIEW

Rabbi Chizkiyah ben Manoach (a thirteenth-century French commentator), known as *Chizkuni* (after his commentary on the Pentateuch), also rejects Rashi's approach in favor of the first opinion in the Jerusalem Talmud.[81] He writes that one cannot reasonably explain that God created multiple languages in order to punish the builders of the Tower of Babel because after the seven days of Creation, God stopped creating new entities *ex nihilo*, and only "manages" that which He has already created. This concept is derived from King Solomon's famous words: "There is nothing new under the sun."[82] Since this principle precludes the innovation of new languages, *Chizkuni* rejects Rashi's approach and concludes, as does Bechor-Schor, that the seventy languages were already in use before the Tower of Babel, and God made each person forget sixty-nine languages as a punishment.

---

77 In his commentary to *Genesis* 11:7.

78 In his commentary to *Genesis* 11:1.

79 *Genesis* 10:5, 10:20, 10:30.

80 In his commentary to *Genesis* 2:20.

81 *Chizkuni* to *Genesis* 11:1; the same is quoted by *Moshav Zekeinim* and Bechor-Schor there.

82 *Ecclesiastes* 1:9.

A DEFENSE OF RASHI

Contrary to this line of thought, Rabbi Levi ben Gershon (1288–1344), known as Ralbag/Gersonides, mentions that God did indeed create the seventy languages as a punishment for the Tower of Babel.[83] It seems that

The Tower of Babel outside of the Bible

Many other cultures—including those who were seemingly not influenced by the Bible—also attest to a story linking the destruction of a tower to the division of languages. The Mexican historian Mariano Veytia (1720–1778) mentions such a story as part of the Toltec (precursors to Aztecs) tradition. See D. & D. Hemingway, *Ancient America Rediscovered* (Cedar Fort, 2000), pgs. 44–54.

Another such story is found in Ancient Sumer literature, which mentions that when a certain overly tall ziggurat was destroyed, the languages were divided (see *Enmerkar and the Lord of Aratta*, Section 1, line 134). Similarly, Hao culture also has a tradition of such a story; see *Religious and Cosmic Beliefs of Central Polynesia* (Cambridge, 1933), pg. 94.

Another account, purportedly basing itself on the biblical account, is told in Irish folklore about King Fénius Farsaid, who traveled to Babel to compile the "perfect language" based on all seventy languages, which were established after the destruction of the Tower of Babel. According to Irish tradition, the language that he developed was the Gaelic language. However, D. Cróinín, *A New History of Ireland* (Oxford University Press, 2005), pg. 462, contends that this story was fabricated in order to reconcile the primitive accounts of Irish origins with Christian theology.

For a more extensive discussion of the division of languages in other cultures and denials of the biblical accounts, see A.D. White, *The Warfare of Science with Theology* (New York, 1896), Ch. XVII, "From Babel to Comparative Philology."

the root of the dispute between *Chizkuni* and Ralbag is where to draw the fine line between what exactly constitutes a completely new creation, and what is merely using (in new ways) that which has already been created. New languages are not necessarily new creations; they are new concepts.

Furthermore, according to Ibn Ezra's explanation that the seventy

83 Ralbag to *Genesis* 11:1.

languages resulted from the dispersal of *Lashon HaKodesh* speakers, even Rashi (who held that God created the seventy languages as a punishment) could agree that the new seventy languages were not a "creation," per se. Rather, they were the natural byproducts of relocating people to separate areas where they lost contact with one another.

RABBI BARUCH EPSTEIN'S NOVEL PROPOSAL

Rabbi Baruch HaLevi Epstein (1860–1940) proposes another explanation, which fits neatly with all the above-mentioned opinions. He writes that before the destruction of the Tower of Babel, each society spoke two languages: one language was used internally amongst the members of that society, and one diplomatic language was used to interact with other groups. All groups had to understand the latter universal language, but needed not understand all of the individual societal languages. The universal inter-societal language understood by all was *Lashon HaKodesh*. When all of humanity decided to join in building the Tower of Babel, they decided to use *Lashon HaKodesh* as their common language. Therefore, when building the Tower, everyone spoke with "one mouth." Thus, when God wished to halt the Tower's construction, He made everyone forget *Lashon HaKodesh* so that the different societal groups could no longer interact with one another. Now they only knew their internal societal languages, but not the common global language. This lack of communication stopped the construction of the Tower of Babel, and brought mayhem and disorder to the world.[84] According to Rabbi Epstein's approach, there is no dispute in the Jerusalem Talmud about whether the pre-Babel civilization spoke *Lashon HaKodesh* or all seventy languages, because the two options are not mutually exclusive.[85]

---

84 *Torah Temimah* to *Genesis* 11:1 §1.

85 The Talmud relates (TB *Sanhedrin* 109a) that the airspace over which the Tower of Babel once stood causes forgetfulness. There, Rashi explains that God had decreed that area to be a place of forgetting, just as the builders of the Tower of Babel forgot their languages. In this explanation, Rashi mentions the "forgetting of languages," not the "creation of new languages." Thus, one could infer that Rashi, like Bechor-Schor, adopts the first opinion mentioned in the Jerusalem Talmud that all seventy languages were spoken pre-Babel (and as a punishment, each person forgot sixty-nine). However, this contradicts Rashi's stance in his commentary to *Genesis*, which reflects the second opinion that only *Lashon HaKodesh* was spoken pre-Babel.

RESOLVING THE OBJECTIONS TO RASHI'S VIEW

Interestingly, according to this understanding, one can refute *Chizkuni* and Rabbeinu Chaim Paltiel's objections to Rashi's view (that God would not create new things), for all seventy languages had already existed and were in use before the destruction of the Tower of Babel. Nonetheless, the disappearance of *Lashon HaKodesh* as the global language still caused a major upheaval.

THE ORIGINS OF LASHON HAKODESH VS. OTHER LANGUAGES

Rabbi Nissim of Gerona (1315–1376) writes that with the exception of *Lashon HaKodesh*, all languages are based on a consensus of individuals.[86] This idea nicely complements Ibn Ezra's explanation mentioned above. The notion that words do not have inherent meaning, and are only defined by their usage, is echoed by the suggestion of the Austrian philosopher Ludwig Wittgenstein (1889–1951) who famously wrote, "The meaning of a word is its use in the language."[87]

LASHON HAKODESH IS NOT MANMADE

In the first chapter of *Ma'aseh Efod*, Efodi writes that *Lashon HaKodesh* (lit. "The Holy Language") is called such because God taught it directly to Adam (or at least gave him the abilities to intuit the language, as we explained previously), as opposed to all other languages that are based on peoples' agreements.[88] Thus, he understands that

---

One way to resolve this contradiction is to posit that Rashi held that the Babylonian Talmud accepts the first opinion cited in the Jerusalem Talmud, and thus his commentary on the Babylonian Talmud reflects the first opinion. However, Rashi himself accepts the second opinion cited in the Jerusalem Talmud, and thus his commentary on *Genesis* reflects this.

According to Rabbi Epstein, there is an easier way of resolving this contradiction. Rashi indeed understood that before the division of languages everyone spoke *Lashon HaKodesh* as a global language, but this was in addition to their local languages. Accordingly, at the division of languages, people *forgot* the one global language and only remembered the local ones.

86 *Pirush HaRan* to TB *Nedarim* 2a. He also acknowledges that the one pre-Babel language was *Lashon HaKodesh*, see L. A. Feldman (ed.), *Pirush HaRan Al HaTorah* (Jerusalem: Machon Shalem, 1968), pg. 145.

87 *Philosophical Investigations* §43.

88 *Ma'aseh Efod* (Vienna, 1865), pg. 28.

the language is called the "Holy Language" because it was taught by the Holy One.

In order to better appreciate this facet of the uniqueness of *Lashon HaKodesh*, we must understand a concept set forth so succinctly by Rabbi Dr. Akiva Tatz:

> In Torah, words always express essence, and close study of the words is rewarded by an understanding of the nature of the ideas which those words describe. In the secular world, words are also revealing: The language of a culture reveals its heart.
>
> If one inclines a sensitive ear to the expression of ideas within a society, one gains insight into its values. In Torah, words express essence because words are in fact the basis for the existence of those things which they describe: the world was created by God's *saying* the words which themselves became the objects of Creation. In Hebrew, the word for a "word" and for a "thing" are the same, *davar* [דבר]; all things in the world are in fact none other than divine words crystallized into material existence. The words are the medium of Creation, and a correct grasp of the words is a correct grasp of the elements of Creation.[89]

Thus, the words of *Lashon HaKodesh* express the very essence of what they describe, while the words of other languages simply represent a consensus shared by several individuals that those words should have those meanings. The meaning of the words of *Lashon HaKodesh* is divinely inherent; the meaning of words in other languages is a practical matter based on the arbitrary whims of human beings.[90]

---

89 A. Tatz, *Worldmask* (Targum Press, 1995), pgs. 89–90. See there for an explanation of why certain words which convey popular cultural ideas are completely absent from *Lashon HaKodesh*. He explains that the absence of those words proves the irrelevance of those ideas. Rabbi Tzvi Inbal (a director of Arachim), a popular lecturer and TV show host on the Hidabroot channel in Israel, regularly speaks about the spiritual significance of *Lashon HaKodesh* and the deeper meanings of its words.

90 As we shall elaborate upon in Appendix C "Prayers in Aramaic," there is quite a commotion about the halachic ramifications of praying in a language other than *Lashon HaKodesh*. Rabbi Elazar Landau (1778–1831) writes (in his glosses to TB *Sotah* 32a) that if one recites a blessing in a language

RABBI S. R. HIRSCH ON THE TOWER OF BABEL

Rabbi Samson Raphael Hirsch (1808–1888) offers a deeper insight as to what exactly transpired at the Tower of Babel, and what part that incident played in the historical development of languages. He explains that before the Tower of Babel, language was an objective means of expression.[91] *Lashon HaKodesh*, in particular, was the medium that God used to express His will to Adam and to each and every person, because its meaning was unambiguous and universally accepted. However, when humanity decided to unite in rebellion against God, they sought to stifle individuality, and instead use language as a global means of turning the population against Him.

---

other than *Lashon HaKodesh*, one's obligation to recite that blessing is only fulfilled if one understands what he said. However, if he does not know the meaning of what he said, then he has not discharged himself from his obligation. Yet, Rabbi Landau notes, if one recites a blessing in *Lashon HaKodesh*, he always fulfills his obligation, even if he does not understand the meaning. Rabbi Yisrael Meir Kagan (1838–1933) asks (*Biur Halacha* to *Orach Chaim* §62): Why is *Lashon HaKodesh* different from all other languages in that one can use it to fulfill his requirement to recite a blessing even if he does not understand it?

Rabbi Asher Arieli, a senior lecturer at Yeshivas Mir in Jerusalem, answers (in his lectures to TB *Nedarim* 3a) that all other languages are simply translations of *Lashon HaKodesh*. Thus, they are simply a means to an end; their validity lies in the fact that they present substitutes for the words of *Lashon HaKodesh*. Therefore, if one does not understand the other language, it is irrelevant to him. Furthermore, because he cannot use that language to serve as a means of relating to *Lashon HaKodesh*, it loses its status as a language. However, *Lashon HaKodesh* is not simply a translation—a means to an end—it is an end in its own right. The words of *Lashon HaKodesh* are the originals, thus they are inherently words. Therefore, if one recites a blessing in *Lashon HaKodesh*, even if one does not understand the meaning, one has nonetheless recited the proper words and thus discharged one's obligation. The deep implications of Rabbi Arieli's explanation echo the concept mentioned above that only the words of *Lashon HaKodesh* possess inherent meaning. Rabbi Moshe Feinstein in *Dibbros Moshe* (*Nedarim* §2:4) offers a similar approach. See *Chiddushei HaGriz HaLevi* (to TB *Sotah* 32b), which offers another explanation of this *halachah* in the name of Rabbi Yitzchak Zev HaLevi Soloveitchik and his son Rabbi Yosef Dov HaLevi Soloveitchik (1915–1981).

Rabbi Yisrael Taplin (in responsa *Orach Yisrael* §4) adds to Rabbi Landau's ruling that Aramaic has the same status as *Lashon HaKodesh* in that if someone recites a blessing in Aramaic, he fulfills his obligation even if he does not understand Aramaic. Rabbi Taplin justifies his position through one of two explanations: Either Aramaic is considered a holy language like *Lashon HaKodesh* because it too is of divine origin, or Aramaic is considered to be one with *Lashon HaKodesh* because it developed from *Lashon HaKodesh* (see below Chapter 8).

91 Interestingly, Rabbi Hirsch writes that although before the Tower of Babel everyone spoke one language, he concedes that different groups spoke different dialects of that one language. See *Chumash Im Pirush HaRav Hirsch* (Jerusalem: Mossad Yitzchak Breuer, 2002), pg. 127.

In response to this effort, God rekindled people's sense of individuality, with all of their personal tendencies and biases. Their individuality overpowered their sense of community, resulting in a shift in the role of language. Language was no longer an objective means of expression. Instead, it became the individual's vehicle of his own personal will and egoist proclivity. Under such circumstances, language could no longer be used as a means of facilitating global cooperation, because each individual heard things the way he wanted to hear them and said things the way he wanted to say them in order to fit his own personal agenda. As a result, the spoken language was no longer *Lashon HaKodesh*—the clear and objective language—rather, the language became fragmented into various subjective languages clouded by the individual perceptions of their speakers.[92]

CHAPTER SUMMARY

In short, the story of the Tower of Babel is one of the most important points in the history of *Lashon HaKodesh*. In that story, we see that those wishing to rebel against God took this language that He graciously gave mankind and used it to unify all people against Him. In the context of that story, we raised several important points about the history and holiness of *Lashon HaKodesh*.

- **History:** The Jerusalem Talmud mentions a dispute between two sages concerning the role of *Lashon HaKodesh* in pre-Babel civilization, a dispute that continued even to medieval times. Nonetheless, it is all but unanimous that *Lashon HaKodesh* was in fact spoken then. We bridged the gap between these opinions by explaining that *Lashon HaKodesh* was used as a diplomatic language between different groups, even though within each group other languages existed. On a historical level, *Lashon HaKodesh*, which was more prominent and widespread before the Tower of Babel, lost its prevalence afterwards.
- **Holiness:** We discussed the differences between *Lashon*

92 *Chumash Im Pirush HaRav Hirsch*, vol. 1 (Jerusalem: Mossad Yitzchak Breuer, 2002), pgs. 132–134.

HaKodesh and other languages, most notably that the former is not manmade like other languages. On a more esoteric level, we explained that only in *Lashon HaKodesh* do words possess inherent divine meaning, while people arbitrarily decide the meanings of words in other languages. Rabbi Hirsch took this idea a step further and explained that *Lashon HaKodesh* represents a clear objective language, unclouded by personal whims, while other languages are the products of individual creativity. On a spiritual level, at the Tower of Babel, humanity no longer focused on one clear goal of following the will of God, but rather splintered into differing goals and objectives with no regard for the will of God.

An artist's rendering of the Tower of Babel (Source: "Tower of Babel" by French artist Paul Gustave Dore (1832–1883). Public domain.)

REWARD FOR THOSE WHO DID NOT JOIN IN

As mentioned above, Noah, Shem, Eber, Assur, and Abraham did not join the rebellion, and refrained from participating in the construction of the Tower of Babel. God rewarded them for their dedication by granting them a special connection to the original pre-Babel language: *Lashon HaKodesh*.

That is, Noah and Shem were rewarded in that the language continued to live on through their descendants. Eber was rewarded in particular in that the language would temporarily use the so-called "Eberite" (*Ivri*) script for writing,[93] and be called "Hebrew" as a tribute to him (as discussed in the next chapter). Assur, the progenitor of the Assyrian nation, was rewarded in that the permanent script used to write *Lashon HaKodesh* would be the so-called "Assyrian" (*Ashuri*) script.[94] In addition, as reward for rejecting Nimrod's scheme, Abraham (then a relatively young man at the age of forty-eight) did not forget *Lashon HaKodesh* like everyone else did. He and his descendants are charged with preserving the Holy Language.[95]

---

93 See Appendix A "The Scripts of *Lashon HaKodesh*."

94 Y. Y. Zilberberg/Di Kasif, *Leshonenu HaKedoshah* (Tel Aviv, 1963), pg. 125. See also *Piskei Tosafos* (TB *Megillah* §23).

95 See Rabbi David Luria's *Chiddushei HaRadal* to *Pirkei D'Rabbi Eliezer*, Ch. 26.

CHAPTER 3:
Abraham the Hebrew

ABRAHAM AND NIMROD'S EARLY ENCOUNTERS

The rebellion at the Tower of Babel was not the first time that Abraham and Nimrod locked horns, nor was it the last. Abraham was born in the city of Ur in Mesopotamia, within the sphere of Nimrod's influence. He and his minions had sought to kill Abraham as a newborn baby.[96] As a result, Abraham was hidden in a cave, where he lived alone for the first thirteen years of his life. The Midrash describes Abraham when he finally emerged from his underground hideaway. It mentions, *inter alia*, that he spoke *Lashon HaKodesh*.

Many years later, Abraham hid himself again to avoid participating in Nimrod's plot to rebel against God with the Tower of Babel. After the Tower of Babel, Abraham gained a reputation for his iconoclastic stance against idolatry. For this "offense," Nimrod—civilization's biggest

---

96 *Pirkei D'Rabbi Eliezer* Ch. 26.

sponsor of idolatry—sentenced him to death by fiery furnace.[97] After Abraham miraculously emerged unscathed from the inferno, his father Terah decided to relocate the family. They moved from Ur (within Nimrod's domain) to the city of Harran in the Aram region,[98] which was relatively free from Nimrod's reign of terror.[99] It was from Harran that Abraham later embarked on his historic journey to the Land of Canaan, which God had promised to give to him and his descendants.[100]

NIMROD WEAKENS

After Nimrod's defeat at the Tower of Babel, he lost prestige and his name was changed to Amraphel (אמרפל) to honor his subjects who had fallen (*naflu*, נפלו) at the Tower of Babel.[101] As a result of the societal upheaval caused by the division of languages, Nimrod lost his dominion over the Mesopotamian region and its Hamitic populace to a different Hamitic king: Chedorlaomer, the king of Elam.[102] Nimrod, who had once

---

97 TB *Pesachim* 118a, *Bereishis Rabbah* §38:13, *Targum Jonathan* (to *Genesis* 11:28), and more. This story occurred when Abraham was fifty years old, see *Sefer HaYashar* (Bene Barak: Mishor Publishing, 2005), pg. 32.

98 Josephus in his *Antiquities of the Jews* quotes the first-century Greek historian Nicolaus of Damascus that Abraham, a "foreigner" from Babylonia, came to Aram. There he reigned as a king for some time until he and his people embarked from there and settled in the Land of Canaan. See *Kisvei Yosef ben Matisyahu, Kadmonius HaYehudim*, vol. 1 (Jerusalem: Reuven Mass, 1939), pg. 31.

99 *Genesis* 11:31.

100 *Genesis* 12.

101 *Sefer HaYashar* (Bene Barak: Mishor Publishing, 2005), pg. 31. TB *Eruvin* 53a states that Nimrod was renamed Amraphel by the Torah for a different reason: Because he proclaimed that Abraham should be cast (*nafal*, נפל) into a fiery furnace. See also *Bereishis Rabbah* §42:4 and *Targum Jonathan* (*Genesis* 14:1), who also assume that Nimrod and Amraphel are one and the same.

102 In his supercommentary to Rashi, Rabbi Eliyahu Mizrachi (1450–1526) explains that Chedorlaomer was actually a Semite. *Genesis* 10:22 lists Elam as a son of Shem. He reasons that if Elam was a Semite, then the nation named after him, as well as its king, were also Semites. This explanation can be seen from Rashi's source *Midrash Tanchuma* (Lech Lecha §15). However, due to some wording issues, the Midrash's intent is not so clear. The Yemenite scholar Rabbi Nesanel ben Yishaya (*Meor Ha'Afeila* to *Genesis* 10:22) takes this idea even further, and writes that Chedorlaomer was Elam himself. According to these views, one must explain that for whatever reason Chedorlaomer decided to ally himself with the Hamites even though he himself was Semitic. Alternatively, one can say that Chedorlaomer himself was of Hamitic descent, and his Elamite subjects were Semitic. Parenthetically, experts have identified the Elamite language as

been an emperor, became merely the local king of Babylon. Chedorlaomer, who had previously been his vassal, now became his overlord.[103]

THE HAMITIC AXIS ATTACKS THE SEMITES

Not long afterwards, Chedorlaomer, Nimrod, and two other Hamitic kings from Mesopotamia made a foray into what would later become the Land of Israel. They subjugated five Semitic city-states in the Jordan River Valley: Sodom, Gomorrah, Admah, Zeboiim, and Zoar. For twelve years, the four-king Hamitic axis ruled over these five Semitic kingdoms, and required them to pay a yearly tribute. In the thirteenth year, the five Semitic kings rebelled by not paying the tribute. They reasoned that it was improper for the Hamites, who were supposed to be slaves to the descendants of Shem and Japheth, to instead rule over them.[104] In the fourteenth year, the Hamitic axis led an expedition to conquer various other nations in the Land of Canaan, including the Rephaim, Zuzim, Emim, and Horites. The five allied Semitic kings from the Jordan River Valley took this as an opportunity to unite their forces and attack the Hamitic army. The nations threatened by the oncoming Hamitic army promised to support them.[105] Nonetheless, the Hamitic axis ultimately defeated the Semitic alliance, plundered their property, and took captives.[106]

---

a linguistic "isolate"; it is not obviously related to any other family of languages. Their language is neither clearly Semitic nor Hamitic, and thus gives no clue as to the ethnicity of its speakers. For reasons not entirely relevant to our discussion, Dr. Yehoshua Meir Grintz of Tel Aviv University (1911–1976) also discusses the placement of Elam amongst the sons of Shem as opposed to amongst the Hamites; see Y. L. Maimon (ed.), *Sinai*, vol. 159 (Jerusalem: Mossad HaRav Kook, 1950), pg. 137 and *Barzilai* (pg. 147).

103 *Sefer HaYashar* (Bene Barak: Mishor Publishing, 2005), pg. 32.

104 In their respective commentaries to *Genesis* 14:2, several Tosafists (including Rabbeinu Yaakov of Vienna, Rabbeinu Chaim Paltiel, and *Paneach Raza*) explain that this was the Sodomites' (who were Semitic) rationale for rebelling against the Hamitic axis. These sources assume that the five city-states were Semitic. However, see *Sefer HaYashar* (Bene Barak: Mishor Publishing, 2005), pg. 30, which says that the settlements of Sodom, Gomorrah, etc. were established by descendants of Ham, not Shem.

105 J. Klugmann (ed.), *Pirush HaRokeach Al HaTorah*, vol. 1 (Bene Barak, 2009), pgs. 136, 138.

106 Rabbi Aharon Marcus in *Kadmonios* (Krakow, 1896), pgs. 50–62, discusses archeological evidence of this war and its major players.

ABRAHAM AND NIMROD MEET AGAIN

Amongst these captives was Lot, Abraham's nephew. A refugee informed Abraham of his nephew's abduction, whereupon Abraham set off to rescue him. Abraham was thrust into the midst of the war—on the side of the Semitic alliance—with three hundred and eighteen members of his household at his disposal (or, according to some Midrashic interpretations, with just his servant Eliezer). Thus, he was once again pitted against Nimrod.[107] Ultimately, Abraham prevailed, killed the four Hamitic kings (including Nimrod), and chased their armies northwards past Damascus.[108]

ABRAHAM AND THE OTHER SEMITES

In the aftermath of the war, two Semitic dignitaries visited Abraham to express their gratitude for his assistance: Melchizedek King of Salem,[109] and the anonymous king of Sodom.[110] According to rabbinic tradition, Melchizedek King of Salem was none other than Shem, the son of Noah—the quintessential Semite. His kingdom, the city-state of Salem, later came to be known as Jerusalem.[111] Shem was grateful to his descendant Abraham for having successfully defended some of the last strongholds of Semitic resistance from the Hamites. However, history would show the Semitic city-states there to be merely temporary footholds in the future Land of Israel; the Semites would eventually lose that entire land to tribes of Canaanites, who were Hamitic.[112]

---

107 According to the *Zohar* (*Lech Lecha* 86b), Nimrod and his allies planned the entire war so that they could finally kill Abraham and stop his anti-idolatry campaign. In fact, the *Zohar* says that they kidnapped Lot under the mistaken impression that he was Abraham, because the two looked very similar.

108 *Genesis* 14:1-15.

109 *Sefer HaYashar* (Bene Barak: Mishor Publishing, 2005), pg. 54, refers to Shem as Adonizedek. However, this is likely a mistake due to confusing the name Melchizedek (the king of Salem mentioned in *Genesis*, who came to greet Abraham) with the name Adonizedek, who is mentioned in *Joshua* 10:1–3 as a later king of Salem.

110 *Genesis* 14:16–24.

111 See *Targum Onkelos* and *Targum Jonathan* (to *Genesis* 14:18), who translate "Salem" as "Jerusalem." Josephus also mentions that the city of Salem over which Melchizedek ruled is Jerusalem. See *Kisvei Yosef ben Matisyahu, Kadmonius HaYehudim*, vol. 1 (Jerusalem: Reuven Mass, 1939), pg. 27.

112 Rashi (to *Genesis* 14:18) adds that Shem also sought to show Abraham that he bore no ill-will

The question is, though, why did Shem accept the killing of his own descendants, regardless of whether they were members of the Semitic alliance or of the Hamitic axis? The answer is that if these Semites were the former, then they were part of the Sodomist society that condoned abhorrent behaviors of which Shem certainly did not approve. Surely if they were part of the Hamitic society, then they participated in the horrible sins encouraged by Nimrod and his ilk. As we shall see below, Shem did not approve of the behavior of most of his descendants, and actually disassociated himself from them. Thus, his lack of resentment toward Abraham was in line with his overall approach toward his descendants.

In fact, several years after the Semitic victory against Chedorlaomer, four out of the five Semitic city-states (Sodom, Gomorrah, Admah, and Zeboiim) were destroyed because of their sins. Their destruction marked the virtual end of Semitic presence in the Holy Land, which was essentially overrun by the Hamitic Canaanites.

EXAMINING ABRAHAM'S LIFE WITH AN EYE FOR LASHON HAKODESH

When viewing the story of Abraham through the lens of linguistics, several important issues need to be addressed.

If all of humanity spoke *Lashon HaKodesh* before the destruction of the Tower of Babel, as mentioned above, then what is the significance of the fact that Abraham spoke *Lashon HaKodesh* after emerging from his subterranean hideout (which occurred before the Tower)? If everyone spoke it, why does *Pirkei D'Rabbi Eliezer* feel the need to stress that it was Abraham's language as well?

We must understand what language Abraham himself spoke and to which languages he was exposed: first in his hometown of Ur, later in Harran, and then in his eventual home in the Land of Canaan. Did it change?

---

toward him for killing his descendants. Rashi's words are perplexing, because Abraham had intervened in the Hamito-Semitic war on behalf of the Semites. If so, which Semites did Abraham kill? The simplest answer is that there must have been incidents of "friendly fire" in which Abraham and/or his men killed other Semites by mistake. Alternatively, one can explain that Abraham killed Semites who were within the ranks of the Hamitic armies. See note above which explains that Chedorlaomer and/or his subjects might have been Semites.

There is a seemingly minor textual particularity that will help shed light upon some otherwise unknown details of the history of *Lashon HaKodesh*. This seemingly minute detail is found in the Torah's account of the war between the five Semitic kings and the four Hamitic kings, where a refugee from said war told Abraham about Lot's abduction. It reads:

> "The refugee came and he told Abraham the *Ivri* [Hebrew]... and Abraham heard that his brother['s son] was captured."[113]

This is the first time that the Bible uses the term *Ivri* to describe someone. Its meaning is unclear and actually subject to dispute. What does it mean that Abraham was an *Ivri*, and what is its significance in the context of the Hamito-Semitic war—and the history of language?

ABRAHAM AS A YOUNG MAN

As mentioned above, Abraham was a young man at the time of the Tower of Babel. This begs the question of why *Pirkei D'Rabbi Eliezer* specifically mentions that Abraham spoke *Lashon HaKodesh* as a child—as though doing so was a novelty—if, as mentioned above, at that time everyone spoke *Lashon HaKodesh*. In his glosses to *Pirkei D'Rabbi Eliezer*, Rabbi David Luria (1798–1855) answers this question by explaining that this Midrash indeed presents a very novel idea: A child who grows up alone without any human interaction will naturally speak *Lashon HaKodesh*.[114] Abraham, while secluded underground from infancy,[115] was able to naturally speak the language as if he had learned it like everyone else. Although this phenomenon does not seem to reflect the current reality,[116] perhaps it was only manifested until

113 *Genesis* 14:13–14.

114 *Chiddushei HaRadal* to *Pirkei D'Rabbi Eliezer* Ch. 26.

115 Rabbi Luria concedes that some Midrashic sources (such as *Sefer HaYashar*) write that Abraham's mother hid with him. However, other Midrashim state that he was alone. J. D. Eisenstein (ed.), *Otzar Midrashim* (New York, 1915), pg. 3, quotes a Midrash saying that as an infant Abraham was alone in a cave without anyone to nurse him.

116 Ibn Ezra in *Safa Berurah* (Fürth, 1839), pg. 2a, rejects a similar idea—that Aramaic is so ingrained in the human mind that command of Aramaic is natural and instinctive. Proponents of this theory claim that if a human was raised isolated from society at birth, with only a mute wet nurse, he would automatically possess the ability to speak Aramaic. They explain that most people do not speak Aramaic because they forgot it when they adopted a learned language. However, Ibn Ezra reasons that a learned behavior does not override an instinctive, natural

אנך (=אנוכי) משע בן כמשית מלך מאב הדיבני. אבי מלך על מאב שלשן שת (=שלו־
שים שנה) ואנך מלכתי אחר אבי. ואעש את הבמת (הבמה) זאת לכמש בקרחה (מצו־
דת העיר) במת ישע כי השעני מכל המלכן וכי הראני בכל שנאי (במפלת שונאי). עמרי
מלך ישראל ויענו את מאב ימן רבן (=ימים רבים) כי יאנף כמש בארצה. ויחליפה בנה
(הוא אחאב) ויאמר גם הא: אענו את מאב. בימי אמר כן. וארא בה (=במפלתו)
ובבתה. וישראל אבד אבד עלם (=לעולמים). וירש עמרי את ארץ מהדבא וישב בה
ימה וחצי ימי בנה ארבען שת וישבה כמש בימי. ואבן את בעלמען ואעש בה האשוח
(=מאגר מים). ואבן את קריתן. ואש גד ישב בארץ עטרת מעלם. ויבן לה מלך ישראל
את עטרת. ואלתחם (ואלחם) בקר (=בעיר) ואחזה (ואחזתי בה) ואהרג את כל העם...
מהקרית לכמש ולמאב. ואשב (=שביתי) משם את אראל (גיבור במואבית) דודה ואס־
חבה לפני כמש בקרית. ואשב בה את אש שרן ואת אשמחרת (שם מקום). ויאמר לי
כמש: לך אחז את נבה (נבו בארץ ראובן) על ישראל. ואהלך בללה ואלתחם בה מבקע
השחרת עד הצהרם ואחזה ואהרג כלה שבעת אלפן גברן וגרן (=גורים, ילדים) וגברת
וגרת (=גורות, ילדות) ורחמת (=עלמות בתולות) כי לעשתר כמש (האלה אשת כמוש)
החרמתה. ואקח משם את כלי ה׳ ואסחבהם לפני כמש. ומלך ישראל בנה את יהץ
וישב בה בהלתחמה (בהלחמו) בי ויגרשה כמש מפני. ואקח ממאב מאתן (מאתיים)
אש כל רשה (=ראשיה או העניים שלה-רשיה) ואשאה ביהץ ואחז הלספת (בנוסף) על
דיבן. אנך בנתי (את) קרחה (=העיר) (את) חמת היערן (מביצורי העיר) וחמת העפל
(=המצודה). ואנך בנתי (את) שעריה ואנך בנתי (את) מגדלתה (המגדלים שלה) ואנך
בנתי בת מלך (בית המלך) ואנך עשתי (את) כלאי האשוח למין (סכר למאגר מים)
בקרב הקר (העיר). ובר אן בקרב הקר בקרחה. ואמר לכל העם: עשו לכם אש בר
בבתה. ואנך כרתי המכרתת (מפעל מים) לקרחה (לעיר) ב(עזרת) אסרי ישראל. אנך
בנתי (את) ערער ואנך עשתי (את) המסלת (הדרך) בארנן. אנך בנתי בת במת (בית
במות) כי הרס הא. אנך בנתי (את) בצר כי עין (עיים=הרוסים) הא באש דיבן חמשן
(הושיב בדיבון חמשים משפחות) כי כל דיבן משמעת (נשמעת לי). ואנך מלכתי...
מאת בקרן אשר יספתי (=סיפחתי) על הארץ. ואנך בנתי (את) מהדבא ודבלתן (דבל־
תיים) ובת בעלמען ואשא שם את... צאן הארץ. וחורנן (חורנים) ישב בה ב...ויאמר לי
כמש: רד הלתחם בחורנן. וארד ואלתחם בקר ואחזה וישבה כמש בימי. ועל משם
עש...שת שדק וא...

"Victory Stele of King Mesha of Moab" written in the Moabite Language (Source: *Explorations in Bible Lands During the 19th Century* by H. V. Hilprecht, page 612. Public Domain). The deciphered text of this artifact is freely available on the Hebrew Wikipedia.

the Tower of Babel, but not afterwards. Nonetheless, as we shall see below, other sources disagree with *Pirkei D'Rabbi Eliezer* and contend that Abraham adopted *Lashon HaKodesh* later on in life.

---

behavior. Thus, if Aramaic is indeed man's inherent language, learning a different language should not cause him to forget Aramaic. Therefore, argues Ibn Ezra, should Aramaic really be so ingrained in the human mind, everyone would naturally speak it and since this is not true, he concludes that Aramaic is not the language of humanity by nature. Ibn Ezra's reasoning applies equally to rejecting *Lashon HaKodesh* as an inborn language.

In discussing such phenomenon, D. Steinberg, *An Introduction to Psycholinguistics* (Longman, 1993), pg. 49, writes, "Likewise it is said that [King] James IV of Scotland [(1473–1513)] also conducted such an experiment with infants. When he heard their first utterings, the king declared that they were in perfect Hebrew!" For discussions of similar ideas and experiments, see M. Idel, *Kabballah in Italy, 1280–1510: A Survey* (Yale University Press, 2011), Appendix 2 "The Infant Experiment: On the Search for the First Language in Italy." See also Y. Y. Stahl (ed.), *Sodei Chumash V'Shar* (Jerusalem, 2009), Appendix 6.

THE HISTORY OF LANGUAGE ACCORDING TO ACADEMIA

Before we examine the languages that Abraham spoke in various locales, let us first summarize how language as a whole developed according to academic opinions. While the academic world has largely rejected the notion that *Lashon HaKodesh* predates all other languages,[117] it has produced some interesting theories about the origins of language that deserve mention. Some scholars are inclined to accept the notion that all of the world's languages evolved from a common linguistic ancestor. This theory is known as "the monogenesis of human language." Although this idea is controversial, it was accepted by Edward Sapir (1884–1934) and Joseph Greenberg (1915–2001), two prominent American linguists.[118]

SEMITIC LANGUAGES

Nonetheless, most linguists trace the origins of language to "families" of similar languages; and even "superfamilies" of related families, but not to one single language.[119] They group Hebrew[120] along with Aramaic and Arabic, as well as Akkadian, Ge'ez (also known as Ethiopic or Abyssinian), and Ugaritic; and view them as offshoots of a hypothetical Proto-Semitic

117 Interestingly, some scholars admit that even English is derived from Hebrew. This idea is expressed in "*Mona Antiqua Restaurata*: An Archaeological Discourse on the Antiquities Natural and Historical" by Henry Rowlands (1551–1616), and "English derived from Hebrew" (S. W. Partridge, 1869) by Robert Govett (1813–1901). The late Rabbi Nathan Glustein wrote *One Language: The Legacy of the Hebrew Language* (Brooklyn, 1991), and Dr. Isaac Mozeson, a contemporary scholar, wrote *The Word* (SP Books, 2002) to prove that English is derived from Hebrew. The latter developed and pioneered an entire field of study known as "Edenics," devoted to discovering elements of other languages that are derived from *Lashon HaKodesh*. Nonetheless, it should be noted, modern-day academia tends to reject and even ridicule this view.

118 See M. Ruhlen, *The Origin of Language: Tracing the Evolution of the Mother Tongue* (Wiley, 1994), pg. 28.

119 Nevertheless, some academic scholars, such as R. Lass, *Historical Linguistics and Language Change* (Cambridge: Cambridge University Press, 1997), pg. 162, remain skeptical of even the widespread notion of universal linguistic families.

120 D. O'Leary, *Comparative Grammar of the Semitic Languages* (London, 1923), pg. 4, writes that although Hebrew, Arabic, Aramaic, et al., are clearly associated and are grouped as Semitic languages, linguists are unable to determine the exact historical relationships between each of these languages in greater detail. This leaves open the possibility that Hebrew is actually the parent language and all the others are its derivatives to some extent or another.

language. In academic parlance, these languages are known collectively as "Semitic languages." As their name implies, they are named after Shem, the son of Noah.

HAMITIC LANGUAGES

Another major linguistic family from the Ancient World is the Hamitic language family, which includes Ancient Egyptian and Coptic, the Berber languages, and various Cushitic and Chadic languages of Northern Africa. The languages in this family are known as "Hamitic languages" after Ham, the son of Noah, whose descendants are traditionally understood to be the native inhabitants of Africa. Just as the Semitic languages are thought by academics to derive from a hypothetical Proto-Semitic language, scholars assume that the Hamitic languages stem from an equally hypothetical Proto-Hamitic language.

Because it has become politically incorrect to speak in racial terms, these languages are generally known as "African" languages, as opposed to "Hamitic" languages, while the "Semitic" languages are often referred to as "Asian." Some scholars take this theory a step further and claim that both of these families are derivatives of a more general Proto-Hamito-Semitic (Proto-Afro-Asiatic) language. Interestingly, while this supposition has only been recently accepted by academia, they do credit Rabbi Yehuda ibn Kuraish (who lived in Algeria during the late Geonic period) for first proposing the correlation between the two families in his Arabic work *Risala*.[121]

LINKING LINGUISTIC AND GENEALOGICAL FAMILIES

Although it is quite tempting to equate these linguistic families with the genealogical families of Noah's sons, the truth is that it is a bit more complicated than that. While the genealogy of different groups can only be mixed through interbreeding, their languages can be mixed through an array of other means. These include political conquest, cultural diffusion, commercial interaction, and the ex-

121 E. Lipiński, *Semitic Languages: Outline of a Comparative Grammar* (Leuven, Belgium: Peeters Publishers & Catholic University of Leuven Department of Oriental Studies, 1997), pg. 23.

change of ideas; not to mention deliberate campaigns to widen one group's linguistic capabilities. Another complicating factor is that sometimes the ruler (or ruling class) of a nation or city-state was a member of one genealogical family, while its subjects (or a majority of its subjects) were members of another. In such instances, the ruling family might have forcibly imposed its own language preferences on its subjects, which complicates efforts to classify languages based on anthropological and genealogical classes.[122] Thus, although it is convenient to assume that the Hamitic and Semitic languages correspond to the Hamitic and Semitic families, this is only a generalization and may not be completely accurate.

THE CANAANITE LANGUAGE ACCORDING TO ARCHEOLOGY

With this in mind, we can now approach the issue of which language was spoken in the Land of Canaan. Archeology has revealed that the language used[123] there was a Semitic language very similar—if not identical—to *Lashon HaKodesh*.[124]

The most significant archeological find relevant to this matter is the Amarna letters—found in Egypt in the late nineteenth century—that contain

122 A similar sentiment is expressed by D. O'Leary, *Comparative Grammar of the Semitic Languages* (London, 1923), pgs. 2–3. He writes that it is preferable to denote language groups by symbols such as letters or figures, rather than by using such names as "Semitic" or "Indo-European," which imply racial or geographical groups. Nonetheless, he notes, once academia had already adopted these terms, it is more convenient to accept them than to invent new terminology.

123 It is important to note that in general, archeological evidence can only decisively prove what the *written* language was, not which language was actually *spoken*. If we posit that the *written* language of the Canaanites matches their *oral* language (usually, but not always, a fairly safe and justified assumption), then we must deal with the conclusion that the Canaanites spoke *Lashon HaKodesh*. However, if we reject this position and instead suggest that their *written* language did not match their *spoken* language, then much of the ensuing discussion below is superfluous and unnecessary. See E. van Dassow, "Canaanite in Cuneiform," *Journal of the American Oriental Society*, vol. 124:4 (2004), pgs. 641–674, who dispels the accepted notion of Akkadian dominance in the ancient Middle East by arguing that Akkadian-influenced *writing* does not prove that those societies *spoke* Akkadian; only that their writing was influenced by Akkadian even though they spoke other (albeit usually Semitic) languages.

124 See A. Saenz-Badillos, *A History of the Hebrew Language*, English ed. (Cambridge University Press, 1988), pg. 53. See also Z. Harris, "Development of the Canaanite Dialects," *American Oriental Series*, vol. 16 (New Haven, Connecticut: American Oriental Society, 1939) who examines the linguistic relationship between the family of Canaanite languages and other Semitic languages.

correspondence between the Egyptian Pharaohs and other kingdoms and empires throughout the ancient world. While most of these letters were written in the Semitic language Akkadian, many of those from the Land of Canaan were written in the Canaanite language,[125] which, as already mentioned, very closely resembles *Lashon HaKodesh*. These letters appear to predate the Jewish conquest of the Land of Canaan (which began in the time of Joshua), yet they show that the native inhabitants there essentially spoke Hebrew.

Similarly, around the same time that the Amarna letters were discovered in Egypt, the Mesha Stele was discovered in present-day Jordan. The Mesha Stele is a stone tablet inscribed with the story of Mesha King of Moab's successful overthrow of the Jewish occupation of Moab. He fought against the allied forces of Jehoshaphat king of Judah, Jehoram king of Israel, and the anonymous king of Edom. This episode is also recorded in the Bible in *Kings* II 3:4–27. The Mesha Stele was written in the Moabite language using the *Ivri* script (which was used to write *Lashon HaKodesh* before the *Ashuri* script[126]). When rendered in *Ashuri* characters, the text of this artifact is fairly understandable to a regular reader of Hebrew. This shows that the Moabite language (in addition to the Canaanite language) was also very similar to *Lashon HaKodesh*.

THE CANAANITE LANGUAGE ACCORDING TO TRADITION

The notion that Canaanites spoke *Lashon HaKodesh* has roots in some classical sources as well. When the prophet Isaiah foretold that Egypt would repent from its idolatry (which ultimately happened after the fall of the Assyrian king Sennacherib[127]), he said:

> "On that day, there will be five cities in the Land of Egypt which will speak the Canaanite language and will swear to God."[128]

Rashi explains that Isaiah was prophesizing that these Egyptians would speak

125 This should not be confused with the Medieval "Knaanic Language," which will be briefly discussed in Chapter 5.

126 See Appendix A "The Scripts of *Lashon HaKodesh*."

127 *Seder Olam Rabbah* (Ch. 23).

128 *Isaiah* 19:18.

the Canaanite language, just as the Jews in the Land of Israel did.[129] This implies that the Jews in the Land of Israel spoke the same language as the Canaanites (who lived there before them).[130] Rabbi Yosef Kara (1065–1135)[131] confirms this assumption by explicitly noting that the "Canaanite language" to which Isaiah referred was *Lashon HaKodesh*. In fact, Ibn Ezra[132] uses this verse to prove that the Canaanites spoke *Lashon HaKodesh*.[133] As we shall see in the next chapter, Rabbi Moshe ben Nachman (1194–1270), better known as Ramban/Nachmanides, also understands that the Canaanites spoke *Lashon HaKodesh*.[134] Although there are other explanations as to why *Lashon HaKodesh* might be called the "Canaanite language,"[135] the consensus is that it is because the Canaanites spoke it.

---

129 Rashi to *Isaiah* ibid. and to TB *Menachos* 109b.

130 See Maharsha (to TB *Menachos* 109b), who writes that Isaiah did not mean that the Egyptians will actually speak *Lashon HaKodesh* as their everyday language. Rather, in the future the Egyptians will literally swear off idolatry, and will utter their oaths in *Lashon HaKodesh* to give them more severity.

131 In his commentary to *Isaiah* 19:18.

132 In his commentary to *Isaiah* there and to *Exodus* 21:2.

133 Rabbi Yosef ibn Kaspi (1279–1340) echoes Ibn Ezra's explanation, but slightly minimizes its impact by proposing that only *most* of the Canaanites spoke *Lashon HaKodesh*, not *all* of them (*Adnai Kesef* to *Isaiah* 19:18).

134 Amazingly, Ramban presents this as if it is his own original idea. He does not note that several other commentators before him already suggested it.

135 Radak (to *Isaiah* 19:18) offers a different approach as to why Isaiah referred to *Lashon HaKodesh* as the "Canaanite language." He explains that Isaiah was prophesying that once the Egyptians repent from their idolatry, and learn from the words and actions of the Jews in the Land of Israel, they would also speak *Lashon HaKodesh*, which would thus become a shared language between them. Isaiah specifically referred to *Lashon HaKodesh* as the "Canaanite language" in order to emphasize the future restoration of the connection between the Land of Canaan (Israel) and Egypt. Mitzrayim (progenitor of the Egyptians) and Canaan were brothers, sons of Ham (*Genesis* 10:10), which means that their lands had initially shared a certain common bond when the Canaanite ruled the Land of Israel. However, once the Semites reconquered the Land of Canaan (when the Jews did so under the leadership of Joshua), the lands lost their common kinship and they no longer had anything in common, for one was Semitic and one was Hamitic. As a result, when Isaiah foretold of Egypt's repentance, he mentioned that they will speak the language of the Jews living there, i.e., *Lashon HaKodesh*. This will rekindle the connection between the two lands: They will speak a common language and share common goals; just as they had shared a common Hamitic kinship when the Land of Israel was ruled by the Hamitic Canaanites. In allusion to this, Isaiah refers to *Lashon HaKodesh* as the "Canaanite language."

In light of Radak's explanation, Abarbanel (there) fiercely rejects Ibn Ezra's use of this verse to prove that the Canaanites spoke *Lashon HaKodesh*. According to Radak, Isaiah referred to *Lashon HaKodesh* as "the Canaanite Language" simply as a way of referring to the future common bond between the lands of Egypt and Canaan—not because the Canaanites spoke *Lashon HaKodesh*.

In light of the fact that the Canaanites spoke *Lashon HaKodesh,* we must now discuss which language Abraham spoke in his early life and later when coming to Canaan. We will also address which language the inhabitants of Canaan spoke upon Abraham's arrival there.

ABRAHAM BROUGHT LASHON HAKODESH TO THE CANAANITES

As quoted earlier,[136] *The Kuzari* notes that Abraham's mother tongue was Aramaic, which he used for all non-holy functions. Since many scholars, both academic and classical, posit that the Canaanites spoke *Lashon HaKodesh*, this might lead us to assume that when Abraham arrived in the Land of Canaan, he adopted *Lashon HaKodesh* from its local inhabitants.[137]

However, according to some authorities it seems that Abraham actually brought *Lashon HaKodesh* to the Canaanites, not vice versa. *The Kuzari* also mentions that *Lashon HaKodesh* was essentially lost during the division of languages at the Tower of Babel and was only preserved by Eber, who possessed this language as an oral transmission from Adam via Noah (and Shem). Although he does not mention this explicitly, *The Kuzari* and others (as we shall soon see) maintain that Eber transmitted *Lashon HaKodesh* to Abraham, who used it for holy purposes. Thus, as Rabbi Yehuda Moscato (1530–1593) proposes in his commentary to *The Kuzari,*[138] Abraham brought the language to the Canaanites, not vice versa.[139]

However, Abarbanel is unclear about whether he rejects Ibn Ezra's entire idea (that the Canaanites spoke *Lashon HaKodesh)* or merely his proof to it.

136 In Chapter 1, "The Language of Adam."

137 Ramban makes two remarks to this effect in a sentence printed in only some editions of his commentary to the Pentateuch. He writes that Abraham could not have brought *Lashon HaKodesh* with him from Ur Kasdim and Harran because the principal language in those places was Aramaic, just as Laban who lived in Harran spoke Aramaic. Furthermore, he writes that it is illogical to assume that *Lashon HaKodesh* was only used by one person, as opposed to being the language of a group of people. Because of these two points, Ramban concludes that *Lashon HaKodesh* must have been the language spoken by the Canaanites (with the implication that Abraham adopted it from them). See C. Chavel (ed.), *Pirush HaRamban Al HaTorah*, vol. 1 (Jerusalem: Mossad HaRav Kook, 1959), pg. 242. If this passage attributed to Ramban is indeed genuine, it is in consonance with his own opinion because, as explained below (Chapter 4), he believes that *Lashon HaKodesh* is not intrinsically holy, but rather is considered holy because of its usage.

138 *Kol Yehuda* (there).

139 *The Kuzari* (Warsaw, 1885), pg. 156.

WHAT ABOUT THE ARCHEOLOGICAL EVIDENCE?

In working with the assumption that Abraham brought *Lashon HaKodesh* to the Canaanites, we must deal with the archeological findings mentioned above. The archeological evidence and Isaiah's prophecy, which seem to suggest that the Canaanites spoke *Lashon HaKodesh*, can be accounted for by explaining that they reflect the period *after* Abraham had already popularized *Lashon HaKodesh* amongst the Canaanites. Thus, the archeological evidence does not contradict the account proposed by Rabbi Moscato because they do not prove that the Canaanites already spoke *Lashon HaKodesh* before Abraham arrived in Canaan.

The Mesha Stele, in particular, cannot be used to prove that the Canaanites spoke *Lashon HaKodesh* at the time of Abraham's arrival for a host of reasons. First, the Mesha Stele refers to events from the Book of Kings, which transpired close to a millennium after Abraham's arrival in the Land of Canaan. Second, as the tablet itself relates, at that time the Moabites had previously been conquered by the Jews and were now rebelling against them, making it quite plausible that they had adopted (or were forced to adopt) the Jews' language. Even if at the point in time that the Mesha Stele was written the Moabites spoke *Lashon HaKodesh*, this does not prove that *Lashon HaKodesh* was their original, native language. Third, according to biblical anthropology, the Moabites are descendants of Lot, Abraham's nephew.[140] Thus, it is likely that Lot, and in turn the Moabites, were influenced by Abraham's own linguistic preferences. Even if the Moabites spoke *Lashon HaKodesh* as their native language, it does not automatically follow that the surrounding Canaanite nations (who were not related) also spoke *Lashon HaKodesh*. Thus, even if the Mesha Stele proves that the Moabites spoke *Lashon HaKodesh*, it proves nothing about what language the Canaanites spoke at the time of Abraham's arrival.

IN DISCUSSING ARAMAIC AS A CORRUPTION OF LASHON HAKODESH, HABACHUR ALSO FOLLOWS THIS APPROACH

Rabbi Eliyahu Ashkenazi HaBachur (1469–1549) apparently also understood that Abraham brought *Lashon HaKodesh* to the Canaanites.

---

140 See *Genesis* 19:29-38.

As we shall discuss in later chapters (notably Chapters 5 and 8), many sources posit that Aramaic is a corruption of *Lashon HaKodesh*. HaBachur writes that it therefore serves to reason that those peoples who spoke Aramaic had once spoken *Lashon HaKodesh* in the generations preceding its corruption.[141] This assertion prompts him to ask when the corruption of *Lashon HaKodesh* occurred, if Aramaic-speaking peoples already existed during the time of the patriarchs.

In other words, if Aramaic—the corrupt form of *Lashon HaKodesh*—existed during the time of the patriarchs, the corruption must have occurred earlier. When did this corruption begin?

He explains that *Lashon HaKodesh* was passed down orally through the generations, beginning with Adam and continuing for ten generations until Noah.[142] After the division of languages, Noah's son Shem continued the tradition of *Lashon HaKodesh*, which had been forgotten by everyone else. By the time Shem died, most of his descendants were already idol worshippers. The corruption of *Lashon HaKodesh* began after his death. They began to call the new language "Aramaic" after Aram, Shem's youngest son,[143] who likely outlived his older brothers. However, Abraham had already emigrated from Mesopotamia to the Land of Canaan before this corruption occurred. In doing so, Abraham transplanted the pure, unadulterated version of *Lashon HaKodesh* to the Land of Canaan.[144]

While HaBachur's theory is quite sound, there is one point that is arguable. HaBachur proposes that the corruption of *Lashon HaKodesh* began after Shem's death. This is somewhat debatable because Shem lived well into Jacob's lifetime, and yet one finds biblical personalities speaking Aramaic even before Jacob's birth (see footnote[145]). Instead, we shall assume

---

141 For example, as previously mentioned (Chapter 1), Laban, the uncle and father-in-law of Jacob, spoke Aramaic. Yet, we also find that he understood *Lashon HaKodesh* (as mentioned later, see note below).

142 See *Avos* 5:2, which states that Noah lived ten generations after Adam. This is also clear from Noah's genealogy in *Genesis* 5.

143 *Genesis* 10:22.

144 Introduction to *Meturgaman*.

145 The fact that Aramaic was already spoken in the time of the patriarchs is evident from *Chizkuni's* explanation (to *Genesis* 24:44) of a discrepancy in the Torah's word choice regarding Rebecca. At first, the Torah (in *Genesis* 24:16) refers to her as a "lass" (*na'arah*, נערה); but afterwards, when detailing Eliezer's account of the story, Eliezer described her as a "lass" (*almah*,

that the corruption of *Lashon HaKodesh* began much earlier—already during the time of Adam, who (as we discussed earlier) spoke Aramaic as well as *Lashon HaKodesh*. Either way, we see that HaBachur understands that Abraham brought *Lashon HaKodesh* to the Canaanites, not vice versa.

WHY WAS ABRAHAM CALLED AN IVRI?

As mentioned above, the Bible refers to Abraham as "Abraham the *Ivri* (עברי)" in the context of the Hamito-Semitic war.[146] The Midrash[147] offers three explanations for why the Torah refers to Abraham as an *Ivri*:[148]

One opinion maintains that it alludes to the fact that if the entire world would be on one "side" (עבר, *ever*) of a scale and Abraham would stand on the other, then because of Abraham's great stature the scale would balance.

A second opinion explains that Abraham was called an *Ivri* as a genealogical marker to show that he descended from Eber (*Ever*, עבר), who was a great-grandson of Shem.

A third opinion explains that he was referred to as an *Ivri* because of his Mesopotamian origins from the other "side" (*ever*, עבר) of the Euphrates River,[149] and because he spoke the *Ivri* language (*Lashon Ivri*,

---

עלמה) using a different word. *Chizkuni* explains that the Torah uses the first word because it is *Lashon HaKodesh*, while Eliezer used the second word in dialogue with Rebecca's family because it is Aramaic. Eliezer thought that Rebecca's family only understood Aramaic to the exclusion of *Lashon HaKodesh*, because they lived in Harran, which is in Aram, where Aramaic was spoken. Nonetheless, *Chizkuni* points out that Rebecca's family did indeed speak *Lashon HaKodesh*, because when the question of her leaving with Eliezer arose, her brother Laban and her mother said, "Let us call the lass (נערה) and we shall ask of her [own] mouth" (*Genesis* 24:57). In that context, they used the *Lashon HaKodesh* word for "lass" as opposed to the Aramaic word.

146 *Genesis* 14:13.

147 *Bereishis Rabbah* §42:8.

148 *Pesikta Rabbasi* (*Pesikta* 33) offers a fourth explanation: When God saw that the entire world was worshipping idolatry and Abraham separated himself by not doing so, He called Abraham an "*Ivri*" to refer to the fact that Abraham took the opposite "side" regarding this pivotal issue than did the rest of the world.

Another Midrash (*Shemos Rabbah* §3:8) explains that the Jews are called "Hebrews" (*Ivriim*, עבריים) because they were destined "to cross over the sea" (*she'avru ha'yam*, שעברו הים). However, according to some commentators there, this Midrash is not explaining the term *Ivri*, but rather the double י in the word *Ivriim*.

149 In *Joshua* 24:3, God says, "And I took your forefather Abraham from across the river and I

(לשון עברי).[150] Most commentators understand that this *Ivri* language is *Lashon HaKodesh* (however, see below). In fact, the English language refers to *Lashon HaKodesh* as "Hebrew," which is the Anglicized form of the word *Ivri*.

The common theme uniting these three explanations is that the term *Ivri* refers to Abraham differing from everyone else in Mesopotamia, whether in terms of Abraham's unparalleled great stature, his uniqueness amongst fellow descendants of Eber, or his distinctiveness in leaving Ur and Harran for the Land of Canaan and speaking *Lashon Ivri*.[151] The bottom line is that *Ivri* means that Abraham was different.

But, in what ways was he different?

ABRAHAM'S ASSOCIATION WITH EBER

Before we examine the significance of the Midrash's assertion that Abraham spoke *Lashon Ivri*, we will first discuss the significance of Abraham's linkage to Eber (by virtue of being called an *Ivri*). This interpretation of the term *Ivri* is found in many early sources in addition to the Midrash. For example, Josephus writes in *Antiquities of the Jews* that the Jews are called "Hebrews" because they descend from Eber.[152]

The special recognition that the Bible gives Eber does not begin with the appellation *Ivri* used to describe Abraham. Rather, it begins earlier when the Torah introduces the genealogy of Shem's family by saying:

---

journeyed him in the entire Land of Canaan." *Targum* (there) translates "across the river" as "across the Euphrates."

150 Rashi seems to follow both the second and third opinions. When explaining why the Bible referred to Abraham as an *Ivri*, Rashi (to *Genesis* 14:13) explains that it is because he came from "across the river;" yet when explaining why Joseph is referred to as an *Ivri* (Ibid. 39:14), he explains that it is because he came from "across the river" *and* because he was a descendant of Eber. Similarly, Ibn Ezra (to *Exodus* 1:16) explains that the Jews enslaved in Egypt were called "Hebrews" for three reasons: because they were descendants of Eber, because they practiced Eber's religion, and because they came from "across the river." He repeats this in his "short commentary" to the biblical passage concerning the "Hebrew bondsman" (ibid. 21:2). In his commentary to said passage, Ibn Ezra also suggests that the Jews are called "Hebrews" because of their language, but he rejects this reasoning in line with his own opinion (mentioned above) that even the Canaanites spoke *Lashon HaKodesh*.

151 Cf. Rabbi Yaakov Tzvi Meklenburg in *HaKsav V'HaKabbalah* to *Genesis* 14:13.

152 *Kisvei Yosef ben Matisyahu, Kadmonius HaYehudim*, vol. 1 (Jerusalem: Reuven Mass, 1939), pg. 28.

> "And Shem also begat [offspring; he is the] father of all the sons of Eber."[153]

Here too, the Bible singles out Eber by mentioning that Shem is the forefather of all of his children,[154] which it does not do for any of Shem's other descendants. The Midrash notes that the phrase "father of the sons of Eber" refers to the fact that Shem was the genealogical forefather of the Jews.[155]

This is hard to understand. Why does the Torah single out Eber as a prominent genealogical indicator for both Shem and Abraham? They shared many other relatives! Also, why are the Jews named after their forefather Eber to the exclusion of other ancestors (except for perhaps Jacob)?

EBER AS THE CONTINUATION OF SHEM

Abarbanel[156] offers the traditional explanation as to why Eber is singled out. He explains that the Torah wanted to teach who exactly Shem was and where his affiliations lay. Shem fathered many children and grandchildren who were the progenitors of various nations. However, the only one whom he truly loved and approved of was his great-grandson Eber (son of Shelah, son of Arphaxad, son of Shem) because he saw that Eber was a wise and righteous person who spent his time engaged in admirable intellectual pursuits. Shem himself was also

---

153 *Genesis* 10:21.

154 Such is evident from the explanations of Radak and Ibn Ezra. However, compare with Rashi (there) who elucidates this passage differently, and explains that Shem was the "father of all the people from the other side of the river." Ramban (to *Genesis* 10:21) accepts Rashi's explanation, and then mentions the view of others who understood that the verse refers to Eber. He rejects this explanation by asking why the Bible would specifically link Shem to Eber and not to any of Shem's other descendants.
However, Abarbanel rejects Rashi's approach, because he reasons that since this verse is written in the genealogical tables of the Semitic family, it makes sense that it would refer to a genealogical group, not a geographical group. Abarbanel points out another difficulty with Rashi's approach: If the Torah refers to Shem as the father of all peoples in the Mesopotamian region, then why did the Torah only mention that region and not any other region where Shem's descendants lived? Another difficulty with Rashi's approach is that it is simply inaccurate (or at least not accurate for all times). As we have already mentioned, there were Hamites who lived in Mesopotamia in addition to Semites, and Shem was not the father of those Hamites.

155 S. Buber (ed.), *Midrash Aggadah* (Vienna, 1894), pg. 24.

156 To *Genesis* 10:2.

a wise and righteous person who followed the path of God, and he saw Eber as his successor. Consequently, Shem identified with Eber—his only descendant to follow in his path—to the exclusion of his other offspring.

Indeed, we find many examples of Eber's righteousness, and of his connection with Shem. Just as the Midrash says that Shem served as an important prophet for four hundred years,[157] so too it says that Eber was a great prophet.[158] One example of Eber's prophetic powers is that he named his son "Peleg" (which means "split" in Hebrew), thus prophetically foretelling the division of languages at the Tower of Babel, which occurred in his lifetime.

Additionally, the Midrash says that when the nations of the world sought to stray from God, He sent two prominent individuals, Shem and Eber, as His emissaries to warn them not to do so.[159]

Rashi mentions that Shem and Eber had their own *Beis Midrash* (study hall),[160] and that every time Rebecca would walk past it during her pregnancy, one of the fetuses inside her would kick as if wishing to escape the confines of its uterine prison to go study Torah. According to *Sefer HaYashar*,[161] in his early years Jacob studied at the *Beis Midrash* of Shem and Eber until Shem died,[162] and the Talmud says that Jacob later studied for another fourteen years in the *Beis Midrash* of Eber, Shem's successor.[163] Even Esau respected Shem and Eber equally, as seen from the Midrash,[164] which says that he was scared of killing his brother Jacob lest he be tried in the "Court of Shem and Eber," even though Shem had already died by then.[165]

157 *Tanna Dvei Eliyahu* Ch. 24.

158 *Bereishis Rabbah* §37:7.

159 *Bereishis Rabbah* §52:11.

160 To *Genesis* 25:22.

161 *Sefer HaYashar* (Bene Barak: Mishor Publishing, 2005), pg. 96.

162 See Maharsha (to TB *Megillah* 17a), who explains that Shem died when Jacob was fifty years old. The Talmud (there) notes that Eber died two years after Jacob went to Harran.

163 TB *Megillah* 16b.

164 *Bereishis Rabbah* §63:6.

165 See *Chizkuni* (to *Genesis* 38:24), who writes that even after the death of Shem, his joint court with Eber continued to be called the "Court of Shem and Eber."

SHEM AND EBER PERPETUATE LASHON HAKODESH

We have seen that Eber was the religious, spiritual, and moral heir of Shem. Abarbanel goes even further and again mentions Eber as the perpetuator of Shem's path in a discussion about the survival of *Lashon HaKodesh.*[166] There, he echoes what we have already quoted from *The Kuzari* above: Following the destruction of the Tower of Babel, only Shem preserved *Lashon HaKodesh.*[167] He taught it to Eber, the most esteemed of his descendants—after whom the language is called "Hebrew"[168]—who, in turn, taught it to his great-great-great-great-grandson and pupil Abraham. In short, Eber was a major stepping-stone in the transmission of Shem's tradition to Abraham. Accordingly, we can now understand that the Torah referred to Abraham as an *Ivri* because of Eber's role in transmitting Shem's tradition to Abraham. For the same reason, the Torah specifically referred to Shem as the father of Eber because Eber was the only one of Shem's descendants to follow in his path.

APPROACH #1: LASHON IVRI IS LASHON HAKODESH

In light of the relationship between Abraham and Eber, we can now harmonize two of the opinions in the Midrash as to why Abraham was

---

166 To *Genesis* 11:1.

167 Interestingly, in *Shalsheles HaKabbalah* (Jerusalem, 1962), pg. 218, Rabbi Gedaliah ibn Yachya writes that before *Lashon HaKodesh* was known after Eber, it was originally called *Lashon Omanah* (לשון אומנה), but he does not offer an explanation of this term. There are two possible ways of explaining it. The term *Lashon Omanah* could mean "the craftsman's language," which is an allusion to the fact that God created the world through *Lashon HaKodesh* (as mentioned in Chapter 1). An alternate meaning of the term is that it is related to the Latin prefix *omni-* which means "all-encompassing." Thus, *Lashon HaKodesh* was called the "Omni-language" because it contains and encompasses the roots of all other languages.

168 Interestingly, this idea is also found in Christian theology. Abarbanel (to *Genesis* 2:21) mentions that the Christian theologian Augustine of Hippo (354–430) writes in *The City of God* (Book 16, Ch. 11) that Hebrew, named after Eber, was the original language spoken by humanity before the division of languages. The Christian poet Dante Alighieri (1265–1321) writes in *De Vulgari Eloquentia,* Book 1, Ch. 6 (translated under the title *Dante's Book of Exile*, University of Nebraska Press, 1990) that the original language, first spoken by Adam and then by all of humanity, was of divine origin. It was preserved until the time of Eber, after whom it was named Hebrew. However, A. Mazzocco notes in *Linguistic Theories in Dante and the Humanists* (Brill, 1993), Ch. 9, that Dante retracted this stance, for he wrote elsewhere [*The Divine Comedy*, "*Paradiso,*" Canto XXVI, translated by Henry Wadsworth Longfellow (1807–1882)] that the language of Adam was only *based on* the divine language, but was not *identical* to it.

called an *Ivri*. He was called *Ivri* because he was a full descendant of Eber—not because he was simply a genealogical descendant of Eber, but because he was the spiritual heir to the religious tradition that Eber had received from Shem. In fact, the Midrash says that during Abraham's encounter with Melchizedek/Shem, he revealed certain secrets of the Torah to Abraham.[169] Thus, we find that Shem viewed Abraham as a continuation of his tradition, someone worthy of accepting the secrets of the Torah. Abraham was also called an *Ivri* because, as part of that religious continuation, he was charged with preserving the unadulterated version of *Lashon HaKodesh*. Therefore, the appellation *Ivri* alludes to two components of Abraham's role in furthering Shem's tradition: continuing the tradition that Shem had transmitted to Eber and continuing the holy language of *Lashon HaKodesh*, which exemplifies this tradition.

SEVERAL UNANSWERED QUESTIONS

We have seen that Abraham is called an *Ivri* because, as a perpetuator of Shem and Eber's tradition, he spoke the pure version of *Lashon HaKodesh*, which he taught to the Canaanites in the Land of Canaan. However, we have not explained why Abraham would teach this pure and holy language to the Canaanites, who were depraved sinners, and why the Canaanites agreed to adopt the language brought to them by an outsider.[170] Furthermore, none of the commentators who describe Abraham as the continuator of Eber's tradition mention that he taught *Lashon HaKodesh* to the Canaanites; that point is pure conjecture, and is weakened by its conspicuous absence in the early commentaries.

APPROACH #2: LASHON IVRI IS A MESOPOTAMIAN LANGUAGE

Given these unanswered questions, we must search for an alternate way of explaining the Midrash that Abraham spoke *Lashon Ivri*. The term *Lashon Ivri* usually refers to *Lashon HaKodesh* and in our context most commentators agree that such is its meaning.[171] However, Rabbi Shmuel

169 *Bereishis Rabbah* §43:6.

170 Perhaps this is related to the association between the Land of Canaan/Israel and *Lashon HaKodesh*, but further analysis is still required before drawing such conclusions. See below.

171 See Rashba, Ritva, and *Tosafos HaRosh* (to TB *Megillah* 8a), who explain so explicitly. See also

Yaffe Ashkenazi (1525–1595) writes that when the Midrash mentioned that Abraham spoke it, it does not mean that he spoke *Lashon HaKodesh*.[172] Rather, *Ivri* in this context refers to a Mesopotamian language[173]—a novelty in the Land of Canaan—that Abraham spoke. It is called *Ivri* because it originated from the other side (עבר) of the Jordan River. According to Rabbi Yaffe, the Canaanites spoke *Lashon HaKodesh*, while Abraham spoke a Mesopotamian language. One advantage of this explanation is that it does not have the difficulties associated with the first explanation. Meaning, this explanation does not need to justify why Abraham taught the holy language to the Canaanites and why the Canaanites, in turn, accepted his teaching.

EXAMPLES OF LASHON IVRI AS A MESOPOTAMIAN LANGUAGE

Rabbi Yaffe's position is strengthened by the fact that there are several other instances in rabbinic literature where *Lashon Ivri* clearly refers to a language other than *Lashon HaKodesh*. The Talmud rules that the Holy Scriptures written in Coptic, Medean, *Ivri*, Elamite, or Greek scripts are considered holy, and one may desecrate the Sabbath in order to save them

---

Bartenura and *Tosafos Yom Tov* to Mishnah, *Yadayim* 4:5, who write that *Lashon Ivri* referred to in that Mishnah is *Lashon HaKodesh*. Nonetheless, the abovementioned commentators to TB *Megillah* concede that there are instances in rabbinic literature where the term *Ivri* does not refer to *Lashon HaKodesh*, but rather refers to the language spoken by other descendants of Eber (discussed below). In those instances, the term *Ashuri* is sometimes used to mean *Lashon HaKodesh* (see *Or Zarua*, *Hilchos Tefillin* §544). Furthermore, rabbinic literature sometimes refers to *Ivri* vis-à-vis *Ashuri*, in which case the former refers to the Paleo-Hebrew Script, while the latter refers to the Assyrian script, both of which have been used to write *Lashon HaKodesh* (see Appendix A "The Scripts of *Lashon HaKodesh*"). See also *Tosafos HaRosh* (to TB *Sanhedrin* 21b), who notes that the term *Lashon Ivri* has multiple meanings.

172 *Yefeh To'ar* to *Bereishis Rabbah* (§42:8).

173 Given the popularity of Akkadian in the ancient world, its similarity to other Semitic languages including *Lashon HaKodesh*, and its geographical epicenter in Mesopotamia, some have claimed that the Mesopotamian language sometimes referred to as *Lashon Ivri* is, in fact, Akkadian. This accounts for the curious absence of any reference to Akkadian in rabbinic literature, despite that language's importance in the ancient world. In other words, it is not absent at all—it is simply known under a different name. However, there is a serious flaw in the theory of identifying *Lashon Ivri* with Akkadian. By the time of the Babylonian exile, Aramaic had already replaced Akkadian as the *lingua franca* of the Ancient World, and Akkadian was barely spoken in the Tannaic and Amoraic periods. It therefore seems unlikely that the Talmud would refer to that language as *Lashon Ivri*.

from being burnt.[174] Rabbi Nosson of Rome (1035–1106)[175] explains that *Ivri* in this context means "the language from across the river," i.e., a Mesopotamian language. Thus, the Talmud means to say that Holy Scriptures written in any of these foreign languages are still considered holy enough to justify desecrating the Sabbath in order to save them.[176]

Similarly, the Talmud rules that the halachic obligation to read the Scroll of Esther on Purim can only be fulfilled with a scroll written in *Lashon HaKodesh* or one's mother tongue.[177] The Talmud specifies that if an ordinary (ostensibly Palestinian) Jew reads the Scroll in Coptic, *Ivri*, Elamite, Medean, or Greek, he has not fulfilled his obligation. However, if a Copt reads it in Coptic, an *Ivri* reads it in *Ivri*, an Elamite reads it in Elamite, etc., then he has fulfilled his obligation. In these sources, the term *Lashon Ivri* refers to a language other than *Lashon HaKodesh*, which is considered just as foreign a language as is Greek. Here, Rashi explains that in this context *Ivri* refers to "the language from across the river," i.e., a Mesopotamian language.[178] In a nutshell, we see in several places that *Lashon Ivri* refers to a Mespotamian language and Rabbi Yaffe assumes that the Midrash about Abraham is another such place.

---

174 TB *Shabbos* 115a.

175 In his Talmudic lexicon *Sefer HaAruch* (s.v. עבר).

176 Rashi (to TB *Shabbos* 115a) explains that in this context *Ivri* refers to "the *script* from across the river."

177 TB *Megillah* 18a.

178 The expression used by the Talmud in this context is *Ivris l'Ivrim* (עברית לעברים). Rabbi Reuven Margolis assumes that the term *Ivri* can only mean *Lashon HaKodesh*, and therefore writes that according to our version of the Talmud this passage cannot be understood (because it is obvious that one fulfills his obligation with a scroll written in *Lashon HaKodesh*). Instead, Rabbi Margolis proposes that a scribal error crept into this Talmudic passage, which should instead read *Aravis l'Aravim* (ערבית לערבים), meaning "Arabic for Arabs." He makes this assertion in no less than three places: *Nitzotzei Ohr* (Jerusalem: Mossad HaRav Kook, 1965), pg. 96; *HaMikra V'HaMesorah* (Jerusalem: Mossad HaRav Kook, 1989), pg. 33; and *Margolios HaYam* to TB *Sanhedrin* 22a §5.

However, I suspected that Rabbi Margolis' textual emendation has no basis in the various manuscripts of the Talmud. Dr. Ezra Chwat (Manuscript Bibliographer at the National Library of Israel), who told me in private correspondence that there is no extant manuscript of the Talmud that has such a variant, confirmed my suspicions. Interestingly, the only other source to use the phrase *Aravis l'Aravim* is Ritva (to TB *Kiddushin* 6a), where he notes that *kiddushin* can be effective if said in one's native language, even if that language is not *Lashon HaKodesh*, and cites as examples *Loez l'Lo'azos, Aravis l'Aravim, v'Yevanis l'Yevanim* (לועז ללועזות ערבית לערבים ויונית ליוונים).

A PROOF TO RABBI YAFFE FROM THE MIDRASH ITSELF

When closely examining the Midrash's assertion that Abraham spoke *Lashon Ivri*, we will notice that the Midrash itself lends support to this explanation. We saw above that the third explanation as to why Abraham was called an *Ivri* is that it reflects his Mesopotamian origins from the other "side" (עבר) of the Euphrates River and because he spoke the *Ivri* language (לשון עברי). According to Rabbi Yaffe, this view in the Midrash states that he is called an *Ivri* to emphasize that he left his origins, i.e., his homeland Mesopotamia and his native Mesopotamian language—not that he spoke *Lashon HaKodesh*. If *Lashon Ivri* refers to *Lashon HaKodesh* like the other commentators assume, then why does the Midrash group Abraham speaking *Lashon Ivri* with him *leaving* Mesopotamia? It is contradictory to explain that the term *Ivri* refers to that which Abraham left *and* that which he adopted. According to Rabbi Yaffe, this problem is a non-starter because the term *Ivri* refers to the Mesopotamian region and language, both of which Abraham rejected.

APPROACH #3: LASHON IVRI AS A CORRUPTION OF LASHON HAKODESH

Others explain that *Lashon Ivri* refers to a language that is linguistically similar (if not identical) to *Lashon HaKodesh*, but is not *Lashon HaKodesh*. In this vein, Rabbi Meir Amsel (1907–2007), the late editor of the rabbinic journal *Hamaor*, writes a lengthy article delineating the difference between *Lashon HaKodesh* and *Lashon Ivri*.

He writes that the term *Lashon HaKodesh* used in rabbinic literature refers specifically to the language used to write the Bible. He cites several instances where the rabbis refer to *Lashon HaKodesh* and do not even mean the language, but rather the Torah itself. It was with this language that God created the world and in which Adam and Eve conversed. Eventually, this language was corrupted and begat linguistic offshoots, some of which are close to *Lashon HaKodesh* (e.g., the Semitic languages), and some of which are less so (e.g., the Hamitic languages).

Aramaic was the first corruption of *Lashon HaKodesh*, beginning in the time of Adam, and thus had much time to deviate from the original. A later corruption of *Lashon HaKodesh,* still bearing a very close resemblance to its parent, is *Lashon Ivri.* It began only after the language had been preserved by Eber. Hence, the language is called *Lashon Ivri* (or *Ivrit*) after Eber. Only Abraham and his descendants, who used *Lashon HaKodesh* for Torah study, preserved *Lashon HaKodesh,* while *Lashon Ivri* gained popularity in the world at large. For generation after generation, only those who were learned in the ways of God and the wisdom of the Torah continued to preserve *Lashon HaKodesh,* for it was used exclusively as a holy language for holy purposes. Nonetheless, even though Abraham was charged with preserving *Lashon HaKodesh,* when he needed a language for mundane uses, and with which to communicate with other people, he used Aramaic—the local language in his Mesopotamian homeland—as well as *Lashon Ivri.*

Because Abraham only used *Lashon HaKodesh* for exalted purposes, he was not forced into perverting the language as others had been. On the other hand, once people began to use it for non-holy (and even unholy) purposes, they were no longer able to maintain the language's purity and instead adulterated the language with foreign influences. In fact, argues Rabbi Amsel, this is the natural outcome of people using *Lashon HaKodesh* for everyday speech, because since it is a holy language and is not equipped for such usage, the only way to use it is by distorting it and submitting it to outside influences. *Lashon Ivri* is the product of such corruption.[179]

Similarly, Rabbi Chaim Aryeh Pam notes that even if *Lashon HaKodesh* and *Lashon Ivri* are linguistically identical, there is an important difference between them. The former is a supernatural language that can support and include in a few words countless deeper meanings, while the latter is a regular language that means what it says and nothing more. The Torah is written in *Lashon HaKodesh* and the rabbis teach that in every line, there are seventy planes of interpretation, all of which are included in the words.

In short, Rabbi Amsel argues that *Lashon Ivri* refers to a corrupt strain of *Lashon HaKodesh.* In line with his reasoning, we can explain that the

179 M. Amsel (ed.), "*Lashon HaKodesh* and Ivrit," *Kovetz Hamaor* vol. 79 (Brooklyn, 1958), pgs. 7–10.

Midrash says that Abraham is called *Ivri* because he left his Mesopotamian upbringings both geographically and spiritually—i.e., by disowning their corruptive tendencies.[180]

According to Rabbi Amsel, *Lashon HaKodesh* is not really a language in the conventional sense. Rather, it is a term used to refer to the language used by the Torah. It cannot be used in everyday speech. When one tries to do so, the result is no longer *Lashon HaKodesh*, but is more akin to *Lashon Ivri* that was a corrupted and adulterated form of *Lashon HaKodesh*. Nonetheless, because the two languages are very similar, the terms used to refer to them are sometimes used interchangeably. Thus, whenever the rabbis refer to *Lashon HaKodesh* or *Lashon Ivri*, one must discern to which language they really refer. He cites several examples in which the rabbis mention *Lashon Ivri* when they intend to refer to *Lashon HaKodesh*, and vice versa.[181]

THE CANAANITES SPOKE LASHON IVRI, NOT LASHON HAKODESH

In the same vein, Rabbi Amsel writes that when Ramban and others explain that the Canaanites spoke *Lashon HaKodesh*, they do not literally mean *Lashon HaKodesh*. Rather, they mean *Lashon Ivri*, which is very similar to *Lashon HaKodesh*, and which the Canaanites had adopted from the Semites who had lived in the Land of Canaan before them.[182] This explanation accounts for the archeological evidence, which seems to point to the fact that the Canaanites spoke *Lashon HaKodesh*, by maintaining that the Canaanites did indeed speak a language very similar linguistically to *Lashon HaKodesh*.

Furthermore, according to this explanation, Abraham did not bring this language to the Canaanites: the Canaanites already spoke it. In a letter penned as a response to Rabbi Amsel's article, Rabbi Uri Langner writes that even if the Canaanites did speak *Lashon HaKodesh*, they did

---

180 This explanation differs only slightly from Rabbi Yaffe's in that he understood that *Lashon Ivri* is a completely separate Mesopotamian *language*, while Rabbi Amsel understood that *Lashon Ivri* is a language very closely related to *Lashon HaKodesh*, but not exactly it.

181 M. Amsel (ed.), "*Lashon HaKodesh* and Ivrit," *Kovetz Hamaor*, vol. 79 (Brooklyn, 1958), pgs. 13–17.

182 Ibid., pgs. 9–10.

not refrain from incorporating words and concepts that profaned its holiness and besmirched its cleanliness. The "clean" version of *Lashon HaKodesh* was what God used to create the world, and what the patriarchs of the Jewish nation spoke.[183] Rabbi Amsel and Rabbi Langner seem bothered by the fact that the morally depraved Canaanites spoke *Lashon HaKodesh*—a language valued for its holiness. They therefore explain that this cannot be taken at face value, and instead propose other interpretations.

CANAANITES AS GUARDIANS OF THE LANGUAGE

However, their explanations may be unnecessary. The fact that the ancient Canaanites spoke *Lashon HaKodesh* does not detract from its religious significance. Just as God arranged for the Canaanites to be keepers of the Land of Israel until the Jews would later conquer it, He also had them preserve the holy language, which is so closely linked to the Holy Land (as we have already mentioned).[184] This point is consistent with Rabbi Moshe Alshich (1508–1593),[185] who writes that the Canaanites spoke *Lashon HaKodesh* and adds "as it was spoken in the generation of the division of languages," which implies that it was not a corruption of the holy language.

CHAPTER SUMMARY

We will now briefly review the various explanations concerning Abraham's role in the history of *Lashon HaKodesh* and how this affects our understanding of the spiritual sanctity of the language:

- We began the chapter by detailing the geo-political background behind the Hamito-Semitic war and Abraham's role therein. We discussed how the Semitic and Hamitic language families recognized by the academic world relate to the participants of that war, and

---

183 M. Amsel (ed.), "*Lashon HaKodesh* and Ivrit," *Kovetz Hamaor*, vol. 81 (Brooklyn, 1958), pg. 6.

184 Also see note above (to Chapter 2) in the name of Rabbi Eliyahu Eliezer Dessler that there is a difference between speaking a language on the surface and truly internalizing the values of the language.

185 *Maros HaTzovos* to *Isaiah* 19:18.

then presented evidence attesting to the fact that the Canaanites (Hamitic peoples) spoke *Lashon HaKodesh* (a Semitic language).

- In the context of the abovementioned war, Abraham is called an *Ivri* because, as the Midrash says, he spoke *Lashon Ivri*. We offered three ways to understand the meaning of that Midrashic passage, especially in light of the evidence (both in tradition and archeology) that the Canaanites spoke *Lashon HaKodesh* or at least a language very similar to it:
    - Some understand that just as in most contexts *Lashon Ivri* means *Lashon HaKodesh*, here too it means *Lashon HaKodesh*. Accordingly, they explain that Abraham is called an *Ivri* because he spoke *Lashon HaKodesh* (which he received from Eber). We extended this explanation to posit that he brought the language to the Canaanites.
    - Rabbi Yaffe explains that while the term *Lashon Ivri* often means *Lashon HaKodesh*, in this case it does not. He understands that here *Lashon Ivri* refers to a Mesopotamian language. According to his understanding, Abraham is called an *Ivri* in allusion to his rejection of that language in favor of the holier and purer *Lashon HaKodesh*.
    - Similarly, others explain that *Lashon Ivri* refers to a corrupted form of *Lashon HaKodesh*. According to this understanding as well, Abraham is called an *Ivri* in allusion to his disassociation with that corrupted language, instead favoring the holier and purer *Lashon HaKodesh*. According to this approach, Abraham received *Lashon HaKodesh* from Shem and Eber and spoke it in tandem with *Lashon Ivri*.

We discussed in great depth the merits and difficulties with each of these approaches and its bearing on how to understand the religious significance of *Lashon HaKodesh*. Now, we shall turn to the next major topic in the history of *Lashon HaKodesh*: the language of the Jews in Egypt.

CHAPTER 4:
The Jews in Egypt

JOSEPH AND PHARAOH'S KNOWLEDGE OF LANGUAGES

The Talmud relates that Pharaoh's royal advisors opposed his plan to appoint Joseph as viceroy over Egypt.[186] They questioned how a slave—bought for a mere twenty silver talents—could rule over Egypt. Pharaoh responded by answering that Joseph's wisdom, courage, and beauty were obvious leadership qualities. The advisors countered that Joseph could only truly have the ability to rule if he knew all seventy languages. The Talmud says that at that point, the angel Gabriel came to Joseph and taught him all seventy languages.[187] The next day, Pharaoh tested

186 TB *Sotah* 36b.

187 Rabbi Yosef Chaim of Baghdad writes (*Ben Yehoyada* to TB *Sotah* 33a) that even beforehand Joseph certainly spoke Egyptian (which is one of the seventy languages), yet the Talmud still says that Gabriel taught him seventy languages as if to imply Joseph did not yet know Egyptian. He explains that previously Joseph was only able to speak the common dialect of Egyptian spoken by the masses, and Gabriel taught him the higher-class dialect of Egyptian spoken by Pharaoh and his noblemen.

Joseph's knowledge of the languages, and Joseph was able to converse in each language in which Pharaoh spoke to him. Furthermore, the Talmud says, Joseph began to speak to Pharaoh in *Lashon HaKodesh*, but Pharaoh was unable to respond in kind because Pharaoh did not understand *Lashon HaKodesh*.[188]

JOSEPH USES AN INTERPRETER TO PRETEND THAT HE DOES NOT UNDERSTAND LASHON HAKODESH

When describing the encounters between Joseph and his brothers, the Torah mentions that Reuven told his brothers that their difficulties were a punishment for their mistreatment of Joseph. The Torah explains that Joseph's brothers felt free to speak frankly about Joseph in front of the Egyptian viceroy, because they did not yet know whom he was and did not realize that he understood *Lashon HaKodesh*. About this, the Torah writes:

> "And they did not know that Joseph was listening because a translator was between them."[189]

Rashi, in his commentary there, explains that throughout his encounters with his brothers, Joseph purposely employed a translator to serve as an intermediary between him and his brothers. Since Joseph pretended to speak only Egyptian, and his brothers only spoke *"Lashon Ivri"*,[190] the translator needed to speak both *Lashon*

---

188 Maharal (*Chiddushei Aggados* to TB *Sotah* 36b) writes that Pharaoh was unable to learn *Lashon HaKodesh* from Joseph because the language was not applicable to him. He explains that mastery over a nation's language represents dominion over that nation. Since the Jews were not yet under Pharaoh's dominion, he was unable to master their language. See Appendix D "Maharal on *Lashon HaKodesh* and Aramaic" for a fuller picture of Maharal's views on what language represents.

Rabbi Shimshon Pincus (1944–2001) offers another explanation as to why Pharaoh was unable to understand *Lashon HaKodesh*. He explains that before Moses brought the Torah down from the Heavens, only those who were already connected to the Torah's spirituality could understand *Lashon HaKodesh*. Afterwards, even a gentile who had no connection to the Torah could potentially understand the language. See *Sichos Rabbi Shimshon Pincus, Pesach* (Jerusalem, 2003), pgs. 204–205. In light of Rabbi Pincus' explanation, one can understand why Pharaoh could not speak *Lashon HaKodesh*, yet (as we have already mentioned in Chapter 2) Balaam could: Pharaoh lived before the receiving of the Torah and Balaam lived afterwards.

189 *Genesis* 42:23.

190 Rabbi Menashe Klein (1924–2011) assumes that Judah certainly knew how to speak Egyptian (because it is a requirement of members of the *Sanhedrin*, and Judah headed the *Sanhedrin* comprised

HaKodesh[191] and Egyptian, implying to Joseph's brothers that the viceroy himself did not understand *Lashon HaKodesh* without the aid of the translator.

APPROACH #1: JOSEPH SPEAKS LASHON HAKODESH TO PROVE HIS IDENTITY

When Joseph finally revealed his true identity to his brothers, he began to speak in *Lashon HaKodesh* without an interpreter.[192] Rashi explains that his purpose in doing so was to prove that he was really whom he claimed to be.[193]

APPROACH #2: JOSEPH SPEAKS LASHON HAKODESH TO PUT HIS BROTHERS AT EASE

However, Ramban writes that the fact that Joseph spoke *Lashon HaKodesh* could not serve as proof of his identity.[194] Ramban reasons

---

of his brothers). Nonetheless, he chose to speak only in *Lashon HaKodesh*, requiring a translator to act as an intermediary between himself and Joseph. See Rabbi Klein's *Shanu Chachamim B'Lashon HaMishnah* (New York: Mishne Halachoth Gedoloth Institute, 1994), pg. 84, who uses this idea as one of his sources for a prohibition against speaking any language other than *Lashon HaKodesh*.

191 In his commentary to the Pentateuch, Rashi writes that the translator spoke Egyptian and *Lashon Ivri*. Nonetheless, in the commentary to *Bereishis Rabbah* generally ascribed to Rashi, he writes (§91:10) that the translator spoke to the viceroy in Egyptian and spoke to Joseph's brothers in either the Canaanite language or in Aramaic. Some have taken this discrepancy in Rashi's explanation to prove that the commentary to *Bereishis Rabbah* was not really written by Rashi, because it contradicts his explanation offered in his commentary to the Pentateuch. See Y. Buxbaum (ed.), *Kovetz Moriah*, vol. 265–266 (Jerusalem: Machon Yerushalayim, 2000), pgs. 125–126.
However, as explained in the previous chapter, there is strong evidence to prove that the Canaanites spoke *Lashon HaKodesh*. Thus, there is no contradiction between Rashi explaining that the translator spoke to Joseph's brothers in *Lashon Ivri* (*Lashon HaKodesh*) and in the Canaanite language. However, a contradiction remains in the alternate language that Rashi proposes because in his commentary to the Pentateuch, he proposes Egyptian, and in his commentary to the Midrash, he proposes Aramaic.

192 Rabbi Zalman Sorotzkin (1881–1966) in his work *Oznayim LaTorah* (to *Genesis* 45:12) explains that Rashi does not literally mean that Joseph sought to prove his identity to his brothers from the fact that he spoke *Lashon HaKodesh*, as per Ramban's objections. Instead, Rabbi Sorotzkin explains that *Lashon HaKodesh* in this context literally means a "holy tongue," and refers to Joseph constantly mentioning God while he spoke to his brothers. This sanctified his speech, making it holy. By pointing out this aspect of his speech, Joseph sought to prove to his brothers that he really was whom he claimed to be.

193 See Rashi, Ibn Ezra, Radak, *Targum Onkelos* to *Genesis* 45:12, and Jubilees 43:15.

194 In his commentary to *Genesis* 45:12.

that it would not have been out of the ordinary for an Egyptian to speak *Lashon HaKodesh* because the inhabitants of neighboring Canaan spoke *Lashon HaKodesh* (as we discussed at length in the previous chapter).[195] Furthermore, it is quite common for the king of a particular nation to be familiar with the languages of nearby countries. An example of this is Nebuchadnezzar, King of Babylon, who spoke *Lashon HaKodesh* even though his advisors answered him in Aramaic.[196] Thus, Joseph would not have proven anything to his brothers by speaking *Lashon HaKodesh,* because, as viceroy, he could be expected to be familiar with neighboring languages. Rather, concludes Ramban, Joseph began to speak *Lashon HaKodesh* merely in order to make his brothers feel more comfortable about the already awkward situation.

LASHON HAKODESH EMBODIES PURITY

There is another reason that Joseph spoke to the brothers in *Lashon HaKodesh*, which is based on what Rabbi Moshe ben Maimon (1135–1204), known as Rambam/Maimonides, writes in his *Guide for the Perplexed.*[197] There, Rambam says that *Lashon HaKodesh* (lit. "The Holy Tongue") is called so because it does not have specific words for the reproductive organs and concepts[198] (including male and female genitalia, as well as the act of intimacy itself[199]), which instead are simply alluded to euphemistically.[200]

---

195 Rabbi Menachem Dov Genack points out that Ramban is also inconsistent with Rashi's abovementioned explanation that before revealing himself, Joseph spoke to his brothers through a translator so that they would not realize that he understood *Lashon HaKodesh*. He reasons that if indeed it was common practice for Egyptians to know *Lashon HaKodesh*, then even if there was a translator they should have suspected that the viceroy understood what they were saying. See Y. Hoffman (ed.), *Beis Yitzchak*, vol. 40 (New York: Yeshivas Rabbeinu Yitzchak Elchanan, 2008), pgs. 259–260.

196 See *Daniel* 2:2–4.

197 *Guide for the Perplexed* 3:8.

198 See Maharal (*Nesivos Olam, Nesiv HaTznius* Ch. 3), who says that Rambam confused the cause and the effect. I.e., the language is not called holy because it does not have words of such concepts, rather it does not have such concepts because it is holy.

199 In rabbinic literature the male organ is called "the limb," "the head of the body," "the forearm," and "the utility"; while the testicles are called "eggs." The female organ is referred to as "that place," "the main part (of a document)," and "the place where the utility threshes." The uterus is referred to as "the source," "the mother," "the grave," and "the place of mercy." The act of intimacy is referred to as "using the bed," "laying with," "entering," and "coming onto."

200 Rabbi Yehonassan Eyebschitz (*Ya'aros Devash*, vol. 2, *Drush* 2) presents an explanation similar to

Ramban[201] questions Rambam's explanation by noting that according to Rambam's reasoning, the language should be called a "clean" language, not a "holy" one. Instead, Ramban explains that *Lashon HaKodesh* is called "holy" because it is in that language that the Torah and the Prophets were written, with which God spoke to His prophets, and in which He called the names of Abraham, Isaac, and Solomon.[202]

Nonetheless, Rabbi Shem Tov ibn Falaquera (1225–1290), in his commentary to Rambam's work, defends Rambam's stance. He states that it is quite appropriate to label detachment from such concepts "holy," as Rashi (to *Leviticus* 19:2) explains that any place where one finds a fence to guard against immorality, one finds holiness.[203] Therefore, even according to Rambam, calling the language "holy" instead of "clean" is justified.

Rambam's. He writes that promiscuous activity can easily be discernible when speaking *Lashon HaKodesh* because it differentiates between masculine and feminine forms of words when it is spoken. An outside listener can easily determine based on the conjugation of the verbs if a man is secluded with a woman (purportedly with immoral intentions), or simply with another man.

However, this method is not necessarily foolproof, because a man can simply talk to the woman as if she was male. An example of this is when Boaz spoke to Ruth as if she was a man, so that those listening would not realize that Boaz had a female visitor to his granary in the middle of the night (see *Rus Rabbah* §7:2). Furthermore, even two secluded men or women can potentially be sinning together. Furthermore, male and female forms of words is not a feature exclusive to *Lashon HaKodesh*, many other languages also differentiate between gender cases, making *Lashon HaKodesh* no different than those languages in this aspect.

201 In his commentary to *Exodus* 30:13.

202 Ritva wrote *Sefer HaZikaron* on the Pentateuch to defend Rambam's *Guide for the Perplexed* against Ramban's dissentions. In his commentary to *Parshas Ki Sisa*, Ritva finds himself unable to defend this passage of Rambam from Ramban's arguments. Similarly, Efodi mentions the dispute between Rambam and Ramban [in *Ma'aseh Efod* (Vienna, 1865), pgs. 177–178], and sides with Ramban. Apparently, they cannot find a way of resolving Rambam's view.

See *Kuntresei Shiurim* (TB *Nedarim*, Shiur 1, end of §7) by Rabbi Yisrael Zev Gustman (1908–1991), who writes that the dispute between Rambam and Ramban is centered on whether *Lashon HaKodesh* is intrinsically "holy" (Rambam), or is only considered holy because of its usage (Ramban). See there also for an explanation as to why Ramban specifically mentioned Abraham, Isaac, and Solomon, but not others.

203 See *Sifsei Chachamim* (to *Exodus* 35:22), a compendium of commentaries to Rashi compiled by Rabbi Shabsai Bass (1641–1718), who writes that Rashi also subscribed to Rambam's view in understanding that *Lashon HaKodesh* does not have explicit words.

A SUPERNATURAL PROPERTY OF LASHON HAKODESH RELATED TO ITS ASSOCIATION WITH PURITY

Based on the understanding of Rambam, Rabbi Moshe Sofer (1762–1839) offers a novel interpretation of the exchange between Joseph and his brothers.

He begins by noting an interesting historical phenomenon. Although the local inhabitants of Poland, Lithuania, and Russia did not speak German at all, it was the main language of the Jews found in those areas. In other words, the Jews of Central and Eastern Europe spoke German (i.e., Yiddish, which is a form of Judeo-German) even though the local populations there did not. Rabbi Sofer explains that most Jews of this region descended from the Jews who had previously lived in Germany (thus they are called *Ashkenazim* which literally means "Germans") and, after being ousted from there, migrated eastwards. Nonetheless, even after many generations they had still preserved this dialect of German as their principal language. He posits that this occurred because each Jewish family raised their children to speak it and had been doing so for hundreds of years.[204]

In view of that, Rabbi Sofer notes that it is quite remarkable that after a mere seventy-year exile to Babylon, the Jews very quickly forgot *Lashon HaKodesh*. The Bible attests to the fact that only half the Jews returning from the Babylonian exile spoke *Lashon HaKodesh*[205] (as we shall discuss in the next chapter), which begs the question: Why was *Lashon HaKodesh* forgotten so quickly, yet German continued to exist in the homes of Jewish families for many generations after they left Germany?

Rabbi Sofer answers that *Lashon HaKodesh* is different from all other languages because only one who maintains a certain degree of holiness can preserve it.[206] Consequently, it can be easily forgotten due to a lapse

---

204 See Rabbi Moshe Feinstein (1895–1986) in his responsa *Iggros Moshe* (*Orach Chaim*, vol. 5 §10) who offers a brief overview of the history of Yiddish. See the next chapter for a more in-depth discussion on the history of Yiddish.

205 *Nehemiah* 13:24.

206 Rabbi Sofer maintains that for this reason *Lashon HaKodesh* is called "holy." He supports this justification by noting that in the entire Bible, *Lashon HaKodesh* is not referred to as such, rather it is known as *Lashon Yehudim*, "The Jewish Language." Only in rabbinic literature is the

in holiness,[207] while German (or other languages) can be passed down for generations, notwithstanding moral degeneration.

APPROACH #3: JOSEPH SPOKE LASHON HAKODESH TO SHOW HIS CHASTITY

Accordingly, explains Rabbi Sofer, Joseph spoke in *Lashon HaKodesh* to prove to his brothers that although he remained in Egypt for many years, he maintained the degree of purity and holiness required to retain the language. He had not defiled himself by pursuing the promiscuous lifestyle[208] epitomized by Egyptian culture.[209]

THE JEWS ARE ENSLAVED IN EGYPT

Joseph's position in Egypt served as the catalyst for Jacob's household to relocate to Egypt. As Joseph and his brothers passed on, Pharaoh disregarded Joseph's contributions to Egypt's success, and cast a malevolent eye upon the Jews, who were by then a vast nation. He subjected them to cruel slave labor in an attempt to reduce their numbers and crush their spirit. The Jewish bondage in Egypt lasted for several centuries. After the Jews underwent this painful, but necessary, ordeal, God led them triumphantly out of Egypt. He afflicted the Egyptians with the Ten Plagues, and orchestrated the miraculous parting of the Red Sea. Then He led them to Mount Sinai, where He be-

---

language known as *Lashon HaKodesh*. He explains that before the return of the exiled from Babylon, this property of *Lashon HaKodesh* was not yet recognized, for it had never been forgotten due to a lapse in holiness. This is especially true according to those opinions (including Ramban himself) that the Canaanites spoke *Lashon HaKodesh*. However, after the return from Babylon when it was quite apparent that *Lashon HaKodesh* could be easily forgotten in such a short period, the rabbis began to call the language "*Lashon HaKodesh*."

207 Rabbi Aharon Rother mentions that this idea is also found within the writings of Rabbi Nachman of Breslov (1772–1810). See his article in *Kovetz Eitz Chaim* (Bobov), vol. 8 (Brooklyn, 2009), pgs. 273–274.

208 Accordingly, one can argue that Rabbi Sofer's explanation only fits with Rambam's explanation of why *Lashon HaKodesh* is called "holy," i.e., because it is a language by which one distances oneself from promiscuity. However, Ramban, who does not interpret the story of Joseph and his brother the same way that Rabbi Sofer does, is consistent with his own opinion that *Lashon HaKodesh* is called "holy" because of different reasons, not because of its correlation to morality.

209 *Toras Moshe* to *Genesis* 45:12; see also *Chiddushim V'Aggados Chasam Sofer*, pg. 147b.

stowed the Torah upon them, thus eternally cementing their privileged status as His Chosen Nation.[210]

◆ ◆ ◆

After examining the significance of Joseph retaining his identity through *Lashon HaKodesh,* we shall now examine the behavior of all the Jews in Egypt and whether or not they too preserved the holy language when exiled to Egypt.

Did Joseph's early descent to Egypt foreshadow the Jews' stay there or did they act differently than he did?

THE JEWS IN EGYPT RETAINED LASHON HAKODESH

The Midrash says that the Jews merited redemption from their exile in Egypt because they did not deviate from their language while in Egypt. The Midrash proves that the Jews spoke *Lashon HaKodesh* from a biblical verse in which Pharaoh's advisors refer to God as "the God of the Hebrews (*Ivriim,* עבריים)."[211] As we mentioned in the previous chapter, the Torah refers to Abraham as a "Hebrew" (*Ivri*) in allusion to his mastery of *Lashon HaKodesh*. Thus, the Midrash deduces that just as in the latter case Abraham spoke *Lashon HaKodesh*, so too in the former case the Jews in Egypt spoke *Lashon HaKodesh*.[212] Indeed, in his introduction to *Meturgaman*, HaBachur cites this Midrash as his source for the contention that the Jews never abandoned the language of *Lashon HaKodesh*—even when exiled to Egypt.

The Midrash relates that when the Jews were in Egypt they banded together and made a pact: They agreed to uphold the covenant of Abraham, Isaac, and Jacob, and to act with kindness to one another.[213] They also agreed to worship only their Father in Heaven, to not forsake the language of the House of Jacob (i.e., *Lashon HaKodesh*), and to not teach their children the Egyptian language because it is the path of idolatry.[214]

---

210 *Exodus* 1–20.

211 *Exodus* 3:18.

212 See *Vayikra Rabbah* §32:5; *Pesikta Rabbasi* 10; *Mechilta, Bo,* 5; *Midrash Socher Tov* on *Psalms* 114.

213 *Tanna Dvei Eliyahu* Ch. 23.

214 *Leviticus* 18:3 prohibits a Jew from following in the statutes of idolaters. When Rabbi Moshe of

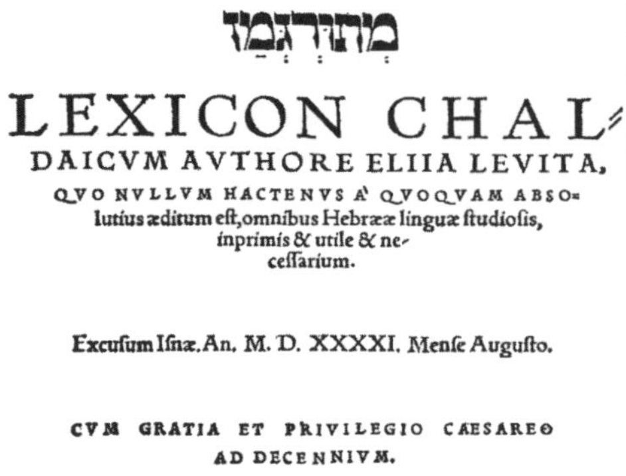
מְתוּרְגְּמָן
LEXICON CHALDAICVM AVTHORE ELIIA LEVITA,
QVO NVLLVM HACTENVS A' QVOQVAM ABSOlutius æditum est, omnibus Hebrææ linguæ studiosis, inprimis & utile & necessarium.
Excusum Isnæ. An. M. D. XXXXI. Mense Augusto.
CVM GRATIA ET PRIVILEGIO CAESAREO AD DECENNIVM.

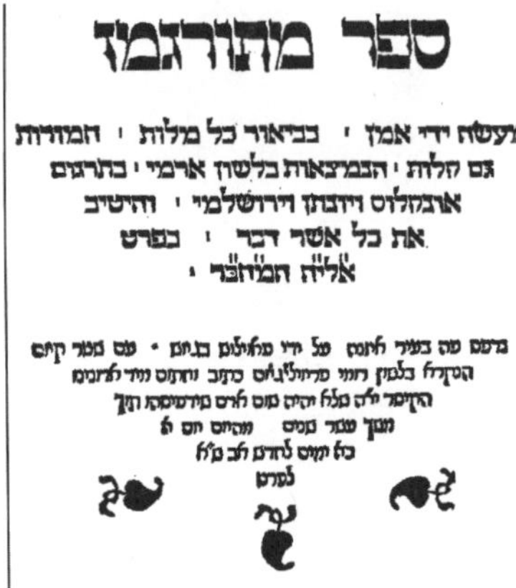
ספר מתורגמן
מעשה ידי אמן · בביאור כל מלות · המוזרות
גם קלות · הנמצאות בלשון ארמי · בתרגום
אונקלוס ויונתן וירושלמי · והיטיב
את כל אשר דבר · בפרש
אליה המחבר ·

The *Shaar Blatt* (title page) of the Latin and Hebrew editions of HaBachur's work *Meturgaman* (Isna, 1541).

In a similar vein, *Mechilta* (to *Exodus* 19:3) says that when God originally commanded Moses to tell the Jews about the Torah, he told Moses to speak to them in *Lashon HaKodesh*. Similarly, *Mechilta* (to *Exodus* 20:1) explains that when the Decalogue (Ten Commandments) was finally delivered to the Jews, it was given in *Lashon HaKodesh*.

THE EGYPTIANS AS FOREIGNERS

In one Psalm, when singing God's praises for the Jews' exodus from Egypt, the Psalmists begins by saying, "When the Jews exited Egypt, the House of Jacob, from 'the foreign nation' (*me'am loez*, מעם לועז)."[215] Why is Egypt called "the foreign nation"? Rashi[216] explains that in this context "the foreign nation" refers to the foreign *language* that the Egyptians spoke (in fact, the word *loez*, לועז is commonly used to refer to a foreign *language*, usually Old French or Latin). Radak adds that the Jews looked at the Egyptians as foreigners because they did not speak

Coucy (a thirteenth century French scholar) codifies this prohibition of not joining idolatrous practices (in his work *Smag*, Negative Commandment #50), he writes that it includes speaking the language of idolaters. Although this point only appears in some versions of *Smag*, Rabbi Menashe Klein in his work *Shanu Chachamim B'Lashon HaMishnah* (a polemic written against translating the Bible and the Talmud into English) decides in practice in accordance with this prohibition.

215 *Psalms* 114:1.

216 To ibid.

Lashon HaKodesh, so their utterances were unintelligible and foreign to the Jews.[217]

Radak asks: How could the Jews view the Egyptians as unintelligible if they had lived in Egypt for many years and presumably spoke the language of the land? He answers by explaining that while the Egyptians enslaved most of the Jews, nonetheless some Jews remained unenslaved. They stayed in Goshen, where they spoke *Lashon HaKodesh* exclusively, and rarely, if ever, interacted with the Egyptians.[218] Even those Jews who went out of Goshen and interacted with the local Egyptians only spoke Egyptian to the locals out of necessity; with their fellow Jews they continued speaking *Lashon HaKodesh*. Thus, Radak argues, *Lashon HaKodesh* remained the Jews' language in Egypt and the Egyptians were viewed as "foreigners" because they did not speak that language.

THE LANGUAGE OF MOSES AND AARON

As we already mentioned (in Chapter 1), Moses initially responded to God's request that he embark on a mission to ask Pharaoh to release the enslaved Jews by saying, "I am not a man of words." The Midrash explains that Moses argued that all the men in Pharaoh's court spoke seventy languages, yet he could not.[219] To this, God responded: "Just as Adam did not learn the seventy

---

217 To ibid.

218 Rabbi Menashe Klein writes in his commentary to *Haggadah Shel Pesach* that even if the Jewish men in Egypt spoke Egyptian as necessary for their work, the Jewish women there did not speak Egyptian at all. See his *Haggadah Shel Pesach Im Maggid Mishnah* (New York: Mishne Halachoth Gedoloth Institute, 1999), pgs. 135–136.

219 Outside of Midrashic interpretation, Rashbam and Ibn Ezra (in their respective commentaries to *Exodus* 4:10) provide a different explanation: Moses responded that he no longer knew how to speak Egyptian because he had fled from Egypt decades ago as a young adult, and was now returning to Egypt decades later. However, many commentators (to *Exodus* 2:19) write that Jethro's daughters assumed that Moses was an Egyptian because he spoke to them in Egyptian. Rabbeinu Chaim Paltiel and *Moshav Zekeinim* (to *Genesis* 50:25) add that because Moses spoke to them in Egyptian instead of in *Lashon HaKodesh*, he did not merit burial in the Land of Israel; as opposed to Joseph who did speak *Lashon HaKodesh* in Egypt and merited to be buried in Israel. These sources seem to assume that Moses did indeed know how to speak Egyptian, despite having left Egypt at a young age. It seems that these two explanations are at odds with each other, yet, interestingly, *Pirush HaRokeach* (to *Exodus* 2:19) explains that Jethro's daughters thought Moses was Egyptian because of the way he spoke and also (to *Exodus* 3:10) explains that Moses told God that he forgot how to speak Egyptian. Barring the ridiculous notion that Moses lied to God, there are two possible ways to answer this contradiction.

languages from anyone, yet he was still able to name each creature in all seventy languages, so too, you, Moses, will be fluent in all seventy languages and will be able to converse properly with Pharaoh and the men of his court."

In practice, Moses insisted on Aaron taking a more prominent role in the divine mission and in fact, the Midrash says in their audiences with Pharaoh, Moses told Aaron what to say in *Lashon HaKodesh*, and Aaron relayed the message to Pharaoh in Egyptian.[220] This discussion also shows that the Jews in Egypt were more inclined toward speaking *Lashon HaKodesh* than to Egyptian.

Did Pharaoh speak Latin?

Rabbi Eliezer ben Eliyahu Ashkenazi (1515–1585) claims in his work *Ma'ase Hashem* (Venice, 1583), pgs. 95b; 134a, that the Egyptians spoke Latin/Italian. He uses that notion to explain the meaning of the names Pharaoh and Potiphar. He explains that the name "Pharaoh" means "master" in Italian (after consulting with experts, we remain unable to confirm this), and the name Potiphar is derived from the Italian phrase *pote fare,* which means "could do," and refers to Potiphar's administrative responsibilities in the court of Pharaoh.

Unless this stance is better clarified, it seems that this idea is little more than a fanciful attempt at homiletic explication. It is all but unanimously clear that the Egyptians spoke Egyptian and not Latin. Academia has offered other explanations of the names Pharaoh and Potiphar. They explain that Pharaoh means "the great house" and Potiphar means "he who is devoted to the house" or "the servant of the house."

Source: S. Leathes, "Foreign Words in the Hebrew Text of the Old Testament," *Journal of the Royal Asiatic Society of Great Britain and Ireland*, New Series, vol. 18:4 (1886), pg. 530.

GOD SPEAKS TO THE JEWS IN EGYPTIAN

While the above sources point to the notion that the Jews in Egypt did not speak Egyptian, there is another Midrash that implies otherwise.

When Moses met Jethro's daughters, he knew the language well enough to speak it in a way that they thought he was Egyptian. However, he had forgotten some of the intricacies of its grammar, syntax, etc., which made him unwilling to speak that language in front of Pharaoh. Alternatively, he forgot the language in the years between first meeting Jethro's daughters and his subsequent mission to Egypt. One also sees from the above sources that there is a connection between *Lashon HaKodesh* and the Land of Israel, an idea already discussed in Chapter 1.

220 See Y. N. Epstein (ed.), *Mechilta D'Rabbi Shimon Ben Yochai* (Jerusalem: Mekize Nirdamim, 1955), pg. 6.

This Midrash likens the Jews in Egypt to a prince who was kidnapped for an extended period of time. Finally, his father the king decided to exact his revenge on the kidnappers and release his son. Upon saving his son, the king conversed with the child in the language spoken to him by the kidnappers. Similarly, explains the Midrash, after God redeemed the Jews from exile in Egypt, He spoke to them in Egyptian.[221]

The Midrash explains that the Jews had been in Egypt for many years, where they had learned the Egyptian language.[222] Therefore, when God wanted to give them the Torah, He began to speak with them in the Egyptian language with which they were already familiar. He began by proclaiming, "I (*anochi*, אנכי) am Hashem, your God...!"[223] According to this Midrash, the word "*anochi*" in this context does not denote the Hebrew word for "I"; rather, it refers to the Egyptian[224] word *anoch* (אנוך), which means "love" and "endearment."[225] One Midrashic source even

---

221 *Pesikta D'Rav Kahane*, *Pesikta* 12.

222 When manna first fell from the sky to nourish the newly freed Jews, they exclaimed, "It is manna" and called their food manna (*Exodus* 16:15). *Pesikta Zutrasa*, *Chizkuni*, Rashbam, and Rabbeinu Yosef Bechor-Schor (there) explain that the word "manna" (*mann*, מן) means "what" in Egyptian. Thus, the Jews were not exclaiming, "It is manna"; rather, they were asking, "What is it?" and called the food "what." From here one sees again that the Jews who exited Egypt spoke Egyptian as their primary language, for it was in that language that they had expressed their curiosity concerning the miraculous food. Nonetheless, it is interesting to note that elsewhere in his commentary, *Chizkuni* (to *Exodus* 16:31) writes that the word "manna" is derived from a Hebrew word meaning to provide food, *vayamen* (וימן).
Building on Rashbam's explanation, *Barzilai* (pg. 59) points outs that the word "what" is also related to another major source of sustenance: water. The first syllable of the word *mayim* (מים, water) is *ma* (מה), which means "what." Interestingly, the same phenomenon is found in German, where the first syllable of the word for water, *wasser*, is *was*, which means "what." (The same is also true in English where the first syllable of "water" is "what.")

223 *Exodus* 20:2.

224 Some explain that the word *anochi* came to Egyptian by way of early Semitic languages (maybe even *Lashon HaKodesh*); see *Barzilai*, pg. 129.

225 See *Pesikta Rabbasi* §21 that explains *anoch* in such a fashion. *Pesikta Zutrasa* (to *Exodus* 20:2) mentions that *anochi* is Egyptian, and refers to the Egyptian word *anoch*, but does not explain what *anoch* means in Egyptian. The *Old Midrash Tanchuma* (Buber), *Yisro* §16, writes that *anoch* is the Egyptian equivalent of the Hebrew word *ani* (אני), and that both words mean "I." See the footnotes from Buber (there and to *Pesikta D'Rav Kahane*) who writes that this Midrash is the source of a *piyyut* (liturgical poem) written by HaKallir for the second day of Shavuot, which states that God gave the Decalogue "in Assyrian script, in Hebrew language, in Egyptian speech." This implies that the entire Decalogue was uttered in Egyptian, a claim also repeated by *Hadar Zekeinim* (to *Exodus* 20:1).

explains that the Jews *forgot Lashon HaKodesh*, which is why God *had to* speak to them in Egyptian.[226]

DID THE JEWS SPEAK LASHON HAKODESH OR EGYPTIAN?

In view of the above, there seems to be a contradiction between these two Midrashic sources. The former sources maintain that the Jews continued to speak *Lashon HaKodesh* in Egypt, while the latter sources maintain that during their exile they spoke Egyptian.

There are several ways to resolve this difficulty.

SOME JEWS WERE BILINGUAL

We can easily resolve this apparent contradiction in light of Radak's

---

This contradicts Abarbanel (*Genesis* 2:19–20), who mentions that the Jews heard the Decalogue in *Lashon HaKodesh*. Rabbi Eliyahu Kramer of Vilna also understood that the Decalogue was spoken in *Lashon HaKodesh*, because he explains (in *Aderes Eliyahu* to *Deuteronomy* 11:29) that the language is called the "Holy Language" because it was in that language that the Holy One spoke to His nation. Since Rabbi Kramer implies that this occurred at the giving of the Torah at Mount Sinai, he must also understand that the Decalogue was related to the Jews in *Lashon HaKodesh*. (However, one could still argue that while most of the Decalogue was delivered in *Lashon HaKodesh*, even Abarbanel and Rabbi Kramer could agree that the first word was said in Egyptian, or at least in a Hebrew word that also has a different connotation in Egyptian.) Furthermore, Ritva (to TB *Megillah* 2b) writes that the language is called *Lashon HaKodesh* because the tablets of the Decalogue were *written* in that language, he does not mention in which language they were *said*.

Interestingly, the *Sifrei* (to *Deuteronomy* 32:2) says that when God revealed Himself when giving the Torah to the Jews, He did not reveal Himself in only one language. Rather, He revealed Himself in four languages: *Lashon HaKodesh*, Arabic, Latin, and Aramaic. See Raavad there for an explanation of how each of these is derived from that verse; cf. M. Kasher, *Torah Shleimah*, vol. 17 (Jerusalem, 1927–1992), pg. 315. This passage seems to imply that God did not speak to the Jews in Egyptian, but He did speak to them in four other languages. However, see *Sifrei Devei Rav* there, who explains that the passage does not only refer to God revealing Himself to the Jews when He gave them the Torah, it refers to Him offering the Torah to other nations (an offer that they refused). According to this Midrash, He revealed Himself to the Edomites in Latin, to the Ishmaelites in Arabic, and to all other nations in Aramaic. See Appendix D "Maharal on Aramaic and *Lashon HaKodesh*," where we discuss the notion that Aramaic is a language not associated with any one nation in particular, but rather with all nations in general.

226 This claim is mentioned in *Pesikta D'Rav Kahane*. When relating this account, *Yalkut Shimoni* (*Yisro* §287), *Midrash Aseres HaDibbros (Otzar Midrashim* pg. 450), and *Pesikta Rabbasi* §21 only mention that they learned Egyptian in Egypt, but omit the claim that they forgot *Lashon HaKodesh* there. There is a serious difficulty with *Pesikta D'Rav Kahane* because if the Jews did not understand *Lashon HaKodesh* and only the first word was said in Egyptian, then how did they understand the rest of the Decalogue?

explanation. As already mentioned, Radak explains that some Jews in Egypt remained isolated in Goshen, where they spoke only *Lashon HaKodesh*, while the Jews who were subjected to slave labor were forced to speak Egyptian with the locals. Thus, according to Radak, some of the Jews in Egypt spoke *Lashon HaKodesh* exclusively, while others were bilingual, speaking *Lashon HaKodesh* to their fellow Jews and Egyptian to the Egyptian locals, when necessary.[227]

THEY SPOKE LASHON HAKODESH, BUT TOOK ORDERS IN EGYPTIAN

Similarly, we can posit that even when exiled to Egypt, the Jews indeed continued to speak *Lashon HaKodesh*. However, they were not accustomed to accepting orders in *Lashon HaKodesh*; their Egyptian taskmasters spoke to them only in Egyptian. Therefore, at Mount Sinai, when God was giving the Jews the Decalogue, He spoke to them in Egyptian, the language in which they were accustomed to "taking orders."[228]

THEY MAINTAINED THE ESSENCE OF LASHON HAKODESH, IF NOT THE ACTUAL LANGUAGE

Even if we assume that the Jews completely forgot *Lashon HaKodesh*, we can still reconcile the contradiction based on a previously mentioned concept set forth by Rambam. Rambam, as we already mentioned, writes that *Lashon HaKodesh* is called so because it lacks the explicitness found in other languages, making it a chaste and holy language. Therefore, one can explain that although the Jews in Egypt spoke the Egyptian language, they did not deviate from the moral standards manifested by *Lashon HaKodesh*. God had to speak to them in Egyptian since that was the only language with which they were familiar. However, they did not change their *manner* of speaking; that is, they internalized the refined and moral linguistic style of *Lashon HaKodesh*, which they maintained even when speaking Egyptian.

---

227 *Eitz Yosef* (to *Shir HaShirim Rabbah* §4:24) also writes that while in Egypt, the Jews spoke *Lashon HaKodesh* amongst themselves and spoke Egyptian when communicating with the Egyptian locals.

228 Rabbi Chananya Jacobson of Los Angeles suggested this explanation to the author.

CHAPTER SUMMARY

In this chapter, we discussed two important points regarding the history of *Lashon HaKodesh* in the Egyptian exile: what did Joseph speak there and what did all the Jews later speak there.

In short, Joseph was fluent in many languages. In addition to his native tongue of *Lashon HaKodesh*, the angel Gabriel taught him the seventy languages so that he would be qualified to serve as the viceroy of Egypt. When Joseph's brothers appeared before him in the Egyptian court, he spoke Egyptian and made use of a translator to convey his words to the brothers in *Lashon HaKodesh*. After he revealed his identity to them, he switched to speaking to them directly—in *Lashon HaKodesh*. We presented three reasons why Joseph did this:

- Rashi says that he did so in order to prove that he was, in fact, their long-lost brother Joseph.
- However, Ramban counters that since *Lashon HaKodesh* was spoken in the neighboring country of Canaan, Joseph's use of the language would not prove his identity. Rather, he spoke the language simply to put his brothers at ease.
- Rabbi Sofer points out that *Lashon HaKodesh* is linked to purity. Thus, Joseph spoke to his brothers in *Lashon HaKodesh* to show them that although he had been living among the morally degenerate Egyptians and had risen to prominence among them, he had still maintained his purity and could continue to speak the holy language.

After discussing Joseph's personal exile to Egypt, we segued into discussing the Jews' collective exile to Egypt. A well-known Midrash states that the Jews in Egypt did not change their language, meaning that they continued to speak *Lashon HaKodesh*. However, another Midrash states that God began presenting the Torah to them in Egyptian, because that was the language that they spoke in Egypt. While these two Midrashim seem at odds with each other, we presented several approaches to reconcile them and give a more concrete answer as to whether the Jews in Egypt spoke *Lashon HaKodesh* or Egyptian:

- Radak explains that there were some Jews who were not enslaved, and they spoke *Lashon HaKodesh* exclusively. Their not-so-fortunate brethren spoke *Lashon HaKodesh* between themselves, and Egyptian with their Egyptian overlords.
- Alternatively, it is possible that all the Jews spoke *Lashon HaKodesh,* yet God presented them the Torah in Egyptian because they were acclimated to accepting orders in that language.
- A third possibility is that since the hallmark of *Lashon HaKodesh* is its embodiment of holiness and purity, even if the Jews forgot the literal language, they could still be said to speak *Lashon HaKodesh*—The Holy Language—if their manner of speech remained holy.

After the Jews exited Egypt and eventually arrived in the Land of Israel, establishing their own rule, it is clear that *Lashon HaKodesh* alone served as their spoken language. This arrangement lasted for several centuries until the language began receding under Babylonian influence, toward the end of the First Temple period.

CHAPTER 5:
Replacing Lashon HaKodesh

WHEN THE TERM "HEBREW" IS USED

The term "Hebrews" (*Ivriim*, עבריים) is used by the Bible to describe the Jews in their encounters with other nations, especially in Egypt. It is never used to describe the Jews in other contexts. The Bible largely stops using the term after the Sinaitic Revelation. We have previously mentioned that the term refers to their usage of *Lashon HaKodesh*, something that continued even when exiled to Egypt. On the other hand, as we shall see in this chapter, throughout history when exiled amongst other nations, the Jews generally succumbed to foreign influences, and to differing degrees replaced the original *Lashon HaKodesh* with other languages.

Rabbi Avraham the Physician of Portleon (*Sha'ar Aryeh*), a sixteenth-century Italian sage, relates an interesting idea. While his idea has some very serious difficulties (see footnotes), it bears mention because of its religious significance, not its accuracy or historical value. He begins by noting that in general each language is known by the nation which speaks it (e.g., "Persian" is spoken by Persians; "Greek," by Greeks; etc.). However, *Lashon HaKodesh* is not usually known as "Hebrew" after the name of its speakers.[229] He explains this anomaly by noting that the term "Hebrew" is found in the Bible regarding Abraham, and only before his ritual circumcision. After he became a full-fledged Jew, he was no longer referred to as a "Hebrew."[230] Similarly, the Torah only describes the Jewish nation as "Hebrews" before the Sinaitic Revelation.[231] Afterwards, they were no longer known as "Hebrews";[232] they were simply called "The Holy Nation."[233] Accordingly, Rabbi Avraham explains that just as all other languages are named after the nation that speaks them, *Lashon*

229 However, see Machon Yerushalayim ed. fn. 2 (there), which cites many instances in rabbinic literature that refer to *Lashon HaKodesh* as *Ivri* ("Hebrew"). He himself attempts to explain away these sources, but his answer is unclear.

230 See M. Herskowitz, "Implications of the Name עברי in Tanakh and Talmudic Sources," *Ohr HaMizrach*, vol. 73 (New York: Religious Zionists of America, 1971), pgs. 25–33, and vol. 77, pgs. 29–38, which discusses and rejects various theories about the appellation *Ivri*, concluding that "Hebrew" is simply a synonym for "Jew." Much of the material he discusses is mentioned in this chapter and the previous ones.

231 Interestingly, most of these examples concern the Jews in Egypt. For example, Joseph is described as a "Hebrew" (*Genesis* 39:14, 41:12), and he claimed to have been kidnapped from the land of the "Hebrews" (ibid. 40:15). The Jewish housewives and midwives are referred to as "Hebrews" (*Exodus* 1:15, 1:16, 1:19, 2:7). In addition, Bithiah described the infant Moses as a "Hebrew" (ibid. 2:6). Furthermore, an anonymous Jewish slave in Egypt who was hit by an Egyptian man was referred to as a "Hebrew man" (ibid. 2:11), as were the two witnesses to Moses' act of retribution toward the Egyptian (ibid. 2:13). The Torah mentions that Egyptians do not eat bread with "Hebrews" (*Genesis* 43:32), and during the story of the Exodus repeatedly refers to God as the "God of the 'Hebrews'" (*Exodus* 3:18, 5:3, 7:16, 9:1, 9:13, 10:3). The appellation appears in the Torah only twice more, both times concerning the laws of the Hebrew male bondsman (ibid. 21:2, *Deuteronomy* 15:12), as well as twice in the prophecies of Jeremiah in that context (*Jeremiah* 34:9, 34:14). See Rabbeinu Bachaya (to *Exodus* 21:6) who explains that the term "Hebrew" connotes a lower spiritual level than the term "Israelite" does. Based on this, Rabbeinu Bachaya explains that it is appropriate to refer to a Jewish slave as a "Hebrew" even after the Sinaitic Revelation because a slave lives on a lower plane of existence than a freedman does (see also *Kli Yakar* and *Ohr HaChaim* there). Besides the instances listed above (and in the next footnote), the term "Hebrew" only appears once more in the entire Bible, when Jonah identifies himself to his shipmates as a Hebrew (*Jonah* 1:9).

232 Nonetheless, he concedes that the name "Hebrew" was renewed during the war between King Saul and the Philistines; see *Samuel* I 4:6, 13:3, 13:19, 14:11, 29:3, and admits that he cannot explain why this name in particular was used in that specific context.

233 *Exodus* 19:6.

HaKodesh is named after the Jewish Nation. Since the Jews are known as the "Holy Nation," their language is called the "Holy Language."[234]

THE HOLY LANGUAGE IS RELATED TO THE HOLY TEMPLE

There is another explanation as to why *Lashon HaKodesh* is called the "Holy Language," which leads to our next discussion. *Targum Jonathan* usually refers to *Lashon HaKodesh* as "*lishon beis kudsha*" (לישן בית קודשא), which literally means "the language of the Holy Temple."[235] This implies that *Targum Jonathan* understands that *Lashon HaKodesh* is called the "Holy Language" because it was the language spoken in the "Holy Temple."[236]

LASHON HAKODESH WAS SPOKEN UNTIL THE DESTRUCTION OF THE FIRST TEMPLE

The association between *Lashon HaKodesh* and the Holy Temple is taken a step further by Rabbi Gedaliah ibn Yachya (1515–1587). He claims (in the name of an anonymous writer) that the Jews spoke and wrote in *Lashon HaKodesh* until the destruction of the First Temple, and that they began to speak Aramaic only upon their exile to Babylon.[237]

Ibn Yachya's claim is echoed by his older contemporary, HaBachur, who writes that during the First Temple period, only select individuals within the king's court understood Aramaic. The rest of the Jews spoke *Lashon HaKodesh* exclusively.

He proves this from the story of Rabshakeh, who made an announcement in *Lashon HaKodesh* before the court that the Assyrian king

---

234 *Shiltei HaGiborim, Ma'amar HaLashon* (Jerusalem: Machon Yerushalayim, 2010), pg. 571.

235 See *Targum Jonathan* to *Genesis* 45:12; *Deuteronomy* 25:7–8.

236 Interestingly, when mentioning the view that *Lashon HaKodesh* was the pre-Babel language, *Targum Jonathan* (to *Genesis* 11:1) deviates from his norm and uses the expression *lishon kudsha* (לישן קודשא), which is a literal translation of "*Lashon HaKodesh*" into Aramaic, instead of using the expression *lishon beis kudsha* (לישן בית קודשא). Nonetheless, in that context and in many others, *Targum Neofiti* (e.g., to *Genesis* 2:19, 11:1, 22:1, 22:11) also refers to the *Lashon HaKodesh* in the same way as *Targum Jonathan*. See *Pirush Yerushalmi* to *Targum Yerushalmi* (*Genesis* 22:11), who explains the reason behind the differences between *Targum Jonathan* and *Targum Yerushalmi* in *Genesis* 22 concerning Abraham speaking *Lashon HaKodesh*.

237 *Shalsheles HaKabbalah* (Jerusalem, 1962), pg. 217.

Sennacherib intended to conquer Jerusalem. King Hezekiah's couriers, Elyakim ben Hilkiyahu, Shebna, and Joach told him to speak only in Aramaic, not in the "Jewish Language."[238] Rashi explains that they did not want the public to hear of what was happening;[239] therefore, they asked Rabshakeh to speak in Aramaic, a language only understood by the diplomats, but not by the public at large. This story occurred approximately 100 years before the Temple's destruction. From this episode, HaBachur proves that *Lashon HaKodesh* continued to be the main language of the Jewish people until the end of the First Temple period. He also claims that the Jewish Nation only lost the language upon their exile to Babylon following the Temple's destruction.[240] While this oversimplification is for the most part accurate, it does not present an entirely precise depiction of the decline of *Lashon HaKodesh*.

EFODI: THE DECLINE OF LASHON HAKODESH BEGAN DURING THE END OF THE FIRST TEMPLE ERA

Efodi writes that *Lashon HaKodesh* began to disappear from the mouths of the Jews even before the destruction of the First Temple.[241] He writes that during the First Temple period, people began to stop delving into the Torah as a written document, which dulled their skills in the sacred tongue.

With this in mind, Efodi explains an episode that occurred approximately forty years before the Temple's destruction. The Bible mentions the surprise and bewilderment of Hilkiah, the Kohen Gadol in the time of King Josiah, when he found a Torah scroll.[242] In fact, the Torah scroll was

---

238 See *Kings* II Ch. 18.

239 To *Kings* II 18:26.

240 Introduction to *Meturgaman*.

241 It seems as if there is a dispute between HaBachur and Efodi, with HaBachur arguing that the language only began its decline at the destruction of the Temple, and Efodi arguing that it began beforehand. However, HaBachur's proof of *Lashon HaKodesh*'s usage at the end of the First Temple period does not necessarily contradict Efodi's proof that the nation lacked fluency in *Lashon HaKodesh* because the latter story occurred half a century after the first story. Nonetheless, if one assumes that HaBachur and Efodi do not argue, it is quite remarkable that *Lashon HaKodesh* went from being the common language to being almost obsolete in only a few decades.

242 *Chronicles* II 34:14–15.

so foreign to King Josiah that he was unable to even read from it. He was forced to ask Shafan, his royal scribe, to read it to him.[243]

Thus, Efodi hypothesizes that the decline of *Lashon HaKodesh* was correlated to the spiritual decline of the Jewish nation, who had become lax in their devotion to studying the Torah. As *Lashon HaKodesh* began its decline, Aramaic rose in popularity, due to Assyrian and later Babylonian influence.[244] Extra-biblical sources attest to the fact that by this period, the Aramaic language had already gained regional prominence and was seen as the *lingua franca* of the ancient world.[245]

THE BABYLONIAN EXILE

After the First Temple was destroyed, the Jews were exiled to Babylon. Seventy years later, the exile officially ended when a stream of Jews began to return to the Land of Israel under the leadership of Ezra and Nehemiah. In discussing these returnees, Nehemiah lamented their linguistic loyalties:

> "During those days, I saw Jews married to Ashdodites, Ammonites, and Moabites—and [of] their children half of them speak Ashdodite and do not know how to speak 'Jewish,' the language of their nation."[246]

Evidently, half of the Jews returning from the Babylonian exile had forgotten *Lashon HaKodesh* during their relatively brief stay in Babylon.[247] While the exact identification of the "Ashdodite language" remains a mystery,[248] Nehemiah's main point was simply

---

243 See TB *Sukkah* 38b, which contrasts the passage mentioned above in Chronicles with another verse in Kings (*Kings* II 22:16), which states that King Josiah himself read from the scroll. From this, the Talmud derives a halachic principle that "one who listens is considered to have recited." See note to Appendix A "The Scripts of *Lashon HaKodesh*" for an alternate explanation of this incident.

244 *Ma'aseh Efod*, Ch. 7.

245 "Aramaic language," *Encyclopedia Britannica* (2011).

246 *Nehemiah* 13:23–24.

247 Rabbi Sa'adya Gaon in Harkavy (ed.), *Sefer HaEgron* (St. Petersburg, 1879), pg. 54, also laments this fact in his poetic outline of the history of *Lashon HaKodesh*.

248 Some have argued that it refers to any non-Semitic language, which should have otherwise been completely unintelligible to Jews of that period. Others argue that the Ashdodite

that many of the returning Jews spoke a foreign language instead of *Lashon HaKodesh*.

WHY BABYLON? WHY ARAMAIC?

The Talmud offers several reasons why God exiled the Jews specifically to Babylon of all places.[249] One explanation states that He did so because Aramaic, the language spoken in Babylon, is so closely related to the language of the Torah. Rabbi Meir Amsel explains that He realized that the Jews would be influenced by the language of their host country. If the Jews would have been exiled to a country whose language differed radically from *Lashon HaKodesh*, then they would risk losing their ability to properly understand and interpret the Torah. In order to minimize this risk, God purposely exiled the Jews to Babylon—whose language was closely related to *Lashon HaKodesh*—so that the Jews would be able to continue living by the Torah.[250]

WHY DID THEY FORGET LASHON HAKODESH SO QUICKLY?

The commentators point out an interesting anomaly: The Jewish exile to Babylon lasted roughly a little more than half a century, yet in such a relatively short period, the Jews forgot *Lashon HaKodesh*, which they had preserved since the beginning of time.

How and why did this happen? The commentators offer several explanations of this phenomenon:

APPROACH #1: LEAVING ISRAEL DETACHED THEM FROM LASHON HAKODESH

As we have seen, the Land of Israel is spiritually linked to the language of *Lashon HaKodesh*. Thus, from a spiritual viewpoint, losing the

---

language was a remnant of the Philistine (Phoenician) language, which was a Semitic language, but differed from *Lashon HaKodesh*. Still others contend that the Ashdodite language was simply a dialect of *Lashon HaKodesh* (apparently of which Nehemiah did not approve). See K. Southwood, "'And they could not understand Jewish Speech': Ethnicity, Language, and Nehemiah's intermarriage crisis," *Journal of Theological Studies*, vol. 62:1 (2011), pgs. 14–16, who summarizes these theories.

249 TB *Pesachim* 87b.

250 M. Amsel (ed.), "*Lashon HaKodesh* and Ivrit," *Kovetz Hamaor*, vol. 79 (Brooklyn, 1958), pg. 11.

language while in exile is completely understandable, because when they are distanced from the Land of Israel they are equally distanced from *Lashon HaKodesh*.

Nonetheless, the commentators offer more complex ways of explaining how and why the exiled Jews so quickly dropped *Lashon HaKodesh* in lieu of Aramaic.

APPROACH #2: BABYLON IS CONDUCIVE TO LINGUISTIC FORGETFULNESS

The Talmud relates that the airspace over which the Tower of Babel once stood is conducive to forgetfulness.[251] Abarbanel explains this idea by noting that Babylon was the epicenter of the division of languages.[252] It was from there that people stopped speaking *Lashon HaKodesh* over a thousand years beforehand. This incident imbued Babylon with the supernatural property of causing people to forget *Lashon HaKodesh*. In other words, the Jews forgot *Lashon HaKodesh* so quickly because they were exiled to the place associated with forgetting *Lashon HaKodesh*. Abarbanel takes this idea further and explains that in the current exile where the Jews mostly emigrated to the West—away from Babylon—they have not forgotten *Lashon HaKodesh* to the same degree, even though this exile is almost thirty times longer than the Babylonian exile.

APPROACH #3: THEY STOPPED SPEAKING LASHON HAKODESH DELIBERATELY

Rabbi Moshe Sofer rules that according to halachah, one should not speak *Lashon HaKodesh* in a place of idolatry. Since Babylon was a country full of idols and idol worshippers, the Jewish sages during the Babylonian exile decreed that Jews should only teach their children to speak Aramaic, not *Lashon HaKodesh*. This edict was enacted so that no one would sin by speaking *Lashon HaKodesh* near an unholy idol, thereby desecrating the holy language. Because the next genera-

---

251 TB *Sanhedrin* 109a.

252 In his commentary to *Genesis* 11:1.

tion never learned the language, *Lashon HaKodesh* was very quickly forgotten.[253]

APPROACH #4: FORGETTING DUE TO SPIRITUAL DETERIORATION

As mentioned in the previous chapter, Rabbi Sofer also explains that the Jews forgot *Lashon HaKodesh* so quickly because the language is correlated to spiritual sanctity. Unfortunately, the Jews in exile were not able to maintain the degree of holiness required to preserve it.[254]

Rabbi Avraham the Physician writes that while exiled to Babylon, the Jews quickly mixed with the gentiles. Because of this intermingling, and the fact that they endured much suffering, they forgot their language very quickly. Nonetheless, he notes, certain individuals preserved the language. These individuals included the likes of Ezra, Nehemiah, Daniel and his colleagues, and Mordecai and Esther. When the Jews returned from their seventy-year exile, these individuals were responsible for rehabilitating[255] *Lashon HaKodesh*.[256]

◆ ◆ ◆

EZRA INSTITUTES PRAYER IN LASHON HAKODESH

In tracing the history of prayer, Rambam writes that once the Jews mixed with the Persians and Greeks (after Nebuchadnezzar had originally

---

253 *Chasam Sofer* to *Shulchan Aruch, Orach Chaim* §85.

254 The author is unsure whether this explanation and the one preceding it are mutually exclusive.

255 Rabbi Avraham the Physician writes that these individuals were responsible for reinstating *Lashon HaKodesh* to its former status. In this, he implies that *Lashon HaKodesh* was restored fully, and that it was unchanged after the exile.

This assumption is contrary to the stance of *The Kuzari* and Ibn Ezra (mentioned below), who write that while much of *Lashon HaKodesh* has been forever lost due to the intensity of the Babylonian exile, the language as a whole was never completely forgotten. Ibn Ezra writes in *Safa Berurah*, pg. 4b, that much of *Lashon HaKodesh* has been lost and only that which has been preserved through canonization, like the Bible, remains. He also mentions this fact in the introduction to his translation of Ptolemy's work on astrolabes *Kli Nechoshes* (Konigsberg, 1845). Rambam also laments the diminution of *Lashon HaKodesh* in his *Guide for the Perplexed* (1:61, 1:67).

Interestingly, Eldad the Danite (who was purportedly from the Ten Tribes) is said to have spoken a pure version of *Lashon HaKodesh* that contained words that were lost to the mainstream Jewish community in their exile; see Rabbi Azariah de Rossi's *Meor Einayim*, vol. 5 (Vienna, 1829), pg. 280b; and J. D. Eisenstein (ed.), *Otzar Midrashim* (New York, 1915), pg. 20.

256 *Shiltei HaGiborim, Ma'amar HaLashon* (Jerusalem: Machon Yerushalayim, 2010), pg. 572.

exiled them to Babylon) and raised the next generation in the diaspora, they became confused in their speech and instead of speaking a pure *Lashon HaKodesh*, they instead spoke a linguistic hodgepodge influenced by multiple languages.[257] As a result, many Jews were no longer able to express their needs in one pure language without distortion, and certainly they were no longer able to express praise of God in *Lashon HaKodesh* without mixing in elements of other languages.

Although according to halachah prayer can be offered in any language, respect for God demands that it be offered in a pure language, not in a garbled and jumbled one.[258] In order to repair the situation, Ezra the scribe and his court institutionalized prayer by composing the exact liturgy to be recited thrice daily. In doing so, they saw to it that a purer form of *Lashon HaKodesh* would once again be the gold standard for prayer, as it had been before the Jews were exiled.

EZRA'S EFFORTS TO REHABILITATE LASHON HAKODESH

Ibn Yachya writes that when Aramaic began to overtake *Lashon HaKodesh*, the Jews also began to forget its rules of vowelization and cantillization—until Ezra restored them.[259]

Efodi, on the other hand, understands that vowels and cantillations did not originally exist in *Lashon HaKodesh*. Rather, when Ezra realized *Lashon HaKodesh's* dismal state, he decided to make the language more palatable to the general public, so in order to ease pronunciation, he established vowelization marks (*nikkudos*) to be written along with the plain letters. He also added cantillation marks (*ta'amim*, טעמים, which literally

257 Laws of *Tefillah* 1:4. See also S. Mirsky (ed.), *Chibbur HaTeshuva L'Rabbeinu Menachem Meiri* (New York: Yeshiva University Press, 1950), pg. 512.

258 See *Ma'aseh Rokeach* to Rambam, *Tefillah* there. Others (including *Ben Yedid* there) explain that Ezra's work was necessary simply because *individuals* are only allowed to pray in *Lashon HaKodesh*—in accordance with the first opinion cited by the *Shulchan Aruch* as elaborated upon in Appendix C "Prayers in Aramaic"—and *communal* prayer was not yet the norm, see also *Divrei Yirmiyahu* (there). Rabbi Moshe Sofer (responsa *Chasam Sofer*, vol. 6, §84) explains that even though prayer in a foreign language is permitted, Ezra and his court still had to institute prayers in *Lashon HaKodesh* because such prayer is only allowed for under short-term provisional circumstances, but not as a fixed policy. Thus, due to the circumstances of the time, Ezra had to institute formalized prayers in *Lashon HaKodesh* as the fixed policy.

259 *Shalsheles HaKabbalah* (Jerusalem, 1962), pg. 217.

means "tastes," or in Yiddish, *trop*, טראָפּ, "emphasis") in order to make reading the *Lashon HaKodesh* of the Bible sweet like music.[260] However, his efforts did not truly come to fruition, as *Lashon HaKodesh* continued its decline throughout the period of the Second Temple.

LASHON HAKODESH REMAINED THE LANGUAGE OF TORAH STUDY

We also find that the Talmud says that Ezra attempted to change the language used for studying Torah from *Lashon HaKodesh* to Aramaic.[261] However, ultimately, *Lashon HaKodesh* prevailed, and that language continued to be the one used for Torah study.

Ezra's rationale for this can be understood from the commentary of Rabbi Naftali Tzvi Yehuda Berlin (1817–1893),[262] where he defines the requirement that everyone write a Torah scroll. He writes that the commandment does not require every person to actually write a Torah scroll. Rather, every individual must ensure that he has access to Torah literature in a form that he can understand.[263] Thus, Ezra advocated that people write Aramaic translations of the Torah so that they could fulfill this requirement; but in the end, the people decided to continue using *Lashon HaKodesh* for Torah study.

ARAMAIC GAINS OFFICIAL RECOGNITION

In the beginning of the Second Temple period, Aramaic replaced *Lashon HaKodesh* as the Jews' main spoken language. From that time and onwards, the rabbis granted Aramaic special recognition. While some believe that the *Targum* (Aramaic translation) of the Torah dates to the

---

260 *Ma'aseh Efod* (Vienna, 1865), pg. 40. See TB *Nedarim* 37b that supports both histories of the vowels and cantillation marks. See also HaBachur's *Mesoras HaMesores*, responsa *Radvaz* (vol. 3 §643), and Rabbi Azariah de Rossi's *Meor Einayim*, vol. 5 (Vienna, 1829), pgs. 286b–292a, for further discussion of when exactly the vowelization and cantellization marks were introduced. Academia contends that the *nikkudot* were instituted by Karaite scholars; however, see *Barzilai*, pg. 106ff who solidly disproves that notion.

261 TB *Sanhedrin* 21b.

262 *Meromei Sadeh* (there).

263 This is based on the ruling of the *Shulchan Aruch* (*Yoreh Deah* §270:2) who writes that nowadays, since people do not study directly from Torah scrolls, there is no commandment to write one; rather, one is obligated to write volumes of the Pentateuch and the Talmud as needed for study.

times of Ezra, or even Moses, there is no doubt that it existed in the time of the Second Temple.[264] Onkelos the Proselyte and Rabbi Yonasan ben Uziel also authored prominent targumim (translations) of parts of the Bible into Aramaic, which were accepted by the rabbis and the Jewish community.[265] These targumim were publicly read in the synagogues for the benefit of the masses who no longer understood pure biblical *Lashon HaKodesh*. The rabbis also instituted a series of prayers to be said in Aramaic for the benefit of the masses, in addition to the previously instituted prayers in *Lashon HaKodesh*.

At this time, Jewish courts regularly issued official documents such as marriage documents (*kesubos*),[266] documents attesting to the performance of *chalitza*,[267] and bills of divorce (*gittin*)[268] in Aramaic. In rabbinic literature—both in works largely written in Aramaic[269] and works largely written in *Lashon HaKodesh*[270]—popular adages are always quoted in Aramaic. In this period, a treatise entitled *Megillas Ta'anis*, which details special minor holidays on which the rabbis forbade fasting, was written in Aramaic. The Talmud attributes this work to an early Tanna named Chananya ben Chizkiyah.[271]

GREEK GAINS PROMINENCE

Decades later, Alexander the Great's forays into the Middle East brought another language to the Jews, adding Greek to their pantheon of languages. In fact, the Mishnah says that during the Second Temple

---

264 See M. Kasher, *Torah Shleimah*, vol. 24 (Jerusalem, 1927–1992), pgs. 1–4.

265 The Talmud (TB *Megillah* 3a) states that Onkelos translated the Torah based on what he learned from Rabbi Eliezer and Rabbi Yehoshua, while Yonassan ben Uziel translated the Prophets based on what he learned from Haggai, Zechariah, and Malachi. See there for a full discussion about these translations.

266 See, for example, Mishnah *Kesubos* 4:7–12.

267 See, for example, JT *Moed Katan* 3:3.

268 See, for example, Mishnah *Gittin* 9:3.

269 Such as the Babylonian Talmud: every time it uses the expression "this is what people say" (*d'amri inshi*, דאמרי אינשי), it then quotes an adage in Aramaic.

270 See, for example, *Bereishis Rabbah* §16:5, §45:10, §84:2, *Midrash Tanchuma* (*Vayichi* §3), and more.

271 TB *Shabbos* 13b.

period, the keepers of the Temple used Greek letters to identify objects,[272] as opposed to Hebrew letters.[273] Rabbi Yehuda ben Binyamin the Physician (1215–1280)[274] and Rabbi Ovadiah of Bartenura (1440–1500)[275] explain that Greek was the common language used by Jews during the Second Temple period. Rabbi Yisrael Lipschitz (1782–1860) adds that during this period, most Jews[276] were more familiar with Greek than they were with *Lashon HaKodesh*.[277]

Under Ptolemaic Greek pressure, Jewish scholars translated the Torah into Greek and produced the work known as the Septuagent.[278] That

---

272 *Shekalim* 3:2.

273 This reflects the opinion of Rabbi Yishmael mentioned in the Mishnah, who writes that the three safes into which people deposited their *shekel*-taxes were marked with Greek letters. However, the anonymous Tanna in the beginning of the Mishnah (likely Rabbi Meir) says that the three safes were labeled with Hebrew letters, not Greek ones. His view is also reflected in another Mishnah (*Ma'aser Sheini* 4:11), which mentions that during the Second Temple period the Jews used to write Hebrew letters on their jugs in order to identify their contents (see also *Tosefta Ma'aser Sheini* Ch. 5), which seems to imply that—to some extent—they used *Lashon HaKodesh*, not Greek.

274 *Pirush Rivavan* to JT *Shekalim* 3:2.

275 Bartenura to Mishnah *Shekalim* 3:2.

276 See Rabbi Yoel Teitelbaum's *VaYoel Moshe* (*Ma'amar Lashon HaKodesh*, §14–16), who proves that even the learned Torah scholars were more familiar with Greek, not just the uneducated masses. See also D. Sperber, *Greek in Talmudic Palestine* (Ramat-Gan: Bar-Ilan University Press, 2012), and D. Sperber, "Rabbinic Knowledge of Greek," *The Literature of the Sages* (Fortress Press, 2006), pg. 627, which document the influence of the Greek language on rabbinic writings.
Later (in Chapter 7), we will discuss several examples of Greek and Greek-influenced words in rabbinic literature. The rabbis considered Greek to be such an important language that, as we have mentioned previously (in a note to Chapter 2), one opinion held that Greek was the language spoken by pre-Babel civilization. The Talmud also teaches (JT *Peah* 1:1) that one may teach his daughter Greek because it is considered an "ornament" (while implying that it is forbidden to teach one's son Greek because during the time he spends learning the language he would not be studying Torah).

277 *Tiferes Yisrael, Yachin* to Mishnah *Shekalim*, Ch. 3, §9.

278 According to the Talmud (TB *Megillah* 9a–b), a Ptolemaic king took seventy-two Jewish elders and housed them in seventy-two separate places and asked them to translate the Torah into Greek. Miraculously, the products of each of these seventy-two elders were exactly the same, and all contained the exact same slight editorial changes in order to circumvent the theological implications of a super-literal translation. This story is mentioned earlier in the Jewish-Greek work *Letter of Aristeas*, who identifies the king as Ptolemy II Philadelphus (285–246 BCE). Philo (*On the Life of Moses* 2:31–44) provides this story as the reason for an annual holiday celebrated on Pharos (an island off the coast of Alexandria, Egypt), but does not mention that there were seventy-two scholars. See also Josephus' *Antiquities of the Jews* (Book XII, Ch. 2). According to *Maseches Sofrim* (1:7), a similar story also happened before this, in which a Ptolemaic king had five Jewish elders translate the Torah into Greek. *Maseches Sofrim* concludes by noting that that day was as difficult for the Jews as the day

translation was the standard edition of the Torah used by many Jews. In fact, Philo Judaeus, a famous Jewish-Greek philosopher in first-century Alexandria, Egypt, was said to have read the Bible only in Greek, not in the original Hebrew.[279] In that century, another famous translation of the Torah into Greek was undertaken by Akylas (Aquila) the Proselyte.[280]

A photograph of one of the caves at Qumran (Cave #4) in the Judean Desert where the Dead Sea Scrolls were discovered. (Source: Dr. Avishai Teicher at Pikiwiki. Creative Commons Attribution 2.5)

THREE LANGUAGES OF THE SECOND TEMPLE

Thus, the Jewish community spoke Greek along with *Lashon HaKodesh* and Aramaic. It seems that this arrangement of three languages—known by linguists as triglossia—remained in the Judean Jewish community well into the seventh century CE, when Muslim conquest forced Arabic upon them.

The use of these three languages side-by-side is exemplified by the so-called "Cave of Letters," discovered in the Judean Desert in 1960. It contained many letters written in *Lashon HaKodesh*, Aramaic, and Greek,

---

that they created the Golden Calf. In the postscript to *Megillas Ta'anis*, the author writes that the day that the Torah was translated into Greek (the eighth of Teves) brought darkness into the world for three days and is to be observed as a fast day.

279 M. Berenbaum & F. Skolnik (eds.), "Philo Judaeus," *Encyclopedia Judaica* 2nd ed., vol. 16 (Detroit: Macmillan Reference USA, 2007), pg. 59.

280 Due to the similarities between Akylas and Onkelos's names and roles, there has been much confusion between the two. See A. E. Silverstone, *Aquila and Onkelos* (Manchester University Press, 1931), who even claims that Akylas and Onkelos were the same person. Cf. *Sefer HaMinhagos* printed in S. Assaf (ed.), *Sifran Shel Rishonim* (Jerusalem: Mekize Nirdamim, 1925), pg. 144, who writes that Onkelos only translated the Pentateuch, while Akylas translated the Hagiography.

dating from the period of the Bar Kochba revolt little more than half a century after the Second Temple's destruction.[281] The Dead Sea Scrolls found at Qumran also contain texts written in these three languages .

◆ ◆ ◆

THE LANGUAGE OF THE MISHNAH

The Mishnah was written in *Lashon HaKodesh* roughly 150 years after the end of the Second Temple era, based on the teachings of the sages who had lived during the entire era.

APPROACH #1: THE GALILEAN DIALECT OF LASHON HAKODESH

According to the Mishnah itself,[282] in its time the Jewish settlement in the Land of Israel was broken up into three major blocs: Judea, Transjordan, and the Galilee. These three blocs were different from each other in that they each spoke a slightly different dialect of *Lashon HaKodesh*.[283] In light of this, the academic world contends that the flavor of *Lashon HaKodesh* used in the Mishnah is specifically that of the Galilee.[284] This idea explains why the brand of *Lashon HaKodesh* used in the Mishnah is more heavily influenced by Aramaic than the *Lashon HaKodesh* used in the Bible.

APPROACH #2: THE MISHNAH REFLECTS POPULAR USAGE

Rambam writes that some claim that the Mishnah uses improper

---

281 Josephus, in describing the final siege of Jerusalem right before the destruction of the Second Temple in his book *The War of the Jews* (Book VI), mentions twice that he was a translator to the Jewish community, relaying the Latin commands of the Roman General Titus to the Jewish public in *Ivri*. See K. Schulman (ed.), *Milchamos HaYehudim*, vol. 2 (Vilna, 1884), pgs. 256, 262. This implies that the Jews at the time of the Second Temple's destruction spoke *Lashon HaKodesh*. However, see footnote (there) of the English theologian William Whiston (1667–1752) to his English translation of Josephus' work, who writes that *Ivri* in this context refers to Syriac (i.e., Aramaic), not to Hebrew.

282 *Kesubos* 13:10.

283 See Rama and other commentaries to *Shulchan Aruch, Even HaEzer* §75:1.

284 This theory is further developed by G. Rendsburg in his article, "The Galilean Background of Mishnaic Hebrew," printed in L. Levine (ed.), *The Galilee in Late Antiquity* (Harvard University Press, 1992), pgs. 225–240.

grammar and inelegant expressions.[285] To this, he counters that the sages of the Mishnah spoke *Lashon HaKodesh* as their main language, and thus their usage of the language in that fashion proves that it is indeed acceptable.[286] That is, Rambam believed that popular usage of the language determines its grammatical rules.

APPROACH #3: RABBINIC HEBREW DIFFERS FROM BIBLICAL HEBREW

Rabbi Avraham ibn Ezra[287] explains that even though one finds that the Mishnah sometimes conjugates its verbs differently than the language of the Bible, the Talmud says that biblical expressions and rabbinic expressions are distinct.[288] Ibn Ezra believes that there are two legitimate strains of *Lashon HaKodesh*: one found in the Bible, and one found in rabbinic literature. (This distinction is also acknowledged in academic circles).[289]

APPROACH #4: A FUSION OF LASHON HAKODESH AND ARAMAIC

Others explain that while the sages of the Mishnah preserved *Lashon HaKodesh* for holy uses,[290] the masses were more familiar with Aramaic,

---

285 In his commentary to the Mishnah *Terumos* 1:1.

286 Rabbi Reuven Margolis notes in *Shem Olam* (Jerusalem: Mossad HaRav Kook, 1989), pg. 15 fn. 15, that this passage of Rambam is based on the introduction of Rabbi Yonah ibn Janach to *Sefer HaRikma*.

287 In his commentary to *Esther* 8:17.

288 TB *Avodah Zarah* 58b.

289 This is especially noteworthy because elsewhere (in his commentary to *Ecclesiastes* 5:1), Ibn Ezra strongly criticizes HaKallir for using rabbinic-style *Lashon HaKodesh* in his liturgical poetry because that style is influenced by foreign languages, as opposed to the biblical *Lashon HaKodesh*, which is purer. He further criticizes HaKallir's style by noting that even words whose origins are in *Lashon HaKodesh* are misused because HaKallir confuses masculine and feminine forms of words, as well as different tense forms. There is much controversy over when exactly HaKallir lived, but according to some opinions (see Tosafos to TB *Chagigah* 13a) HaKallir was actually a Tannaic sage. If so, then Ibn Ezra's criticism of HaKallir is weakened because Ibn Ezra himself acknowledges that biblical Hebrew and Mishnaic Hebrew are two valid strands of *Lashon HaKodesh*. HaKallir was simply using the latter instead of the former.

290 *Mizrachi* notes (in his commentary to *Deuteronomy* 26:5) that the style of *Lashon HaKodesh* used by the Mishnah closely resembles the *Lashon HaKodesh* of the Torah. He explains that by the time of the Mishnah's composition, *Lashon HaKodesh* had already significantly declined and much of it was lost. However, the Tannaic sages retained *Lashon HaKodesh* based both on tradition and on unpublished books from the Biblical Era which used *Lashon HaKodesh* in its proper form. (Rabbi Shmuel Strashun independently proposes the same idea in his *Hagahos*

and even the sages spoke Aramaic for mundane matters. Therefore, the sages used their intimate knowledge of both *Lashon HaKodesh* and Aramaic to fuse the two languages together and create a new entity, which is reflected in the language of the Mishnah. This new language had elements of both Hebrew and Aramaic grammar and vocabulary. The advantages of this language was that it made the laws of the Mishnah accessible even to the untrained layman, while also preserving the holy status of *Lashon HaKodesh* as the language of Torah study.[291]

BORROWING FROM OTHER LANGUAGES

In Chapter 7, we will revisit this topic and describe several ways in which the rabbis of the Mishnah regulated the language in their times, especially in regard to the introduction of foreign influences into *Lashon HaKodesh*. In addition to this, the rabbis added more words to *Lashon HaKodesh* than existed in the Bible[292]—even for ideas and concepts for which words already existed in the Bible[293]—and sometimes even changed the meanings of pre-existing words.[294]

HaRashash to TB *Nedarim* 2a.) Thus, they had a richer *Lashon HaKodesh* vocabulary than was widely available.

Rabbi Moshe Sofer (*Toras Moshe* to *Genesis* 11:1) admits that *Lashon HaKodesh* does indeed have a paltry vocabulary compared to other languages. He explains the dearth of words by noting that while all other languages have evolved through contributions and additions, *Lashon HaKodesh* is limited to those words spoken by God to His prophets. He adds that even words that were introduced by the sages of the Mishnah and the Talmud are not considered *Lashon HaKodesh*, for God Himself did not speak them. Rabbi Sofer's explanation follows Ramban's stance (as cited in Chapter 4). In other words, God did not speak the language of *Lashon HaKodesh*; whatever God spoke became *Lashon HaKodesh*. See Rabbi Yoel Teitelbaum's *VaYoel Moshe* (*Ma'amar Lashon HaKodesh* §28), who attempts to reconcile Rabbi Sofer's explanation with that of *Mizrachi*.

291 *Ma'amar Al Dikduk Lashon HaKodesh* (printed in the beginning of the standard Vilna Mishnayos) written by the Hungarian historian Solomon Löwisohn (1788–1821). See there for several specific examples.

292 For example, the word *tzarich* (צריך), "needs," is used countless times in the Mishnah and throughout rabbinic literature, but is absent from the Bible. The same is true of the word *shtar* (שטר), "document"; *efshar* (אפשר), "possible"; *chatul* (חתול), "cat" ; and *pagum* (פגום), "blemished."

293 For example, in biblical *Lashon HaKodesh*, the word for "sun" is *shemesh* (שמש), "tree" is *eitz* (עץ), and "how" is *eich* (איך). In rabbinic literature, the words *chamah* (חמה), *ilan* (אילן), and *keitzad* (כיצד) are commonly used instead.

294 For example, the word *olam* (עולם) in the Bible usually refers to temporal infinity, while in rabbinic usage refers to spatial infinity. The verb *koreh* (קורא) in the Bible means to "call," while in Rabbinic literature it means to "read." The word *chafetz* (חפץ) means "desire" in the Bible,

Efodi points out that even the Mishnah, which was largely written in *Lashon HaKodesh*, needed to borrow words from other languages in order to describe things for which the *Lashon HaKodesh* words were not known. The Orders of *Taharos* and *Zera'im* of the Mishnah are especially replete with such instances.[295] The reason for this is that by that time, *Lashon HaKodesh* had waned as an everyday language. In fact, the Talmud relates that even in the time of Rabbi Yehuda HaNassi, the famed redactor of the Mishnah,[296] some Torah scholars required the assistance of others to understand certain obscure words in *Lashon HaKodesh*.[297]

THE LANGUAGE OF THE TALMUD

The Babylonian Talmud was written roughly four centuries after the destruction of the Second Temple. Efodi and HaBachur explain that the Talmudists had chosen—for lack of alternative—to adopt Aramaic as their principal language. The Talmud was written in Aramaic and not *Lashon HaKodesh*, for by then *Lashon HaKodesh* was all but forgotten.[298] Rabbi Yehuda HaChasid (1150–1217)[299] confirms that the Talmud was written in Aramaic because the ignorant masses did not understand *Lashon HaKodesh*.[300]

---

while in Rabbinic literature it means "object." Rabbi Baruch Epstein (*Tosefes Bracha* to *Numbers* 16:22) points out that the meanings of several words and phrases have changed since Biblical times. Amongst his examples, he notes that *seter* (סתר) in the Bible means "hidden" while in Rabbinic litature refers to "destroying," and *keles* (קלס) in the Bible refers to mockery and derision, while in Rabbinic writings it is a form of praise. The word *neis* (נס) is used in the Bible to mean a "mast," "sign," or "flag," and is only used to mean "miracle" in later writings.

295 Interestingly, Efodi asserts that had the Book of Remedies been extant then, the Mishnah would not have needed to use foreign words for flora and fauna; their *Lashon HaKodesh* equivalents would have been known. But alas, the book had been hidden by King Hezekiah, as mentioned in the Mishnah (*Pesachim* 4:9).

296 Rabbi Yehuda HaNassi, as mentioned in the footnotes to Chapter 8, declared that Aramaic is useless because one could speak either Greek or *Lashon HaKodesh* in its stead. Despite his support for the reclamation of *Lashon HaKodesh* under Roman occupation, some Torah scholars in his time were apparently not entirely fluent in that language.

297 See TB *Rosh HaShanah* 26b.

298 *Ma'aseh Efod* (Vienna, 1865), pg. 41.

299 *Sefer Chassidim* (§785).

300 Rambam (in his Introduction to *Mishnah Torah*) mentions the same point and notes that Talmudic Aramaic was only understood by the masses during the Amoraic Period. Therefore, he explains, much elucidation and explanation is needed in latter generations in order to fully

◆ ◆ ◆

As the generations progressed, *Lashon HaKodesh* as a spoken language was relegated to relative obscurity, understood only by Jewish scholars and other aficionados, to the exclusion of the general masses.[301] In general, as the Jews spread across the world, they began to speak the local languages and/or their own "Jewish" dialects of those local languages. These dialects, although heavily influenced by *Lashon HaKodesh* and Aramaic, replaced those languages as the vernacular.[302] Nonetheless, even during the medieval period and later, new words were coined that entered the lexicon of *Lashon HaKodesh*.[303] In fact, Rashi alone is reputed to have invented over 1,500 neologisms![304]

JUDEO-GREEK

As we have already mentioned, during the Second Temple period and thereafter, the Jews in Judea spoke a triglossia of languages: *Lashon HaKodesh*, Aramaic, and Greek. The strain of Greek spoken by the Jewish community from that era through the Byzantine period was not pure

---

understand the Talmud. Rambam viewed his own role as translating the complex halachic code of the Talmud from the obscure language of the Talmud to the more clear, concise, and understandable language of the Mishnah. See Rabbi Shmuel Ashkenazi's elaboration on this theme in his article first published in the journal *Leshonenu L'Am*, vol. 158 (Jerusalem: The Academy of the Hebrew Language, 1965), pgs. 139–174, and later again in Y. Y. Stahl & E. Y. Brodt (eds.), *Asufa* (Jerusalem, 2014), pgs. 87–108.

301 Rabbi Shlomo ibn Parchon (circa. twelfth century) writes that during his time, Jews in Arabic-speaking countries were not accustomed to speaking *Lashon HaKodesh*. This was unlike Jews in European countries, who spoke *Lashon HaKodesh* to communicate with Jews of different nationalities who spoke different languages. See Z. Gottleib (ed.), *Machaberes HaAruch* (Bratislava, 1844), pg. xiii.

302 Much of the material for this section was culled from Dr. Bernard Spolsky's *The Languages of the Jews* (Cambridge University Press, 2014), which offers a comprehensive survey of the various linguistic preferences in different parts of the Jewish diaspora. His book is written from a sociolinguistic perspective, and contains much important historical data. I thank Dr. Spolsky for making his then-unpublished manuscript available to me. *Encyclopedia Judaica* is another invaluable resource for the information contained in this section. See also G. Jochnowitz, "Yiddish? Why Don't We Speak Judeo-French?", *Midstream*, vol. 54:4 (July/August 2008), pgs. 32–34.

303 For example, the word *teva* (טבע), which means "to mint" in rabbinic literature, was first used by medieval commentators to mean "nature." The word *dfus* (דפוס), which means "print," obviously only came into use in that context after the invention of the printing press (discussed below), while beforehand it was a generic term used to refer to any cast mold.

304 O. Chen, *HaKsav V'HaMichtav* (Bene Barak: Machon HaRav Matzliach, 2014), pg. 84.

Greek; they used a variety of Greek heavily influenced by *Lashon HaKodesh* and Aramaic—a Judeo-Greek dialect. Subsequently, Judeo-Greek continued to exist outside of Judea, primarily in some Jewish communities in Turkey, Greece, and the Balkans. Some of those communities in Greece continued to speak Judeo-Greek until the Nazis obliterated them during the Holocaust (1939–1945).

THE JEWS' INTRODUCTION TO ARABIC

In Babylonia, where Greek never gained much traction, the Jewish communities mainly spoke *Lashon HaKodesh* and Aramaic (with significant Persian influence). This arrangement remained intact until the Muslim conquest of the Holy Land in the seventh century. The Muslim invaders promptly imposed Arabic on the many civilizations that came under their domain. The prominence of Greek (in the Byzantine Levant); Persian (in modern-day Iraq and Iran); Coptic (in modern-day Egypt); Latin (in Spain and certain parts of North Africa); and the Berber languages (in North Africa) dwindled under Muslim rule. Arabic replaced them as the vernacular, making it the language that unified the Muslim territories. Arabic's rapid spread within the Jewish community was aided by the fact that Arabic is a Semitic language, so it was similar to their native *Lashon HaKodesh* and Aramaic. While there may be evidence of Arabic-speaking Jews (whether converts or migrants) in Arabia, Ethiopia, and Yemen even before the Muslim conquest, the language's popularity only swelled afterwards.

JUDEO-ARABIC

Nonetheless, under the early seventh-century Muslim rule, non-Muslims (including Christians and Jews) were purposely excluded from taking advantage of the linguistic advances of Arabic (Muslim law forbade non-Muslims to learn Classical Arabic). Instead, they developed their own brand of Arabic known as Middle Arabic, as opposed to the Muslims' Classical Arabic (in which the Quran was written). The Jewish community developed Judeo-Arabic, a dialect of Middle Arabic that was written in Hebrew script. In the ensuing centuries, many Jewish communities gradually replaced *Lashon HaKodesh*, Aramaic, and Greek with Judeo-Arabic.

Judeo-Arabic became *the* language used by Jews in everyday speech, and even in writing; unlike most other Jewish dialects which, for the most part, remained spoken but not written. In tenth-century Babylonia, Rabbi Sa'adya Gaon (882–942), one of the foremost Geonim, authored a translation of the Bible into Judeo-Arabic (known as the *Tafsir*, "explanation"), as well as several philosophical and polemic works. In the next century, Rabbi Yehuda HaLevi, in Islamic Spain, authored his seminal work *The Kuzari* in Judeo-Arabic (as well as many beautiful Arabic-influenced poems in *Lashon HaKodesh*, a genre first introduced by Rabbi Shmuel HaNaggid). Rambam was born in Islamic Spain in 1135 and lived in various places under Muslim control (including North Africa and the Holy Land). He wrote most of his works in Judeo-Arabic. An exception is his *magnum opus*, *Mishnah Torah*, which he wrote in pure *Lashon HaKodesh*.[305]

All of these Judeo-Arabic works, plus many more, were translated into *Lashon HaKodesh*—some even during the lifetimes of their authors. However, the fact that they were originally written in Judeo-Arabic attests to the prevalence of that language in medieval times. In fact, most of the texts discovered from that period at the Cairo Geniza are written in Judeo-Arabic.

JUDEO-ARABIC SPEAKERS STUDIED LASHON HAKODESH

Nonetheless, the Spanish scholars of that time were very interested in understanding the systematic grammar of *Lashon HaKodesh*. For example, Rabbi Yonah ibn Janach (990–1050) wrote two works in Judeo-Arabic on *Lashon HaKodesh*, which were subsequently translated into *Lashon HaKodesh* by Rabbi Yehuda ibn Tibbon (1120–1190). Rabbi Menachem ibn Saruk, another prominent tenth-century Spanish scholar, produced one of the earliest dictionaries of *Lashon HaKodesh*: the *Machaberes*. His

305 Interestingly, Rambam himself writes that he later regretted writing his main works in Arabic instead of in *Lashon HaKodesh*. See Y. Shalit (ed.), *Iggros HaRambam* (Maale Adumim: Shilat Publications, 1995), pgs. 233, 409.

interlocutor Donash (920–990) famously debated with him regarding the various rules governing *Lashon HaKodesh*'s grammar and lexicon. Ibn Ezra, who started out in Spain and traveled to many different Jewish communities to escape persecution, translated several Arabic works into *Lashon HaKodesh* and was a prolific writer in *Lashon HaKodesh* himself.

OTHERS JEWISH LANGUAGES IN THE MUSLIM EMPIRE

In some regions under Muslim control, the Jews ended up speaking languages besides Arabic, although these were the exceptions rather than the rule. In the areas of modern-day Iran and Iraq, even though Arabic gained prominence, Farsi (Persian) continued to be spoken in everyday speech. The Jewish communities there developed a form of Judeo-Persian, an umbrella term that includes the languages spoken by the Jews in Dagestan, Uzbekistan, and Azerbaijan. Similarly, after the expulsion of Jews from Spain and Portugal, many went to Turkey and other areas of the Ottoman Empire where they spoke Judeo-Spanish, not Judeo-Arabic.

JUDEO-SPANISH

With the Muslim conquests of Spain, Judeo-Arabic made its way to the Jews living on the Iberian Peninsula. In that region,[306] the Spanish language had developed as a Latin-based Creole with significant influences from other Romance languages, Arabic, and even some Germanic languages. The Jews cast out from Spain in 1492 (which was ruled by a Catholic king at the time) spoke their own brand of Judeo-Spanish (also known as *Judezmo* or "Ladino"). Historians have debated whether this dialect existed in the Jewish communities of Spain before the expulsion.[307]

306 Judeo-Provençal, a local Jewish dialect in Provençe (southern France) bears closer resemblance to Judezmo than to the supposed Judeo-French (see below). The Jewish communities of Southern France were disconnected from the Jewish communities of Northern France, and were more closely associated with the Jewish communities of Spain. For example, two famous Provençal Talmudic scholars, Raavad and Meiri, are more closely associated with the Sephardic tradition than with the French-German Tosafist tradition, even though both traditions certainly influenced their writings.

307 M. Berenbaum & F. Skolnik (eds.), "Ladino," *Encyclopedia Judaica* 2nd ed., vol. 8 (Detroit: Macmillan Reference USA, 2007), pgs. 427–435.

On the other hand, it seems that Jaquetía, the Judeo-Spanish dialect spoken in Northern Africa (in Morocco and Algeria) and Gibraltar, was indeed spoken by the Jewish population in Spain before the expulsion.[308]

FRENCH JEWS

At the turn of the millennium, Jews in Arabic-speaking countries used Judeo-Arabic as both a written and spoken language. However, in France (which was not under Muslim rule) most Jews spoke Old French[309] and wrote in *Lashon HaKodesh*.[310] The strongest evidence of this notion is found in the writings of Rashi and the Tosafists. They wrote in highly advanced *Lashon HaKodesh*, yet offered a multitude of definitions and translations of Hebrew and Aramaic terms into Old French, their spoken language.

Even though they spoke Old French, the French scholars were also heavily interested in *Lashon HaKodesh*—the language in which they wrote. Rashi; his grandsons Rabbeinu Tam (1100–1171) and Rabbi Shmuel ben Meir (1085–1158), known as Rashbam; Rabbi Yosef Kara; *Chizkuni*; and other French scholars wrote extensively on the grammar and vocabulary of *Lashon HaKodesh*. In fact, Rabbeinu Tam and the Kimchi family from Provençe also engaged in the arguments between Donash and Ibn Saruk, siding with Donash more often than not.

The French Jewish community also spanned northwards to England, from where the Jews were expelled by the end of the thirteenth century. The Anglo-French scholars were also interested in *Lashon HaKodesh*. In fact, two of the few remaining works by English Tosafists deal with the grammar and vowelization of *Lashon HaKodesh:* Rabbi Moshe ben Yitzchak HaNessiah of England's *Sefer HaShoham* (first printed by Mekize Nirdamim in Jerusalem, 1945), and Rabbi Moshe ben Yom Tov of London's *Darchei HaNikkud V'HaNigginos* (Hanover, 1847). By the

---

308 M. Berenbaum & F. Skolnik (eds.), "Jaketía," *Encyclopedia Judaica* 2nd ed., vol. 8 (Detroit: Macmillan Reference USA, 2007), pgs. 243–244.

309 Old French was a variety of Latin, which was heavily influenced by the various tribes who had inhabited and invaded ancient Gaul.

310 The existence of an early Judeo-French dialect is subject to controversy among historians. See M. Berenbaum & F. Skolnik (eds.), "Judeo-French," *Encyclopedia Judaica*. 2nd ed., vol. 11 (Detroit: Macmillan Reference USA, 2007), pg. 545.

end of the fourteenth century, the Jews had been expelled from all of France, to return only centuries later. From France, they emigrated in all possible directions: northeast to Germany, southwest to Spain, and southeast to Italy.

LASHON HAKODESH IN ITALY

Throughout the generations, several different varieties of Judeo-Italian (also called Judeo-Roman) developed in central and southern Italy. However, *Lashon HaKodesh* played a more prominent role in Italy than in many other places. As the printing press was beginning to wax in popularity and the Italian Renaissance was in full swing, the interplay of cultures gave way to a renewed interest in Judaism—and especially the Hebrew language—amongst Italian Christians. This newly-found interest in the Hebrew language begat the Christian Hebraist movement, which consisted of Christian scholars interested in studying the inner workings of *Lashon HaKodesh*. HaBachur was one of the most prominent figures in this movement in fifteenth and sixteenth-century Italy, as he tutored several prominent Christians in Hebrew and Jewish mysticism. Other figures from this period include Rabbi Avraham de Balmes (d. 1523), an Italian Hebraist who also taught many Christian pupils.

YIDDISH

The most famous—and arguably the most esteemed—of local Jewish dialects is the Judeo-German dialect known colloquially as "Yiddish" (lit. "Jewish").[311] It developed in Germany (*Ashkenaz*) before the end of the first millennium. Jews came to Germany from three directions: from France in the west, from Italy in the south, and from Bohemia and Kievian Russ[312] (and possibly Jewish Khazaria) in the east. Like all Judeo

311 This language was historically known as *Lashon Ashkenaz*, *taytsh* (*Deutsch*, meaning German), and "jargon."

312 While Kievian Russ (Russia) was an important center of Jewry in the twelfth and thirteenth centuries, it is almost unheard of in the centuries before that. The community there is not mentioned in the rabbinic literature of the time because its members were largely ignorant and unsophisticated, not scholarly. This dismal state of Eastern Europe was noted by Rabbi Meir of Rothenberg (1215–1293) in his responsa *Teshuvos Mahram Bar Baruch* (Lemberg, 1860) §112. Nonetheless, there may be one notable exception to this generalization. In recent years, a five-

dialects, *Lashon HaKodesh* and Aramaic influenced it, but Yiddish was also shaped by *Loez* dialects (i.e., Judeo-French and Judeo-Italian) and later by a Slavic influence. Yiddish is traditionally written in Hebrew script.

Persecution, including mass murders and expulsions, gradually drove most Western European Jews eastward to countries such as Czechoslovakia, Hungary, Romania, Poland, Lithuania, Ukraine, and Russia. Yiddish is divided between Western Yiddish (spoken in Germany and Holland[313]), and Eastern Yiddish (spoken in the Eastern European states); the latter of which is further subdivided into the northern "Lithuanian" and the southern "Galician" varieties. Before World War II, seventy-five percent of World Jewry spoke Yiddish.[314]

THE HASKALAH'S REACTION TO YIDDISH

In Western Europe, the so-called "Jewish Enlightenment" (*Haskalah*) advocated adopting the local language. Thus, in Germany their preferred tongue was German, not Yiddish. In Eastern Europe, the *Haskalah* movement also opposed Yiddish at first, instead favoring the use of local gentile languages. However, they realized that they could not easily uproot an established institution such as Yiddish, which had already been ingrained in the Jewish community for hundreds of years. Instead, they opted to embrace Yiddish as a language representative of "Jewish culture"

---

volume commentary to the Pentateuch was published under the name *Sefer Russaina*, written by an eleventh century commentator, Rabbi Shmuel of *Russaina* (Jerusalem: Mossad HaRav Kook, 1976–1996). The editor of that work, Dr. M. Weiss, argued that *Russaina* means Russia, and that this work was written by the only known Russian Torah scholar of that time. However, see the journal *Tarbiz*, vol. 72:4 (Jerusalem, 2003), pgs. 567–580, where Dr. Y. M. Ta-Shma argues that the author of this work was really from Southern Italy, not Russia. Two other scholars from Eastern Europe during this time period are Rabbi Moshe ben Yaakov the Exile, and Rabbi Zechariah ben Aharon HaKohen, discussed by M. Taube, "Transmission of Scientific Texts in 15th-Century Eastern Knaan," *Aleph*, vol. 10:2 (Indiana University Press, 2010), pgs. 16–24.

313 Rabbi Shabsai Bass writes that he had, on occasion, visited Amsterdam and witnessed in the study halls of the Sephardic community there that its members spoke *Lashon HaKodesh* from a very young age, which contributed to their proficiency in Bible studies, Hebrew grammar, and Hebrew poetry. See his *Sifsei Yesheinim* (Amsterdam, 1678), pg. 8a. This, however, is only reflective of the Sephardic community there. The Yiddish-speaking Ashkenazic community in Holland only burgeoned afterwards.

314 M. Berenbaum & F. Skolnik (eds.), "Jewish Languages," *Encyclopedia Judaica* 2nd ed., vol. 11 (Detroit: Macmillan Reference USA, 2007), pg. 302.

devoid of any religious meaning. These secular "Yiddishists" hijacked the traditional language of Ashkenazic Jewry and used it to further spread their non-religious and anti-religious philosophies. The Jewish-communist "Bundist" movement also followed this path. Their efforts were briefly supported by the Soviet government, which viewed Yiddish as archetypical of the "Jewish proletarian/workman's culture"; as opposed to Hebrew, which it viewed as a nationalist language that could compete with Soviet interests.[315] In the 1898 census, ninety-eight percent of Russian Jews named Yiddish as their native language.[316] In the next chapter, we will further explore how the dynamics of the debate between Yiddish and Hebrew played out in the context of Zionism.

THE KNAANIC LANGUAGE

Linguists have recently begun to acknowledge another Jewish dialect that contributed to the development of Yiddish. The "Knaanic language" (*Lashon Canaan*, לשון כנען) is a Jewish dialect of the Slavic language spoken during the Middle Ages in Bohemia (roughly the western two-thirds of modern-day Czech). This language is referenced by several medieval commentators across Europe. These commentators, including the German Rabbeinu Gershom Meor HaGolah (tenth century),[317] the French Rashi (eleventh century),[318] Rabbi Avraham ben Ezriel of Bohemia (early thirteenth century),[319] and Rabbi Yitzchak Ohr Zarua of Vienna (mid-thirteenth century),[320] sometimes refer to words in the Knaanic language.[321] Knaanic should not be confused with the Canaanite language

315 See D. Shneer, *Yiddish and the Creation of Soviet Jewish Culture* (Cambridge University Press, 2004).

316 D. Margolis, "The Language Where Jews Lived," *Jerusalem Report* (December 17, 2001) [http://www.davidmargolis.com/article.php?id=36].

317 In his commentary to *Chullin* 8b.

318 E.g., *Deuteronomy* 3:9, and his commentary to TB *Shabbos* 20b; *Avodah Zarah* 28b, 51b.

319 The Knaanic glosses cited in his work *Arugas HaBosem* are indexed in E. Auerbach (ed.), *Sefer Arugas HaBosem*, vol. 4 (Jerusalem: Mekize Nirdamim, 1963), pgs. 292–293.

320 For example, see S. Klein (ed.), *Ohr Zarua HaShaleim*, vol. 1 (Jerusalem: Machon Yerushalayim, 2010), pgs. 96, 103, 114, 119. See also I. Markon, "Die slawischen Glossen bei Isaak ben Mose Or Sarua," *Monatsschrift für Geschichte und Wissenschaft des Judentums* (Breslau, 1905), pgs. 707–721, who indexes many of the Knaanic glosses found in *Or Zarua*.

321 See also A. Kohut, *Aruch Completum*, vol. 1 (Vienna, 1878), pg. VII.

Why are Slavs called Canaanites?

Another question baffling linguists about Knaanic is its name. Scholars assume that it refers to some similarity between Slavs and Canaanites. In translating the seventy biblical nations into more contemporary terms, *Yossiphon* (Ch. 1) writes that some understand that the Sclaveni (Slavs) are descendants of Japheth, while others understand that they descend from the ancient Canaanites.[1] The latter view is reflected in Radak's comment (to *Obadiah* 1:20) that the Canaanites who were chased out of the Holy Land by Joshua resettled in Europe were still called "Canaanites" in his time.[2]

Rabbi Binyamin of Tudela (1130–1173) writes that Prague and the surrounding area (Bohemia) is known as the "Land of Canaan," because the peoples in those areas are known to sell their sons and daughters to foreigners.[3] He seemingly refers to the Romani (known colloquially as Gypsy) population, who are known to be involved in human trafficking.

Others explain that the term alludes to the fact that the Slavs were kept by Europeans as slaves and engaged in the trade of human beings. In fact, the English word "slave" is etymologically derived from the word "slav." *Oxford English Dictionary* explains that the Slavonic populations in parts of Central Europe were reduced to a servile condition by conquest.[4] If the Slavs are in fact descendants of the Canaanites, then the term "slave" is an appropriate description because Canaan, the son of Ham, was cursed by his grandfather Noah that his descendants should be slaves. Even if they do not genetically descend from the Canaanites, they can reasonably be called "Canaanites" simply because they were customarily the local slaves.[5]

---

1. *Yossiphon* (Jerusalem: Oraysoh Publishing, 1999), pg. 51.
2. However, Radak seems to be discussing Western European Germans, not Eastern European Slavs because he refers to "Alemania," the Spanish word for Germany.
3. *Massaos Rebbi Binyamin* (Sulzbach, 1783), last page; *Massaos Rebbi Binyamin* (Munkatch, 1895), pg. 18b; and M. Adler (ed.), *Massaos Rebbi Binyamin* (London, 1907), pg. 72. However, in some editions of this work, this line does not appear. For example, *Massaos Rebbi Binyamin* (Warsaw, 1844), pg. 20b; and J. D. Eisenstein (ed.), *Otzar Massaos* (New York, 1926), pg. 44, do not contain this line. Apparently, discussing human trafficking was deemed inappropriate and did not pass intact through censorship.
4. See "slave, n.," *Oxford English Dictionary Online* 3rd ed. (Oxford University Press, June 2011). See also K. Bertheloy, J. E. David, & M. Hirshman (eds.), "'Canaanites' in Medieval Jewish Households," *The Gift of the Land and the Fate of the Canaanites in Jewish Thought* (Oxford University Press, 2014), pgs. 285–296.
5. I first overheard this theory at the Abrams Research Library of Beth Medrash Govoha in Lakewood, NJ. I have since found it in several academic works, including P. Wexler, *Explorations in Judeo-Slavic Linguistics* (Leiden: Brill, 1987), pg. 5. See also D. Katz, "Knaanic in the Medieval and Modern Scholarly Imagination," in O. Bláha, R. Dittmann & L. Uličná (eds.), *Knaanic Language: Structure and Historical Background* (Prague, 2014), who traces the rediscovery of these explanations in modern-day academia.

(spelled differently to differentiate between the two), for the latter is an Ancient Semitic language, while the former is a Medieval dialect of the Indo-European Slavic variety.

KNAANIC INFLUENCE ON YIDDISH

Apparently, when early Yiddish speakers still lived in Germany, they came into contact with Bohemian Jews who provided Yiddish with a Slavic influence. Later, when the German Yiddish-speaking Jews migrated eastwards to Poland, Polish also played an important role in the Slavization of Yiddish.[322] Some scholars claim that since Eastern Yiddish has stronger Czech influence than does Western Yiddish, the two languages must not have evolved from a singular Proto-Yiddish parent. Rather, they emerged concurrently but independently. Under this model, the Eastern strain of Yiddish developed within the Knaanic-speaking Jewish communities. Therefore, it understandably exhibits a much greater Czech influence than does its Western counterpart. However, this theory is at odds with the perceived Jewish populations of Eastern Europe in the early second millennium, because it grants Eastern Europe more clout and influence than their population then would have suggested. Another question baffling linguists is how the Knaanic language was so thoroughly displaced by Yiddish that by the fourteenth century it had completely disappeared.[323] The study of Knaanic is still a budding field where scholars encounter more questions than answers.

CHAPTER SUMMARY

The pinnacle of *Lashon HaKodesh*'s existence as a spoken language was when the Jews lived in the Land of Israel during the time of the First Temple. As that period came to an end, the language's usage began to dwindle and with the destruction of the Temple and the Jews' exile to Babylon, Aramaic entered the fray, gaining prominence and recognition

---

322 M. Berenbaum & F. Skolnik (eds.), "Jewish Languages," *Encyclopedia Judaica* 2nd ed., vol. 11 (Detroit: Macmillan Reference USA, 2007), pg. 302.

323 For more information about the Knaanic language and early Eastern European Jewry, see M. Taube, "Transmission of Scientific Texts in 15th-Century Eastern Knaan," *Aleph*, vol. 10:2 (Indiana University Press, 2010), pgs. 11–42.

within the Jewish community. When some Jews later returned to the Land of Israel from the Babylonian exile, many of them no longer spoke *Lashon HaKodesh*.

We discussed several reasons for this phenomenon in which the Jews very quickly forgot the Holy Language that they had preserved since the beginning of time:

- Since *Lashon HaKodesh* is mystically connected to the Land of Israel, when the Jews were distanced from the Holy Land during the exile, they were also distanced from the Holy Language.
- Similarly, others explain that the Jews forgetting *Lashon HaKodesh* is directly correlated to their spiritual deterioration. That same spiritual deterioration that brought about the destruction of the Holy Temple also served as an impetus for them to forget the Holy Language.
- Abarbanel explained that Babylon itself is a catalyst for forgetfulness and just as we find that the sinners at the Tower of Babel forgot *Lashon HaKodesh*, so too the Jews exiled to Babylon forgot *Lashon HaKodesh*.
- Rabbi Moshe Sofer proposes that the rabbinic leadership of the Jewish community in Babylon purposefully enacted a policy of minimizing *Lashon HaKodesh* so that the language would not be used in the presence of idolatry—a common item in Babylon.

While Ezra, the leader of the Jews who returned to Israel after the exile, sought to rehabilitate the dying language, it never truly recovered after this fatal blow. From then on, Aramaic—and later Greek as well—became officially recognized as a language important to the Jews. This plurality of language remained dominant during the Second Temple period and as the Jews later spread out across the world in their current exile, they replaced *Lashon HaKodesh* and Aramaic with a host of other "Jewish languages." In modern times, some of these dynamics have changed (see footnote for examples[324]), although these specifics are not entirely relevant to our discussion.

In general, *Lashon HaKodesh* ceased to be the common language at the start of the post-Second Temple period, but there are several notable exceptions. As we have already mentioned, many Jewish communities continued to use *Lashon HaKodesh* for writing, even if they spoke other Jewish languages. Most serious works of rabbinic scholarship were written in *Lashon HaKodesh* (with the exception of some in Judeo-Arabic), except for those geared specifically for women and/or the unlearned, which were usually written in the local vernacular (albeit commonly in Hebrew script). In fact, people who ostensibly did not even speak *Lashon HaKodesh* in their day-to-day life were the ones who wrote the most important works of Hebrew grammar and vocabulary.

Furthermore, *Lashon HaKodesh* was always preserved. Jews continued to pray and study in that language, even if they spoke a different language outside of the synagogues and study halls. *Lashon HaKodesh* also served as a common language among Jews who would otherwise have no other way of communicating with one another. In a letter first printed in 1853, Rabbi Yishaya Horowitz (1565–1630) writes of his experience travelling from Germany to the Land of Israel via Syria. He writes that he spent about a month in Aleppo, where the local Jewish population spoke *Lashon HaKodesh*, and he mentions that he received much honor from the community and even had the opportunity to deliver lectures in *Lashon HaKodesh*.[325] Throughout the ages, this role of the language has remained important to travelling Jews, especially in trade and commerce, and has been greatly amplified by the ingathering of Jews from different countries to the nascent state of Israel.

---

324 For example, Jews in North Africa began speaking French when the French colonized those countries in the nineteenth century; and the partitioning of Germany after World War II has created the current reality where most of Germany's Jews are now Russian speakers. In present times, the Orthodox Jewish community has largely created and sustained its own dialect of English known as "Yeshivish" or "Yinglish," which is a brand of English heavily influenced by *Lashon HaKodesh*, Aramaic, and Yiddish. The most important work on this subject is C. M. Weiser, *Frumspeak: The First Dictionary of Yeshivish* (Aaronson, 1995).

325 M. Katz (ed.), *Shnei Luchos HaBris*, vol. 1 (Haifa: Machon Yad Rama, 1997), pg. 26.

CHAPTER 6: The Language Wars

THE TRUE STATE OF LASHON HAKODESH

Eliezer Ben-Yehuda (1858–1922) is commonly considered the father of the "Modern Hebrew" language. He is credited with resurrecting the language, which had long been pronounced "dead."

While he certainly had a huge effect on the history of Hebrew, he was not the first person to advocate speaking *Lashon HaKodesh*. As we mentioned in the previous chapter, whenever Jews of differing backgrounds encountered each other and had no other means of communicating, they resorted to *Lashon HaKodesh* as a common language. Also, as we have seen, Jews preserved *Lashon HaKodesh* by using it for daily prayer and study, and in rabbinic writings. Consequently, even when the language was no longer spoken, it remained dormant within the Jewish linguistic repertoire to be used when needed. Thus, *Lashon HaKodesh* was never really "dead," it was only "sleeping"! Furthermore, even in the period before modern Zionism, *Lashon HaKodesh* was not in decline, as we shall soon see.

KABBALISTS FOR LASHON HAKODESH

Even as usage of *Lashon HaKodesh* had significantly waned over the centuries, many of the leading Kabbalists sought to strengthen their connection to the language so significant to Judaism.

Rabbi Moshe Cordovero (1522–1570) is reputed to have been careful to speak only *Lashon HaKodesh* within his inner circle during the week, and with any Torah scholar on the Sabbath (provided there were no strangers present).[326]

His slightly younger colleague, Rabbi Yitzchak Luria (1534–1572), also known as Arizal, is said to have been careful to exclusively speak *Lashon HaKodesh* on the Sabbath, and only use foreign languages as needed to clarify elaborate Torah-related complexities.[327]

Rabbi Yishaya Horowitz advocated that the masses speak *Lashon HaKodesh*. He writes that it is praiseworthy for one to accustom oneself to speak *Lashon HaKodesh* even on weekdays.[328]

Despite such rabbinic approval, *Lashon HaKodesh* remained a rarity amongst the general populace. In fact, there was even some rabbinic opposition to speaking *Lashon HaKodesh*, as we shall discuss below.

REB ELIYAHU BAAL LASHON HAKODESH

In 1809, Rabbi Hillel Rivlin (1758–1838), a student of Rabbi Eliyahu Kramer of Vilna (1720–1797), led a group of Rabbi Kramer's students in establishing the first non-Hassidic Ashkenazic settlement in Jerusalem. This Jerusalemite community is known today as the *Perushim*. Rabbi Hillel Rivlin's son, Rabbi Eliyahu Rivlin (1821–1865), served as registrar and secretary of the fledging community. He was known within the Jerusalem community as *Reb Eliyahu Baal Lashon HaKodesh* because of his peculiar routine of speaking only *Lashon HaKodesh* and demanding that others answer him only in that language. Reb Eliyahu actively sought

---

326 Y. M. Toledano (ed.), *Otzar Genazim* (Jerusalem: Mossad HaRav Kook, 1960), pg. 49.

327 *Pri Eitz Chaim, Sha'ar HaShabbos* (end of Ch. 21). A later account of Arizal's behavior mentions that he was particular not to speak to anyone—even his wife—in a language other than *Lashon HaKodesh*. See S. Ashkenazi, *Doros B'Yisrael* (Tel Aviv: Don Publishing House, 1975), pg. 165.

328 *Shelah* (*Shabbos, Ner Mitzvah* §60).

to encourage the use of *Lashon HaKodesh* and even organized a society of Ashkenazic and Sephardic Jews to advance this ideal. In the messianic fervor that was typical of Rabbi Kramer's students in Jerusalem, Reb Eliyahu claimed that speaking Yiddish—which he called "jargon" and referred to as the "Amalekite language" (possibly because of its association with German)—was delaying the arrival of the Messiah.[329]

Though Reb Eliyahu's influence was limited, one of his notable followers was Rabbi Moshe Nechemia Kahanoff (1817–1887). Rabbi Kahanoff served as the Rosh Yeshiva of Jerusalem's most prestigious yeshiva at the time, Yeshivas Eitz Chaim. He is reputed to have spoken to his students only in *Lashon HaKodesh*[330] (though some reports minimize the significance of his devotion to *Lashon HaKodesh*[331]).

Although Reb Eliyahu's efforts never truly took off, they do represent an early effort at reviving *Lashon HaKodesh* in Jerusalem.

OTHER JERUSALEMITES WHO SPOKE LASHON HAKODESH

Dr. Yosef Yoel Rivlin (1889–1971),[332] a great-grandson of Reb Eliyahu, documented many of the interesting characters who made their home in the Jerusalemite community of Meah Shearim.

Two of the characters whom he describes only spoke *Lashon HaKodesh*: Rabbi Yaakov Zilberman (known as *Reb Yankele Midaber Lashon HaKodesh*), and Rabbi Avraham Chen-Tamim (nicknamed *Avraham HaIvri*).

Before relocating to Jerusalem, Rabbi Zilberman was the rabbi of a small town in Europe. He was staunchly opposed to speaking Yiddish, which he considered a form of idol worship that was delaying the end of the exile. He showed through puns how many common Yiddish words have

---

329 C. H. Rivlin, *Chazon Tzion* (Tel Aviv, 1956), pgs. 140, 142.

330 E. Horowitz, *Mossad HaYesod* (Jerusalem, 1958), pg. 72.

331 D. Tidhar, *Encyclopedia L'Chalutzei HaYishuv U'bonav*, vol. 1 (1947), pg. 58, discuses Rabbi Kahanoff's linguistic habits: He reports that Rabbi Kahanoff spoke only *Lashon HaKodesh* in the yeshiva and in his study hall and, on Shabbos and festivals, even in his house. Only under dire circumstances did he use Yiddish words to explain himself. Nonetheless, according to Tidhar's report, Rabbi Kahanoff's speeches and lectures were always delivered in Yiddish, not *Lashon HaKodesh*, so that his listeners could better understand him.

332 He was the late father of Reuven "Ruvi" Rivlin, current President of the State of Israel and former Speaker of the Knesset.

hidden unholy meanings,[333] and tried to convince people to stop speaking the language. He would regularly cite proofs from the Bible and rabbinic literature to the effect that if all Jews would speak *Lashon HaKodesh*, then the Messiah would immediately arrive.[334] He lived a long life and was still alive when Ben-Yehuda's efforts to spread Modern Hebrew were taking hold. When he was confronted with the fact that *Lashon HaKodesh* had been "taken" by the secularists (with the implication that the religious should therefore not speak the language) he would respond, "And if they wore tefillin (phylacteries), then we should refrain from wearing tefillin?"

Rabbi Zilberman tried to deliver public lectures, but no one attended them because they could not understand his unique flavor of *Lashon HaKodesh*.

Rabbi Avraham Moshe Chen-Tamim (1854–1914), an ascetic Jew, also spoke *Lashon HaKodesh*. Every day he would fast until nightfall and only then eat at night. He would sometimes stand in the middle of the street and preach to the local Arabs (who highly respected him) in Arabic, while to his Jewish brothers he would only speak *Lashon HaKodesh*. According to Rivlin, Chen-Tamim supported himself by teaching Hebrew and Arabic grammar.[335]

Thus, we see that even before the endeavors of Ben-Yehuda, *Lashon HaKodesh* was already beginning its resurrection as a spoken language in Jerusalem (albeit by a handful of fringe individuals).[336]

---

333 For example, he claimed that the common Yiddish word *shtender* (שטנדר, lectern) was really a portmanteau for the phrase *satan dar* (שטן דר, the Satan dwells).

334 Interestingly, J. D. Eisenstein, *Otzar Yisrael*, vol. 7 (New York, 1912), pg. 314, mentions that some believe that *Lashon HaKodesh* will be the universal language of the Messianic Era. This belief is based on the prophecy of Zephaniah (*Zephaniah* 3:9) who foretells that in the future the entire world will call out the name of God in a *Safa Berura* (lit. "clear language"). The phrase *Safa Berura* (שפה ברורה) is equal in numerical value to "in *Lashon HaKodesh*" (בלשון הקודש). Radak (in his commentary there) alludes to this explanation in the name of Ibn Ezra (yet interestingly, when discussing that verse in his commentary to *Deuteronomy* 6:3, Ibn Ezra does not spell out this explanation). Rabbi Azariah de Rossi ascribes this idea to the Christian thinker Thomas Aquinas (1225–1274); see his *Meor Einayim*, vol. 5 (Vienna, 1829), pg. 279a. *Reb Eliyahu Baal Lashon HaKodesh* and Rabbi Yaakov Zilberman evidently understood this idea to mean that speaking *Lashon HaKodesh* is a prerequisite for the Messiah to come.
Rabbi Diskin and others (see below) apparently understood that speaking *Lashon HaKodesh* is something reserved for the Messianic Era, to begin only once the Messiah had already arrived, and that until then it should not be spoken.

335 For more about Chen-Tamim and his works, see D. Tidhar, *Encyclopedia L'Chalutzei HaYishuv U'bonav*, vol. 2 (1947), pgs. 615–616.

336 Y. Rivlin, *Meah Shearim* (Jerusalem, 1947), pgs. 173–175.

THE HASKALAH ACCEPTS LASHON HAKODESH

As we have already mentioned in the previous chapter, the *Haskalah* movement sought to undermine traditional Jewish values and replace them with secular values in order to facilitate Jewish integration into the gentile world at large. Although the movement had already adopted Hebrew as its language long before Ben-Yehuda's birth,[337] Hebrew was not systematically sanctioned as a means of fostering Jewish nationalism until Ben-Yehuda's time. Nonetheless, it seems that the style of Hebrew used by these *Maskillic* activists was originally based solely on biblical Hebrew.[338] Even before Ben-Yehuda was born, a *Maskillic* grammarian named Yehuda Leib Ben-Zev (1764–1811) compiled a work on the Hebrew language. His work was considered innovative inasmuch as unlike its predecessors, it incorporated post-biblical words and usage into its understanding of Hebrew.[339] Thus, rabbinic Hebrew gleaned from the Mishnah and other post-biblical sources was eventually incorporated into Modern Hebrew.

RABBINIC OPPOSITION TO THE HASKALAH'S USE OF LASHON HAKODESH

Rabbi Yaakov Tzvi Meklenburg (1785–1865), a champion in the defense of Orthodoxy from the onslaughts of the *Haskalah*, lamented the fact that in his times the general populace began using *Lashon HaKodesh* for obscene and lowly purposes.[340] He is an early example of rabbinic opposition to the *Haskalah* movement adopting *Lashon HaKodesh* as its

---

337 "Recent Arabic and Hebrew Literature" in *American Presbyterian Review of 1871* (pg. 646) mentions Hebrew as a spoken language on the continent of Europe and in New York City. This article pre-dates the publication of Ben-Yehuda's manifesto by almost a decade and claims that Hebrew was already spoken then. However, this article does not necessarily prove anything except that the common gentile misconception that Yiddish is in fact Hebrew was already prevalent at that time. In fact, it is quite common for those who speak neither language to confuse Hebrew and Yiddish, since both languages are associated with the Jews. Alternatively, the article was referring to the *Maskillic* community who had by then already adopted Hebrew as its language.

338 Since the platform of many *Maskillim* was to eliminate rabbinic authority, it makes sense that they would try to deemphasize the importance of rabbinic literature in the history of *Lashon HaKodesh*.

339 *History of the Hebrew Language: The Modern Division* (Tel Aviv: The Open University of Israel Press, 1994), pg. 18.

340 See *HaKsav V'HaKabbalah* to *Genesis* 2:23.

primary language, and his lamentation was written before Ben-Yehuda was even born.

ENTER BEN-YEHUDA'S PROPOSAL

On March 30, 1879, Eliezer Ben-Yehuda published his manifesto for the direction of Jewish nationalism in the Viennese monthly journal *HaShachar*. In that article, entitled "A Serious Question," Ben-Yehuda asserted that the continuation of the Jewish Nation was dependent on the establishments of a common homeland, language, and culture.[341] Hence, Ben-Yehuda proposed the revival of *Lashon HaKodesh* as a means of fostering Jewish nationalism. However, Ben-Yehuda conceded that the vocabulary of *Lashon HaKodesh* would not suffice to meet the demands of modernity. Therefore, he proposed modifying the language by adding new words and changing the meanings of existing words. The resulting linguistic concoction is the Modern Hebrew language.[342] After moving to Jerusalem, Ben-Yehuda dedicated the rest of his life to promoting his vision.

CHOOSING THE LANGUAGE OF ZIONISM

In 1896, Theodore Herzl (1860–1904), the father of Modern Zionism and a product of the Western European *Haskalah*, published his work *Der Judenstaat* in which he laid out his vision of a secular Jewish state. In his description of that nationalistic dream, he envisioned that German would replace Yiddish as the language spoken by Jews.[343] This view, it seems, was largely rejected by his colleagues, and instead two other candidates were presented as the language of the future Jewish state. The Jewish communists known as the "Bundists" supported Yiddish as the state's language, while others, including the *Haskalah* intelligentsia, followed Ben-Yehuda's proposal and supported Hebrew.[344]

---

341 J. A. Fishman (ed.), *Readings in the Sociology of Jewish Languages* (Brill, 1985), pg. 31.

342 M. Berenbaum & F. Skolnik (eds.), "Ben-Yehuda, Eliezer," *Encyclopedia Judaica* 2nd ed., vol. 3. (Detroit: Macmillan Reference USA, 2007), pgs. 386–388.

343 B. Wein, *Triumph of Survival* (New York: Shaar Press, 1990), pg. 237.

344 See R. Kuzar, *Hebrew and Zionism* (Berlin: Mouton, 2001), who documents the various Jewish groups of that time and their linguistic affinities.

THE LANGUAGE WARS

The battles between adherents of these two views were fierce and often times violent, but in the end, Ben-Yehuda's plan was accepted. In the 1920s and 1930s, the "Battalion for the Defense of the Language" used terrorist-like tactics to promote their Hebraic agenda in Palestine. They tore down signs written in "foreign" languages and disturbed Yiddish theater gatherings.[345]

Other accounts of their activities report that they functioned with military precision. Some units promoted and disseminated propaganda, while others intimidated and publicly embarrassed Yiddish-speakers. They threw stink bombs and inkwells at public functions that were not conducted in Modern Hebrew, and plastered the country with signs warning, "Jew, speak Hebrew" (*Yehudi daber Ivrit*, יהודי דבר עברית).[346] Even the famous Modern Hebrew poet Chaim Nachman Bialik (1873–1934)[347] was victimized for daring to speak Yiddish in public![348]

Despite their unconventional methods, the "Hebraist Zionists" prevailed and ultimately, the budding Zionist movement adopted Modern Hebrew in accordance with Ben-Yehuda's proposal.

THE IMPLICATIONS AND MOTIVES OF BEN-YEHUDA'S CAMPAIGN

In reality, Ben-Yehuda stumbled upon part of the esoteric underpinnings of the world. It seems that at some level, he realized that

---

345 J. A. Fishman & O. Garcia (eds.), *Handbook of Language and Ethnic Identity*, vol. 2 (Oxford University Press, 2011), pg. 72.

346 S. Feinstein, *Sunshine, Blossoms and Blood: H. N. Bialik in His Time* (Lanham, Maryland: University Press of America, 2005), pg. 177.

347 Bialik studied in Volozhin Yeshiva for a year and a half where he was reputed to have almost memorized the entire TB *Kesubos* with Tosafos in his first few months. However, after some time, the *Haskalah* movement (which by then had made inroads into Volozhin Yeshiva), influenced him and led him astray. For more information about Bialik's time in Volozhin Yeshiva and his attitude toward religion in general, see N. Kamenetsky, *Making of a Godol: A Study of Episodes in the Lives of Great Torah Personalities* (Jerusalem: Hamesorah Publishers, 2002), pgs. 893–902.

348 S. Feinstein, *Sunshine, Blossoms and Blood: H. N. Bialik in His Time* (Lanham, Maryland: University Press of America, 2005), pgs. 182–183.

there was an unbreakable bond between the Land of Israel and *Lashon HaKodesh* (an idea which we have already seen several times in this work).

Ben-Yehuda, a decidedly non-religious Jew, unwittingly undertook a campaign that saw to the fulfillment of this deeply religious concept. Nonetheless, his intentions were not pure. He purposely tried to empty *Lashon HaKodesh* of its innate holiness and use it for purely nationalistic ambitions. In fact, some scholars have labeled Ben-Yehuda's engineering of the Hebrew language the "ideological secularization of Hebrew terms."[349] Ben-Yehuda undermined the historical and religious integrity of *Lashon HaKodesh* by changing the accepted meanings of words and adding new words. His decidedly secular slant ensured that Modern Hebrew would not reflect the values and standards of the Torah's *Lashon HaKodesh*.

WHAT IS MODERN HEBREW?

In the decades since the resurrection of *Lashon HaKodesh* as Modern Hebrew, linguists have struggled to classify the language in their own terms:

---

349 One common example of this is the Hebrew word *kayheh* (כהה) which is used in the Bible to mean "dim" (*Genesis* 27:1; *Leviticus* 13:6, 21;26, 28;56; *Isaiah* 42:3, 61:3; and *Zechariah* 11:1). It was reused by the compilers of Modern Hebrew to mean "dark." Such redefining of biblical words creates utter confusion for Modern Hebrew-speaking biblical scholars, who cannot properly understand the meaning of the texts which they study. Another famous example is the meaning of the word *aggadah* (אגדה) which, in rabbinic literature, refers to non-halachic discussions. In Modern Hebrew, the word means "folktale," so that one encountering a passage of *aggadah* would have the preconceived notion that the passage is meant as simply a made-up folktale devoid of any factual deeper meaning.
Other examples of Ben-Yehuda's changes to *Lashon HaKodesh* include redefining *shulaim* (שולים, bottom) as "side," *harbatzah* (הרבצה, crouching) as "beating," *aizor* (אזור, belt) as "area," *tarboos* (תרבות, education) as "culture," and *bilui* (בילוי, wearing out) as "fun pastime." Similarly, the word *achuz* אחוז used in the Bible refers to the numerator of a fraction, while Modern Hebrew has redefined the word to mean a percentage.
See A. Yadin & G. Zuckermann, "*Blorít*—Pagans' Mohawk or Sabras' Forelock?: Ideological Secularization of Hebrew Terms in Socialist Zionist Israeli," *The Sociology of Language and Religion: Change, Conflict and Accommodation. A Festschrift for Joshua A. Fishman on his 80th Birthday* (London: Palgrave Macmillan, 2009) for further specific examples. See also H. Kantor, "Current Trends in the Secularization of Hebrew," *Language in Society*, vol. 21:4 (Cambridge University Press, 1992) for numerous examples of the secularization of Modern Hebrew. J. D. Eisenstein, *Otzar Yisrael*, vol. 7 (New York, 1907–1913), pg. 317 also mentions several examples.

252 — החבצלת עת השבע עצרה — רנב

דרשות לבית ישראל.

לכבוד התורה ולכבוד למודית.

Newspaper article describing the excommunication of Eliezer Ben-Yehuda by the Sephardic community in Jerusalem (*Havazelet*, July 8, 1887). The archives of this newspaper were digitized by the National Library of Israel's Historical Jewish Press Society [http://www.jpress.org.il] and are reproduced here with their written permission.

Using "*Chashmal*" as Electricity

The word *chashmal* (חשמל) is used by Ezekiel to describe a mysterious fiery spectacle which he saw in his famous vision of the Heavenly Chariot (*Ezekiel* 1:27). In Modern Hebrew, this word's mystical and elated meaning is distorted to simply mean "electricity"—this holy and exalted concept was demoted by the creators of Modern Hebrew to an everyday technological routine. (See *Barzilai*, pgs. 307–308, who favors translating חשמל as "amber.")

For this reason, Rabbi Yosef Greenwald (1903–1984), the Pupa Rav, writes in the introduction to his father's work *Vayaged Yaakov*, vol. 1, that his father, Rabbi Yaakov Yechezkiya Greenwald (1882–1941) especially opposed using the word *chashmal* to mean electricity. He argued that the word originally referred to some elated spiritual entity and was defiled when redefined to refer to a regular physical reality. Parenthetically, the senior Rabbi Greenwald's uncle, Rabbi Eliezer Dovid Greenwald of Satmar (1867–1928), was also a staunch opponent of Modern Hebrew, as discussed in Rabbi Binyamin Rabinowitz's *Mishkenos HaRoim* (vol. 2, pg. 394).

In a letter penned as a response to Rabbi Greenwald's harsh words, Rabbi Yissocher Dov Goldstein (1915–1988) disagreed with his approach. He noted that the word *chashmal* used by Ezekiel was not necessarily a strictly spiritual entity, but was rather a physical entity used by Ezekiel as a metaphor for some higher spiritual idea. Accordingly, Rabbi Goldstein argues that using the word *chashmal* is not really "defiling" the word, even though it is probably an inaccurate usage. For this reason, Rabbi Goldstein concludes that one need not refrain from using the word *chashmal* any more so than other words from *Lashon HaKodesh* that were redefined by Modern Hebrew. See Rabbi Goldstein's responsa *Ohel Yissocher* (§76).

This *post facto* acceptance of the Modern Hebrew word *chashmal* is found in the writings of other prominent rabbis. For example, Rabbi Avraham Yishaya Karelitz and Rabbi Shlomo Zalman Auerbach (1910–1995) both use the word repeatedly in their respective works (although, in his first published work, Rabbi Auerbach uses the Yiddish term אלקטריא, which means "electricity"). When questioned about this, Rabbi Auerbach justified his approach by noting that the word *chashmal* used by Ezekiel was simply a description of something holy about God, but was not the name of the Holy One Himself. Accordingly, explains Rabbi Auerbach, there is no problem in using that word to refer to something that is not holy. In short, Rabbi Auerbach writes that while optimally it is not right to take words used for holy meanings and redefine them, *post facto* those words should not be rejected. Rabbi Menashe Klein (responsa *Mishne Halachos*, vol. 6 §95) concurs with this approach and cites several other authorities who apparently shared this view.

Sources: Y. Buxbaum (ed.), *Kovetz Moriah*, vol. 193–196 (Jerusalem: Machon Yerushalayim, 1990), pgs. 130–132; and *Meorei Aish HaShalem*, vol. 2 (Jerusalem: Otzaros Shlomo, 2010), pgs. 809–810.

1. Some consider Modern Hebrew to be a Semitic language because it is built on the original ancient *Lashon HaKodesh*.
2. Others consider Modern Hebrew an Indo-European language, claiming that, for the most part, it is Yiddish relexified. That is, the lexicon of Yiddish (the mother tongue of most Hebrew revivalists) was replaced with *Lashon HaKodesh*, but its syntax remained largely intact. The resultant language is considered Indo-European because of its syntax and grammar, even though it is comprised of a Semitic-based vocabulary.
3. In his many books and articles, Dr. Ghil'ad Zuckermann argues for a middle ground. He believes that Modern Hebrew—or Israeli (as he insists on referring to the language)—is a mosaic synthesis built primarily on both a resurrected *Lashon HaKodesh* and a relexified Yiddish, as well as other Jewish languages.[350]

BEN-YEHUDA SUCCEEDS BECAUSE THE JEWS ALREADY SPOKE LASHON HAKODESH

Ben-Yehuda's campaign had an early advantage in that, as we have already mentioned, *Lashon HaKodesh* had always continued to exist latently within the Jewish community. People already more or less *knew* the language; he only had to convince them to speak it.

As the British historian Cecil Roth (1899–1970) so poignantly wrote, "Before Ben-Yehuda, Jews *could* speak Hebrew, after him they *did*."[351]

◆ ◆ ◆

350 G. Zuckermann, "Realistic Prescriptivism: The Academy of the *Hebrew* Language, its Campaign of 'Good Grammar,' and *Lexpionage*, and Native *Israeli* Speakers," *Israel Studies in Language and Society*, vol. 1 (2008); G. Zuckermann, "Hybridity versus Revivability: Multiple causation, forms and patterns," *Journal of Language Contact*, vol. 2 (2009), pgs. 40–67; and G. Zuckermann & M. Walsh, "Stop, Revive, Survive: Lessons from the Hebrew Revival Applicable to the Reclamation, Maintenance and Empowerment of Aboriginal Languages and Cultures," *Australian Journal of Linguistics*, vol. 31:1 (2011), pg. 114.

351 C. Roth, "Was Hebrew Ever a Dead Language," *Personalities and Events in Jewish History* (Philadelphia, 1953), pg. 136.

MODERN HEBREW IN THE RELIGIOUS SECTOR

Modern Hebrew was created as a means of fostering Jewish secularism and nationalism and played a prominent role in shaping the character of the State of Israel. Although *Maskillic* and secular forces initiated the revival of the language, Religious Zionists also accepted it and viewed the language as the present-day form of *Lashon HaKodesh*—or at the very least its spiritual heir. They believed that the changes that the language experienced created a new brand of *Lashon HaKodesh* similar to the way that the rabbis of the Mishnah and medieval times modified the *Lashon HaKodesh* of the Bible. They not only embraced Modern Hebrew as their own language, but they also attached to it religious significance.

Is Yiddish the holy language?

Decades after the issue of Modern Hebrew ceased to be at the forefront, Rabbi Shlomo Wolbe (1914–2005), *Mashgiach* of Yeshivas Be'er Yaakov, still preferred to use Yiddish. One time, he complained that because his yeshiva accepted students from thirteen different countries, many different languages could be heard in the study hall. To rectify this situation, he announced "Everyone must speak *Lashon HaKodesh* [in this context meant literally as "the holy language"]—Yiddish." Rabbi Wolbe explained that nowadays the true "holy language" is Yiddish, which has been absorbed into the souls of Jewry for hundreds of years.

Source: *Avnei Shlomo* (Jerusalem, 2006), pg. 61.

However, the "Ultra-Orthodox" (*Chareidi*) community's view of Modern Hebrew is more complicated. They view Modern Hebrew as clearly based on *Lashon HaKodesh*—but lacking its status. In the Ultra-Orthodox community, there were proponents for and against the masses speaking *Lashon HaKodesh* as an everyday language. Those against speaking *Lashon HaKodesh* were following the general Ultra-Orthodox approach of rejecting political Zionism. Zionism developed in the wake of the *Haskalah*. In the spirit of nationalism that swept Europe at the time, Zionism attempted to redefine the Jews as being just like any other nation: existing by virtue of having a common language, homeland, and culture. This was in sharp contrast to the traditional view that a Jew is Jewish by virtue of adherence to Judaism. Just as the Ultra-Orthodox opposed other facets of Zionism, they also opposed Modern Hebrew.

RABBINIC OPPOSITION TO MODERN HEBREW

At the same time that Ben-Yehuda was spearheading the effort to revive Modern Hebrew, many of the leading religious personalities of the Old Yishuv of Jerusalem strongly condemned Ben-Yehuda's efforts. Instead of accepting Modern Hebrew, they resisted Ben-Yehuda's efforts by strengthening their dedication to Yiddish, which—in one form or another—had been the spoken language[352] of Ashkenazic Jewry

---

352 It is worthwhile to stress that while there was extreme rabbinic opposition to accepting *Lashon HaKodesh* as a spoken language, there was no such objection to using *Lashon HaKodesh* in writing. In fact, as we have already seen, even communities that replaced *Lashon HaKodesh* and Aramaic with other Jewish languages in speech continued to write in *Lashon HaKodesh*. Thus, for example, even Rabbi Yoel Teitelbaum, who was a harsh critic of speaking Modern Hebrew, embraced using *Lashon HaKodesh* as a written language, as was customary amongst Torah scholars for hundreds of years. See L. Glinert & Y. Shilhav, "Holy Land, Holy Language: A Study of an Ultra-Orthodox Jewish Ideology," *Language in Society*, vol. 20:1 (Columbia University Press, 1991).

Interestingly, the works of Rabbi Yisroel Dovid Harfenes (a leading rabbi in the Williamsburg neighborhood of Brooklyn, NY) are a notable exception to this rule. His works are written mostly in *Lashon HaKodesh*, but he would sometimes require foreign words to refer to newer things and ideas for which words in *Lashon HaKodesh* were not extant. As a student of Rabbi Teitelbaum, Rabbi Harfenes sought to refrain from legitimizing Modern Hebrew and thought to use English and Yiddish words, but on the other hand realized that his works would not be practical for an Israeli audience if they did not use words in Modern Hebrew. Thus, Rabbi Harfenes writes in the introduction to his responsa *Nishmas Shabbos*, vol. 4 (Brooklyn, 2003), pgs. 10–11, that he was originally unsure of how to refer to modern-day technology in his halachic works. He turned to one of the leading students of Rabbi Teitelbaum for an approach in solving this predicament. That rabbi told Rabbi Harfenes that there is no reason to worry if his works are mostly written in *Lashon HaKodesh,* but sporadically used Modern Hebrew words for modern-day inventions, when absolutely necessary. However, Rabbi Harfenes writes that after he published the first edition of his work, another leading student of Rabbi Teitelbaum, Rabbi Binyamin Rabinowitz (d. 2002), the first *Mishkenos HaRoim* Rebbe, disagreed with this approach. Rabbi Rabinowitz noted while he agreed with the first rabbi's ruling, Rabbi Harfenes should nonetheless act more stringently so as not to give the appearance of legitimizing the language that Rabbi Teitelbaum had so vehemently opposed. For this reason, Rabbi Harfenes redacted subsequent editions of his work and switched all instances of Modern Hebrew words to English or Yiddish words. [I thank Rabbi Eli Nemetzky for pointing out this source.]

While Rabbi Harfenes does not explicitly reveal the identity of the first rabbi who justified the more lenient approach to Modern Hebrew, he offers a hint to the rabbi's identity by purposely misspelling the word רמה as רמא in describing the rabbi. The author realized that in doing so, Rabbi Harfenes was insinuating that Rabbi Moshe Aryeh Freund (1894–1996), the Chief Rabbi of the *Eidah Chareidis* in

for centuries. The religious community in Jerusalem—including the Sephardic leaders—excommunicated Ben-Yehuda and all those who espoused his views. While the Sephardic Jews eventually warmed up to the idea of Modern Hebrew, the Ashkenazic Jews largely resisted it.

On his deathbed, Rabbi Eliyahu David Rabinowitz-Teomim (1845–1905) wrote a letter explaining that his deathly illness was a result of his extreme distress over the fact that Modern Hebrew became the language of instruction in Jewish schools, replacing the more traditional Yiddish.[353]

OPPOSITION TO SPEAKING LASHON HAKODESH

According to tradition, Rabbi Yehoshua Leib Diskin (1818–1898) refused to speak to a certain Torah scholar in Jerusalem because that scholar spoke *Lashon HaKodesh*. One time, the latter entered Rabbi Diskin's home and began to pose a question to Rabbi Diskin in *Lashon HaKodesh*. At that point, Rabbi Diskin strongly reprimanded the scholar and exclaimed, "Leave my house! Throughout our exile, we will only speak Yiddish!"[354] Thus, Rabbi Diskin opposed speaking *Lashon HaKodesh*—even without the secular implications of its usage.

RABBI TEITELBAUM: MODERN HEBREW IS LIKE A TORAH SCROLL WRITTEN BY A HERETIC

In 1957, the Satmar Rebbe, Rabbi Yoel Teitelbaum (1887–1979), delivered a fiery speech against Modern Hebrew and mentioned that Ben-Yehuda died a sudden death on Shabbos night with a pen in his hand. Whether or not this was literally true is irrelevant; the fact of the matter is that Ben-Yehuda died an unrepentant sinner who put

---

Jerusalem, was the rabbi who offered that ruling because his initials are רמא. This hypothesis was confirmed by Rabbi Harfenes himself in a telephone conversation with the author, in which he admitted that Rabbi Freund was indeed the first rabbi, but his identity was hidden in deference to the views of his dissenters.

353 A facsimile of this letter, which was addressed to his student Rabbi Benzion Yadler (1871–1962), "the Maggid of Jerusalem," was published in the book *Tohar HaLashon* (Jerusalem, 2008), pg. 56. That important book on the history of *Lashon HaKodesh* was subject to ridicule by Yair Ettinger in a *Ha'aretz* newspaper article entitled "Language Wars—Round Two" (March 28, 2008).

354 Y. M. Sofer & M. M. Gerlitz, *Mara D'Ara D'Yisrael*, vol. 2 (Jerusalem, 2003), pg. 185.

his efforts to spread Modern Hebrew before the will of God. Rabbi Teitelbaum compared Modern Hebrew to a Torah scroll that was written by a Jewish apostate, about which Rambam rules that it—including its instances of God's name—should be burnt.[355] So too, argued Rabbi Teitelbaum, Modern Hebrew, which was instituted by Jewish apostates, should be shunned—even though it has holy elements to it.[356] Rabbi Teitelbaum later printed his anti-Zionist polemic *VaYoel Moshe*, a large portion of which is dedicated to elaborating on his nuanced stance against Modern Hebrew.

THE "HOLY LANGUAGE" IS NO LONGER HOLY

Some authorities asserted that once people began to use *Lashon HaKodesh* for mundane purposes, its holiness became desecrated. Thus, the resulting Modern Hebrew can no longer be considered *Lashon HaKodesh*, but a new language.[357] A prominent member of a society dedicated to Modern Hebrew—who was known to espouse heretical views—once approached Rabbi Shmuel Salant (1816–1909), the Chief Rabbi of Jerusalem, and asked why he opposed that society's efforts to fight for the spread of the new language. Rabbi Salant replied with an analogy that in the Bible, language is compared to wine, as it says, "And may your utterances be like the finest wine."[358] "Therefore," explained Rabbi Salant, "just as wine is used for many holy purposes in Jewish ritual, such as the libations on the altar in the Holy Temple, as well as *Kiddush* and *Havdalah,* but if a gentile touches it, it immediately becomes treated like idol sacrifices, so too..." His intent was clear even before he finished his

---

355 Laws of *Yesodei HaTorah* 6:8.

356 M. Amsel (ed.), *Kovetz Hamaor*, vol. 74 (Brooklyn, 1957), pg. 29.

357 Rabbi David Menachem Babad of Ternopol (1754–1838) makes this assertion in his responsa *Chavatzeles HaSharon* (vol. 1, *Orach Chaim* §10). He repeats *The Kuzari*'s claim that previously, *Lashon HaKodesh* was used solely for holy purposes, and Aramaic dialects were used for other purposes. He reasoned that when one uses *Lashon HaKodesh* for all purposes, including such profanity as "love songs," the language can no longer be considered "holy." Based on this assertion, Rabbi Babad rules that it is forbidden to teach Modern Hebrew in the courtyard belonging to a synagogue because the latter is a holy place and should be used only for holy purposes. Rabbi Babad's death predated Ben-Yehuda's birth by twenty years.

358 *Song of Songs* 7:10.

sentence: he opposed Modern Hebrew because he viewed it as a perversion of *Lashon HaKodesh*.[359]

RABBI SONNENFELD'S RELUCTANT RECOGNITION OF MODERN HEBREW

Rabbi Moshe Blau (1885–1946), the leader of Agudath Israel in the British mandate of Palestine, records several anecdotes in his autobiography concerning the views of the leading rabbis of his time on the topic of Modern Hebrew. He writes that when a certain Talmud Torah in Petach Tikvah was considering Modern Hebrew as its language of instruction, the matter was presented to Rabbi Yosef Chaim Sonnenfeld (1848–1932), the first Chief Rabbi of the *Eidah Chareidis* of Jerusalem. Rabbi Sonnenfeld ruled that if the parents of the school demanded that their children be instructed in Modern Hebrew, then there should be no reason to oppose such a request. Rabbi Sonnenfeld then commented that he regrets that the early leaders of the Old Yishuv did not adopt *Lashon HaKodesh* as their official language, for such action would have preempted the efforts of the secular Zionists in trying to influence Palestinian Jewry through language.[360]

---

359 S. Ashkenazi, *Doros B'Yisrael* (Tel Aviv: Don Publishing House, 1975), pg. 173.

360 In 2005, a new volume of Rabbi Sonnenfeld's writings was published. There, in a letter dated 1928, he responds to someone who inquired about the permissibility of opening a school outside of Jerusalem that teaches in Modern Hebrew. While Rabbi Sonnenfeld ultimately allowed for the school to teach in Modern Hebrew, he also outlined his objections to that idea and his advice for avoiding some of the problems. Rabbi Sonnenfeld's objection to using Modern Hebrew as the language of instruction is three-fold: First, he argues that teaching in that language will expose the students to the works of Jewish apostates and secularists, which can negatively influence their young minds by poisoning them with anti-religious ideas. He notes that this is especially true if the language is taught as a separate subject (i.e., as opposed to just being used as the language of instruction for other subjects) because the books on the grammar and lexicon of Modern Hebrew were not written by the most upstanding Jews. Secondly, he argues that teaching in Modern Hebrew might lower the standards of the school, for if they decide to teach only in Modern Hebrew, they are limiting themselves and they might not always be able to find the best teachers who can teach in that language. Furthermore, he notes that even the best teachers could likely become corrupt by trying to familiarize themselves with Modern Hebrew by reading works in that language. Thirdly, Rabbi Sonnenfeld points out that teaching Modern Hebrew as a separate subject would waste precious time that could have otherwise been spent for higher purposes (e.g., the study of Torah). All in all, Rabbi Sonnenfeld allows for Modern Hebrew to be used as the language of instruction but with the warning that the language should not be viewed as an objective in and of itself, rather it should only be taught as a means of understanding the curriculum. Furthermore, Rabbi Sonnenfeld recommends that while

Rabbi Blau tells another story illustrating Rabbi Sonnenfeld's reluctant acceptance of Modern Hebrew. One time, in the presence of Rabbi Sonnenfeld, someone added the expression, "May his name be blotted out," in reference to Ben-Yehuda. Because this expression is customarily reserved for the most heinous of villains, Rabbi Sonnenfeld admonished the individual who used it in referring to Ben-Yehuda and opined that there is some good outcome from Ben-Yehuda's efforts.[361]

MODERN HEBREW'S PROBLEMATIC SEPHARDIC PRONUNCIATION

Nonetheless, Rabbi Blau notes that acceptance of Modern Hebrew was far from unanimous. Rabbi Yosef Tzvi Dushinsky (1867–1948), the former Chief Rabbi of Galanta (in Slovakia) and Rabbi Sonnenfeld's successor, followed Rabbi Rabinowitz-Teomim's view and opposed the acceptance of Modern Hebrew as the spoken language. Rabbi Dushinsky explained that his main reason for opposing Modern Hebrew was technical: its form of pronunciation mimics the Sephardic tradition and can cause halachic issues for an Ashkenazic Jew when mixed into prayer and Torah reading.[362]

---

the school should make an extra effort to teach the children Modern Hebrew in its early years, once the language has already gained a foothold within the student body, the school need no longer concentrate on teaching Modern Hebrew as an independent subject because anyway the older students will train the newer, younger students to quickly adopt the language, even without specifically being taught it. See *Teshuvos Rabbi Yosef Chaim Sonnenfeld* (Jerusalem: Machon Keren Ram, 2005), pgs. 240–242.

While Rabbi Sonnenfeld's first two objections are arguably no longer applicable (because of the plethora of non-heretical works written in Modern Hebrew), his third objection (that studying the language takes time away from Torah study) is still relevant nowadays.

361 M. Blau, *Al Chomosayich Yerushalayim* (Tel Aviv, 1946), pg. 115.

362 Rabbi Moshe Feinstein rules in his responsa (*Iggros Moshe, Orach Chaim*, vol. 4 §5, vol. 4 §23, and *Even HaEzer*, vol. 4 §104) that any manner of pronouncing *Lashon HaKodesh* accepted by a given community may be considered halachically legitimate for that community, but people cannot switch from one mode of pronunciation to another.

In a series of letters written on the subject, Rabbi Kook writes that the Jewish Yemenite tradition of pronouncing *Lashon HaKodesh* is the most exact, seconded by the Sephardic tradition, and then followed by the Ashkenazic tradition. In spite of this, Rabbi Kook still writes that it is forbidden for people to switch from one mode of pronunciation to another (although it does not, *post facto*, halachically disqualify his ritual utterances). Rabbi Uziel disagrees with Rabbi Kook and is more permissive in allowing people to switch from one mode to another. See Rabbi Kook's responsa *Orach Mishpat* (§17–18) and the correspondence between him and Rabbi Uziel printed at beginning of the latter's work *Mishpatei Uziel*, vol. 1.

MODERN HEBREW HAS FOREIGN INFLUENCES

Rabbi Dushinsky also noted that Modern Hebrew is not really *Lashon HaKodesh*, but is rather a creole of languages fused together to facilitate communication between Jews of different origins. Thus, it contains many imported words, idioms, and slang from other languages. He looked with great suspicion at the influence of these foreign elements.[363]

Some have attributed to him a straw man argument that Modern Hebrew should be shunned because it exhibits foreign influences, and then proceed to dismantle his reasoning by noting that *Lashon HaKodesh* always had foreign influences. Of course, a rabbi of his vast knowledge was certainly aware of this. Therefore, it seems that Rabbi Dushinsky's objection to Modern Hebrew is not as simple as his detractors make it out to be. While we shall see in the next chapter that foreign influences always affected the development of *Lashon HaKodesh* in one way or another, these influences were always monitored by the watchful eyes of the rabbis. They decided exactly how to introduce foreign words into the holy language, and set barriers to prevent matters from going too far. Modern Hebrew, on the other hand, is a largely unregulated language, which reflects the secular culture that has unfortunately crept into Jewish society.

LEADING RABBIS TAKE A HARD STANCE

Following in the footsteps of the rabbinic leadership in Jerusalem, several rabbis outside of Israel also made clear their objections to Modern Hebrew. These figures include the Satmar Rebbe, Rabbi Yoel Teitelbaum; the Bobover Rebbe, Rabbi Ben Zion Halberstam (1874–1941); the Tzeilemer Rav, Rabbi Eliezer David Greenwald (1867–1928); and others.[364]

RABBI KOOK'S PRONUNCIATION OF HEBREW

One time, the rabbis from many of the early Jewish settlements met to discuss the spiritual welfare of the settlers. The rabbis gathered at the home of Rabbi Reuven Katz (1880–1963), the Chief Rabbi of Petach

---

363 M. Blau, *Al Chomosayich Yerushalayim* (Tel Aviv, 1946), pgs. 117–118.

364 *Tohar HaLashon* (Jerusalem, 2008), pg. 63–64.

Tikvah, to discuss several proposals for strengthening the deteriorating situation. One attendee proposed teaching Torah subjects in Yiddish instead of Modern Hebrew. He argued that if the younger generation would be more accustomed to speaking Yiddish, they would distance themselves from secular Modern Hebrew-speaking influences. However, Rabbi Zev Gold (1889–1956), president of the Religious Zionist World Mizrachi branch in America, vehemently disagreed with this proposal. He launched into a diatribe detailing the religious significance of speaking *Lashon HaKodesh* and the need for unity amongst the different sectors of world Jewry.

In the middle of his speech, he mentioned that the late Rabbi Avraham Yitzchak HaKohen Kook used to speak *Lashon HaKodesh* with the Sephardic pronunciation characteristic of Modern Hebrew when speaking of mundane matters, and would speak *Lashon HaKodesh* with his traditional Ashkenazic pronunciation when praying and learning. Rabbi Gold explained that Rabbi Kook did this in accordance with the idea set forth by *The Kuzari* that Abraham spoke *Lashon HaKodesh* for holy purposes and Aramaic for other purposes. In mentioning this anecdote, Rabbi Gold preempted Rabbi Dushinsky's objection to Modern Hebrew by proposing that one could use the Sephardic pronunciation for day-to-day speech, all the while keeping the traditional Ashkenazic pronunciation for holy matters. However, as Rabbi Gold himself admitted, most people are not able to maintain this fine distinction, implying that even should one try, issues would still arise.[365]

MODERN HEBREW IS A MANMADE LANGUAGE

As we explained in the second chapter, one of the unique traits of *Lashon HaKodesh* is that it is the only language whose words bear inherent meaning. The lexicons of all other languages represent merely a group consensus to associate those particular sounds with those particular meanings. This leads to another reason why Modern Hebrew can be considered objectionable. The Modern Hebrew language was governed by the Hebrew Language

365 S. Mirsky (ed.), *Talpiyos* vol. 4:3– 4 (New York: Yeshiva University Press, 1950), pgs. 793–809.

Council,[366] and later by its successor, the Academy of the Hebrew Language (האקדמיה ללשון העברית),[367] which legislates the development of the language according to its standards. The makeup of Modern Hebrew is literally agreed upon by an actual committee that convenes to approve or reject suggested words and grammatical rules. By conferring such authority over the language to ordinary human whim, the language has certainly been demoted from its status as *Lashon HaKodesh*, a language not based on the consensus of humans, but rather on divine wisdom. (However, we should note that by now the committee's rulings are largely symbolic, technically only binding upon government agencies, and for the most part left unimplemented or implemented on only a small scale.[368])

THE RABBIS NEVER ADVOCATED SPEAKING LASHON HAKODESH

Rabbi Meir Amsel mentions an important historical observation. He notes that while *Lashon HaKodesh* has been in use by rabbis for hundreds of years, we never find that these rabbis instituted that the general populace should speak *Lashon HaKodesh*. To the contrary, *Lashon HaKodesh* has generally been a language in use by the rabbinic elite and not the masses. He explains that the rabbis purposely did not want the masses to speak *Lashon HaKodesh*, so as not to corrupt it.

---

366 I. Aytürk, "Revisiting the language factor in Zionism: The Hebrew Language Council from 1904 to 1914," *Bulletin of the SOAS*, vol. 73:1 (School of Oriental and African Studies, 2010), pgs. 45–64, documents the rise and fall of that institution's influence in the early twentieth century.

367 Ironically, this body has repeatedly come under fire for using the Greek word "academy" in its name, which clearly shows foreign influence and does not reflect a purely Hebrew language. However, in an equally ironic twist of fate, I have discovered that in a passage likely unbeknownst to the founders of the Academy, Rabbi Azariah de Rossi in *Meor Einayim*, vol. 5 (Vienna, 1829), pg. 278b, writes that the word "academy" actually has a source in *Lashon HaKodesh*. He writes that it is related to the phrase "gathering-house for shepherds (*beis akad roim*, בית עקד רועים)" found in the Bible (*Kings* II 10:12). Rabbi Yosef Shlomo Delmedigo (1591–1655) also makes this connection between the phrase "gathering house for shepherds" and "academy," see his *Mitzaref L'Chachma* (Warsaw, 1890), pg. 85.

368 In January 2014, the Academy began to allow open access to the database of their Historical Dictionary Project, which seeks to produce a concordance of all Hebrew words ever used in the history of the language spanning several millennia [http://maagarim.hebrew-academy.org.il/Pages/PMain.aspx]. This project has the potential to stimulate much important research pertaining to the history of Hebrew.

Instead, they allowed and even encouraged—to some extent—the masses to adopt the languages of their surroundings. For example, instead of promoting *Lashon HaKodesh* as a language for all the Jews exiled in Babylon, the rabbis instituted that the Torah be read in both *Lashon HaKodesh* and an Aramaic *Targum* so that the masses could understand it. In doing so, they lent credence to the acceptance of Aramaic as a spoken language (as we mentioned in the previous chapter). The rabbis even instituted several prayers in Aramaic so that everyone could understand them, instead of insisting that everyone should speak *Lashon HaKodesh*. He explains that the rabbis encouraged this arrangement to clearly demarcate the holy and the non-holy. *Lashon HaKodesh* was reserved for holy uses; other languages were used for other purposes.[369]

While Rabbi Amsel does not explicitly mention this, he implies that accepting Modern Hebrew as a language for everything achieves the exact opposite of the rabbis' objective: It blurs the line between the holy and the non-holy.

ADVOCATES FOR SPEAKING LASHON HAKODESH

While in general Rabbi Amsel's assertion that the rabbis never advocated *Lashon HaKodesh* for the masses is true, there are several notable exceptions. For example, several notable Kabbalists, and especially Rabbi Yishaya Horowitz, as mentioned in the beginning of this chapter, felt that it is important to speak *Lashon HaKodesh*.

In discussing the various subjects (besides Torah studies) in which a father is obligated to instruct his children, Rabbi Yosef Chaim of Baghdad (1832–1909) stresses that one must teach his children *Lashon HaKodesh*. He notes that the Torah was written in *Lashon HaKodesh* and that language is destined to be the standard global language in the Messianic Era.[370] He rhetorically asks, "How can a Jewish man not be able to speak *Lashon HaKodesh* properly?" He points out that it is an embarrassment that in Baghdad even the Torah scholars do not know how to speak

---

369 M. Amsel (ed.), "*Lashon HaKodesh* and Ivrit," *Kovetz Hamaor*, vol. 79 (Brooklyn, 1958), pgs. 12–13.

370 See note above.

and write *Lashon HaKodesh* and that certainly the general populace does not know the language.[371] Rabbi Baruch Epstein likewise stresses the importance of raising children to speak *Lashon HaKodesh*.[372] Rabbi Yehonassan Eyebschitz also laments the reality in his time that people did not teach their children *Lashon HaKodesh*, even though they taught their children other languages.[373]

CHAZON ISH SOFTENS THE OPPOSITION TO MODERN HEBREW

Rabbi Avraham Yishaya Karelitz (1878–1953), known as Chazon Ish after his *magnum opus*, sought to soften the religious community's militant stance against Modern Hebrew. He personally told Rabbi Yaakov Edelstein, the Rosh Yeshiva of Yeshivat HaSharon in Ramat HaSharon, to open his yeshiva with Modern Hebrew as the language of instruction. That way Sephardic students (whose families had already embraced Modern Hebrew a generation earlier) and Ashkenazic students who did not grow up speaking Yiddish could benefit. Chazon Ish told him to do so even though it meant that certain known donors would refrain from supporting his yeshiva.[374] In fact, Chazon Ish regularly interacted with students of Hebrew-speaking Talmudei Torah, thereby showing his recognition of the legitimacy of such institutions.

When asked why he offered his support to such institutions, he famously responded with a parable about a retired general. If a retired general, who was successful in previous wars, is called back into service, he cannot simply mobilize his army at the front-lines where he had once successfully led his campaigns. The war must be fought at the current front-lines; the front-lines of past battles are obsolete. So too, explained Chazon Ish, in the past the issue of Modern Hebrew had been a battlefront in the general war fought by religious Jews against Secularism. However, he felt that in his times Modern Hebrew was no longer the issue at the forefront. With this, he justified not combating the rise of Modern

371 Y. Salam (ed.), *Os Chaim* (Jerusalem, 1998), pgs. 222–223.

372 *Safa L'Ne'emanim* (Warsaw, 1893), pg. 13.

373 *Ya'aros Devash*, vol. 2, *Drush* 12.

374 T. Yabrov, *Ma'aseh Ish*, vol. 3 (Bene Barak, 2000), pg. 39.

Hebrew within the religious sector.[375] Due to his most amicable stance, even the most prominent of yeshivas and rabbinical courts in Israel have reluctantly adopted Hebrew as their official language, abandoning Yiddish, the traditional language of Ashkenazic Jewry. Nonetheless, a few stalwart exceptions exist, especially in the Hassidic world.[376]

CHAPTER SUMMARY

To recap the early history of *Lashon HaKodesh* in its latest incarnation as Modern Hebrew, there are two major points:

- Ben-Yehuda and others recognized that a common language had to be created and imposed post haste in order to facilitate the advancement of the idea of a Jewish state. Modern Hebrew was the natural candidate for such a language because it was already familiar to most Jews (although there were attempts to use German and/or Yiddish). Ben-Yehuda built Modern Hebrew upon the foundations laid by earlier scholars of the *Haskalah* and used it to further the Zionist cause.
- In response, the Ultra-Orthodox rejection of this construct was fierce. Some argued that since *Lashon HaKodesh* is holy, it is not supposed to be used for mundane, and even inappropriate, matters. Doing so makes it lose its status as *Lashon HaKodesh*.[377] The language was manmade, as opposed to divine. Furthermore, they believed that since Modern Hebrew deliberately incorporated secular influences in an unregulated fashion, it was tainted by the unholy intentions of its creators. Some concern was also expressed at the halachic ramifications of the fact that an Ashkenazic Modern Hebrew-speaker would have difficulty maintaining Ashkenazic pronunciation for praying and reading from the Torah.

---

375 T. Yabrov, *Ma'aseh Ish*, vol. 1 (Bene Barak, 1999), pgs. 47–49.

376 See S. D. Baumel, *Sacred Speaker: Language and Culture Among the Haredim in Israel* (Oxford: Berghahn Books, 2006) who offers a curious study of the linguistic habits of several Ultra-Orthodox sects in Israel.

377 See above (end of Chapter 3) where we discussed the view that *Lashon HaKodesh* becomes perverted when one attempts to use it for everyday things. The resulting language, though very similar, is no longer *Lashon HaKodesh*.

At first, the Ultra-Orthodox community strongly opposed adopting Modern Hebrew as a spoken language. Their rejection of the language was part and parcel of their rejection of the secular and nationalistic agenda that came with it. In time, use of Modern Hebrew became less of an issue of dogma, and more of practicality. Thus, even in the Israeli *Chareidi* community, it gradually became widely (though not exclusively) used. Ultimately, Modern Hebrew has largely prevailed in Israel.

MODERN HEBREW OUTSIDE OF ISRAEL

Outside of Israel, Modern Hebrew did not fare as well. Yiddish continued to be the main language spoken by Ashkenazic Jewry until the Holocaust. After the Holocaust, usage of Yiddish waned, especially in America (and to a lesser extent in Europe), although it remains in use by some Ultra-Orthodox sects and through the revival efforts of secular Yiddish enthusiasts.

In the diaspora, Jews have generally accepted the languages of their host countries, albeit under heavy influence from *Lashon HaKodesh* and Aramaic, as we discussed in the previous chapters. Usage of Modern Hebrew outside of Israel is numerically insignificant. However, in recent years, many Israeli expatriates have brought Modern Hebrew to more far-flung places. In addition, certain pedagogical policies practiced in France and in some schools in America (especially in South America) who teach Hebrew/Jewish studies in Modern Hebrew (known as *Ivrit B'Ivrit)*[378]

---

378 This method is especially touted in the Modern Orthodox/Religious Zionist community in America. Nonetheless, many of the leading post-Holocaust rabbis in America opposed such a teaching method. For example, Rabbi Aharon Kotler (1891–1962) strongly disallowed using *Ivrit B'Ivrit* in Bais Yaakov of Boro Park; see M. Amsel (ed.), *Kovetz Hamaor*, vol. 128 (1963), pgs. 34–36 (albeit in that discussion the alternative was teaching in Yiddish, not English). Rabbi Yosef Eliyahu Henkin (1881–1973) also opposed the practice in general, but was more accepting of it for English-speaking students; see Rabbi Henkin's article first printed in S. Elberg (ed.), *Kovetz HaPardes*, vol. 35:5 (1960), pgs. 2–3, 6, and later printed in *Kisvei HaGaon Rabbi Yosef Eliyahu Henkin zt"l* (New York: Ezras Torah Press, 1989), pgs. 78–80. The general objection to this method is that teaching students a subject in a language with which they are not familiar (or not as familiar) will cause them to not properly understand the material and will weaken their interest in that subject.
In the spring of 1990, Dr. Joel Wolowelsky, a contributing editor of *Ten Da'at* wrote an article for that publication, calling on all Orthodox schools to accept this method regardless of their

has led to Modern Hebrew being somewhat more commonplace there, although this prevalence is virtually intangible and rarely extends beyond the scholastic arena. Ultimately, Modern Hebrew has barely made an impact outside of Israel.

stance on Zionism. His article elicited varied responses with some scholars mentioning anecdotal evidence supporting the arguments of those opposed to this method. The original article and the responses to it are available online in the archives of the Lookstein Center for Jewish Education [http://www.lookstein.org/articles/ivrit.htm].

CHAPTER 7:
Foreign Influences on Lashon HaKodesh

FOREIGN WORDS IN LASHON HAKODESH

The passage from *The Kuzari* (which we quoted in Chapter 1) sings the praises of *Lashon HaKodesh* by stating, "One never finds that the stories and descriptions in the Torah needed to borrow foreign words. One never finds that the Torah needs to borrow foreign words for the names of peoples, birds, stones..."

However, this assertion is not accepted by all sources. Some commentators understand that even in the Bible, *Lashon HaKodesh* borrows words from other languages—and certainly extra-biblical *Lashon HaKodesh* does.[379] (For the purposes of this discussion, Aramaic and

379 However, Rabbi Moshe Sofer (previously mentioned in a footnote to Chapter 5) wrote that *Lashon HaKodesh*, by definition, only refers to the language used in the Bible and nothing beyond that.

Lashon HaKodesh are given equal standing; see the next chapter for the justification of such an approach.)

EXTRA-BIBLICAL WORDS IN LASHON HAKODESH

Whether the holiness of *Lashon HaKodesh* is intrinsic or acquired through usage, the language itself is not static, but rather evolves. Thus, new words can be and were incorporated into *Lashon HaKodesh*. When confronted with such instances, most commentators will admit that the words are of foreign origin (although some claim that the foreign words originated in *Lashon HaKodesh*), while others will expound the word through puns and the like to explain its meaning in *Lashon HaKodesh* or Aramaic. While on the surface these two approaches seem irreconcilable, there is a way to synchronize them.

THE WORD SANHEDRIN

In this discussion, we will draw heavily on examples to illustrate our points. The first of these is the word *sanhedrin* (סנהדרין), which is used in rabbinic writings to refer to the legislative/judicial High Court. The word *sanhedrin* is never found in the Bible; it appears for the first time in post-biblical rabbinical writings.

HaBachur writes that *sanhedrin* is actually a Greek word, which means "chairs."[380] Rabbi Gershon Shaul Yom Tov Lipman Heller (1578-1654) writes that the word is Aramaic.[381]

However, Rabbi Yaakov Moelin (1365–1427) writes that the word is derived from the Hebrew phrase *soneh hadras panim badin* (שונא הדרת פנים בדין, roughly translated as "despises favoritism in justice").[382] Bartenura also mentions this explanation in his commentary to the Mishnah.[383]

This case is typical of words that are not found in the Bible but are used in later *Lashon HaKodesh*. Some commentators explain that they are

---

380 *Sefer HaTishbi* (Bene Barak: Machon HaRav Matzliach, 2005), pgs. 188–189. Rabbi Yisrael Yaakov Algazi (1680–1756) in *Kehillos Yaakov*, vol. 2 (Lemberg, 1898), pg. 16a, quotes this explanation in the name of Tashbatz.

381 *Tosafos Yom Tov* in his introduction to Tractate *Sanhedrin*.

382 *Minhagei Maharil, Likutim* no. 6.

383 *Sotah* 9:11.

portmanteau or abbreviations of phrases in *Lashon HaKodesh*, and some explain that they are of foreign origin.

THE WORD GEMATRIA

Another example of a popular extra-biblical word used in *Lashon HaKodesh* is *gematria* (גימטריא). The Mishnah lends credence to this concept[384]—the numerology of the Hebrew alphabet—which links together multiple words or phrases because of their numerical equivalence. Rabbi Akiva Eiger Schlussel (1927–2011) offers a simple explanation of the term and its meaning. He reasons that *gematria* is a portmanteau of *gamma* and *trio*. *Trio* means "third" in Greek, and *Gamma* was the third letter of the Greek Alphabet. Thus, the word *gematria* alludes to the numerical values of letters.[385]

However, for some reason, the classic commentators explain the word differently and do not mention this relatively simple explanation.[386] They agree that the word *gematria* is of Greek origin, but explain that it is derived from the Greek word γεωμετρία ("geometry").[387] Others add that even though "geometry" literally refers to the study of measuring the earth ("geo-" means earth and "-metria" means measurement), the rabbis adopted this phrase to refer to all forms of calculations[388] and mathematics. Thus, the Mishnah's

384 *Avos* 3:18.

385 A grandson of the late Rabbi Schlussel shared this thought with the author.

386 Rabbi Yosef Karo writes (*Kllalei Gemara* to *Halichos Olam*, Gate 7, §29) that the word *gematria* is a portmanteau of the *Lashon HaKodesh* word *gay* (גיא, valley) and the Aramaic word *meturia* (מטוריא, from mountains). Thus, *gematria* means "a valley from between mountains." This probably alludes to the idea that *gematria* can connect two different things (that would otherwise have no relation), just as a valley can connect two separate mountains.

Rabbi Yishaya Horowitz (in *Shelah*, Oral Torah, *Drushim V'Aggados* 4:17) also quotes this portmanteau without explaining it. By doing so, he seems to eschew the idea that the rabbis adopted words from other languages and incorporated them into *Lashon HaKodesh*. Indeed, one finds that Rabbi Horowitz writes elsewhere in *Shelah* (Oral Torah, *Pesachim*, *Matzah Ashira* §3) that a little bit of *Lashon HaKodesh* is mixed into each language, instead of admitting that *Lashon HaKodesh* itself is influenced by other languages, see below.

387 See the anonymous commentator printed with Rambam's Laws of *Kiddush HaChodesh* 18:13.

388 The anonymous medieval work *Kolbo* (§122) mentions that the Targumim translate "the census of the nation" as *yas gamator* (ית גמטור), which shows that the Targumim understood the meaning of *gematria* to refer to any type of calculation. However, upon examination, one will find that none of the popular Targumim translate the phrase as such. See *Targum Jonathan* to *Samuel* II 24:9, and *Targum Rav Yosef* to *Chronicles* I 21:5, who translate the phrase as *yas chush-*

use of the word in reference to the numerology of the Hebrew alphabet[389] is appropriate.[390] However, the Mishnah does not actually use the word "geometry"; it uses the word *gematria*, which is derived from "geometry." The word the rabbis use is not identical to the Greek word, albeit it is quite similar.

From this discussion, we see two important points:

- The classical commentators do not shy away from explaining that certain words in *Lashon HaKodesh* are actually adopted from other languages.
- When the rabbis adopted words from foreign languages, they did not do so verbatim; they slightly altered the actual form or meaning of the word. Rabbi Yisrael Lipschitz first takes note of this phenomenon and writes that before the rabbis accepted any Greek word into rabbinic Hebrew, they would first "Judaize" the word by altering its pronunciation.[391]

DEFINING THE WORD AFIKOMEN

The Mishnah rules that after eating the meat from the Paschal sacrifice, one should not eat *afikomen* (אפיקומן).[392] The commentators evidently understood that *afikomen* means dessert, which is traditionally served at the end of the meal. They explain that *afikomen* is an abbreviation of the Aramaic phrase *afiku minei* (אפיקו מיני), "take out [different] types of [food]," which is the typical call for dessert.[393]

---

ban minyan (ית חושבן מנין). Rabbi Yaakov Schor of Kitov (1853–1924) notes this in his glosses to HaBachur's *Sefer HaTishbi* (Bene Barak: Machon HaRav Matzliach, 2005), pg. 58.

389 Rabbi Avraham Zacuto (1452–1515) writes (*Sefer Yuchasin Ma'amar* 1, *Rabbi Eliezer Chisma*) that in the context of the Mishnah in question, the word *gematria* actually does refer to the measurement of the earth, not the numerology of the Hebrew alphabet. See Dr. Alexander Kohut (1842–1894), *Aruch Completum* (Hebrew ed.), vol. 2 (Vienna, 1878–1892), pg. 309.

390 See *Tosafos Yom Tov* and *Tiferes Yisrael* to *Avos* 3:18 and *Sefer HaTishbi* by HaBachur (s.v. גימטריא).

391 *Tiferes Yisrael*, *Boaz* (*Pesachim* Ch. 10 §3), see there for several other examples.

392 *Pesachim* 10:8.

393 Many medieval sages quote this explanation in their respective commentaries to the *Haggadah Shel Pesach*, including Raavan, Rokeach, Shibolei HaLeket, and Abudraham. The earliest source for this explanation is Rashi's *Issur V'Heter* (Berlin, 1928), pg. 21. It is also quoted by *Sefer HaMichtam* (to TB *Pesachim* 119b), *Machzor Vitry* (§72), Bartenura to the Mishnah *Pesachim* 10:8, and *Levush Mordechai* (*Orach Chayim* §478:1). This explanation is also alluded to by Rashi

HaBachur asks why the commentators had to explain the word *afikomen* in such a strained fashion. They could have simply explained that the word *afikomen* refers to *epikomion,* the Greek word for dessert.[394]

Rabbi Yaakov Emden (1697–1776) answers HaBachur's question by explaining that *Lashon HaKodesh* is the mother of all languages—including Greek. If anything, Greek adopted the word from *Lashon HaKodesh*, not vice versa.[395] He writes that the above-mentioned commentators were not seeking to explain what *afikomen* actually means; they were simply trying to find a hint to its meaning through phonetic homilies in *Lashon HaKodesh* and Aramaic.

As we have already mentioned, before the rabbis incorporated Greek words into rabbinic Hebrew, they would first "Judaize" the words by modifying its pronunciation.[396] Based on this premise, some answer HaBachur's question by explaining that the commentators were not trying to explain the meaning of the word *afikomen*—they knew it was Greek for "dessert." Rather, they were trying to understand why the rabbis changed the Greek word *epikomion* into *afikomen.*[397] To answer that question, they showed that *epikomion* had to be rendered specifically as *afikomen* by expounding on the word *afikomen* as above. If the rabbis had not used the term *afikomen*, they would have prevented the commentators from providing their explanation.

Here again, we see that when the rabbis wanted to add a foreign word to *Lashon HaKodesh*, they would first modify the word slightly (in this case by slightly altering its pronunciation), and give it a "Jewish flavor"; they did not simply copy the word from Greek as is.[398]

---

and Rashbam (to TB *Pesachim* 119b). See *Midrash Talpiyos* (s.v. *Afikomen*) by Rabbi Eliyahu HaKohen of Izmir (1659–1729), who also understands that *afikomen* is an abbreviation, but offers other explanations of the term.

394 See HaBachur's *Sefer HaTishbi* (s.v. אפיקומן). Rabbi Eliezer ben Eliyahu Ashkenazi (in his work *Ma'ase Hashem* in his commentary to the *Haggadah Shel Pesach*), actually does note that the word *afikomen* is of Greek origin. Perhaps it was HaBachur's remark that had encouraged him to do so.

395 *Ezer Ohr* (Emden's glosses to *Sefer HaTishbi*) there.

396 *Tiferes Yisrael, Boaz* (*Pesachim* Ch. 10 §3); see there for several other examples.

397 *Sefer HaTishbi* (Bene Barak: Machon HaRav Matzliach, 2005), pgs. 26–28.

398 A. S. Yahuda, *The Language of the Pentateuch in its Relation to Egyptian* (Oxford University Press, 1933), discusses the influences of various ancient languages, especially Egyptian, on the language of the Bible. He writes there (pg. xxviii): "The most striking, nay, astonishing feature in all this is the creative energy of the Hebrew linguistic genius. For in all these transformations

JUDAIZING THE WORD APIKORUS

Interestingly, the accepted way of pronouncing the Mishnaic Hebrew word for "heretic" (אפיקורוס) is *apikorus*. The commentators give two different etymologies for the word.

In his commentary to the Mishnah,[399] Rambam writes that the word is derived from the Aramaic word *hefker* (הפקר), which denotes lawlessness and anarchy. Rambam's explanation thus implies that a heretic is one who rejects authority and promotes unruliness.

Alternatively, Rabbi Yosef Elbo (1380–1444) explains that the word *apikorus* is derived from the name Epicurus (Επίκουρος), an ancient Greek philosopher who preached indulgence in worldly pleasures as a legitimate—and even idealized—lifestyle.[400] It would therefore seem that Rambam and Rabbi Elbo disagree whether the word is of Aramaic or Greek origin. However, in light of the above suppositions, one can reason that the two commentators are not really arguing. Rabbi Elbo explains the actual origins of the word, which is related to Epicurus, while Rambam explains how this word was "Judaized" into *apikorus* so that it could also fit into an Aramaic meaning.

ROMAN PLACE NAMES IN ISRAEL

The name of the Galilean city Tiberias is another example of this idea. Josephus writes that this city was built by King Herod's son and was named after the Roman Emperor Tiberius (42 BC–37 AD).[401] However, according to rabbinic tradition, the city dates to biblical times[402] and is

under the influence of languages of diverse origins, Hebrew, despite the many heterogeneous elements that impinged upon it, always proceeded creatively, in that it recoined the foreign elements in its own spirit and fitted them to its own linguistic usage; so much so that the newly acquired treasures were so easily assimilated to the older store that their foreign origin can hardly be detected." His work is a treasure trove of information pertaining to the subject of foreign influences on *Lashon HaKodesh*.

399 *Sanhedrin* 10:1.

400 *Sefer HaIkkarim, Ma'amar* 10, Ch. 1.

401 Josephus' *Antiquities of the Jews* (Book XVIII, Ch. 2).

402 However, see M. Avi-Yonah, "The Foundation of Tiberias," *Israel Exploration Journal*, vol. 1:3 (1950-51), pgs. 160-169, who dates the founding of the city to Herodian times and concludes quite assertively that the city was founded in the year 18 CE.

known in the Bible under other names. The Talmud explains that Tiberias (טבריה) is called so because the city is located "at the middle [lit. 'navel'] of the Land of Israel." Although it seems that these two sources offer incompatible explanations as to the onomastic origin of Tiberias, they can be reconciled. When analyzing the proper names of places in the Land of Israel in rabbinic literature, one notices an interesting phenomenon. Sometimes the rabbis adopt the Roman names for those places like Tiberias, Caesarea (קסריה), and Sepphoris (צפורי). Yet, in other instances,[403] the rabbis rejected the Roman names and favored Hebrew names, as is the case with Eleutheropolis, which the rabbis called Beit Guvrin (בית גוברין), and the Roman city Aelia Capitolina (built on the ruins of Jerusalem), which the rabbis continued to call Jerusalem. Regarding Tiberias, the rabbis chose the former approach and justified their decision by showing how the city's Roman name also bears significance in *Lashon HaKodesh*.

THE RABBIS' ROLE IN SHAPING LASHON HAKODESH

This idea (that the rabbis sometimes took foreign words and "Judaized" them before introducing them to *Lashon HaKodesh*) was proposed relatively recently. However, it has a precedent in the Talmud, which shows that the rabbis influenced how Jewish society used language. For example, the Mishnah mentions different slang words for taking vows of prohibition, sacrifices, Nazirite status, and oaths.[404] According to one opinion in the Talmud,[405] these words originated in foreign languages. However, a dissenting view (there) held that the

---

403 The ancient city of Acre, which is a Roman name, is known in the Bible and in rabbinic literature as Akko (עכו), which is very similar. However, in this case, the Romans corrupted the name of a pre-existing city rather than the rabbis granting a name that closely resembled the Roman one. In fact, archeology has revealed through the Amarna letters that the city of Akko is quite ancient and was known by that name well before the Jewish exodus from Egypt. See M. Berenbaum & F. Skolnik (ed.), "Acre," *Encyclopedia Judaica*, vol. 1. 2nd ed. (Detroit: Macmillan Reference USA, 2007), pgs. 364–368. Such ancient Semitic place names in Israel have been used to prove that the Semites in fact ruled that land before the Hamitic Canaanites arrived there; see Y. Elitzur & Y. Kil (eds.), *Atlas Da'as Mikra* (Jerusalem: Mossad HaRav Kook, 1998), pgs. 11, 62. Nonetheless, as we have already noted in Chapter 3, Semitic linguistic features were not necessarily exclusive to Semitic peoples.

404 *Nedarim* 1:2.

405 TB *Nedarim* 10a.

rabbis coined them for religious reasons. The rabbis suspected that if people used the real biblical *Lashon HaKodesh* words for those concepts, they might inadvertently end up saying God's name in vain (because in the Bible those words are usually followed by God's name). According to this opinion, it is clear that the rabbis had a hand in shaping how *Lashon HaKodesh* was spoken. Perhaps even the former opinion would agree that these words, although of foreign origin, were adjusted by the rabbis before they entered the Jews' vernacular.

FOREIGN WORDS IN THE BIBLE

While it is almost universally agreed upon that the rabbis used foreign words (or, more accurately, foreign-influenced words) in their writings, there is a controversy about whether the Bible uses foreign words.

Various commentators have presented evidence that foreign languages have influenced even the *Lashon HaKodesh* of the Bible. In describing tefillin, the Torah thrice mentions that they should be "*totafos* (טטפת) between your eyes."[406] The Talmud mentions a Tannaic dispute as to the source of the law that the tefillin worn on the head must have four sections.[407] Rabbi Yishmael expounds that the word *totafos*, which is in plural form, means at least two. Then, he expounds the repetition of the word to teach that one needs four sections. Rabbi Akiva disagrees and instead derives this law by expounding the word *totafos* itself. He explains that *tota* means "two" in the Coptic language,[408] and *fos* means "two" in the Phrygian language.[409] Thus, the word *totafos* itself already teaches that there should be four sections in the tefillin. In this, the rabbis of the Talmud seemingly endorse the notion that even the Torah borrows words from other languages and adopts them as part of *Lashon HaKodesh*.[410]

---

406 *Exodus* 13:16; *Deuteronomy* 10:8, 11:18.

407 TB *Sanhedrin* 4b.

408 See M. Jastrow, *A Dictionary of the Targumim, the Talmud Babli, and Yerushalmi, and the Midrashic Literature* (Philadelphia, 1903), pg. 682.

409 *Afriki* mentioned in the Talmud does not mean "African" as some mistakenly think. Rather, as Rabbi Binyamin Schmerler (1860–1941) in his commentary to *Targum Jonathan* (*Ahavas Yehonassan* to *Genesis* 10:2) proves, it refers to the Phrygian language. See also M. Jastrow, *A Dictionary of the Targumim, the Talmud Babli, and Yerushalmi, and the Midrashic Literature* (Philadelphia, 1903), pg. 108.

410 Rabbi Yaakov Tzvi Meklenburg posits that the word *totafos* is actually Aramaic in origin, and

THE GREEK "ONE" IN THE TORAH

Similarly, the Torah rhetorically asks, "Now Israel, what does Hashem your God ask of you?" It answers, "Only to fear Hashem your God."[411] From this verse the Talmud proves that fear of Heaven is all that matters to God in This World.[412] The Talmud then offers another verse to support this assertion. The Book of Job says that God told man, "Behold (*hen*, הן) fear of God is wisdom."[413] However, since the word "*hen*" means "one" in Greek (ἕνας), the verse can also be read as "One [meaning "only"] fear of God is wisdom."[414]

This pun is repeated elsewhere in the Talmud in expounding another verse.[415] The Torah says, "And a man who 'takes' a woman and her mother, it is a scheme, he and they (*ve'es'hen*, ואתהן) shall be burnt by fire so that there shall not be schemes within you."[416] A literal reading of the Torah seems to implicate both women. However, Rabbi Yishmael understood that in reality only the man and the second woman are liable for the death penalty, for they alone had sinned—the first woman is innocent. Rabbi Yishmael proves his view by stating that the word *ve'es'hen* (ואתהן), "and they," can be read as *ve'es hen* (ואת הן). "*Ve'es*" (ואת) means "and" in *Lashon HaKodesh*, and "*hen*" (הן) means "one" in Greek. Thus, the phrase *ve'es hen* means "and one [of them]." According to this interpretation, the original verse reads "he and one [of them, i.e., the second woman] shall be burnt by fire."

---

means "appeasement." Indeed, *Targum* (to *Kings* II 12:9) translates appeasement as *ve'itafsu* (ואיטפסו). However, in other instances, such as *Genesis* 34:15, 34:22 and 34:23, *Targum* translates it as *ve'itfas* (ואיתפס). He accounts for the double ט by explaining that it denotes continual appeasement, which can be achieved through the commandment of tefillin. He further writes that the abovementioned Talmudic exegesis is based on a tangential point about alternate meanings of the word in other languages, but does not refer to the literal meaning of the word in *Lashon HaKodesh*. See Rabbi Meklenburg's *Siddur Iyun Tefillah* (Tel Aviv, 1954), pg. 95, for further elaboration. See insert for more discussion about the meaning of the word *totafos*.

411 *Deuteronomy* 10:12.

412 TB *Shabbos* 31b.

413 *Job* 28:28.

414 Rabbi Yerucham Levovitz (1873–1936) notes (*Da'as Torah* to *Genesis* 10:2) that these exegeses are also true in German and Yiddish where the word for one is *ein*.

415 *Sanhedrin* 76b, cited by Rashi to *Leviticus* 20:14.

416 *Leviticus* ibid.

Did Pharaoh wear eyeglasses?

In addition to the explanation offered in the Talmud as to the origin of the word *totafos*, the medieval commentators present several other explanations. Rabbi Avraham Saba (1440–1508), in his commentary to the Pentateuch *Tzror Hamor* (there), quotes *Nabataean Agriculture* who writes that eyeglasses worn on the head by ancient Egyptians to optimize their sight are called *ataf* (אטף). He proposes that the word *totafos* is related to that. Abarbanel (there) also writes that *totafos* is Egyptian, but explains that it is related to the Egyptian word for "brain."

Rabbeinu Meyuchas (there) explains that the word is Aramaic and is related to the Aramaic word *atif* (אטיף), which refers to something noticeably exceptional.

See M. Kasher, *Shema Yisrael* (Jerusalem, 1980), pgs. 324—327, who presents more than thirteen additional etymologies for the word *totafos*.

It is notable that Rabbi Yishmael uses this technique to prove his point, since, as mentioned above, he rejects Rabbi Akiva's exegesis linking the word *totafos* to Coptic and Phrygian. Thus, while they may disagree on a particular case, it seems that all the sages of the Talmud unanimously hold that homonyms (similar-sounding words) from other languages can be taken into account when attempting to understand biblical verses written in *Lashon HaKodesh*. This seems to imply that the Bible uses words from other languages.

IDENTIFYING FOREIGN WORDS IN THE BIBLE

Some commentators note that when the Bible uses a term and then defines it, the fact that the Bible felt the need to define that term shows that it is likely from a foreign language.[417] Another method of identifying

417 E.g., in mentioning Joseph's incarceration in Egypt, the Torah writes, "Joseph's master took him and placed him in the *Beis HaSohar*, [which is] the place where the king[dom]'s prisoners are imprisoned. And he remained there in the *Beis HaSohar*" (*Genesis* 39:20). Ibn Ezra there writes that he is unsure whether the phrase *Beis HaSohar* is in *Lashon HaKodesh* or is an Egyptian phrase, which is why the Torah had to define it. Abarbanel justifies the Torah's definition of the term, even if it is *Lashon HaKodesh*. He explains that the Torah meant to stress that Joseph was not put in a jail with common criminals who were sentenced to incarceration by local magistrates; rather he was placed in the *Beis HaSohar*, where those dignitaries sentenced to imprisonment by the king himself were imprisoned.

foreign words is based on the roots (*shorashim*) of the words. Every word in *Lashon HaKodesh* has a root of one, two, or three letters that makes up the core of the word. The roots are then modified to fit the exact meaning and context. However, there are some words in the Bible whose roots seem to have four letters (known as quadrilateral roots). Ibn Ezra acknowledges the existence of these roots, but writes that they are rare because it is difficult for a human to pronounce words with four-letter roots. He also notes that some words that are thought to have four-letter roots[418] are actually from foreign languages.[419] Elsewhere, Ibn Ezra writes that in general these roots are either compound roots that are made up of multiple roots fused together or are from a language other than *Lashon HaKodesh*.[420]

Rabbi Meir Leibush Weiser (1809–1879), known as Malbim, writes[421] that rabbinic tradition agrees with the view of the Hebrew grammarians who held that biblical words with quadrilateral roots are from foreign languages.[422] This view is also attributed to HaBachur,[423] and is quoted several times by Rabbi Baruch HaLevi Epstein[424] and Rabbi Meir Simcha HaKohen of Dvinsk (1843–1926) in his name.[425]

WHY DOES THE BIBLE USE FOREIGN WORDS?

Why would the Bible use a word from a foreign language, especially in cases where words in *Lashon HaKodesh* exist to fit those needs?

---

418 *Targum* is a word whose root is four letters. Interestingly, some scholars have claimed that the word *targum*, (תרגום) which usually means "translation," is borrowed from the Ugaritic language. In Ugaritic, the root RGM (רגם) means "to say" or "to speak" (similar to אמר and דבר in *Lashon HaKodesh*). With a ת prefixed to it, it means "he shall speak." (In Hebrew, the root RGM means "to stone.") See Rabbi Loyfer's introduction to *Targum Onkelos* appended to *Otzar Rishonim*, vol. 1 (Brooklyn, 2013). [Rabbi Loyfer writes a regular column about *Lashon HaKodesh* in the *Hamodia* newspaper in Israel.]

419 *Sefer Tzachus B'Dikduk* (Berlin, 1769), pg. 51a.

420 *Moznei Lashon HaKodesh* (Offenbach, 1791), pg. 42a.

421 In the introduction to his commentary to *Leviticus*, *HaTorah V'HaMitzvah*, *Ayeles HaShachar* §1.

422 Malbim (in his commentary to the *Sifra*, *Parshas Vayikra* §152) discusses this idea further and cites many examples of such words in the Bible and how the rabbis expounded those words into *Lashon HaKodesh* and Aramaic.

423 HaBachur writes this in his work *HaBachur* (*Ma'amar* 4, §3) and in his introduction to *Sefer HaHarkava*.

424 *Torah Temimah* to *Genesis* 2:14 §32, 15:2 §1; *Tosefes Bracha* to *Deuteronomy* 7:3; and *Safa L'Ne'emanim* (Warsaw, 1893), pg. 23.

425 *Meshech Chachmah* to *Deuteronomy* 23:3.

Rabbi Baruch HaLevi Epstein, without actually addressing this question in specific, offers a fascinating answer. In the Torah, Abraham mentioned that if he did not sire an heir, then his household fellow "*Damesek* Eliezer" (דמשק אליעזר, commonly translated as "Damascus Eliezer") would inherit his assets.[426] The Talmud explains that Eliezer was called "*Damesek* Eliezer" because he "would draw (דולה) from the Torah of his master [Abraham] and pour it (ומשקה) for others."[427]

How did the Talmud see this alluded to in the name "*Damesek* Eliezer"?

Rabbi Epstein begins his explanation by quoting HaBachur, who writes that any word whose root is more than three letters does not originate in *Lashon HaKodesh*.[428]

Based on HaBachur's rule, Rabbi Epstein reasons that the word *damesek* does not originate in *Lashon HaKodesh*. Rather, he argues, it is related to the French word *"domestique,"* meaning domestic servant, which is an accurate description of Eliezer's role in Abraham's house. Accordingly, Rabbi Epstein explains why the Talmud felt the need to expound on Eliezer's title. Whenever the Bible deviates from its normal wording, it alerts the rabbis that something deeper is alluded to in the text.[429] The fact that the Bible chose to use a foreign word to describe Eliezer showed the rabbis of the Talmud that there is a deeper significance to the usage of that word in particular. In other words, the Bible uses a foreign word on purpose in order to teach an extra lesson. Therefore, they expounded the word in the abovementioned manner. The Bible uses foreign words in the same way that it uses other textual anomalies, i.e., as a way of noting that in those places there is room for the Oral Torah to add an additional layer of exegetical interpretation.

The Bible thus uses words from foreign languages as an anomaly to prompt the rabbis to engage in exegetical analysis.

---

426 *Genesis* 15:2.

427 TB *Yoma* 28b.

428 *Torah Temimah* to *Genesis* 15:2.

429 Rabbi Epstein notes another anomaly in the term "Damascus Eliezer." The gentilic demonym precedes Eliezer's personal name as opposed to coming after it, unlike the norm in the Bible (e.g., Yiftah the Giladite, Eliyahu the Tishbite, Ittai the Gathite, etc.). This could be another reason that the Talmud saw that further elucidation was required.

EXPOUNDING AN EGYPTIAN WORD

With this in mind, we can reconcile another instance in which the commentators seem to be at odds with one another. Ibn Ezra writes that the word for necromancers in the Bible (*chartumim*, חרטומים) is either Egyptian or Aramaic,[430] both because it has a four-letter root and because the Bible only uses it in connection with Egyptian[431] and Chaldean necromancers.[432] However, Ramban disagrees with Ibn Ezra's theory.[433] Instead, he favors Rashi's approach that *chartumim* is an abbreviation of the *Lashon HaKodesh* phrase "those who disturb the bones of the dead" (*hanecharim betimei meisim*, הנחרים בטימי מתים).[434]

In this discussion, the commentators take two approaches: Ibn Ezra understands that the word is foreign, while Rashi and Ramban understand that it is a contraction of a *Lashon HaKodesh*/Aramaic phrase.

These two opinions can be synchronized in light of what we have already explained. The Bible uses foreign words in order to facilitate rabbinic exegetical interpretation. Accordingly, Ibn Ezra explained that the word is in fact Egyptian or Aramaic, while Rashi and Ramban offered rabbinic exegesis precisely because the Bible used a foreign word.[435]

RABBI HIRSCH: THE BIBLE DOES NOT USE FOREIGN WORDS

This approach is not universally accepted. In fact, Rabbi Samson Raphael Hirsch seems to outright reject the idea that the Bible would use words from other languages. Instead, he regularly seeks to find other explanations (albeit sometimes very strained ones) for words with four-letter roots.

---

430 To *Exodus* 7:11.

431 I.e., *Genesis* 41:8, 41:24, *Exodus* 7:11, 7:22, 8:3, 8:14, 8:15, 9:11.

432 I.e., *Daniel* 1:20, 2:2, 2:10, 2:27, 4:4, 4:6, 5:11.

433 In his commentary to *Exodus* 7:11.

434 Rashi to *Genesis* 41:8 and *Daniel* 1:20 (see also *Pirush Rasag* there).

435 Another case: The Torah prohibits one from eating the Paschal sacrifice *na* (נא) (*Exodus* 12:9). In this context, the Targumim translate *na* as "undercooked." Rashi explains that, in fact, *na* means "undercooked" in Arabic. The Tosafists question Rashi's explanation by rhetorically asking whether the Torah was written in Arabic. Instead, they propose that in this context the word *na* means "now" or "please," as it does in other places. Thus, God was requesting of the Jews to "please" delay eating the sacrificial meats or to not eat them "now" but rather after they are cooked fully. See J. Gellis (ed.), *Tosafos HaShalem*, vol. 7 (Jerusalem: The Harry Fishel Institute, 1987), pgs. 73–74.

For example, in the case of *chartumim*, Rabbi Hirsch explains that it is related to the word *cheret* (חרט, inscriber) in *Lashon HaKodesh*.[436] This refers to the necromancers' expertise in hieroglyphics, which was the source of their wisdom of necromancy. In the case of *totafos*, Rabbi Hirsch admits that he does not know how to explain the root of the word, despite the fact that the Talmud and Rashi already explained that the word is made up of Coptic and Phrygian words.[437]

There is a general dispute amongst commentators whether or not foreign words (especially Arabic ones) can be used for understanding the Bible, and that dispute is correlated to the discussion about whether the Bible, in fact, uses foreign words.[438]

FOREIGN LANGUAGES USE LASHON HAKODESH

Some commentators take a different approach to this subject. They argue that *Lashon HaKodesh* does not borrow from other languages—other languages instead borrow from *Lashon HaKodesh*.

Rabbi David HaLevi Segal (1586–1667) writes that the word *totafos* used in the Bible is not derived from the Coptic and Phrygian words, as the Talmud seems to imply. Rather, the Talmud means that the Coptic and Phrygian words serve as proof of the meaning of an otherwise indecipherable Hebrew word.[439] This explanation echoes that of Rabbi Yehoshua ibn Shuaib (a fourteenth-century student of Rashba) who wrote that these words were originally *Lashon HaKodesh* and are only found in the Coptic and Phrygian languages as relics of the pre-Tower of Babel language spoken by all of humanity, i.e., *Lashon HaKodesh*.[440]

---

436 In his commentary to *Exodus* 7:11.

437 In his commentary to *Exodus* 13:16.

438 See A. M. Glanzer, *Maayanei Agam* (Antwerp, 2003), pgs. 115–130, for further discussion about this.

439 *Divrei David* to *Deuteronomy* 6:8.

440 See Z. Metzger (ed.), *Drashos Ibn Shuaib*, vol. 1 (Jerusalem: Machon Lev Sameach, 1992), pg. 19. Rabbi Yerucham Levovitz in *Da'as Torah* (to *Exodus* 13:16) offers the same explanation. Chazon Ish also alludes to such an explanation; see T. Yabrov, *Ma'aseh Ish*, vol. 3 (Bene Barak, 2000), pg. 93. Rabbi Chaim Yosef David Azulai (1724–1806) in his work *Nachal Kedumim* (to *Deuteronomy* 6:8) quotes a similar explanation in the name of Rabbi Eliezer Nachum (c. 1660–1764). He also mentions that Maharal saw in a dream that the word *totafos* was written by using foreign languages to allude to the halachah that one can read the passages of the *Shema* (of which the

Similarly, Rabbi Raphael Immanuel Chai Ricchi (1688–1743) explains that every language is based on *Lashon HaKodesh*. God used certain words in the Bible that are also used in other languages in order to show that all languages include certain elements of *Lashon HaKodesh*.[441] This explains why the Bible uses the word *totafos* to refer to the four sections of the tefillin, for the Bible specifically used words that appear in other languages to convey that all languages derive from *Lashon HaKodesh*. He takes this a step further by arguing that this explains why the rabbis specifically use the word *gematria*, which he claims is a word in *Lashon HaKodesh*. The rabbis introduced the word *gematria*—which closely resembles the Greek word for "geometry"—into the Mishnah to testify that all languages are derivatives of *Lashon HaKodesh*.

THE ACADEMIC APPROACH

The academic world accepts that the language used by the Bible had been influenced by foreign languages. In addition to Aramaic, Greek, and Egyptian influences (which are readily acknowledged by the sages of the Talmud, as mentioned above), the academic world also sees Ugaritic, Akkadian, and other Semitic languages as having influenced the *Lashon*

---

passages concerning the tefillin are part and parcel) in any language. This halachah is mentioned four times in the Talmud Babli: *Sotah* 32b, *Brachos* 13a, *Megillah* 17a, and *Shevuos* 39a (see Azulai there who explains the significance of the fact that this halachah is mentioned four times).

Rabbi Yissocher Ber Eilenberg also offers an explanation very similar to Ibn Shuaib's. Furthermore, in his commentary *Tzeidah L'Darech* (to *Exodus* 13:16), Rabbi Eilenberg quotes in the name of his teacher Rabbi Mordechai Yaffe that tefillin represents God's divine way of sustaining the world. The box of the tefillin worn on the head represents God's dominion that is on top of all existence. The leather straps that descend from the box symbolize God's influence, which reaches to the inner core of the world (represented by the wearer's torso). He further explains that tefillin are called *totafos*, a word based on Phrygian and Coptic, in allusion to the fact that God's rule encompasses the entire world from Phrygia to Egypt (which he assumes are on opposite ends of the globe). *Eitz Yosef* to *Midrash Tanchuma* (*Bo* §14) also quotes Rabbi Yaffe's explanation. Rabbi Tzvi Yechezkel Michelson (1863–1943) in his work *Tirosh V'Yitzhar* (§154) elaborates on Rabbi Yaffe's explanation.

Rabbi Elazar Strashun explains (responsa *Amud Aish* §9) that the Torah uses a foreign word in the context of the commandment of tefillin to teach that this commandment is applicable even when in foreign places (i.e., outside of the Land of Israel); see there for his exact way of explaining this.

441 *Hon Osher* to the Mishnah (*Avos*, end of Ch. 3).

HaKodesh used in the Bible.[442] Based on this approach, some scholars use the degree and style of foreign influence to date books of the Bible.

For example, some argue that *Song of Songs* was written later than the rest of the Bible because the language used in that book seems to reflect *Lashon HaKodesh* as spoken in the Second Temple period more so than other books of the Bible. One of the proofs they offer is the book's usage of the words *apiryon* (אפריון, canopy) and *pardes* (פרדס, garden or paradise), which are *hapax legomenon* in the Bible because they appear only once within that entire corpus of text—in *Song of Songs* 3:9 and *Song of Songs* 4:13, respectively. These words are purportedly of Greek and/or Persian origin.

However, this is not evidence that *Song of Songs* was written later. The fact that the word does not appear elsewhere in the Bible does not prove that it is not of Hebrew origin—lack of evidence is not evidence of lack.[443] In fact, it is equally plausible that the word does indeed originate in *Lashon HaKodesh* and was already in use during the First Temple period, but was only used once in the Bible because it was not used in literature, it was only used colloquially.[444] Furthermore, in cases like these, it is difficult to discern who borrowed the word from whom. It is possible that the Persian word is derived from the Hebrew word, not vice versa.

Similarly, academia points to the usage of the letter ש in *Song of Songs* and *Ecclesiastes* to mean "that" and "of" (a convention quite common in later rabbinic writings) instead of the Hebrew word *asher* (אשר) used in earlier books of the Bible. From this, scholars see that those books were written later than the rest of the Bible and so their form of *Lashon HaKodesh* more closely resembled that of the later rabbinic writings than other books of the Bible do.[445]

---

442 S. Leathes, "Foreign Words in the Hebrew Text of the Old Testament," *Journal of the Royal Asiatic Society of Great Britain and Ireland*, New Series, vol. 18:4 (1886), pgs. 527–542, offers a listing of numerous foreign words used in the Bible.

443 This important logical argument used in refuting proofs is first mentioned in the Mishnah (*Ediyos* 2:2).

444 A. Hakham (ed.), *Da'as Mikra Shir HaShirim* (Jerusalem: Mossad HaRav Kook, 1990), pgs. 12–13.

445 See also R. Holmstedt's article "The Grammar of ש and אשר in Qohelet," printed in M. Boda, T. Longman, & C. Rata (eds.), *The Words of the Wise Are like Goads: Engaging Qohelet in the 21st*

However, this argument is easily countered in light of archeological evidence of Phoenician and Sumerian inscriptions that attest to such usage of the letter ש in Semitic languages at an earlier period. Such usage is even found in the Mesha Stele (which dates to biblical times), thus dispelling the notion that these books were only written later.[446] While this does not answer why the Bible never used the ש in such a fashion in other books, it certainly refutes the idea that such usage is only a later development.

◆ ◆ ◆

Rabbinic literature is replete with examples of Hebrew words that are created by combining other Hebrew words. However, there are also numerous examples of Hebrew words (both in the Bible and in rabbinic literature) which are constructs of words from other languages. The following table illustrates some examples of this phenomenon:

Hebrew Word:	Source language(s):	Source words:	Explanation:
Pilegesh **(פלגש) Concubine**	**Aramaic and Hebrew**	**"Half" in Aramaic *Peleg* (פלג) & "Wife" in Hebrew *isha* (אשה)**	**A concubine has half the status of a full wife.**
Androginus **(אנדרוגינוס) ermaphrodite**	**Greek**	**"Man" in Greek *Anthro* (άνθρωπος) & "Woman" in Greek *Gini* (γυναίκα)**	**A hermaphrodite has the characteristics of both genders.**
Cartigni **(קרטיגני) Carthage**	**Aramaic and Greek**	**"City" in Aramaic *karta* (קרתא) & "Woman" in Greek *Gini* (γυναίκα)**	**The city of Carthage is reputed to have been founded by a woman known as Queen Elissa (the former Princess Dido of Tyre).**
Vayehi **(ויהי) And it was**	**Aramaic and Hebrew**	**"Woe" in Aramaic *vay* (וי) & "Woe" in Hebrew *he* (הי)**	**The Talmud explains (TB *Megillah* 10b) that the term "it was" connotes a painful experience.**
Terumah **(תרומה) Tithe**	**Aramaic and Hebrew**	**"Two" in Aramaic *trei* (תרי) & "from one hundred" in Hebrew *m'me'ah* (ממאה)**	**The Mishnah (*Terumos* 4:3) teaches that the average person tithed one fiftieth of his produce as *Terumah*. (Two hundredths equals one fiftieth.)**

Century (Winona Lake, Indiana: Eisenbrauns, 2013), pgs. 283–307.

446 *Barzilai*, pgs. 275–276, 287.

CHAPTER SUMMARY

In this chapter, we presented evidence to the notion that the Mishnah and even the Bible incorporated foreign words into their *Lashon HaKodesh* text. Examples of such words include *sanhedrin*, *gematria*, *afikomen*, *apikorus*, *totafos*, *damesek*, and *chartumim*. We showed that the rabbis regulated this exchange of words and saw to it that foreign words were not adopted verbatim—the pronunciation and/or meaning were altered before accepting the words as *Lashon HaKodesh*.

- We mentioned two ways of identifying foreign words in the Bible:
    - When the Bible uses a term and then defines it, the fact that the Bible felt the need to define that term shows that it is likely from a foreign language.
    - Many grammarians state that words with quadrilateral roots are generally from foreign languages.
- We offered a very important discussion of why the Bible sometimes uses foreign words. It does so in the same way that it uses other textual anomalies, i.e., as a way of noting that in those places there is room for the Oral Torah to add an additional layer of exegetical interpretation. In these instances, some commentators will explain that the word is of foreign origin, while others will offer rabbinic exegesis precisely because the Bible used a foreign word. Although superficially these commentators appear to contradict each other, in reality they are addressing different questions. The first group explains the word's origin, while the second group answers why the Bible chose that word to begin with.
- Some argue that *Lashon HaKodesh* does not borrow from other languages; other languages borrow from *Lashon HaKodesh*. Therefore, all of the "foreign" words in the Bible and Mishnah are actually in *Lashon HaKodesh*, but these words were also adopted into foreign languages. Sometimes the meaning of a word in *Lashon HaKodesh* is unknown, so the commentators try to

decipher it by searching for the word in the context of other languages, where the meaning is known. According to this approach, statements that a given word in the Mishnah or the Bible is actually from a foreign language are not to be taken at face value. They are merely identifying which foreign language had adopted the otherwise inscrutable *Lashon HaKodesh* word.

- Taking this idea a step further, some propose that the Bible and Mishnah deliberately use words that are also found in foreign languages to show that all other languages derive from *Lashon HaKodesh* (by providing examples of foreign words which originate in *Lashon HaKodesh*).

CHAPTER 8:
Development of Aramaic

THE RELIGIOUS SIGNIFICANCE OF ARAMAIC

Some commentators lend religious significance to Aramaic because it developed out of *Lashon HaKodesh*. Some of them even explain that because of this Aramaic and *Lashon HaKodesh* are considered one language. However, others view Aramaic's development from *Lashon HaKodesh* in a negative light. They argue that Aramaic is a corruption of *Lashon HaKodesh*, making it a disgraceful language. In this chapter, we will explore these varying stances and the basis for their opinions.

IS ARAMAIC CONSIDERED A SEPARATE LANGUAGE?

Rambam rules that bills of divorce (*gittin*) written in more than one language are invalid.[447] In trying to fully understand Rambam's stance, Rabbi Moshe Isserles (1520–1572), known as Rama, and his second cousin Rabbi Shmuel Yehuda Katzenellenbogen (1521–1597) debate whether

447 Laws of *Gittin* 4:8.

Aramaic is considered distinct from *Lashon HaKodesh*.[448] In doing so, they clarify the significance of Aramaic as a religious language and its interplay with *Lashon HaKodesh*. Their debate is printed in Rama's responsa as an exchange of letters between the two.[449] Their overall discussion is quite pertinent to understanding the traditional view of the development of Aramaic and its religious (especially halachic) implications.

ARABIC AS A CORRUPTION OF LASHON HAKODESH

Before we examine their discussion of Aramaic's role, we must first discuss Arabic. Many early commentators write that Arabic is simply a corruption of *Lashon HaKodesh*. This opinion plays a significant part in the discussion between Rama and Rabbi Katzenellenbogen.

Rabbi Katzenellenbogen opens the exchange by expressing his opinion that Aramaic and *Lashon HaKodesh* are considered one language (and thus *gittin* written in both languages are valid). He supports this assertion by stating that just as *The Kuzari* wrote that Arabic is a corruption of *Lashon HaKodesh*, Aramaic is also a corruption of *Lashon HaKodesh*. However, as Rabbi Zvi Hirsch Chajes (1805–1855) points out *The Kuzari* writes no such thing. In a subsequent letter, Rabbi Katzenellenbogen admits that he mentioned *The Kuzari* from memory and that the idea was actually said slightly differently from how he had quoted it. However, *The Kuzari* does say something quite similar in order to defend the honor of *Lashon HaKodesh* against Arabic.[450] As we mentioned quoted in Chapter 1, *The Kuzari* writes:

> Even Abraham spoke Aramaic, the local language in his homeland Ur Kasdim, because Aramaic was indeed the language of the Chaldeans there. Nonetheless, though Abraham

448 The other intricacies they discuss regarding *gittin* written in Aramaic and *Lashon HaKodesh* need not concern us.

449 *Teshuvos HaRama* §126–130.

450 Interestingly, the atmosphere of perceived competition between Arabic and *Lashon HaKodesh* in vying for the title of "most beautiful language" prompted Rabbi Moshe ibn Ezra (1055–1138) to author *Kitab al Muharada wal-Mudhakar* (translated by Dr. Benzion Halper into Hebrew under the title *Shiras Yisrael*, Leipzig, 1924), and Rabbi Yehuda al Harizi (1165–1225) to write *Tachkemoni*. These works sought to prove *Lashon HaKodesh*'s superiority to Arabic.

> held Hebrew to be a special and holy language, he held Aramaic to be merely a mundane language. Ishmael brought *Lashon HaKodesh* to Arabia. These three languages, Aramaic, Hebrew, and Arabic, use similar nouns and rules of grammar, but Hebrew is the most esteemed of them.[451]

While some have attempted to read *The Kuzari* as arguing that Arabic and Aramaic are derivatives of *Lashon HaKodesh*,[452] this argument is not stated explicitly. He simply writes that they are related (as are all Semitic languages). However, the idea that Arabic derives from *Lashon HaKodesh* is certainly implied in the words "Ishmael brought *Lashon HaKodesh* to Arabia." Arabic presumably developed from the *Lashon HaKodesh* that Ishmael brought to Arabia. Although *The Kuzari* does not mention this idea explicitly, several others do:

1. Rambam writes in a letter to the translator Rabbi Shmuel ibn Tibbon (1150–1230) that Arabic is most certainly a corrupted form of *Lashon HaKodesh*.[453] He repeats this assertion again in one of his medical writings.[454]
2. Ibn Ezra writes that *Lashon HaKodesh*, Aramaic, and Arabic are all considered one language.[455] He notes that they all use the same—or very similar—letters, and have other similarities (see there for more specific examples).[456]
3. Efodi, in discussing the relationship between *Lashon HaKodesh* and Arabic, writes that the latter is a corruption of the former.

---

451 *Iggeres HaBikores* (Pressburg, 1853), pg. 39a.

452 See *Otzar Nechmad* to *Sefer HaKuzari* (Vilna, 1905), pg. 78a.

453 *Chovos HaLevavos* (Jerusalem: Mesoras Yisrael, 1993), pg. 84.

454 See *Pirkei Moshe* (Lemberg, 1834), pg. 53a; S. Muntner (ed.), *Pirkei Moshe B'Refuah* (Jerusalem: Mossad HaRav Kook, 1940), pg. 361; and Y. Kapach (ed.), *Iggros HaRambam* (Jerusalem: Mossad HaRav Kook, 1994), pg. 150.

455 Similarly, Ibn Ezra (in his commentary to *Genesis* 30:37) explains that the word *luz* (לוז) mentioned in the Torah means "almonds," because that is the meaning of the word in Arabic (لوز), and "we have already established that *Lashon HaKodesh*, Arabic, and Aramaic are from the same family of languages." Interestingly, Rabbi Yaakov Emden (in *Migdal Oz, Beis Middos, Aliyas HaLashon*) adds that Greek—in addition to Arabic and Aramaic—is also a direct derivative of *Lashon HaKodesh*.

456 *Safah Berurah* (Fürth, 1839), pg. 2b.

> He stresses that one cannot argue that *Lashon HaKodesh* is a corruption of Arabic because *Lashon HaKodesh* is clearly older than Arabic.[457]

These sources (and many others) state that Arabic is a corruption of *Lashon HaKodesh*. Although Rabbi Katzenellenbogen does not mention these sources, he understands that they believe that Aramaic is also a corruption of *Lashon HaKodesh* (which Ibn Ezra wrote explicitly, as already mentioned).

"TO GIVE" IN ARAMAIC

In his first letter, Rabbi Katzenellenbogen offers fascinating proof of his position that Aramaic is a corruption of *Lashon HaKodesh* and therefore they are considered one language. He notes that in multiple instances, the Targumim (that usually translate the Scriptures from *Lashon HaKodesh* to Aramaic) change words from *Lashon HaKodesh* into other *Lashon HaKodesh* synonyms, or leave them untranslated—even in instances where Aramaic equivalents for those words definitely do exist.

Rabbi Katzenellenbogen notes that this phenomenon is especially prevalent in the future-tense form of the verb "to give." For example, in *Genesis* 27:28, the Targumim (Onkelos, Jonathan, and Neofiti) leave the word *v'yitein* (ויתן, you will give) untranslated as *v'yitein*, instead of translating it into the Aramaic *v'yahaveh* (ויהבה). The Targumim's substitution of a *Lashon HaKodesh* word for an Aramaic one shows Rabbi Katzenellenbogen that the two languages are interchangeable and could really be considered one.[458]

RAMA'S REPLY

While Rama's response to his cousin's initial letter has not been published, we can glean what he wrote from Rabbi Katzenellenbogen's second letter, which was penned as a response to Rama's reply. It seems that Rama holds that Aramaic is separate from *Lashon HaKodesh*, and therefore

457 *Ma'aseh Efod* (Vienna, 1865), pg. 33.

458 In fact, Rabbi Avraham ben Eliyahu Kramer of Vilna (1765–1808) authored a work entitled *Tirgem Avraham* (Jerusalem, 1896), in which he sought to prove that every word used in *Targum Onkelos* and *Targum Jonathan* has a source in *Lashon HaKodesh*.

rejects Rabbi Katzenellenbogen's proposition. He brings two proofs for his position. The first involves *Shnayim Mikra V'Echad Targum*, a practice mentioned in the Talmud whereby every Jew is obligated to maintain his connection to the Jewish community by reading that week's Torah portion twice in the original *Lashon HaKodesh* and once in an Aramaic *Targum*.[459] Rama states that many authorities write that the reason why *Shnayim Mikra V'Echad Targum* should be done with the *Targum* is that it was given to Moses at Mount Sinai (an idea which Rama leaves unexplained until the end). These authorities do not write that the advantage of *Targum* is its status as a derivative of *Lashon HaKodesh*. From this conspicuous absence, Rama proves that Aramaic is not a form of *Lashon HaKodesh*. Secondly, it seems Rama argued, the fact that the Targumim leave the word *v'yitein* in its *Lashon HaKodesh* form does not prove that Aramaic is an offshoot of *Lashon HaKodesh* because many languages share words with *Lashon HaKodesh*, yet are not its direct descendants in the sense that Aramaic is.

RABBI KATZENELLENBOGEN'S RESPONSE

Rabbi Katzenellenbogen refutes both of these arguments. He explains that those authorities who mention that *Targum*'s advantage is its Sinaitic origins are explaining the advantage of using *Targum* as opposed to Rashi for *Shnayim Mikra V'Echad Targum*. Both commentaries are written in languages similar to biblical *Lashon HaKodesh*, yet only the *Targum* was actually "given at Mount Sinai." Additionally, Rabbi Katzenellenbogen clarifies that his proof from the *Targum* not translating the word *v'yitein* is contingent upon the fact that an Aramaic equivalent for that word exists. The fact that the *Targum* does not use the available Aramaic word proves that the languages are interchangeable. He did not mean to write, as Rama apparently misunderstood, that the fact that the word *v'yitein* has the same meaning in both Aramaic and *Lashon HaKodesh* proves that the two languages are one.

RAMA CLARIFIES HIS POSITION

In his first letter printed on this matter, Rama clarifies his position and his objections to Rabbi Katzenellenbogen's proofs.

---

459 TB *Brachos* 8a.

He writes that the "authorities" to whom he referred who write that *Targum* is optimal for *Shnayim Mikra V'Echad Targum* were discussing *Targum* as opposed to other possible languages, not *Targum vis-à-vis* Rashi. He points to a ruling by *Hagahos Maimonios*[460] that mentions that some people assume that one should ideally fulfill *Shnayim Mikra V'Echad Targum* either through a commentary on the Pentateuch (such as Rashi) or with a translation of the Pentateuch into one's mother tongue,[461] rather than by reciting the *Targum*. *Hagahos Maimonios* himself rejects this position by noting that the Talmud specifically said that *Shnayim Mikra V'Echad Targum* should be performed in *Targum* (Aramaic) because God gave that language to the Jews at Mount Sinai. It is unclear whether *Hagahos Maimonios* only rejects using one's mother tongue for *Shnayim Mikra V'Echad Targum* or also rejects using a commentary.

Rama explains that since *Hagahos Maimonios* notes that only Aramaic was given to the Jews at Mount Sinai,[462] he rejects any language other than Aramaic for *Shnayim Mikra V'Echad Targum*.[463] Rama repeats his earlier argument that the fact that *Hagahos Maimonios* wrote that Aramaic's advantage is that it was "given at Mount Sinai"—and not the stronger argument that it is a derivative of *Lashon HaKodesh*—proves that it is not a derivative of *Lashon HaKodesh*. Furthermore, Rama wonders how one can reconcile the fact that Aramaic was given at Mount Sinai with Rabbi Katzenellenbogen's assertion that it is a corruption of *Lashon HaKodesh*.[464]

Because of these questions, Rama concludes that Aramaic is not a corruption of *Lashon HaKodesh*; rather it is a separate language entirely.

---

460 To Rambam's Laws of *Tefillah*, Ch. 13.

461 See *Rosh* (TB *Brachos* 1:8) and Tosafos (TB *Brachos* 8a), who also reject this possibility.

462 Maharsha to TB *Nedarim* 37b also makes this claim.

463 Obviously, *Lashon HaKodesh* was also given to the Jews at Sinai. Thus, Rama allows one to fulfill *Shnayim Mikra V'Echad Targum* by reading a commentary in either Aramaic or *Lashon HaKodesh*. Rabbi Katzenellenbogen, however, disagrees.

464 Interestingly, Rabbi Yoel Teitelbaum (*VaYoel Moshe, Ma'amar Lashon HaKodesh* §25) assumes that the explanation that Aramaic was given at Mount Sinai complements the explanation that it is a corruption of *Lashon HaKodesh* (a fusion of the opinions of Rama and Rabbi Katzenellenbogen). Based on this assumption, he reasons that if Aramaic, which was given at Mount Sinai and is to be considered a "holy" language, is still considered disgraceful by the angels because it is a corruption of *Lashon HaKodesh* (see below), then surely Modern Hebrew, which is a manmade corruption of *Lashon HaKodesh*, should be considered at least equally disgraceful.

In the end of his letter, Rama concedes that although Aramaic is not a derivative of *Lashon HaKodesh*, in regard to *gittin* it is not considered a separate language, because both languages were given at Mount Sinai and are thus interconnected.[465]

THE TORAH USES ARAMAIC

Rama raises an interesting point in his final letter to Rabbi Katzenellenbogen. He mentions the Midrash that quotes Rabbi Shmuel bar Nachmani that "one should not look lightly upon the Aramaic[466] language because God 'honored' that language in all three parts of the Bible (Torah, Prophets, and the Hagiography)."[467] The Midrash then proceeds to quote examples of Aramaicisms in the Bible (elaborated upon below). Rama notes that HaBachur also quotes this Midrash (in his introduction to *Meturgaman*). HaBachur understands that the Bible uses Aramaic because it is so similar to *Lashon HaKodesh,* just as Ibn Ezra (mentioned above) writes that Aramaic is a corrupt form of *Lashon HaKodesh*. In this, Rama acknowledges that some earlier commentators held like Rabbi Katzenellenbogen, but he then proceeds to ask a question that delivers a final blow to that view:

Why does the Midrash write that one should not look lightly upon Aramaic because "God 'honored' that language," and not because that language itself is a derivative of *Lashon HaKodesh*?

Rama once again uses the "conscious absence" argument to prove conclusively that Aramaic is not a derivative of *Lashon HaKodesh*—however

---

465 Rama remains consistent with his position. He writes in his glosses to *Shulchan Aruch* (*Even HaEzer* §126:1) that even according to the opinion that *gittin* written in two languages are invalid, a *get* written in *Lashon HaKodesh* and Aramaic is not invalid because both languages are of divine origin and are similar enough to be considered one language (see also *Darchei Moshe* there). Rabbi David HaLevi Segal (*Turei Zahav* there) rejects both the approach of Rama and his cousin Rabbi Katzenellenbogen and, while agreeing to their ruling, he argues that *gittin* written in *Lashon HaKodesh* and Aramaic are valid because they are not considered written in two different languages. Rather, he explains, they are written in "the language of the Talmud," which is largely Aramaic with strong *Lashon HaKodesh* influences, but is considered a third language of its own, rather than two separate languages.

466 Some editions of the Midrash read "Persian language." Nonetheless, many commentators (see *Eitz Yosef* and Rabbi David Luria's *Chiddushei HaRadal* there) have already suggested emending the *Midrash Rabbah*'s version to fit with the Jerusalem Talmud, which reads "Sursi" (see below).

467 *Bereishis Rabbah* §74:12.

similar they might be. He therefore concludes that the only advantage that Aramaic has over other languages is the fact that it was given at Mount Sinai. Finally, Rama explains that "given at Mount Sinai" refers to the fact that the language is sometimes used in the Bible (i.e., entire sections of the Bible are written in Aramaic just as *Lashon HaKodesh*, even though as we have shown previously the Bible uses words from other languages as well).

◆ ◆ ◆

ARAMAIC AS A RESPECTED LANGUAGE

Both Rama and Rabbi Katzenellenbogen view Aramaic as a "holy language," either because it developed out of *Lashon HaKodesh* or because it was given at Mount Sinai. Their view seems to reflect that of rabbinic tradition, as evidenced by Rabbi Shmuel bar Nachmani's warning not to look lightly upon Aramaic. His warning is also quoted in the Jerusalem Talmud,[468] which states that one should not look lightly upon the Sursi language because that language is used in all three parts of the Bible.[469] According to the commentators, "Sursi" is the Syriac dialect of Aramaic spoken in the areas surrounding Aram Zoba (Aleppo), which roughly

468 JT *Sotah* 7:2.

469 The Talmud states (TB *Bava Kamma* 82b) that Rabbi Yehuda HaNassi said that one in Palestine has no need for the Sursi Language. Instead, one can use *Lashon HaKodesh* or Greek, which are clearer, more concise languages. Then the Talmud states that one in Babylon need not speak Aramaic because one can instead use *Lashon HaKodesh* or Persian.

Elsewhere (TB *Pesachim* 61a), Rabbi Yehuda HaNassi himself defines the word *b'michsas* (במכסת) found in the Bible (*Exodus* 12:4) in *Lashon HaKodesh* based on its meaning in the Sursi dialect of Aramaic. From this passage, it is evident that there is a need for Sursi—to help define unknown words in *Lashon HaKodesh*. So why did Rabbi Yehuda HaNassi himself say that the language has no purpose? Rabbi Yosef Shalom Elyashiv (1910–2012) notes (*Ha'aros* to TB *Pesachim* 61a) this discrepancy and explains that Rabbi Yehuda HaNassi did not mean to say that the Torah used a Sursi word. Rather, the Torah used a word in *Lashon HaKodesh* whose meaning is unknown, so the Talmud used the meaning of that word from another language to prove its meaning in *Lashon HaKodesh*. Consequently, Rabbi Yehuda HaNassi said that there is no need for Sursi because *Lashon HaKodesh* was not relying on Sursi, Sursi was relying on *Lashon HaKodesh*. This explanation is similar to the explanation of Rabbi David HaLevi Segal mentioned above (Chapter 7) regarding *totafos*. Nonetheless, this explanation is somewhat lacking because ultimately Sursi does have a use: to help restore the definition of *Lashon HaKodesh* words that have lost their meaning.

corresponds to modern-day Syria.[470] In fact, Rabbi David Frankel (1704–1762), in his commentary to the Jerusalem Talmud,[471] readily acknowledges that Sursi is the dialect of Aramaic spoken in Syria and the dialect of Aramaic used in the Jerusalem Talmud.[472]

After quoting Rabbi Shmuel bar Nachmani's pronouncement, both the Talmud and the Midrash proceed to note examples of Aramaicisms in each of the three sections of the Bible:[473]

1. First, they quote the passage in the Torah (mentioned in Chapter 1) in which Laban refers to the site of his covenant with Jacob as "*yegar sehaddusa*," which means "witness mound" in Aramaic.
2. Second, they cite a verse in the Prophets where Jeremiah said an entire sentence in Aramaic.[474]

---

470 See Rabbi Nosson of Rome's *Sefer HaAruch* (s.v. סרס), Rashi (to TB *Sotah* 49b), and Tosafos (to TB *Bava Kamma* 83a, and TB *Bava Basra* 90b). The Tosafists attempt to prove that Sursi is actually Aramaic by citing the Midrash mentioned above. This lends credence to the editions of the Midrash that read "Aramaic" as opposed to "Persian" (see note above).

471 *Korban HaEida* (there).

472 See HaBachur's introduction to *Meturgaman*, where he draws a distinction between the Aramaic used by the Jerusalemic Targumim (like *Targum Jonathan* and *Targum Yerushalmi*) and the Babylonian Targumim (like *Targum Onkelos*). He writes that the former is a blend because it also incorporates other languages such as Babylonian, Persian, Greek, and Roman (Latin), all of whose kingdoms once ruled Jerusalem. The Babylonian Targumim are written in pure Aramaic. Perhaps the fact that the language of the Jerusalem Talmud is more complex, due to multiple foreign influences, accounts for the perception that the Jerusalem Talmud is more difficult to understand than the Babylonian Talmud. See A. Kashet, *Amri B'Ma'arava* (Netanya, Israel, 2010), pg. 161, for several other explanations as to why the language used in the Jerusalem Talmud is more difficult to comprehend than the language of the Babylonian Talmud.

473 See also Rabbeinu Bachaya (*Deuteronomy* 33:25), who cites more examples of Aramaic in the Bible. Rabbi Elazar Fleckeles (1754–1826) writes (responsa *Teshuva M'Ahavah*, vol. 1 §198) that only Aramaic phrases that are two words or more are significant, but a single Aramaic word used in the Bible does not constitute "honoring" that language. Similarly, Rabbi Baruch Epstein writes in *Safa L'Ne'emanim* (Warsaw, 1893), Ch. 3, that only because those verses contained Aramaic *phrases*, not just Aramaic *words*, did the Talmud use them to prove the importance of Aramaic. However, he notes, the mere fact that the Torah would use an individual word from another language would not prove that language's importance, because it is quite common for languages to borrow words from each other. See above (Chapter 7) for a fuller discussion of the influence of foreign languages on *Lashon HaKodesh*.

474 See *Jeremiah* 10:11.

3. Third, they note an example of Aramaic in the Hagiography is found in the Book of Daniel, which is written largely in Aramaic.[475]

The Talmud continues by quoting a statement by Rabbi Yonasan of Beis Guvrin, who claims that there are only four languages that are truly valuable to the world: Greek for song, Latin for battle, Sursi for elegy, and Hebrew for speech. The Talmud parenthetically notes that some include Assyrian in this list for its script. According to these sources, Aramaic is indeed a worthy language, not a disgraceful one.

ARAMAIC AS A DISGRACEFUL LANGUAGE

Other sources, however, view Aramaic as a disgraceful language. The Talmud[476] states that one should not offer personal prayers in Aramaic because the ministering angels do not understand Aramaic.[477] There are several ways of explaining this passage (as we shall elaborate upon in Appendix C). Among them, Rabbi Asher ben Yechiel (1250–1328), also known as *Rosh*, explains that the Talmud does not mean to say that angels lack the ability to understand the Aramaic language. He argues that if they can read the minds of human beings,[478] then they can surely understand Aramaic. Rather, the Talmud means that since Aramaic is disgraceful in the eyes of the angels, they do not bother listening to prayers said in that language.[479] Indeed, the *Zohar*[480] teaches that while the ministering angels actually do understand Aramaic, since they view the language as overly disgraceful, they do not attend to prayers in that language.

---

475 *Daniel* 2:4–7:28 is written in Aramaic.

476 TB *Shabbos* 12b.

477 See Appendix C "Prayers in Aramaic" for a survey of various traditional prayers that are recited in Aramaic.

478 See *Divrei Chamudos* (there) who questions Rabbi Asher's source for this assertion. See also Tosafos (to TB *Shabbos* 12b) who assume that angels can indeed read the thoughts of human beings. For a more extensive treatment of this issue, see *Biur HaGra (Orach Chaim* §101:12); *Mor U'Ketziah* (to *Orach Chaim* §101); *Sdei Chemed* (Letter *Mem*, §202); and *Megadim Chadashim* (to TB *Shabbos* 12b).

479 *Piskei HaRosh*, *Brachos*, Ch. 2, §2.

480 *Lech Lecha* 89a.

DISGRACEFUL BECAUSE IT IS A CORRUPTION

Rabbi Gershon Shaul Yom Tov Lipman Heller[481] clarifies Rabbi Asher's position by first posing a question: Why do the angels look down upon Aramaic, if Aramaic is so similar to *Lashon HaKodesh*?

He answers that therein lies the key to understanding Rabbi Asher's explanation. Aramaic is so closely related to *Lashon HaKodesh* precisely because it is a corruption of it. Therefore, since it is a corruption of the holy language, the angels ignore all requests made in that language, for it is a disgraceful language.[482]

OPPOSING VIEWS ON ARAMAIC

Rabbi Yissocher Ber Eilenberg (1550-1623),[483] as well as several other commentators, point out that there is a contradiction in the rabbinic attitudes toward Aramaic.[484] On the one hand, Aramaic is praised as an important language that should not be taken lightly. Yet, on the other hand, Aramaic is considered disgraceful—because it is a corrupted version of *Lashon HaKodesh*—so the ministering angels ignore requests made in that language. Similarly, we find that on the one hand Aramaic is a language that is well-suited for Torah literature (e.g., the Talmud and Targumim were written in Aramaic), yet Jacob was punished for causing Aramaic to be introduced to the Torah (as mentioned in Chapter 1). This dichotomy is indeed a curious anomaly, which several commentators have already noted but not solved. It remains a conundrum.

CHAPTER SUMMARY

We opened this chapter with the debate between Rama and his cousin Rabbi Katzenellenbogen concerning the relationship between *Lashon HaKodesh* and

---

481 In his commentary *Ma'adanei HaMelech* to Rabbi Asher's rulings (there).

482 However, concedes Rabbi Heller, according to this reasoning, the same should apply to Arabic. That is, since Arabic is also a corruption of *Lashon HaKodesh* (as mentioned above), it should also be a language ignored by the angels. Accordingly, Rabbi Heller cannot explain why the Talmud singles out Aramaic. See also *Elya Rabbah* (*Orach Chaim* §101).

483 *Beer Sheva* to TB *Sotah* 33a.

484 See also *Olas Tamid* (to *Orach Chaim* §101) and Rabbi Yaakov Emden's *Mor U'Ketziah* (to *Orach Chaim* §101). Rabbi Yosef Palagi discusses this question in *Yosef Es Echav* (Izmir, 1896), pgs. 4b–6b. See also indices to responsa *Maharsham*, vol. 5, §9, who points out this inconsistency.

Aramaic. Rabbi Katzenellenbogen claimed that just as earlier commentators write that Arabic is to be viewed as a corruption of *Lashon HaKodesh*, Aramaic should also be viewed as such. Rama, it seems, disagreed with that analysis. Both rabbis, however, agree that Aramaic is considered a valuable language on par with *Lashon HaKodesh* for its religious significance.

After discussing the debate between these two authorities and the conclusion that their argument has no practical ramifications, we turned to other sources that seem to point to the notion that Aramaic is considered a disgraceful language, not a worthy one. These sources understand that precisely because Aramaic developed out of *Lashon HaKodesh* and it is considered a corruption of that language, Aramaic should be viewed in a negative light. We noted the great disparity between these two approaches and we ultimately were not able to reconcile the differences between them.

APPENDICES

Appendix A: The Scripts of Lashon HaKodesh

The subject of the scripts used to write *Lashon HaKodesh* is complex and expansive, but nonetheless requires special attention in a work on the history of *Lashon HaKodesh*. Therefore, we will present an overview of the various opinions and their implications, but we shall refrain from delving into the intricacies of the topic. The controversy centers on the two scripts:

1. *Ivri* script ("Eberite script," known in academia as the "Paleo-Hebrew" script)
2. *Ashuri* script (known as the "Assyrian" script)

While the latter is the Hebrew script commonly used today, the question is when and how each one of these scripts was used. Much of the discussion concerns a certain passage in the Talmud and its implications. The Talmud in *Sanhedrin* explains:

Mar Zutra ([or as] some say Mar Ukva) said:

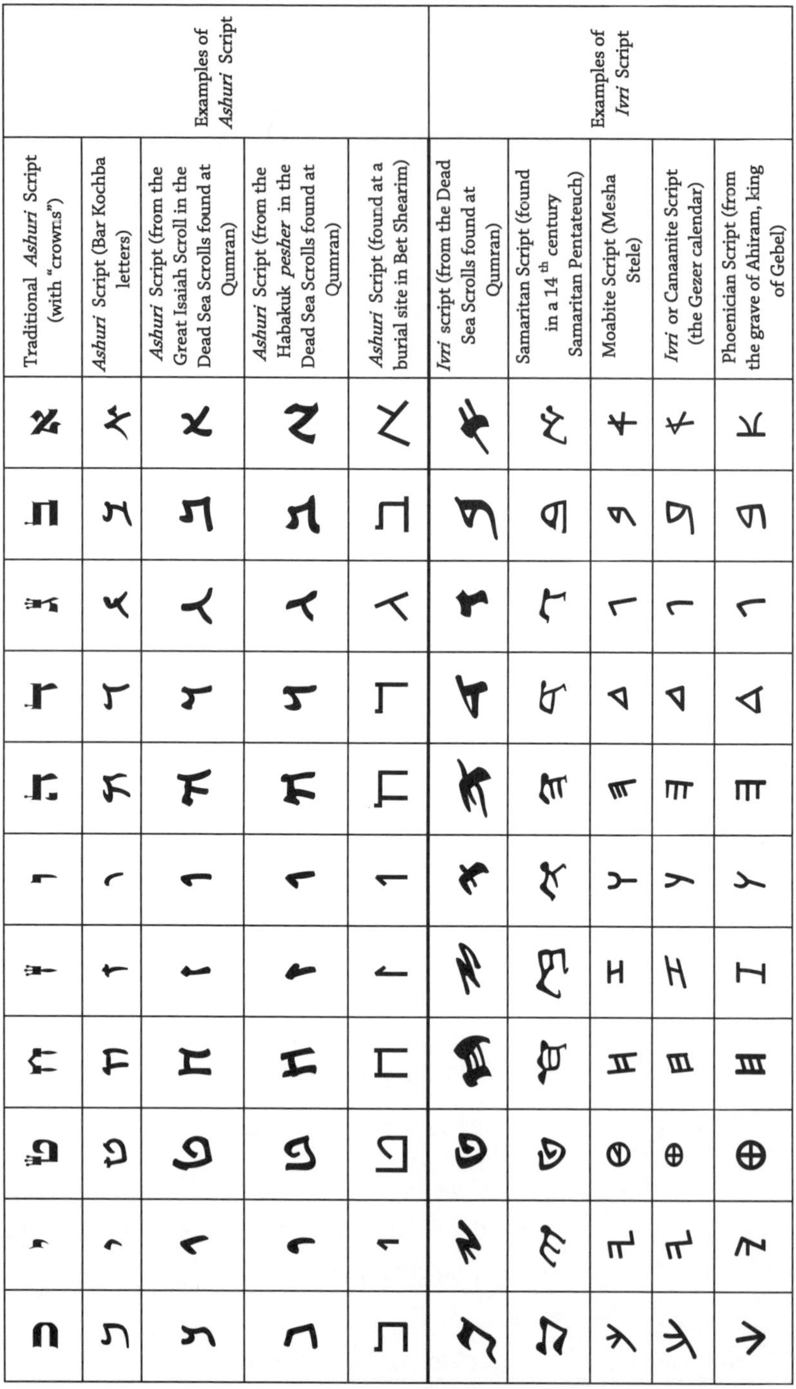
Examples of *Ashuri* Script
Traditional *Ashuri* Script (with "crowns")
Ashuri Script (Bar Kochba letters)
Ashuri Script (from the Great Isaiah Scroll in the Dead Sea Scrolls found at Qumran)
Ashuri Script (from the Habakuk *pesher* in the Dead Sea Scrolls found at Qumran)
Ashuri Script (found at a burial site in Bet Shearim)
Examples of *Ivri* Script
Ivri script (from the Dead Sea Scrolls found at Qumran)
Samaritan Script (found in a 14th century Samaritan Pentateuch)
Moabite Script (Mesha Stele)
Ivri or Canaanite Script (the Gezer calendar)
Phoenician Script (from the grave of Ahiram, king of Gebel)

These fonts were designed by Dr. Yoram Gnat of the Culmus Project based on significant archeological finds. They are licensed under GNU-GPL.

In the beginning, the Torah was given to the Jews in *Ivri* script and *Lashon HaKodesh* and then it was given again to them in the days of Ezra in *Ashuri* script and the Aramaic language. The Jews chose for themselves *Ashuri* script and *Lashon HaKodesh* and left *Ivri* script and the Aramaic language for the "simpletons."

Who are the "simpletons"? Rav Chisda said they are the Samaritans.[485]

What is *Ivri* script? Rav Chisda says *Lebonae* (ליבונאה)...

Why is it called *Ashuri* (אשורי)? Because it came up with them from Assyria (אשור).

We have learned [in a *Braisa*] Rabbi Yose says Ezra was worthy that the Torah should have been given through him, if not for the fact that Moses preceded him...even though the Torah was not given through him, but the script was changed through him..."[486]

WHY IS IVRI SCRIPT CALLED LEBONAE?

Before continuing to quote the rest of this Talmudic passage, we will first interject by listing several explanations as to why the Babylonian Talmud calls *Ivri* script *Lebonae.*

Rashi (there) explains that this refers to a large block (לבנה means "brick") script, but other commentators offer other explanations.

LEBONAE: REVERSE STENCIL

They explain that it is called so because it is a script "written" in reverse stencil. That is, one masks off the form of the letters and marks the space around the form of the letters, so that when removing the mask the background creates a form of that letter, while the marks become

485 Some argue that one of the reasons that the script changed was to separate the Jews from their Samaritan neighbors (whom Sannecherib imported when he displaced the Jews of the Ten Tribes), who adopted *Ivri* script as their own and used it to further their own mockery of the Bible; see *Barzilai*, pgs. 93–94.

486 TB *Sanhedrin* 21b.

the background.[487] With such a style, the script will appear in white (the default background color) while the background will be black (the usual color for writing). This is in stark contrast to the standard whereby the script is written in black and the background is white. According to this explanation, the name *Lebonae* refers to the fact that the script is "written" in white (*lavan*, לבן).

OTHER WAYS OF EXPLAINING LEBONAE

However, other commentators reject these explanations because they only refer to the different size of or technique used in writing the script, which they feel does not justify calling it a completely new script. Thus, they provide other explanations. Some explain that Rashi means that *Lebonae* refers to a special script traditionally used in writing amulets.[488]

Towards the beginning of his work *Mikneh Avram* (Venice, 1523), Rabbi Avraham de Balmes (1440–1523) prints this version of what he calls the alphabet of the *Ivri* script in the name of an ancient work . However, Rabbi Azariah de Rossi in *Meor Einayim* vol. 5 (Vienna, 1829) pg. 276a writes that de Balmes is mistaken and that the script which he printed does not reflect the archeological evidence. The script printed by de Balmes is very similar to the scripts used in descriptions of various amulets in the book *Raziel HaMalach*. For more information, see "Additions and Corrections."

487 For example, this could be accomplished by putting a paper in the shape of the letter "A" on a white background, then spray painting black over it.

488 See Tosafos, *Tosafos HaRosh*, *Rabbeinu Yonah*, *Yad Ramah*, and *Chiddushei HaRan* there.

The Geonim explain that *Lebonae* is a portmanteau for the expression *libo na'eh* (לבו נאה, his heart is pleasant); though they note that such an expression is never[489] found elsewhere in the Talmud.[490]

Rabbi Shmuel Eidels (1555–1631), better known as Maharsha, writes that it is called so after Laban, the maternal patriarch of the Jews, from whom the Jews adopted the script until they got the Assyrian script from Assyria.[491]

This is the ancient (pre-Ezra) Hebrew alphabet as published by the Christian brothers Johann Theodor (1561–1623) and Johann Israel (1565–1609) de Bry in their Latin work *Alphabeta et Characteres* (Frankfurt, 1596).

Alternatively, Tosafos (there) quote Rabbeinu Tam's explanation that *Lebonae* refers to the name of a place. According to the textual emendations *Hagahos HaRashash* by Rabbi Shmuel Strashun (1794–1872), Rabbeinu Tam understood that this place was Lebanon. Interestingly, preliminary research has revealed that the Paleo-Hebrew Alphabet is quite similar to the alphabet used by the Phoenicians who occupied

489 This assertion is not entirely accurate. The Mishnah (*Sotah* 1:5) mentions that during the special ceremony in which a woman suspected of adultery drinks the *sotah* waters, part of the ceremony includes disgracing her by publicly ripping her clothes. The Mishnah says that the officiating Kohen should rip her shirt until the tear reveals "her heart" (chest). The Tanna Rabbi Yehuda opines that if "her heart [chest] is pleasant" then the Kohen should not do so (so that the sight will not arouse the spectators to sin). In this context, Rabbi Yehuda uses the phrase *libah na'eh* (לבה נאה).

490 A. Harkavy (ed.), *Zichron L'Rishonim V'Gam L'Acharonim, Teshuvos HaGeonim* (Berlin, 1887), pg. 181.

491 See Maharsha (there) who writes that the Jews used *Lashon HaKodesh* (which they received via tradition through Jacob) as their *language* even though they used *Lebonae* as their *script* (which they received via tradition through Jacob's father-in-law, Laban). Nonetheless, my colleague Rabbi Yisroel Aryeh Gradmann notes that Maharsha writes elsewhere (TB *Megillah* 3a) that the Jews also received Aramaic as their *language* in a tradition dating to Laban.

Lebanon. This lends credence to Rabbi Strashun's reading of Tosafos that the *Ivri* script originated in Lebanon.

Others explain that place known as *Lebonae* is actually Nablus (the city built on the ruins of Biblical Shechem.) That city is capital of the Samaritans, who are closely associated with *Lebonae*. According to this explanation, the rabbis rearranged the letters of the city's name so as not to refer to it explicitly.[491a]

What does it mean that *Ashuri* script was *ro'etz*?

The Talmud mentions that Rebbi says that the *Ashuri* script became *ro'etz* before it was later restored. The meaning of the term *ro'etz* in this context is unclear and is a point of contention amongst the various commentators:

- According to the Jerusalem Talmud (JT *Megillah* 1:9), *Ra'atz* (רעץ) or *Da'atz* (דעץ) was another name for the *Ivri* script.
- Rabbi Nosson of Rome (in *Sefer HaAruch*, s.v. רעץ) writes that the word means "pain," but he does not explain how it fits into this context.
- Rashi (to TB *Sanhedrin* 22a) explains that it means "forgotten," so that when the Jews began to sin, they "forgot" *Ashuri* and used *Ivri* in its stead until *Ashuri* was later restored.
- Maharsha (to TB *Sanhedrin* 22a) explains that it means "broken", so when the Jews began to sin, they (perhaps miraculously) switched from the rich and elegant *Ashuri* to the "broken" and less elegant *Ivri*.
- Interestingly, other sources have a variant reading of the Talmud, which reads *do'etz* (דועץ) instead of *ro'etz*. Rabbeinu Chananel writes that the proper version is *do'etz* and notes that this word is related to the word *v'da'itz* (ודעיץ, wedged) as used by *Targum* (to *Genesis* 30:38), although he also does not explain how it fits into this context.

LEBONAE IS NAMED AFTER JERAH

Rabbi Avraham the Physician offers a fascinating theory as to why the *Ivri* script would be called *Lebonae*. He explains that the Torah tells that

Eber's youngest son, Joktan, had a son named Jerah (ירח).[492] Jerah's name means "moon" in Hebrew, and is synonymous with the word *levanah* (לבנה), which also means "moon."[493] Thus, argues Rabbi Avraham the Physician, the *Ivri* script was called *Lebonae* (ליבונאה) after Jerah the grandson of Eber.[494]

◆ ◆ ◆

The Talmud in *Sanhedrin* then continues by quoting a Tannaic dispute about the history of the scripts:

> Rebbi says the Torah was originally given in this [*Ashuri*] script and when the Jews sinned, it became *ro'etz* (רועץ) and when they repented, it returned to them...Why is it called *Ashuri*? Because its writing is "fortunate" (מאושר)[495]...
>
> Rabbi Shimon ben Elazar says in the name of Rabbi Eliezer ben Parta in the name of Rabbi Eliezer HaModai the script never changed at all.[496]

THREE OPINIONS: THE TORAH'S ORIGINAL SCRIPT

In which script was the Torah originally written? To summarize, there are three Tannaic opinions on the matter:

Rabbi Yose held that the Torah was originally given in *Ivri* script and Ezra switched it to *Ashuri*.

491a This idea was proposed by Rabbi Dr. Moshe Katz of Ramat Shlomo. See A. Buxbaum (ed.), *Kovetz Moriah*, vol. 391–393 (Jerusalem: Machon Yerushalayim, 2014), pgs. 252–254 and vol. 394–396, pgs. 359–360.

492 Genesis 10:26.

493 This theory can also offer an alternate etymology of the name of the region of Lebanon. Lebanon is generally thought to come from the Hebrew word *lavan* (לבן, white), in reference to the snow-capped Mount Lebanon; see A. Room, *Placenames of the World* (MacFarland, 2005), pgs. 214–215.

494 *Shiltei HaGiborim Ma'amar HaLashon* (Jerusalem: Machon Yerushalayim, 2010), pgs. 577–578.

495 Rambam (in his commentary to the Mishnah *Yadayim* 4:5) explains that *Ashuri* is considered "fortunate" because each letter is distinct from the other, so one cannot confuse letters; and because, unlike other forms of (cursive) writings, the letters do not run into each other, which can cause confusion.

Rabbeinu Chananel (to TB *Sanhedrin* 22a) adds that another reason why the script is called *Ashuri* is because it is *meyushar b'osiyoseha*, "its letters are straight" (מיושר באותיותיה). Perhaps this refers to the squareness of the *Ashuri* script.

496 TB *Sanhedrin* 22a.

Rebbi held that the Torah was originally given in *Ashuri* script, which was subsequently lost and temporarily replaced by *Ivri* until Ezra restored it.

Rabbi Eliezer HaModai held that they always used *Ashuri*.

These three Tannaic opinions are also recorded in the Tosefta,[497] as well as in the Jerusalem Talmud.[498] The Amora Rav Chisda seems to accept the view of Rabbi Yose, because, as quoted above, he offers two explanations in accordance with that view.

We will examine how this dispute has been handled throughout the ages with each commentator building on the opinions of his predecessors.

THE GEONIM AGREE WITH RABBI ELIEZER HAMODAI: ASHURI WAS ALWAYS USED

The Geonim unequivocally write that the halachah is in accordance with Rabbi Eliezer HaModai, who held that the script never changed and that the Torah was originally given in *Ashuri*.[499]

Rabbeinu Chananel (965–1055), who bridged the eras of the Geonim and Rishonim, rules in accordance with the Geonim,[500] as does Rabbi Meir Abulafia (1170–1244).[501] Ibn Ezra also seems to follow this view.[502]

---

497 *Sanhedrin* 4:5.

498 JT *Megillah* 1:9.

499 A. Harkavy (ed.), *Zichron L'Rishonim V'Gam L'Acharonim, Teshuvos HaGeonim* (Berlin, 1887), pgs. 181–182; and C.Z. Taubs (ed.), *Otzar HaGeonim L'Maseches Sanhedrin* (Jerusalem: Mossad HaRav Kook, 1967), pgs. 161–163.

500 In his commentary to TB *Sanhedrin* 21b–22a.

501 *Yad Ramah* to TB *Sanhedrin* 21b. See *Shiltei HaGiborim, Ma'amar HaLashon* (Jerusalem: Machon Yerushalayim, 2010), pg. 574–580 who also rejects Rabbi Yose's opinion.

502 Ibn Ezra writes in his *Sefer Tzachus B'Dikduk* (Berlin, 1769), pg. 7b, that there is a disagreement over whether the script that we now use is the original one used to write *Lashon HaKodesh*, and is called *Ashuri* because its letters "are fortunate;" or is not the original script, and is called *Ashuri* because it comes from Assyria. This is seemingly an allusion to the dispute between Rabbi Yose (who held that the Torah was originally written in *Ivri* and Ezra switched it to *Ashuri*), and Rebbi/Rabbi Eliezer HaModai (who held that the Torah was originally written in *Ashuri*). Regarding this difference of opinions, Ibn Ezra later writes (ibid. pg. 9b) that in his view the script that we use today is the original. (See also Ibn Ezra to *Exodus* 1:16 where he repeats this assertion.)

PROOF FROM THE DECALOGUE THAT THE TORAH WAS ORIGINALLY GIVEN IN ASHURI

Rabbeinu Chananel verifies this ruling from the fact that the Talmud in *Megillah* mentions that Rav Chisda said that the final *mem* (ם) and the *samech* (ס) on the tablets of the Decalogue stood by way of miracle.[503] A miracle was needed because the letters were engraved in the tablets in such a way that the engraving went through to the other side of the stone. Thus, these two letters, which are completely closed, would ordinarily have a middle piece fall out. The Talmud explains that the middle piece was miraculously suspended in the air. This miracle could only take place in *Ashuri* script, in which the final *mem* and the *samech* are closed characters. However, in *Ivri* script, wherein they are not closed characters (and final letters are not even differentiated from other letters), such a miracle is not necessary. Thus, the fact that the Talmud explains that there was a miracle on the tablets shows that the Talmud understood that the tablets were written in *Ashuri,* not *Ivri*.

RABBEINU CHANANEL: RAV CHISDA RULES AGAINST RABBI YOSE

Rabbeinu Chananel was perplexed by the apparent contradiction in Rav Chisda's view. On the one hand, in Tractate *Sanhedrin* he seemed to support Rabbi Yose (that the Torah was originally given in *Ivri*). On the other hand, in Tractate *Megillah* he maintained that the final *mems* and *samechs* in the Decalogue were miraculous—a feat that is only possible if *Ashuri* was used. Rabbeinu Chananel concludes that Rav Chisda's personal position is that the Torah was given in *Ashuri* and that in Tractate *Sanhedrin* he was merely explaining Rabbi Yose's view.

Nonetheless, a thorough reading of the Jerusalem Talmud renders Rabbeinu Chananel's entire proof obsolete.[504] The Jerusalem Talmud quotes the early Amora Rabbi Levi, who said that according to the opinion that the Torah was originally given in *Ashuri* script, then the final *mem* and the *samech* were miraculous (as mentioned above), and according to

---

503 TB *Megillah* 2b; *Shabbos* 104a.

504 JT *Megillah* 1:9.

the opinion that the Torah was originally given in *Ra'atz* (or *Da'atz)* script, then the letter *ayin* was miraculous.[505] Accordingly, when Rav Chisda said that the final *mem* and the *samech* of the tablets were miraculous, he was explaining the miracle in terms of the view that the Torah was originally given in *Ashuri*. However, this does not necessarily mean that he personally subscribed to that view. His statement that there was a miracle remains true even if the Decalogue was written in *Ivri*.

MEDIEVAL COMMENTATORS: EVERYONE AGREES THAT THE DECALOGUE WAS WRITTEN IN ASHURI

Many medieval commentators offer another way of resolving the issue. Their approach also minimizes the implications of the original dispute between the Tannaic sages. These Rishonim include Ibn Shuaib in the name of Rambam,[506] Ritva,[507] Rabbi Yaakov ibn Chaviv (1460–1516),[508] Rabbi David ben Zimra (1479–1573),[509] and Maharal.[510]

They explain that all three Tannaic sages agreed that the tablets of the Decalogue were originally written in *Ashuri* script.

Rabbi Yose (who said that *Ivri* was the original script) maintained that the Jews realized immediately that the *Ashuri* script was so incredibly holy that they decided from the onset not to use *Ashuri* for themselves—even for holy purposes (such as writing Torah scrolls).[511] Instead, they wrote their private Torah scrolls only in *Ivri*, which was the script used by Shem and Eber (hence the name "*Ivri*"). Even the Torah scrolls that Moses wrote

---

505 In the Paleo-Hebrew script, the letter *ayin* is a closed letter and very closely resembles a *samech* in *Ashuri*. If one carefully examines different examples of the Paleo-Hebrew script, one will find that there are several other letters besides the *ayin* which are also closed letters, and, if written on the tablets, should have necessitated a miracle.

506 Z. Metzger (ed.), *Drashos Ibn Shuaib*, vol. 2 (Jerusalem: Machon Lev Sameach, 1992), pg. 354.

507 In his commentary to TB *Megillah* 2b. Rabbi Chaim Yosef David Azulai, in his work *Pesach Einayim*, revisits the topic in light of the objections of Rabbi Shmuel Yaffe Ashkenazi (in several places) to Ritva's explanation.

508 *Ein Yaakov, HaKoseiv* to TB *Megillah* ad loc.

509 Responsa *Radvaz*, vol. 3 §442. He also offers several explanations as to what changed in Ezra's time to allow *Ashuri* to be used in writing Torah scrolls.

510 *Tiferes Yisrael* Ch. 64.

511 Some say that they could not even look at the tablets of the Decalogue because it shined so strongly from its sheer holiness.

and gave to the Jews before he died were written in *Ivri*, although the Torah scroll that Moses wrote and was stored in the Holy Ark was, in fact, written in *Ashuri*. As the generations progressed and the Holy Ark containing the original tablets were hidden, people began to forget the *Ashuri* script.

Nonetheless, even though *Ashuri* was never in popular use, Moses taught the script to select individuals, who passed the tradition down from generation to generation. Thus, when the angel wrote on the wall of Belshazzar, Daniel was able to decipher the script based on his previous knowledge of it through tradition, even though no one else could do so.[512]

Upon their exile to Assyria, the Jews once again encountered the *Ashuri* script (perhaps because the Assyrians had earlier plagiarized it from the Jews), so they began to use it from Ezra's time and onwards, at which point it became the standard script used to write Torah scrolls.

Essentially, these medieval commentators viewed the dispute between the Tannaic sages as being minute:

- Rabbi Yose held that the Decalogue was originally given in *Ashuri*, but the Jews wrote their Torah scrolls in *Ivri* from the onset.
- Rebbi believed that everyone originally used *Ashuri* to write Torah scrolls, and only once the Jews began sinning did the rabbis decide to stop using *Ashuri* and replace it with *Ivri*.
- Rabbi Eliezer HaModai diverges the most from these two opinions, and maintains that *Ivri* never replaced *Ashuri*, which was used for writing the Torah from the onset.

---

512 In light of this, Rabbi Reuven Margolis offers an original explanation of another biblical account. The Bible (*Chronicles* II 34:14–15) mentions that when Hilkiah, the Kohen Gadol in the time of King Josiah, found a Torah scroll he was unable to read from it, and instead had Shafan, his royal scribe, read the scroll to him. Rabbi Margolis explains that even the most literate people were not expected to read the *Ashuri* script, which was used only for the tablets of the Decalogue and the Torah scroll that Moses wrote and stored in the Holy Ark. Accordingly, explains Rabbi Margolis, the Torah scroll referred to in this passage was actually *the* Torah scroll originally written by Moses and stored in the Holy Ark. Since this scroll was written in *Ashuri* and most people at that time only read and wrote *Ivri*, it is quite understandable that even the Kohen Gadol was unable to read from the scroll. Instead, he had Shafan, a scribal specialist and likely a Torah scholar who received training from the leading prophets of his time, read the scroll. See Rabbi Margolis' *HaMikra V'HaMesorah* (Jerusalem: Mossad HaRav Kook, 1989), pg. 31. See above (Ch. 5) for another explanation of this episode.

RAV CHISDA IS COMPATIBLE WITH RABBI YOSE

According to the view of these Rishonim, one can believe that the tablets were written in *Ashuri*, and also believe that *Ivri* was the original script used for writing the Torah.[513] As a result, there is no contradiction in Rav Chisda's opinion. In Tractate *Megillah*, he maintained that the tablets were written in *Ashuri*, and in Tractate *Sanhedrin* he agreed with Rabbi Yose that the original script used for the Torah was *Ivri* until Ezra switched it to *Ashuri*.[514]

FOLLOWING RABBI YOSE'S OPINION

In light of the two ways of reconciling Rabbi Yose's opinion with Rav Chisda's statement in *Megillah*, Rabbi Yosef Elbo, along with other Rishonim, expresses his willingness to adopt Rabbi Yose's approach (even though the Geonim held otherwise).[515] Accordingly, he assumes that the

---

513 Nonetheless, Radvaz (cited below) points out that this explanation is inconsistent with Rabbi Levi in the Jerusalem Talmud. As mentioned above, Rabbi Levi understood that according to the opinion that the Torah was given in *Ivri*, the *ayin* on the tablets was miraculous, while only according to the opinion that the Torah was given in *Ashuri* were the final *mem* and the *samech* miraculous. This is inconsistent with the explanation at hand, because according to this view, there is no opinion that states that the tablets were given in *Ivri*.

Radvaz resolves this difficulty by modifying his view and asserting that everyone agreed that the *original* pair of tablets that God gave to Moses at Mount Sinai were written in *Ashuri*. However, just as they argued about in which script Torah scrolls were originally written, they also argued about in which script the second pair of tablets was written. According to this explanation, Rabbi Levi was only discussing the second pair of tablets, because everyone agrees that the first pair was written in *Ashuri* (and that the final *mem* and the *samech* therein were miraculous).

Rabbi David Tevel Rubin (1794–1861) also came to this conclusion, and then notes that he later saw the idea in Radvaz; see his *Beis David* (Jerusalem, 1904), pg. 32a. See also Y. Zilberstein, *Ma'ase L'Melech* (Vacs, 1913), pg. 3b, who independently arrives at the same conclusion as Radvaz. Rabbi Yaakov Emden also proposed such an explanation (see *Migdal Oz, Beis Middos, Aliyas HaKesiva*), but ultimately rejected it.

514 See also Maharal's *Chiddushei Aggados* to TB *Sanhedrin* 21b, where he explains the differences between Moses' role and Ezra's role in the dissemination of Torah. Rabbi Yitzchak Hutner (1906–1980) elaborates upon and explains some of the more esoteric concepts mentioned by Maharal; see his *Pachad Yitzchak Chanuka (Ma'amar* 10 §3).

515 The only thing stopping Rabbi Elbo from fully adopting Rabbi Yose's view is the fact that Rebbi argued with it. To counter this, he suggests that perhaps even Rebbi might agree to the historical account portrayed by the Rishonim. According to the Rishonim, Rav Chisda, an Amora, supports Rabbi Yose's view. Although Rebbi said that the Torah was originally given in *Ashuri*, perhaps he referred only to the tablets of the Decalogue and not to the Torah scrolls. Further-

Torah was, in fact, originally written in *Ivri* and Ezra switched it to *Ashuri*. He explains that Ezra wanted to institute a memorial within Judaism's rituals to commemorate the Jews' redemption from the Babylonian exile. Thus, he adopted *Ashuri* script to testify to that redemption.[516] (Ezra also decided to use the Babylonian names of months for the same reason; see Ramban to *Exodus* 12:1.)

ARCHEOLOGICAL SUPPORT FOR RABBI ELBO'S CONCLUSION

Rabbi Elbo follows up by noting that when Ramban first arrived in the Land of Israel,[517] he found an ancient silver coin in Acre with a picture of the manna and Aaron's staff engraved upon it. The coin contained a text written in a script that Ramban could not understand. He took the coin to a Samaritan who explained that it was written in the ancient *Ivri* script, which the Samaritans had preserved (as mentioned in the Talmudic passage quoted above). In that script, the text read "*Shekel* of the *Shekalim*" (שקל השקלים). This anecdote reflects Rabbi Elbo's conclusion that *Ivri* was the original script.[518]

Rabbi Elbo and others sought to prove through archeology that the Torah was originally written in *Ivri* from the fact that *shekel* coins have

---

more, Rabbi Elbo notes, even though Rebbi argues with Rabbi Yose's position, Rebbi's opinion is that of one individual. Thus, even if Rebbi would not concede the point above, his opinion is voided by the consensus view. These two rationales allow Rabbi Elbo to decide in accordance with Rabbi Yose.

516 Rabbi Reuven Margolis claims that archeological evidence has proven that even the Assyrians did not use the script known as the Assyrian script. Accordingly, he explains that the script was merely called "Assyrian" to commemorate the Jewish redemption from their exile to Assyria and Babylon, but has nothing to do with Assyria. See *Margolios HaYam* to TB *Sanhedrin* 22a, §2. Rashi (to TB *Sanhedrin* 22a) explains that the new script was revealed through the angel in the story of the writing on the wall (*Daniel* 5). Even though *Ashuri* was *revealed* through Daniel, it was not *instituted* as the used script until Ezra did so. Rabbi Shamai Ostreicher in his work, *Machamadeha M'yimei Kedem to Daniel* (*Shaar* 2, Ch. 1), links this idea to a statement quoted in the Talmud in several places (TB *Sanhedrin* 24a, *Kiddushin* 49b, *Pesachim* 87a) that Elam—i.e., Daniel and his colleagues (see Rashi there)—merited to *learn* but did not merit to *teach*. Rabbi Ostreicher explains that this alludes to the fact that Daniel merited to *reveal* the *Ashuri* script, but not *spread* its usage.

517 Ramban mentions this story about himself in short in the epilogue to his commentary on the Pentateuch. See C. Chavel (ed.), *Pirush HaRamban Al HaTorah*, vol. 2 (Jerusalem: Mossad HaRav Kook, 1960), pg. 507.

518 *Sefer HaIkkarim, Ma'amar* 3, Ch. 16.

been discovered that contain *Ivri* text, not *Ashuri* (a discovery already mentioned by Ramban, above, and Rambam, as cited below[519]).

However, in a letter penned as a response to one such person, Rabbi Moshe Al-Ashakar (1466–1542) writes that the script used on coin inscriptions has no bearing on our discussion because it proves nothing about what language they used to write the Torah. It only shows that the Jews used *Ivri* script for some things, a fact that nobody denies.[520] Instead, he tells his recipient that he understands that he saw what Rabbi Yosef Elbo wrote in his work (mentioned above), and that this explanation is illegitimate and that the truth is in accordance with the Geonim.[521] Nonetheless, a slightly later scholar, Rabbi Azariah de Rossi (1513–1578), highly praises the opinion of Rabbi Yosef Elbo (and only then proceeds to quote Al-Ashakar) who decided like Rabbi Yose that Ezra switched the script for writing the Torah from *Ivri* to *Ashuri*.[522]

---

519 Rabbi Eliyahu ben Binyamin HaLevi in his responsa *Zekan Aharon* (Constantinople, 1634), pg. 82b, understood that Ramban offered his account of the coin that he found as proof of Rabbi Yose's view. However, argues Rabbi Eliyahu HaLevi, one can reject Ramban's proof by explaining that the coin was actually Samaritan in origin. Thus, it used *Ivri*—the Samaritan script—while the Jews always used *Ashuri*. See there for further elaboration on this topic. Similarly, Rabbi Yaakov Loyfer argues (in a lecture freely available at *Kol HaLashon*) that usage of *Ivri* script in coinage dated to the Hasmonean period does not prove that that script continued to be used then. He explains that the Hasmoneans likely revived the script—which already fell into disuse by then—as a means of promoting a sense of Jewish entitlement and culture by using the historic script. This is similar to the way the Israeli government uses the *Ivri* script on New Israeli Shekel coins.

520 Another point must be made when discussing the archeological evidence about this topic. All ancient coins discovered thus far date at earliest to the Second Temple period. This obviously post-dates Ezra's policy change. It would therefore seem that in order for a coin to prove Rabbi Yose's stance, that coin must have pre-dated the Second Temple period. The likelihood of this is quite slim, which is another reason to reject Rabbi Elbo's proof.
Similarly, the fact that many of the biblical texts of the Dead Sea Scrolls found at the Qumran were written in *Ivri* script does not prove that that script was ever used for writing the Torah for several reasons. Firstly, the community at Qumran was not of normative Judaism; it was a sect that rejected the mainstream traditional Judaism of its time. Secondly, the Qumran community almost certainly lived after Ezra switched to *Ashuri* script, so anyway they were going against the prevailing Jewish custom. Thirdly, those texts were possibly not used as ritual scrolls; they were just books used for study.

521 Responsa *Maharam Al-Ashakar* §74.

522 *Meor Einayim*, vol. 5 (Vienna, 1829), pg. 276.

OTHERS WHO RULE LIKE RABBI YOSE

Rabbi Yaakov ben Asher (1270–1340), known as *Baal HaTurim,* also seems to follow Rabbi Elbo's view. In his commentary to the Pentateuch,[523] he mentions that Ezra instituted a new script (*Ashuri*) for writing the Torah, implying that beforehand a different script was used (*Ivri*)—like Rabbi Yose explained. Rabbi Menachem Meiri (1249–1310) also seems to agree with Rabbi Elbo's decision because when he summarizes the Talmudic discussion on this topic, he only mentions Rabbi Yose's opinion (that the Torah was originally given in *Ivri* script and Ezra later switched it to *Ashuri*). The only additional comment that Meiri offers is the caveat that the entire discussion only concerns which *script* (of *Lashon HaKodesh*) was used, not which *language*.[524]

IVRI FOR MUNDANE PURPOSES, ASHURI FOR HOLY PURPOSES

As seen above, some scholars note that the fact that the Jews used *Ivri* in coinage is found in several earlier sources (besides Ramban) and seems to support the notion that the Jews used *Ivri* for non-holy purposes and *Ashuri* for holy purposes.

The Mishnah mentions in several places that the rabbis decreed that the physical scrolls of the Holy Scriptures are considered ritually impure.[525] They did this so that *Kohanim* would not store their *terumah* (holy tithes given to the *Kohanim*) with the scrolls, which would attract mice who would then eat away at the parchment and thereby desecrate the holy scrolls.[526] Nonetheless, the Mishnah[527] declared that there is an exception to this decree— scrolls written in *Ivri* script—since they are not considered holy scrolls. Rambam[528] explains that *Ivri* script refers to the script that the Samaritans use, which differs from the traditional *Ashuri* script. Bartenura adds that historically the Jews also used *Ivri* script for non-

523 *Baal HaTurim* to *Exodus* 15:25.

524 *Beis HaBechira* to TB *Sanhedrin* 21b–22a.

525 *Keilim* 15:6; *Zavim* 5:12; *Yadayim* 3:2.

526 See Rambam's commentary to the Mishnah ad loc.

527 *Yadayim* 4:5.

528 In his commentary to the Mishnah ad loc.

holy purposes (before rejecting it entirely). He bases himself on archeological evidence in which ancient coins found in the Jewish kingdoms used that script, and not the traditional *Ashuri* script. However, he writes that nowadays the traditional script used for writing *Lashon HaKodesh* is *Ashuri,* which was the script used in the tablets of the Decalogue which God gave to Moses at Mount Sinai.

Bartenura's words are echoed in a recently published responsum from Rambam, who writes that the Torah was originally given in *Ashuri* and the tablets were originally written in *Ashuri,* as were the Torah scrolls (which is in accordance with the Geonim's view). Therefore, Rambam rules, since *Ashuri* is a holy script, it is forbidden to write anything with it other than the Holy Scriptures.[529] He writes that historically, the Jews only used *Ashuri* script for holy purposes and used *Ivri* for all other uses. This is why ancient *shekel* coins that are discovered always contain text in the *Ivri* script, not *Ashuri.*[530]

---

529 Rabbi Aharon HaKohen of Lunel adds (*Orchos Chaim, Hilchos Talmud Torah* §9) that for this reason the Sephardic Jews traditionally write in a script that is different enough from traditional *Ashuri* that it can be considered an entirely different script. They use what is colloquially known as "Rashi Script" (which is a misnomer because the script has nothing to do with Rashi). This prohibition is codified by Rabbeinu Yerucham (*Nesiv* 2, §50) and by Rama (*Yoreh Deah* §284:2). Rama (*Teshuvos HaRama* §34) is inclined to rule that one can treat Torah materials written in the popular script differently than an actual Torah scroll because the former is not written in the real *Ashuri* and is therefore not as holy as a Torah scroll. About the origins of these supplementary scripts, Rama theorizes that perhaps they grew out of necessity. Since technically there is a prohibition to write the Oral Torah, people used these alternate scripts to write the Oral Torah without transgressing the prohibition. One can add that these scripts likely grew out of necessity of avoiding the prohibition of using *Ashuri* script for non-holy purposes, as well.

Rabbi Moshe Feinstein (*Iggros Moshe Yoreh Deah*, vol. 3 §120) rules that the prohibition of using *Ashuri* script for non-holy purposes only applies to the exact traditional *Ashuri* used in writing a Torah scroll. But not, for example, to the square versions of the script prevalent in Hebrew publishing, which are mostly considered invalid for writing a Torah scroll (see also responsa *Chavos Yair* §109). Rabbi Feinstein also uses this logic to rule that one is allowed to bring a Hebrew newspaper written in *Ashuri* script into the bathroom (see *Iggros Moshe Yoreh Deah*, vol. 2, end of §76). Nonetheless, this second ruling is somewhat controversial, and is discussed by several recent authorities in their various responsa (see *Be'er Moshe*, vol. 3 §183 and vol. 8 §127; *Tzitz Eliezer*, vol. 15 §7; *Minchas Yitzchak*, vol. 1 §17–18; *Rivivos Efrayim*, vol. 7, §390, and *Teshuvos V'Hanhagos*, vol. 2 §462). Even Rabbi Feinstein's first ruling is not accepted by everyone. For example, Rabbi Aizik Ausband (1915–2012), basing himself on *Aruch HaShulchan* and *Gilyon Maharsha*, extends the prohibition to the popular *Ashuri* script and not just the traditional one. See M. Amsel (ed.), *Kovetz Hamaor*, vol. 27 (Brooklyn, 1952), pg. 10.

530 A. Friemann (ed.), *Teshuvos HaRambam* (Jerusalem: Mekize Nirdamim, 1934), pgs. 5–6; and D. Yosef (ed.), *Pe'er HaDor* (Jerusalem: Machon Yerushalayim, 1984), pg. 17.

TALMUDIC SUPPORT FOR RABBI YOSE

Despite the controversy over whether the Torah was originally written in *Ivri* or *Ashuri* script, later commentators seem to follow Rabbi Yose's view. They explain that in two instances the Talmud seems to unanimously adopt his view that the Torah was originally in *Ivri*, without even alluding to dissenting views. In one place, the Talmud writes:

> Rav Yehuda said in the name of Rav: When Moses ascended to the Heavens, he found God sitting and tying crowns to letters. He [Moses] said to Him, "Master of the Universe, who is stopping You [from revealing the meaning of those crowns to the world right now]?" He [God] said to him, "There is one man who is destined to be after several generations and his name is Akiva ben Yosef. He is destined to expound mounds and mounds of laws on each part [of these crowns attached to the letters]"... He [Moses] said to Him, "Master of the Universe, there is such a person [who will live] and you give the Torah through me [and not through him]?" He [God] said to him, "Quiet! Such has arisen in [My] thoughts."[531]

Rabbi Yitzchak Zev HaLevi Soloveitchik (1886–1959) explains this story by tying it to the topic of the scripts used in writing *Lashon HaKodesh*. He begins by assuming that the concept of "crowns" attached to the letters only exists in *Ashuri* script, and not in *Ivri* script. As such, he explains that when Moses saw God tying the crowns to the letters, he asked why He did not simply reveal the Torah in the *Ashuri* script from the beginning, so that these crowns could already be expounded upon.

To this, God answered that Rabbi Akiva, who would live in a future generation, was destined to reveal the meanings of the crowns. Because He did not wish to reveal the crowns on the letters yet, He originally gave the Torah in *Ivri* script. Eventually, Moses asked God why He decided to reveal the Torah through himself (and in *Ivri)* and not reveal the Torah in *Ashuri* through Rabbi Akiva. God did not answer this question. Instead,

---

531 TB *Menachos* 29b.

He silenced Moses and noted that He already decided that Moses should first reveal the Torah in *Ivri* and that later, after Ezra would switch the script to *Ashuri*, Rabbi Akiva would reveal the meanings of the crowns. Thus, according to Rabbi Soloveitchik, this Talmudic passage adopts the view of Rabbi Yose that the Torah was originally given in *Ivri* and only in Ezra's time was it switched to *Ashuri*.

Based on this explanation, Rabbi Soloveitchik explains an otherwise enigmatic passage in *Sefer HaTagin*, an ancient work about the crowns on the letters. Ramban[532] writes in the name of *Sefer HaTagin* that in the times of Ezra, they copied the crowns from the text of the stones upon which Moses wrote the entire Torah.[533] Why did they need to copy the crowns based on the texts of those stones? Were there not many Torah scrolls in existence from which they could copy the exact usage of the crowns in writing the text of the Torah?

Rabbi Soloveitchik answers that all of this is in congruence with Rabbi Yose's opinion that the Torah was originally written in *Ivri*, and only in the time of Ezra did they switch to *Ashuri*. Accordingly, there were no Torah scrolls that could serve as an example of how to write the crowns on the letters of the *Ashuri* script, because until Ezra's time they used the *Ivri* script that did not have crowns. Instead, they had to look to the stones of Moses whereupon the Bible was transcribed in seventy languages,[534] which ostensibly included the *Ashuri* script as well.[535]

THE PROOF IS CONTESTED

Nonetheless, Rabbi Yitzchak Zev HaLevi Soloveitchik's son, Rabbi Meshullam David Soloveitchik, points out that according to a variant reading of *Sefer HaTagin*,[536] this transcription occurred in the time of Eli the Kohen in the period of the Judges, and was based on the stones which were written by Joshua (see *Joshua* 8:32).[537] The problem with the senior Rabbi Soloveitchik's explanation is compounded by the fact that even a cursory

532 In his commentary to *Deuteronomy* 27:8.
533 *Deuteronomy* 27:1–8.
534 See TB *Sotah* 32a and Rashi to *Deuteronomy* 27:8.
535 *Chiddushei Rabbeinu HaGriz HaLevi* (stencil) to TB *Menachos* 29b.
536 See S. Horowitz (ed.), *Machzor Vitri*, vol. 2 (Nuremberg, 1923), pg. 673.
537 *Shiurei Rabbeinu Meshullam David HaLevi* to TB *Menachos* 29b.

glance at Ramban's commentary reveals that he never wrote that *Sefer HaTagin* was written in or after Ezra's times. In actuality, Ramban writes in the introduction to his commentary to the Pentateuch that *Sefer HaTagin* already existed in the time of King Hezekiah, who lived about two hundred years before Ezra! In other words, the senior Rabbi Soloveitchik misquoted Ramban and built his discussion upon that misunderstanding.

ANOTHER SUPPORT FOR RABBI YOSE

There is a second Talmudic passage that seems to adopt Rabbi Yose's view, thus lending credence to the notion that his opinion is the one to be followed. The Talmud[538] says that each of the three prophets of the Second Temple (Haggai, Zechariah, and Malachi) played an important role, and then explains an important prophecy told by each of those prophets. While not all the sages quoted there agree on which prophecies were the most important, Rabbi Eliezer ben Yaakov says that one of those prophets' most important prophecy is that the Jews should switch the script for writing the Torah in *Ivri* to writing it in *Ashuri*.[539] In this, Rabbi Eliezer ben Yaakov assumes that the Torah was originally written in *Ivri* and only later was switched to *Ashuri*, in accordance with Rabbi Yose's view.

Rabbi Menachem Kasher adds to this the oft-mentioned Talmudic dictum that "the teachings of Rabbi Eliezer ben Yaakov are measured and clean," meaning that we always follow Rabbi Eliezer ben Yaakov's view (even though he did not issue many rulings). Although it is debatable whether this rule applies only to his statements recorded in the Mishnah, or to all of his statements, many authorities maintain that this rule even applies to his statements recorded in *Braisos* (Tannaic material quoted by the Talmud that was not codified in the Mishnah). Thus, this Talmudic passage proves that in practice we follow Rabbi Yose's view.[540]

538 TB *Zevachim* 62a.

539 Although this passage implies that one of the three prophets switched the script—not Ezra—the contradiction can be easily reconciled with a third Talmudic passage (TB *Megillah* 15a), which states that Ezra and Malachi are actually one and the same.

540 *Torah Shleimah*, vol. 22 (Jerusalem, 1927–1992), pg. 138; see *Barzilai* (pgs. 92, 330) who also proves from this that the halachah is in accordance with Rabbi Eliezer ben Yaakov's view. Nonetheless, this reasoning is somewhat flawed because the matter at hand is not a halachik discussion, it is an aggadic discussion.

APPENDIX SUMMARY

In summation, the Talmud mentions a dispute between Tannaic sages whether the Torah was originally written in *Ivri* and was later switched by Ezra to *Ashuri*, or if the Torah was originally written in *Ashuri*, switched to *Ivri* and then restored by Ezra to *Ashuri* or if the Torah was always written in *Ashuri*. This early dispute continued to be a matter of contention amongst later authorities:

- The Geonim (and others) follow the opinion of Rebbi and Rabbi Eliezer HaModai that the Torah was originally written in *Ashuri*.
- Many medieval commentators (such as Rabbi Yosef Elbo and others) and later commentators (such as Rabbi Yitzchak Zev Soloveitchik) follow Rabbi Yose that the Torah was originally written in *Ivri* and Ezra changed it to *Ashuri*. Some of these commentators soften their stance by explaining that the tablets of the Decalogue were given in *Ashuri*, whereupon (due to *Ashuri*'s incredible holiness) the Jews immediately decided to use *Ivri*. Thus, as Rabbi Yose says, from the outset Torah Scrolls were written in *Ivri*, which remained the script of choice until Ezra instituted the use of *Ashuri*.

In truth, we have only scratched the surface of this topic. It has been discussed at greater length and with much erudition by various figures including Rabbi Menachem Kasher,[541] Rabbi Reuven Margolis,[542] the Belgian scholar Rabbi Henri Infeld,[543] two previous Chief Rabbis of the *Rabbanut*; Sephardic Chief Rabbi Ben-Zion Meir Chai Uziel (1880–1953)[544] and Ashkenazic Chief Rabbi Shlomo Goren (1917–1994),[545] and, most recently, the *Talmudic Encyclopedia*.[546]

---

541 *Torah Shleimah*, vol. 22 (Jerusalem, 1927-1992), pgs. 127–146, and vol. 29, pgs. 1–70.

542 *HaMikra V'HaMesorah* (Jerusalem: Mossad HaRav Kook, 1989), pgs. 30–34; and *Margolios HaYam* to TB *Sanhedrin* 21b–22a.

543 Z. Infeld, *Ksav Ivri Ksav Ashuri* (Feldheim, 2008).

544 *Mikmani Uziel*, vol. 1 (Tel Aviv, 1939), pgs. 9–26.

545 See *Machanayim*, vol. 106 (Jerusalem: Rabbinate of the Israel Defense Forces, 1966), pgs. 7–13. However, see Y. Cohen (ed.), *Ohr Torah*, vol. 2:10 (Ashkelon, 1970), pgs. 270–279, who systematically takes Rabbi Goren to task for lack of consistency and unacceptable conclusions, and then offers his own take on the issue.

546 *Talmudic Encyclopedia*, vol. 32 (Jerusalem: Yad HaRav Herzog, 2013), pgs. 509–518.

Appendix B: Egyptian Names in the Bible

As mentioned in Chapter 1, *The Kuzari* posits that the most ancient people, including Adam, Eve, Seth, Kayin, and Noah, spoke *Lashon HaKodesh*. He proves this from the fact that their names have meanings in *Lashon HaKodesh* that suit them. For example:

- The name Adam is derived from the Hebrew word for ground, *adamah* (אדמה), which is an appropriate description because he was created from the dirt of the ground.[547]
- Similarly, the name Eve is derived from the word *chai* (חי, meaning life) because Eve was the mother of all living people.[548]

Although rabbinic authorities almost unanimously accept *The Kuzari*'s basic premise that these ancient figures spoke *Lashon HaKodesh*, his proof from the meanings of their names leaves room for debate.

---

547 *Genesis* 2:7, 3:19.

548 Ibid. 3:20. See also footnote above to Chapter 2 where Ibn Ezra and others reject the proof offered from Eve's name.

DOES THE BIBLE TRANSLATE NAMES?

In discussing the validity of this proof, some commentators point out that in theory these names could have originally been in a different language, based on words in that language. Then, when the Torah was written, those names would have been translated in a way that rendered them similar to the equivalent words in *Lashon HaKodesh* on which their names were based.

Abarbanel counters that when translating a text, one leaves the proper nouns intact—transliterating them, if need be—and only translates the surrounding text.[549]

However, other commentators understand that the Bible does indeed translate names. The most notable case of such an occurrence is the name of Moses, a central character in the Torah. The Bible first introduces the name "Moses" by saying that Bithiah named him *Moshe* (משה, Moses)[550] "because I drew him from the waters (משיתיהו, *meshisihu*)."[551]

The Tosafists ask how Bithiah could have named him "*Moshe*," which refers to him "having been drawn" in *Lashon HaKodesh*, if she did not speak *Lashon HaKodesh*.

MOSES WAS NAMED IN EGYPTIAN

The Tosafists answer that she really gave him an Egyptian name that meant something related to him having been drawn from the waters,[552]

---

549 To *Genesis* 2:23.

550 The Midrash (*Vayikra Rabbah* §1:3) explains that the Bible refers to Moses by ten different names: Jared, Avigdor, Heber, Avisoho, Jekuthiel, Avizanoah (all of these in *Chronicles* I 4:18); Toviah, Shemaiah, ben Nethanya the Scribe (in *Chronicles* I 24:6); and Moses. *Pirkei D'Rabbi Eliezer* (Ch. 48) offers an opinion that maintains that his name was Tov (as opposed to Toviah). The Talmud (TB *Bava Basra* 15a) writes that "Heiman" (a character mentioned several times in *Psalms*) is also another name for Moses. See R. Duke, "Moses' Hebrew Name: The Evidence of the 'Vision of Amram,'" *Dead Sea Discoveries* vol. 14:1 (2007), pgs. 34-48 who discusses evidence of an early tradition that Moses' Hebrew name was: Melchi, Melakhiyah, and/or Melchiel.

551 *Exodus* 2:10.

552 See J. Gwyn Griffiths, "The Egyptian Derivation of the Name Moses," *Journal of Near Eastern Studies*, vol. 12:4 (Oct. 1953), pgs. 225–231, who offers a scholarly explanation of the Egyptian origins of Moses' name. Interestingly, as mentioned there, the publication of that article was sponsored in part by Cecil B. DeMille, who is famous for producing two movies under the title *The Ten Commandments* (1923, 1956).

Is the name "Phineas" of Egyptian origin?

Abarbanel writes (in his commentary to *Numbers* 25:11) that the name Phineas (פינחס, *Pinchas*) is Egyptian.[1] He proves this by noting the similarity between the name Phineas and the name of the Egyptian city Tahpanhes (Daphnae), the place to where the Jews of Jerusalem fled following the destruction of the First Temple, as told in *Jeremiah* 42. The name Phineas also bears a striking resemblance to the name of Tahpenes, the Queen of Egypt mentioned in *Kings* I 11:19 (whose sister married Hadad king of Edom[2]).

Egyptologists in the academic world also assume that the name Phineas is of Egyptian origin and was, in fact, a common Egyptian name, which meant "The Nubian" in Egyptian.[3]

Rabbi Yaakov Emden claims that Phineas was named after his ancestor Joseph (see Rashi to Numbers 31:6) because the first three letters of the name *Pinchas* (פנח) correspond to the letters in Joseph's Egyptian name (פענח).[4]

Interestingly, *The Chronicles of Yerachmiel* (a tenth century Italian work) writes that Pinchas was the name of a son of Magog, son of Japheth, who was appointed as the leader of the post-Deluge family of Japheth.[5]

---

1. According to Abraham Epstein (1841–1918), Abarbanel's source for this etymology of the name of Phineas is the work *Tzafnas Pan'each* by the fourteenth century scholar Rabbi Elazar Ashkenazi ben Nassan HaBavli, who was proficient in Ancient Coptic. See A. Epstein, *M'Kadmonius HaYehudim* (Vienna, 1887), pg. 126. Rabbi Ashkenazi's work was printed for the first time by Solomon Rappaport as *Tzafnas Pan'each* (Johannesburg, 1965).
2. See Ibn Ezra (to *Genesis* 36:31), who writes that this refers to Mehetabel, who is mentioned in the Torah as the wife of Hadad, king of Edom.
3. A. H. Gardiner, "The Egyptian Origin of Some English Personal Names," *Journal of the American Oriental Society*, vol. 56:2 (American Oriental Society, 1936), pgs. 191–192; and M. Berenbaum & F. Skolnik (eds.), "Phinehas," *Encyclopedia Judaica* 2nd ed., vol. 16 (Detroit: Macmillan Reference USA, 2007), pg. 115.
4. *Kovetz Yeshurun* vol. 30 (Jerusalem, 2014), pg. 135.
5. See E. Yassif (ed.), *The Chronicles of Yerachmiel* (Ramat Aviv: Tel Aviv University, 2001), pgs. 120; 122.

and the Torah referred to him by its *Lashon HaKodesh* equivalent.[553] In doing so, the Torah translated the meaning of Moses' Egyptian name into *Lashon HaKodesh*, producing the name *Moshe*. Ibn Ezra also mentions such

---

553 *Da'as Zekeinim* to *Exodus* 2:10.

an approach and writes that Bithiah actually named him Monius,[554] which means, "having been drawn"[555] in Egyptian, and the Torah translated his name[556] as Moshe (משה) because it has the same meaning in *Lashon HaKodesh*.[557] Ibn Ezra notes that *Nabataean Agriculture*[558] also writes that his name was Monius, as do various Greek philosophers. In light of this, Ibn Ezra and some Tosafists evidently understand that the Torah does indeed translate proper nouns, unlike the view presented by Abarbanel and assumed by *The Kuzari*.

---

554 Rabbi Gedaliah ibn Yachya in his *Shalsheles HaKabbalah* (Jerusalem, 1962), pg. 225, mentions this as one of three possible original names for Moses. Alternatively, he writes that Moses was actually named *Tamar* (תמר, date fruit), which is the Egyptian word for "raising" (as in "raising" a foster child). However, the exact spelling of this word is almost certainly a typo. In fact, in two early prints of *Shalsheles HaKabbalah* this name is spelled *Tamur* (תמור); see *Shalsheles HaKabbalah* (Venice, 1587), pg. 95b, and *Shalsheles HaKabbalah* (Amsterdam, 1697), pg. 87b. This spelling is quoted by Rabbi Yechiel Halpern (1660–1746) in his work *Seder HaDoros* in the name of the *Shalsheles HaKabbalah*. The earliest source for the spelling *Tamar* (תמר) is *Shalsheles HaKabbalah* (Warsaw, 1881), pg. 42b, a relatively late print of the work.
Ibn Yachya also mentions that some explain that Moses' original name was Mosh, which is the Egyptian word for "water" (for Bithiah drew baby Moses from the "water"). This explanation gives way to an interesting halachic discussion. Rabbi Shmuel HaLevi Segal (1625–1681) writes in his work *Nachlas Shivah* (on the laws of documents) that someone whose name is Moses and is nicknamed Mosh need not write in his documents "Moses who is nicknamed Mosh," because according to Ibn Yachya the name Moses itself already comes from the name Mosh. However, Rabbi Yosef Shaul Nathanson (1808–1875) disagrees with Rabbi Segal's assertion in his glosses *Chelek L'Shivah* (to *Nachlas Shivah*) and argues that since Ibn Ezra was a greater expert in foreign languages than was Ibn Yachya, we should assume that Moses' original name was Monius, as Ibn Ezra explained. Therefore, he writes that the name Moses is not a derivative of the name Mosh, so someone named Moses who is nicknamed Mosh should in fact write in his documents, "Moses who is nicknamed Mosh." See *Nachlas Shivah HaShalem*, vol. 2 (Jerusalem: Machon Otzar HaPoskim, 2006), pgs. 926–927.

555 Rabbi Baruch Epstein writes in *Safa L'Ne'emanim* (Warsaw, 1893), pgs. 17–18, that he found in some journal that the word *Moshe* means "boy" in Egyptian. S. Leathes, "Foreign Words in the Hebrew Text of the Old Testament," *Journal of the Royal Asiatic Society of Great Britain and Ireland*, New Series, vol. 18:4 (1886), pg. 532, conjectures that *Moshe* in Egyptian means "son of water" or "delivered from the water."

556 See *Moshav Zekeinim* (to *Exodus* 2:10), who writes that it was Moses himself who translated this when he was transcribing the Torah (ostensibly by God's dictation).

557 According to this explanation, the fact that the names Monius and Moshe bear some slight resemblance is merely coincidental, because each name is derived from the phrase meaning "to be drawn from waters" in its own language.

558 The work *Nabataean Agriculture* was written in Arabic by the ninth century Muslim philosopher Abu-Bakr Ibn Wahshiyya and is supposedly an Arabic translation of an ancient Syriac text describing the beliefs of the Sabian religion. Academia believes this work to have been forged (at least in part) by Ibn Wahshiyya himself.

According to these commentators, if proper nouns are also translated, then *The Kuzari's* proof that the original people spoke *Lashon HaKodesh* falls apart because the names of Adam, Eve, et al., could have been translated from another language in a way that their meanings remained.

NAMES LOSE THEIR MEANINGS FROM ONE LANGUAGE TO ANOTHER

However, others explain that when proper nouns are converted from one language to another, they are not translated based on their meaning. Rather, they are adapted to the orthography and naming conventions of the object language so that the reader can better pronounce the names. In other words, the name is not translated; rather, it is adjusted to sound more similar to the host language. Names do not change very much in this manner of adaptation, which is neither translation nor transliteration. For example, the name "Charles" in English and French is the equivalent of "Carlos" in Spanish, "Karl" in German, "Karlo" in Polish, and "Károly" in Hungarian. Similarly, Moses' original name might have been *Monius* in Egyptian. However, the Bible changed it to *Moshe* in order for it to fit better into *Lashon HaKodesh*. When the name *Moshe* was Anglicized (via Greek), it underwent a similar process of modification which rendered it "Moses."

Thus, the meaning of the name only exists in the original language. When the name is modified to fit another language, that meaning might be lost. That is, in the new language the name may not have any real meaning and only reflects the original name with slight changes.[559] Rabbi Yehuda Moscato defends *The Kuazri*'s proof of the antiquity of *Lashon HaKodesh*[560] in light of this method of converting names. He argues that if the names of Adam, Eve, et al. were originally from a different language, then they would have lost their meanings (while maintaining a semblance of their pronunciation in their original language). Thus, from

559 According to this explanation, the fact that the Bible says (*Exodus* 2:10) that Bithiah named the baby *Moshe* is merely coincidentally related to the next clause which states "for she had drawn him from the waters (משיתיהו)." The Bible used the word Moshe simply because it is orthographically similar to *Monius*, not because it is derived from the word *meshisihu* (משיתיהו). It seems that according to this view, the Hebrew meaning of *Tzafnas Pane'ach* is also of mere coincidence, for the name was simply a Hebraization of a similar-sounding Egyptian one (see below).

560 *The Kuzari* (Warsaw, 1885), pg. 154.

the fact that the meanings of their names in *Lashon HaKodesh* do fit them, one can prove that their names were originally given in that language.

MOSES WAS NAMED IN LASHON HAKODESH

The discussion above is based on the assumption that the name *Moshe* was originally given in Egyptian. However, others argue that Moses' name is not of Egyptian origin at all. As alternate explanations to the one quoted above, Ibn Ezra and the Tosafists[561] propose that Bithiah, the daughter of Pharaoh, learned *Lashon HaKodesh* from the Jews enslaved in her country, and named the child *Moshe* in *Lashon HaKodesh*.

Alternatively, Abarbanel explains that when the Torah says, "And she said, 'Because he was drawn from the waters,'" the antecedent of the word "she" refers not to Bithiah, but to Moses' mother Jochebed; so Moses' mother, then, gave him his name, not Bithiah.[562] It is understandable that she would name him in *Lashon HaKodesh* because she was Jewish and spoke that language. Abarbanel notes that this does not contradict what Ibn Ezra wrote in the name of *Nabataean Agriculture* that Moses' Egyptian name was Monius. According to the Ibn Ezra, his original name was "Moshe" in *Lashon HaKodesh* and adapted into Egyptian, is rendered Monius. He explains the variance between these two names by arguing that the *sh*-sound in the *Lashon HaKodesh* version morphed into an *s*-sound[563] in Egyptian, and the linguistic conversion somehow added an extra *n*-sound.[564] (See there for further information.)

---

561 *Da'as Zekeinim* to *Exodus* 2:10.

562 To *Exodus* ibid.

563 A famous example of the *sh*-sound morphing into an *s*-sound is already found in the Bible (*Judges* 12:5–6 and Radak there). When Jephtah massacred the Ephraimites, he was able to discern who was from the tribe of Ephraim by asking them to say the word *shibboles* (שיבולת), which they pronounced as *sibboles* (סיבולת). This phenomenon is found amongst Lithuanian Jews, some of whom confuse the *sh*-sound with the *s*-sound (see *Barzilai*, pg. 100). See also Rashi to *Amos* 7:14. Incidentally, in explaining that episode, Radak uses the letter ת (without a dot) to denote the *s*-sound, which is reflective of the Ashkenazic custom (as opposed to the Sephardic custom of pronouncing both ת and תּ as a *t*-sound). This is noteworthy because Radak was a Provencal scholar, and, as we have previously mentioned (in a note to Chapter 5), Provence was in general more strongly influenced by Spanish Jewry than by French Jewry.

564 See Rabbi Shmuel Strashun's *Hagahos HaRashash* (to TB *Yoma* 34b), who notes in a totally unrelated discussion that *Lashon HaKodesh* words converted to Aramaic commonly have an extra *n*-sound.

THE NAME TZAFNAS PANE'ACH IS EGYPTIAN

Similarly, when the Torah mentioned that Pharaoh called Joseph "*Tzafnas Pane'ach*" (צפנת פענח, which can mean "decipherer of mysteries"[565] in *Lashon HaKodesh),* Ibn Ezra[566] writes that he is unsure whether this name is Egyptian or a *Lashon HaKodesh* translation of an Egyptian name. Ibn Ezra's uncertainty is reflected in his two opposing explanations of Moses' name where he explained that the name is either from Egyptian or from *Lashon HaKodesh* (as mentioned above).

Other commentators (including Ralbag there) assume that it is indeed an Egyptian name.[567] Rashbam writes that Pharaoh gave Joseph an Egyptian name,[568] just as Nebuchadnezzar gave Daniel and his colleagues Aramaic names.[569]

Radak also sides with these commentators and questions those who maintain that the name *Tzafnas Pane'ach* is *Lashon HaKodesh* by asking how Pharaoh knew *Lashon HaKodesh*.[570] This question is strengthened based on the sources mentioned in Chapter 4, which all assume that the Pharaoh in Joseph's time did not speak *Lashon HaKodesh*. Furthermore, the word *pane'ach* does not appear anywhere

---

565 See M. Kasher, *Torah Shleimah*, vol. 6 (Jerusalem, 1927–1992), pgs. 1554–1556, who cites several other interpretations in this manner. Interestingly, he cites *Mincha Belulah* (to *Genesis* 41:45), who writes that Joseph's Egyptian name was Monius, which bears the same meaning as *Tzafnas Pane'ach* does in *Lashon HaKodesh*. Rabbi Kasher writes that this explanation is simply a mistake, for it was Moses whose Egyptian name was Monius (as mentioned above), not Joseph.
See also Rabbi Naftali Tzvi Yehuda Berlin's *Chumash HaEmek Davar* (to *Genesis* 41:45), who offers a different explanation of the meaning of *Tzafnas Pane'ach* in *Lashon HaKodesh*.

566 To *Genesis* 41:45.

567 Rabbi Aryeh Kaplan (1934–1983) in *The Living Torah* (New York: Maznaim Publishing Corporation, 1985), pg. 207, shows how to write this name in Egyptian hieroglyphics and explains its meaning as either "lord of life", "Neth speaks life", or "The god speaks and [this man] lives." S. Leathes, "Foreign Words in the Hebrew Text of the Old Testament," *Journal of the Royal Asiatic Society of Great Britain and Ireland*, New Series, vol. 18:4 (1886), pg. 532, writes that the term means "redemption of the age" or "savior of his time." Egyptologists have proposed several other meanings of this name, explaining that it can mean "the man who knows things," "the God has said: "he will live," "food, sustenance of the land, is living," or "[he] who is called 'Ip-Ankh ['who recognizes life']." See J. K. Hoffmeier, *Israel in Egypt* (Oxford University Press, 1996), pg. 86.

568 To *Genesis* 41:45.

569 *Daniel* 1:7.

570 To *Genesis* 41:45.

else in the Bible, which leads one to believe that the word is not *Lashon HaKodesh*.[571]

These commentators must have understood that the Torah either translated or otherwise adapted the Egyptian name into *Lashon HaKodesh*.

THE NAME TZAFNAS PANE'ACH IS LASHON HAKODESH

On the other hand, Ibn Ezra and the Tosafists (cited above) explain that just as Moses' name was originally given in *Lashon HaKodesh*, Pharaoh named Joseph *Tzafnas Pane'ach* in *Lashon HaKodesh*. They explain that Pharaoh understood *Lashon HaKodesh* and therefore gave Joseph a Hebrew name.

Similarly, Ramban and Rabbeinu Bachaya write that since Canaan, where the spoken language was *Lashon HaKodesh*, was geographically so close to Egypt, it is quite understandable that Pharaoh spoke *Lashon HaKodesh*.[572] In this, Ramban remains consistent with his own opinion (as mentioned above in Chapter 4) that *Lashon HaKodesh* was the language spoken by the Canaanites.

However, these commentators, who evidently understood that Pharaoh did speak *Lashon HaKodesh*, are clearly at odds with the Talmud (as mentioned in Chapter 4), which asserted that he did not.[573]

Alternatively, Ramban proposes that Pharaoh asked Joseph to translate the description of "decipherer of mysteries" into *Lashon HaKodesh*, and gave him that as a name.

TZAFNAS PANE'ACH IS NOT A NAME

Interestingly, Rabbi Mordechai Corcos (1890–1954) explains that *Tzafnas Pane'ach* was not a name at all:[574] it was simply a title or description that Pharaoh conferred upon Joseph. Accordingly, since it was not a

---

571 Ibn Kaspi writes (*Mishneh Kesef* to *Genesis* 41:45) that this argument is invalid, because the fact that the Bible does not use a word does not prove that the word is not *Lashon HaKodesh*, for there are many words in *Lashon HaKodesh* that are not mentioned in the Bible. In fact, he writes, much of *Lashon HaKodesh* has been lost and only some of its words have been preserved, a notion already discussed several times in this work.

572 In their commentaries to *Genesis* 41:45.

573 Perhaps they understood that Pharaoh originally did not know *Lashon HaKodesh* and was initially unable to learn it from Joseph, but was subsequently able to pick up the language.

574 *Gedulas Mordechai* (Bene Barak, 1978), pg. 176.

name, rather a title, one could easily argue that the Bible translated the meaning of this title, even though in general, proper nouns are not to be translated. This explanation fits with the Talmudic understanding that Pharaoh did not speak *Lashon HaKodesh*, while still maintaining that *Tazfnas Pan'each* is in *Lashon HaKodesh*.

APPENDIX SUMMARY

We began this section by again mentioning *The Kuzari*'s assertion that the first humans spoke *Lashon HaKodesh*, which he supports by pointing out that their names were in *Lashon HaKodesh*. He proves this by pointing out that their names bear relevant meanings in that language. However, the commentators present a few approaches as to whether and how names are translated. These approaches have ramifications on the validity of *The Kuzari*'s proof:

- Abarbanel states that names are never translated; they are merely transliterated (in which case the names lose their meaning in the new language).
- Others disagree with him, and believe that names are translated based on their meanings.
- A third group says that names are neither transliterated nor translated. They are adapted to sound similar to the new language (usually divesting them of their meaning in the original language).

We discussed these ideas in the context of the names *Moshe* and *Tzafnas Pane'ach*.

- *Moshe*:
    - Some assume that Moses was originally given an Egyptian name, whose meaning was related to him having been drawn from the waters. This may have been *Monius* (as attested to by ancient historians) and the Bible then translated or adapted this Egyptian name into *Lashon HaKodesh*.
    - *Abarbanel*, on the other hand, argues the opposite: his true, original name was *Moshe* (in *Lashon HaKodesh*), while

the Egyptians adapted this name and called him *Monius*. Assuming that Moses was originally named *Moshe* in *Lashon HaKodesh*, the entire discussion of whether and how the Bible translated his name is moot.

- *Tzafnas Pane'ach:*
  - Similarly, we discussed whether Joseph's name *Tzafnas Pane'ach* was in Egyptian or *Lashon HaKodesh*. The claim of some commentators that it was in Egyptian is strengthened by the fact that the Talmud states that Pharaoh did not speak *Lashon HaKodesh*.
  - However, others say that *Tzafnas Pane'ach* was, in fact, a *Lashon HaKodesh* name. They explain either that Pharaoh spoke *Lashon HaKodesh* or that he asked Joseph to translate "decipherer of mysteries" into *Lashon HaKodesh* and gave him that as a name.

◆ ◆ ◆

COMPOSITION OF EGYPTIAN NAMES

In a somewhat related topic, Rabbi Yaakov Kamenetsky (1891–1986) offers a fascinating discussion on Egyptian names in the Bible. He writes that all Egyptian names mentioned in the Torah have at least two out of the first three letters of Pharaoh's name (פרעה). The name Potifera (פוטיפרע) has three of those letters. Similarly, Shifra (שפרה) and Puah (פועה)—the Egyptian names of the Jewish midwives[575]—also contain letters from Pharaoh's name.[576] The same is true of the Egyptian place-names Ramses (רעְמסס) and Ra'amses (רעַמסס).

575 See TB *Sotah* 11b.

576 Rabbi Kamenetsky (*Emes L'Yaakov* to *Exodus* 7:27) also suggests, for the same reason, that the word *tzefardea* (צפרדע, the second of the Ten Plagues, commonly translated as "frog") is Egyptian, and therefore need not conform to the grammatical standards of *Lashon HaKodesh*. HaBachur (*HaBachur, Ma'amar* 4, §3) already posited that the word *tzefardea* (צפרדע) is not from *Lashon HaKodesh* in line with his rule that we mentioned above (Ch. 7), that any word whose *shoresh* has more than three letters is likely foreign.

THE NAME "EPHRAIM" IS EGYPTIAN

Based on this premise, Rabbi Kamenetsky posits that the name Ephraim (אפרים) is also Egyptian. This indicates that Ephraim was more immersed in Egyptian culture than was his brother Menashe (מנשה), for the latter's name is in *Lashon HaKodesh*.

Another indicator of this is that although Rashi[577] writes that Menashe spoke *Lashon HaKodesh* and served as Joseph's translator, one does not find that Ephraim spoke *Lashon HaKodesh*. Menashe was the older of the two siblings and grew up less immersed in Egyptian culture, because his father Joseph had not yet settled comfortably in Egyptian social life. It was only by the time of Ephraim's birth that Joseph was socially accepted in Egypt, so Ephraim was raised under a stronger Egyptian influence.

In light of all this, Rabbi Kamenetsky explains that it is understandable why Jacob sought to give the more prominent blessing to Ephraim, even though Menashe was the firstborn.[578] Ephraim needed a stronger blessing in order to be on par with Reuben and Simeon, and overcome the evils of Egyptian influence.[579]

JARHA AS AN EGYPTIAN NAME

Although Rabbi Kamenetsky does not mention this, there is another name in which his theory can be reconfirmed. Ibn Ezra in *Sefer Tzachus B'Dikduk* writes that the combination of letters חע (in that order) is non-existent in *Lashon HaKodesh* because it is very difficult to pronounce properly. He then points to a possible difficulty from a biblical passage,[580] which says that Sheshan married his Egyptian servant Jarha (ירחע) to his daughter, and the name Jarha uses this unique combination of letters. Ibn Ezra answers that the name "Jarha" is actually Egyptian, not *Lashon HaKodesh*, so it can understandably use a combination of letters that is generally absent in *Lashon HaKodesh*.[581]

---

577 To *Genesis* 42:23.

578 See ibid. 48:13–20.

579 *Emes L'Yaakov* to *Genesis* 41:51, 48:5.

580 *Chronicles* I 2:35.

581 *Sefer Tzachus B'Dikduk* (Berlin, 1769), pg. 7b.

This name not only conforms to Rabbi Kamenetsky's formula (it contains the letters ר and ע from Pharaoh's name), but also supports his basic premise that foreign words used in the Bible need not necessarily conform to the normal rules of *Lashon HaKodesh*.[581a]

Interestingly, none of the Egyptian names mentioned above fit with Rabbi Kamenetsky's rubric for identifying Egyptian names in the Bible. That is, Monius,[582] Phineas, Tahpanhes, and Tahpenes (see insert) do not contain any letters from the Pharaoh's name. The two-word name for Joseph, *Tzafnas Pane'ach*, does contain two out of the three letters of the Pharaoh's name, but only one per word.

581a In 2015, a new volume of Rabbi Kamenetsky's work *Emes L'Yaakov* was printed. This volume is a commentary to the Prophets/Hagiography and in several places, Rabbi Kamenetsky again discusses this idea (see Samuel I 17:5; Kings I 4:9, 6:8; Kings II 17:6; and Daniel 3:5).

582 The same is true of the two other possible Egyptian names for Moses that Ibn Yachya quoted (mentioned above).

Appendix C: Prayers in Aramaic

ANGELS DO NOT UNDERSTAND ARAMAIC

As we mentioned in Chapter 8, the Talmud warns one not to offer personal prayers in Aramaic because the ministering angels do not recognize prayers offered in that language.[583]

What does this mean? There are several approaches:

Some Tosafists[584] take the Talmud's assertion at face value and assume that angels literally do not understand Aramaic.[585]

---

583 TB *Shabbos* 12b.

584 See *Tosafos HaRosh* (to TB *Sotah* 33a and *Shabbos* 12b), Tosafos Shantz/Évreux (to TB *Sotah* 33a), *Akeidas Yitzchak* (Gate 58), and *Pri Chadash* (*Orach Chaim* §101).

585 Maharsha (TB *Sotah* 33a) notes that the angel Gabriel knows Aramaic because, as mentioned above (Ch. 4), he taught all seventy languages to Joseph. However, explains Maharsha, one should still not pray in Aramaic because Gabriel is probably not the angel charged with presenting prayers to God. See *Zohar* (*Pekudei* 245a) that lists the names of those angels charged with presenting prayers before God and, indeed, Gabriel's name is not mentioned there. (In this, Maharsha assumes that Aramaic is considered one of the seventy languages; see Appendix D "Maharal on *Lashon HaKodesh* and Aramaic" for Maharal's view on this point.)
When Nebuchadnezzar saw Ezekiel's miraculous resurrection of the dead at the Valley of Durah, he began to sing God's praises. The Talmud (TB *Sanhedrin* 92b) declares that had an angel not

ANGELS ONLY UNDERSTAND LASHON HAKODESH

Some of these commentators explain that the angels only understand *Lashon HaKodesh*,[586] to the exclusion of every other language.[587] Some explain that the angels only understand *Lashon HaKodesh* because it alone is a "natural language," while all other languages are artificial and man-made.[588]

ANGELS DO UNDERSTAND ARAMAIC

However, Rabbeinu Tam feels that the Talmud did not really mean that the angels do not understand Aramaic. Rather, they actually do understand it, but for whatever reason do not listen to prayers in that language.[589] Support of this view can be seen in *Daniel* 5, which records the story of the "writing on the wall" where an angel wrote an Aramaic

---

come to hit Nebuchadnezzar on his mouth and stop him, his eloquent praises would have put King David's *Psalms* to shame. Maharsha (there) asks how the angel knew that Nebuchadnezzar was singing the praises of God, if Nebuchadnezzar spoke Aramaic and the angels do not understand Aramaic. Maharsha answers that only accusatory angels do not understand Aramaic, but these angels were angels of mercy (who were trying to help preserve the Jews' monopoly on singing God's praises), and angels of mercy do indeed understand Aramaic. (Other answers to Maharsha's question include the notion that Nebuchadnezzar did not sing God's praises in Aramaic, rather he sang them in another language, perhaps Sumerian or even *Lashon HaKodesh*.)

Rabbi Chaim Shraga Feivel Frank (*Toldos Zev* to TB *Shabbos* 12b) questions Maharsha's assumption that angels of mercy do indeed understand Aramaic. If so, why does the Talmud advise that one should not pray in Aramaic? The angels of mercy understand Aramaic, and one would be better off if the accusatory angels did not understand his prayers! Thus, Rabbi Frank concludes that the Talmud itself contradicts Maharsha's explanation. Instead, he offers an alternate answer to Maharsha's question by explaining that the angel who stopped Nebuchadnezzar's singing was actually Gabriel who—as Maharsha himself agrees—understands Aramaic. See also *Shibbolei HaLeket* (§282) who lists Gabriel, Michael, and Metatron as angels who understand Aramaic.

586 So, why did the Talmud only warn against praying in Aramaic? Maharsha (TB *Sotah* 33a) explains that the Talmud singled out Aramaic to note that even though Aramaic is important because it was given at Mount Sinai (as explained above in Chapter 8), one should still pray only in *Lashon HaKodesh*, not Aramaic. Alternatively, Rabbi Yaakov Emden (*Mor U'Ketziah* to *Orach Chaim* §101) writes that the Talmud singled out Aramaic because at the time it was the most commonly spoken language besides *Lashon HaKodesh*.

587 Raavad in responsa *Tamim De'im* §184.

588 See Maharal's *Chiddushei Aggados* (TB *Sotah* 33a).

589 According to Tosafos Shantz (to TB *Shabbos* 12b), Rabbeinu Tam understood that because the angels do not normally speak Aramaic, they choose to ignore prayers in that language. This requires further explanation.

phrase on the wall of King Belshazzar's palace and only Daniel was able to read it properly. If the angel's message was in Aramaic, then the angel was obviously familiar with that language. This position is also evident from the *Zohar* and from *Rosh*, who, as mentioned in Chapter 8, explain that the angels ignore requests offered in Aramaic because they view that language as disgraceful.

WHY ANGELS IGNORE PRAYERS IN ARAMAIC

Rabbi Yehuda bar Yakar (1150–1250) explains that angels understand all languages—especially Aramaic, which is very similar to *Lashon HaKodesh*. However, God commanded them to ignore prayers offered in Aramaic to prevent people from neglecting to study *Lashon HaKodesh* and ending up living as ignoramuses.[590] Rabbi Perachya ben Nissim (a twelfth to thirteenth-century Talmudist) takes a similar position.[591] He writes that the Talmud means that there is a punishment for those who "do not bother" to learn *Lashon HaKodesh* and instead rely on Aramaic for prayer. God punishes them by having the angels "not bother" to listen to their prayers. According to this explanation, the angels do understand Aramaic, but they ignore the prayers of those who "cannot bother" to learn *Lashon HaKodesh*.[592]

---

590 Rabbi Yehuda bar Yakar's explanation is also printed in Y. Lipschitz (ed.), *Leket Rishonim Sotah* (Jerusalem: Mossad HaRav Kook, 1998), pgs. 34–36, and is quoted by Raavad in responsa *Tamim De'im* §184.

In his commentary to the *Siddur* (Jewish prayer book), Rabbi Yehuda bar Yakar writes that Aramaic is actually a clearer and more concise language than *Lashon HaKodesh*. If the angels would understand Aramaic, then people would pray in that language, allowing *Lashon HaKodesh* to fall to the wayside. Since this would result in disrespect for *Lashon HaKodesh*, God arranged that the angels would not be able to understand Aramaic, forcing *Lashon HaKodesh* to be used for prayer. He explains that in a similar vein the rabbis instituted *Shnayim Mikra V'Echad Targum* be said twice in *Lashon HaKodesh* and only once in Aramaic, in order to avoid disrespecting *Lashon HaKodesh* by affording it the same honor given to Aramaic. See S. Yerushalmi (ed.), *Pirush HaTefillos V'HaBrachos (Ri bar Yakar)*, vol. 1 (Jerusalem: Meor Yisrael Publications, 1979), pgs. 19–22.

591 In his commentary to TB *Shabbos* 12b.

592 According to Rabbi Perachya's explanation, only one who does not know *Lashon HaKodesh* should not pray in Aramaic, but one who knows *Lashon HaKodesh* may. However, Rabbi Yaakov Emden writes the exact opposite. He contends that the Talmud only means to say that one who knows *Lashon HaKodesh* should not pray in another language, but one who does not know *Lashon HaKodesh* may pray in whatever language he does know (see below).

◆ ◆ ◆

CASES IN WHICH THE TALMUD ALLOWS FOR PRAYERS IN ARAMAIC

The Talmud itself notes two exceptions to the rule of not praying in Aramaic:

The first exception is for prayers recited in an ill person's presence when praying for his recovery, which may be said in Aramaic. The Talmud justifies this exception by noting that God's Holy Presence is in the company of a sick person. Rabbi Perachya justifies this exception by explaining that a sickly person is an exception to this rule because since he is praying out of pain and desperation and he humbles himself before his Lord, he is granted a special charm from Heaven that allows for his prayers to be heeded to—even if he prays in Aramaic.

The Talmud elsewhere offers an exception for any prayer offered in the presence of a communal gathering of Jews (*minyan*).[593] It implies that such prayers may be recited in Aramaic because the Holy Presence joins in when a community gathers in prayer. When one prays alone, angels function as messengers who deliver one's prayers to God. Thus, it is critical that the angels understand the prayer and are willing to deliver it properly. However, when one prays with a *minyan*, God's Presence is there; the prayer goes to Him directly without being routed through the angelic messenger service. Rashi adds that God never ignores the prayers of a community.[594]

---

593 TB *Sotah* 33a.

594 Rashi simply cites the verse, "Behold, God is mighty and does not despise" (*Job* 36:5), which he understands as referring to God never rejecting communal prayer. Rabbi Yehuda Roseannes (1657–1727) in his *Parshas Derachim* (§13) poses a fairly simple question to Rashi's explanation. Why did Rashi invent a new explanation for why communal prayer can be offered in Aramaic, if he could have simply explained that the Holy Presence of God appears before any congregation of Jews (as evident in TB *Brachos* 6a)? Meaning, just as the Talmud explained that a sick person can pray in Aramaic because the Holy Presence is in front of him, the same explanation could be used for understanding why communal prayer can be offered in Aramaic, yet Rashi opted for another avenue. See Y. Ohana (ed.), *Parshas Derachim* (Jerusalem, 1992), pg. 157, and responsa *Amudei Aish* §3:31 for answers to this question.
Talmidei Rabbeinu Yonah (to TB *Brachos* 13b) write that communal prayers may be said in Aramaic because a congregation of people praying does not require an intermediary for their prayers to be heard by God, but he does not explain why. *Tanya Rabasi* (*Hilchos Rosh HaShanah* §72) writes that while the angels who forward individual prayers to God do not understand Aramaic, those angels charged with forwarding communal prayers to God do in fact understand Aramaic.

SELICHOS AND OTHER COMMUNAL PRAYERS

This latter exception accounts for several notable prayers in Aramaic, including *Kaddish* (קדיש)[595] and *Brich Shmay* (בריך שמיה), which are only recited in communal prayer.[596]

Another example of communal prayers in Aramaic is the *Selichos* (סליחות) prayers, which are recited annually in the days leading up to Rosh Hashanah and Yom Kippur. These prayers are a mixture of scriptural verses, poetic prayers of repentance, and requests for forgiveness. Although most of the various poems and liturgy that make up the *Selichos* prayers are in *Lashon HaKodesh*, several passages are recited in Aramaic. Rabbi Yosef Chaim of Baghdad explains that the *Selichos* prayers were intended to be said publicly to show the power of community. The community does not need the intervention of angels—they can appeal directly to God for their needs. Therefore, he explains, some of these prayers were intentionally written in Aramaic to show that the community can manage even without the angels (who do not understand Aramaic). However, notes Rabbi Yosef Chaim, since *Lashon HaKodesh* is actually preferable for prayer, most of the *Selichos* prayers are in that language.[597]

ARAMAIC IS ONLY A PROBLEM WHEN PRAYING TO ANGELS

Though not accepted in halachah, a minority opinion holds that one may sometimes beseech angels in prayer instead of God Himself.[598]

595 See H. L. Ehrenreich (ed.), *Sepher Ha-Pardes* (Budapest, 1924), pg. 326, where Rashi offers reasons as to why *Kaddish* is recited specifically in Aramaic (see also Tosafos to TB *Brachos* 3a). When mentioning in *Deuteronomy* 33:2 that God gave the Torah to the Jews, the Torah uses an Aramaic word to describe God "coming" to them (אָתָה instead of בא). Rabbi Moshe Alshich explains (*Toras Moshe* there) that the Torah uses an Aramaic word in this context so that the angels would not understand the full implications of God giving the Torah to the Jews. This would prevent them from being jealous of the Jews' exalted position in God's legions. Alshich explains that the rabbis instituted that *Kaddish* be said in Aramaic for this reason. This would prevent the angels from being jealous of the Jews singing God's praises, for *Kaddish* is a prayer sanctifying God's name and his eternal sovereignty. See also S. Assaf (ed.), *Sifran Shel Rishonim, Sefer HaMinhagos* (Jerusalem: Mekize Nirdamim, 1925), pg. 139.

596 *Divrei Chamudos* (to *Piskei HaRosh, Brachos* 2:2, §6).

597 Responsa *Torah Lishmah* §49 and *Ben Yehoyada* to TB *Sotah* 33a.

598 See Tashbatz (to TB *Brachos* 13a) and Rabbi Shimon HaMeilli's *Sefer HaMeoros* (to TB *Brachos* 64a). In a recently published responsum, Rabbi Avigdor Kara (d. 1439) discusses whether or not one is al-

According to this opinion, the Geonim explain that the Talmud means that when praying to angels, one should not do so in Aramaic because they do not understand Aramaic. However, when praying directly to God, one may pray in any language, for God obviously understands all languages.

Why does Rambam not discuss prayer outside of *Lashon HaKodesh*?

Rambam in his Laws of *Tefillah* seems to completely ignore the entire discussion of prayer in foreign languages and does not at all mention that prayer can ever be said in a language other than *Lashon HaKodesh*. Rabbi Elazar Fleckeles (in responsa *Teshuva M'Ahavah*, vol. 2, *Orach Chaim* §222) explains the rationale for Rambam's ommitance of this concept by offering two possibilities:

- Rambam understood that while one could theoretically pray in foreign languages, the entire discussion is moot because practically one would have to somehow insert all the deeper and hidden mystical meanings of prayer into foreign words in the same way that Ezra and his court inserted such elements into the original liturgy that they instituted in *Lashon HaKodesh*. Since doing this is almost an impossibility, and if even one letter is off-place the entire endeavor would be faulty, Rambam omitted this entire discussion altogether.
- Alternatively, Rabbi Fleckeles suggests that since the Jews are presently scattered across the entire world, if each Jew would copy the traditional prayers into his personal language, then the concept of communal prayer would no longer be possible for travelers because he will not understand the prayers in places where a different language is spoken. Thus, Rambam saw a great disadvantage in allowing for prayer in languages other than *Lashon HaKodesh*, so he omitted that option entirely.

---

lowed to pray to angels in lieu of praying to God Himself. Parenthetically, he also notes that the Talmud means that angels are not particularly fond of Aramaic (or any other language save for *Lashon HaKodesh*), not that they do not understand it. See *Kovetz Yeshurun* vol. 30 (Jerusalem, 2014), pgs. 69–73.

GEONIM: ARAMAIC IS NEVER REALLY A PROBLEM

Nonetheless, the Geonim conclude that one need not be concerned with this passage and may offer prayers in Aramaic, if one chooses to do so.[599] Rabbi Zecharia Aghmati (1120–1195) mentions[600] that such was the opinion of Rabbi Hai Gaon (969–1038), who asserts that the halachah is not in accordance with the Talmudic passage in discussion.[601] In other words, the Geonim ignore the Talmud's warning about praying in Aramaic.

THE RULINGS OF THE SHULCHAN ARUCH

However, Rabbi Yosef Karo (1488–1575), in his work *Shulchan Aruch*,[602] does not ignore the Talmud's warning about praying in Aramaic and makes three rulings on the topic:

> He first rules according to the opinion that the angels only understand *Lashon HaKodesh*. He states that any language[603] may be used for communal prayer, but individual prayers must be in *Lashon HaKodesh*.
>
> He further qualifies this ruling by explaining that an individual's

599 A. Harkavy (ed.), *Zichron L'Rishonim V'Gam L'Acharonim, Teshuvos HaGeonim* (Berlin, 1887), pgs. 188–190.

600 In his work *Sefer HaNer* (to TB *Brachos* 13a).

601 M.D. Ben-Shem (ed.), *Sefer HaNer Brachos* (Jerusalem: Machon Torah Shleimah, 1958), pgs. 18–19. See also Y. Y. Stahl (ed.), *Sefer Gematrios* (Jerusalem, 2005) pg. 190

602 *Orach Chaim* §101:4.

603 Rabbi Efrayim Zalman Margolis (1762–1828) evidently rules that even in cases where one can pray in languages other than *Lashon HaKodesh*, one should not pray in invented languages and/or inferior forms of the language. Instead, Rabbi Margolis rules one can only pray in an original form of one of the original seventy languages.

Rabbi Moshe Sofer (responsa *Chasam Sofer*, *Choshen Mishpat* §193) argues with Rabbi Margolis' ruling and allows one to pray in any language that he understands, even if it is not one of the original seventy. Rabbi Sofer adds a caveat that one should only pray in a language befitting to be spoken in the court of the ruling government and not in inarticulate slang or "street talk." Although Rabbi Sofer allows for praying in a foreign language, he notes elsewhere (responsa *Chasam Sofer*, vol. 6, §84) that this is only allowed under short-term provisional circumstances, but to do so as an official fixed policy is forbidden. Rabbi Mordechai Leib Winkler of Madd (1845–1932) in his responsa *Levushei Mordechai* (*Orach Chaim*, vol. 1 §9) also follows the ruling of Rabbi Sofer. He writes that in the times of Rabbi Sofer, a certain community in Hamburg adopted German as their official language of worship and that community was excommunicated, with the rabbis of that time forbidding one to enter their synagogues or pray from their prayer books. See also *Aruch HaShulchan* (*Orach Chaim*, §101:9).

obligation to pray in *Lashon HaKodesh* applies only in regard to personal requests (e.g., the recovery of a sick person), but even individuals may recite the established communal prayers in any language.

Then *Shulchan Aruch* offers a more lenient view in accordance with the opinion that the angels understand every language except for Aramaic. According to this approach, he rules that an individual may offer any prayer, including personal requests, in any language other than Aramaic.[604]

Nonetheless, within the Jewish liturgy, there are several prayers in Aramaic, which one may recite even without a minyan. This phenomenon seems contrary to even the most lenient ruling of the *Shulchan Aruch*, who never intimated that an individual could pray in Aramaic.

SOME ARAMAIC IN PRAYER IS ACCEPTABLE, IF IT IS MOSTLY LASHON HAKODESH

Rabbi Chaim Shraga Feivel Frank writes that the Talmud does not mean that every single passage of all prayers has to be in *Lashon HaKodesh*.[605] Rather, the general language of prayer should be *Lashon HaKodesh*. Therefore, he explains, there is no problem for some prayers to be recited in Aramaic, if the bulk of the prayers are still said in *Lashon HaKodesh*. This answers most of the following examples of Aramaic prayers, because those are only short passages.

---

604 As we have previously mentioned, this opinion understands that the angels especially detest Aramaic because it is a corruption of *Lashon HaKodesh* and is thus considered a bastardized language. In light of the view of Rabbi Teitelbaum and other authorities who view Modern Hebrew as a perversion of *Lashon HaKodesh*, *Piskei Teshuvos* (to *Mishnah Berurah* vol. 1, *Orach Chaim* §101:7) rules that it is preferable to offer prayers in any language—even completely foreign ones—than to pray in Modern Hebrew.
However, those who view Modern Hebrew as a continuation and successor to *Lashon HaKodesh* would vehemently disagree with such a ruling. Meiri (to TB *Shabbos* 12b) explains that the main reason not to pray in Aramaic is the fact that since people are not used to speaking that language every day, it is harder to properly concentrate on meaning when using it to pray. According to this, Modern Hebrew, even if it is a corruption of *Lashon HaKodesh*, should be acceptable for prayer because it is in fact used in everyday speech.

605 *Toldos Zev* to TB *Shabbos* 12b.

OTHER REASONS THAT PRAYERS IN ARAMAIC ARE PERMITTED

However, even without relying on Rabbi Frank, other commentators provide several exceptions to the rule that prayers may not be offered in Aramaic:

Firstly, the prohibition of praying in Aramaic is limited to prayers that are requests.

Secondly, just as God's Presence manifests Itself when prayers are said with a minyan, and thus these prayers may be recited in Aramaic (as explained above), so too since God's Presence manifests on Shabbos, prayers recited on Shabbos may be in Aramaic.

Thirdly, prayers that the angels could use to prosecute the Jews are purposely said in Aramaic (so that the accusatory angels will not comprehend them).

Now we shall examine several prayers that rely on these and other more specific exceptions.

THE ARAMAIC KEDUSHA

The first example is the *Kedusha* (קדושה) prayer, which is customarily recited three times in *Shacharis* (the morning services). This prayer consists of two biblical verses, which record the praises that the angels sing to God: "Holy, Holy, Holy is God [Master of] legions, the whole world is filled with His honor,"[606] and "Blessed is the honor of God from His place."[607] Sometimes a third verse is added, which proclaims God's everlasting sovereignty.[608] This formula is recited three times: during the benedictions attached to the *Shema*, in the public repetition of the *Shemona Esrei*, and in *U'va L'Tzion* (ובא לציון). Of these three times, only the middle *Kedusha* must be said with a minyan; even an individual worshipper recites the other two *Kedushas*. In the *Kedusha* in *U'va L'Tzion*, the scriptural verses in *Lashon HaKodesh* are accompanied

---

606 *Isaiah* 6:3.

607 *Ezekiel* 3:12.

608 Sometimes that verse is "God should reign forever; the lord of Zion, for generation and generation, Hallujah" (*Psalms* 146:10), while sometimes that verse is "God should reign forever" (*Exodus* 15:18).

by the *Targum's* Aramaic translations. The *Zohar*[609] compares this to *Shnayim Mikra V'Echad Targum*: the first two *Kedushas* are in *Lashon HaKodesh*, while the third is also in Aramaic.

How may an individual recite the third *Kedusha* in Aramaic?

The answer to this question is clear from a close examination of the Talmudic passage, which literally says that one should not "ask his needs" in Aramaic. However, this is not a prayer of "asking one's needs," i.e., submitting personal requests. Rather, one reciting the *Kedusha* recounts God's praises and accepts His sovereignty. This type of prayer is perfectly acceptable in Aramaic.

YEKUM PURKAN

Two more Aramaic prayers, beginning with the words "*Yekum Purkan*" (יקום פורקן), are found at the beginning of the *Mussaf* services on Shabbos. Only the first of these is reserved exclusively for communal worship, while the second prayer is recited even by an individual.[610] These prayers ask God to bestow specific blessings upon rabbinic and communal leaders and their families. Rabbi Efrayim Greenblatt (1932–2014)[611] explains in the name of Rabbi Yitzchak Yaakov Weiss (1902–1989) that this Aramaic prayer is permissible because it is not a prayer of *request*, but rather is a prayer of *blessing*. Therefore, since it is a blessing, not a request, even an individual can recite it, even though it is in Aramaic. Nonetheless, Rabbi Greenblatt himself questions the validity of this distinction on several grounds.

SHABBOS HYMNS

However, there is another reason to permit an individual to recite *Yekum Purkan*, which the commentators provide regarding the special hymns customarily recited and/or sung on Shabbos (*zemiros*). Most of these hymns are written in *Lashon HaKodesh*, but some are written in Aramaic. The Aramaic hymns include those written by Rabbi Yitzchak

609 *Terumah* 132b.

610 See Rabbi Efrayim Zalman Margolis' *Sha'arei Efrayim* (10:26) who is the source for this custom. However, Rabbi Yisrael Meir Kagan (*Mishnah Berurah* to *Orach Chaim* §101:19) rules that both paragraphs are reserved exclusively for communal worship.

611 In his responsa *Rivivos Efrayim* (vol. 1 §216).

Luria and the hymn *Kah Ribon Olam* (י-ה רבון עלם), written by Rabbi Luria's contemporary Rabbi Yisrael Najara (1555–1625).

Based on the second ruling of the *Shulchan Aruch* that one may pray established communal prayers in Aramaic, Rabbi Tzvi Pesach Frank (1873–1960) reasons that these poems may be recited by an individual, even though they are written in Aramaic, because they do not contain specific requests. They are songs that contain praises of God and general requests for the welfare of the Jewish people.[612]

However, his nephew, Rabbi Chaim Shraga Feivel Frank (1908–1973), notes that the last stanza of *Kah Ribon Olam* includes a specific request calling for the Final Redemption of the Jewish people and the rebuilding of the Holy Temple. How can this Aramaic stanza be recited by individuals if it contains specific requests?

To answer this question, the younger Rabbi Frank proposes a novel idea. He proves from kabbalistic sources that the Holy Presence of God rests upon one who properly keeps Shabbos. Therefore, he reasons that on Shabbos, since the Holy Presence is upon him, one does not need the angels to deliver prayers to God, for he has a direct line to God on that Holy Day. Therefore, on Shabbos, one can say prayers in Aramaic, even though the angels do not understand it.[613] This reasoning serves to exonerate not only *Kah Ribon Olam*, but also *Yekum Purkan*.

PASSOVER NIGHT INVITATION

Another prayer recited in Aramaic is the introduction to the *Maggid* section of the Passover *Seder*, *Ha Lachma Anya* (הא לחמא עניא), which invites all those who are needy to partake of the Passover meal. Most of this paragraph is written in Aramaic, while the rest of *Maggid* is in *Lashon HaKodesh*.

Rashi writes that this passage is in Aramaic because the demons do not understand Aramaic. If they understood Aramaic, they would take this "open door policy" as an opportunity to attack those celebrating Pesach.[614]

---

612 Responsa *Har Tzvi* (*Orach Chaim*, vol. 1 §64); *Har Tzvi Al HaShas-Mo'ed* (to TB *Shabbos* 12b); and S.A. Pardes & S. Elberg (eds.), *Kovetz HaPardes*, vol. 29:1 (1954), pg. 5.

613 *Toldos Zev* to TB *Shabbos* 12b.

614 H. L. Ehrenreich (ed.), *Sepher Ha-Pardes* (Budapest, 1924), pg. 92; see also Ritva to *Haggadah*

Similarly, Rabbi Yom Tov ben Avraham of Seville (1250–1330), known as Ritva, and Abudraham write that this passage is recited in Aramaic because the prosecuting angels do not understand Aramaic and therefore would be unable to prosecute the Jews in the Heavenly Courts. Otherwise, while the Jews would pray for the Final Redemption, these angels would remind God of the Jews' sins to prove that they are unworthy of salvation.

Afterwards, Ritva explains that since this section was instituted by Amoraic sages—not Tannaic sages—it was written in Aramaic, just as the Talmud is written in Aramaic and the Mishnah is written in *Lashon HaKodesh*. Similarly, Raavan explains that this passage was instituted in Babylon, where the general populace spoke Aramaic. Abudraham adds that the laymen did not understand *Lashon HaKodesh,* so for their benefit this passage was instituted in Aramaic. (This could have been true even in Israel and not only in Babylon.) Tashbatz and *Orchos Chaim* write that it was instituted in Aramaic so that even the children would understand it, and be aroused to ask the questions of the *Mah Nishtanah*.

"NEXT YEAR IN JERUSALEM" IN LASHON HAKODESH

However, the concluding words of this prayer, *L'shanah haba'ah b'yerushalayim* (לשנה הבאה בירושלים), "Next year [we should merit to be] in Jerusalem," are written in *Lashon HaKodesh*.

Tashbatz explains that even the children, who normally spoke Aramaic exclusively, were familiar with this phrase in *Lashon HaKodesh*. Thus, it could be said in *Lashon HaKodesh* without compromising the children's understanding. However, *Orchos Chaim* says that the last line was written in *Lashon HaKodesh* so that the Arameans (Persians?) who understood Aramaic would not suspect that the Jews wished to rebel against them.

Based on the idea already mentioned several times that *Lashon HaKodesh* is particularly associated with the Land of Israel, it seems quite appropriate that this line, which expresses the Jewish yearning for a return to Zion, would be recited in *Lashon HaKodesh*.

Shel Pesach. See *Shibolei HaLeket*, *Tosafos HaRid*, and Abarbanel, who discuss this understanding at great length; see also *Kovetz Yeshurun*, vol. 10 (Jerusalem: 2002), pgs. 72–73.

NULLIFYING THE LEAVENED BREAD

The explanation that prayers are recited in Aramaic to prevent angelic prosecution is also offered regarding the Aramaic[615] formula *Kol Chamira* (כל חמירא). This formula is recited at the burning of the leavened bread (*biur chametz*) before Passover. Rabbi Moshe ben Machir (a sixteenth-century sage from Safed) explains that this prayer in particular was written in Aramaic because it is a declaration that denigrates the importance of bread. Denigrating bread is sometimes considered a sin,[616] so one should only say this prayer in Aramaic so that the ministering angels will not understand the denigration and prosecute him for this sin.[617]

USHPIZIN ON SUKKOS

This idea comes up again in another, closely related, discussion. According to Kabbalah, on each day of the seven-day Sukkos festival, one of seven historical Jewish forefathers "visits" all the Jews' *sukkos* as a spiritual guest known as *Ushpizin* (אושפיזין, "guests" in Aramaic). Customarily, a special prayer in Aramaic is recited each night to "welcome" them. Rabbi Yosef Palagi (1815–1896) explains why this prayer is written specifically in Aramaic. He argues that if it was in *Lashon HaKodesh,* then the ministering angels would prosecute those who recite these prayers for only inviting these "spiritual guests" on Sukkos, but not inviting poor people as guests year-round. Therefore, those prayers are recited in Aramaic so that the ministering angels will not understand them.[618]

APPENDIX SUMMARY

We began our examination of prayers in Aramaic with the Talmud's

---

615 Rama (*Orach Chaim* §434:1) mentions that this formula was written in *Lashon HaKodesh*. Rabbi Yaakov Reischer (1661–1773) in his glosses there (*Chok Yaakov*) points out that it is not written in *Lashon HaKodesh*, it is written in Aramaic. He mentions that some commentators propose changing the text of Rama's comment. However, he himself favors leaving Rama's comment intact, while explaining that Aramaic is considered a "holy language" when compared to other languages. In truth, there is no basis for Rabbi Reischer's question; Rama himself (as elaborated upon in Chapter 8) agrees to Rabbi Katzenellenbogen in some ways that Aramaic and *Lashon HaKodesh* can be considered one language. See also responsa *Maharsham*, vol. 5, §9.

616 E.g., see TB *Brachos* 50a.

617 *Seder HaYom* (*Seder Biur Chametz*) cited by *Magen Avraham*, *Orach Chaim* §434:6.

618 *Yosef Es Echav* (Izmir, 1896), pg. 5b.

warning not to offer prayers in Aramaic because the ministering angels do not recognize prayers offered in that language. Amongst the commentators there are several approaches in dealing with this passage:

- Some commentators take this literally and conclude that angels do not understand Aramaic.
- Some go as far as to say that angels only understand *Lashon HaKodesh*.
- However, other commentators say that although angels do understand Aramaic, they do not listen to prayers in that language so as to preserve the people's familiarity with and respect for *Lashon HaKodesh*.

Nonetheless, the Talmud itself allows prayers to be recited in Aramaic in places where God's Presence manifests, namely in an ill person's vicinity and a place where there is a *minyan*. Examples of prayers in Aramaic that are only said with a *minyan* include *Kaddish*, *Brich Shmay*, and *Selichos*.

Yet, in practice, there are other Aramaic prayers which are said without a minyan. Rabbi Frank permits such prayers on the grounds that *Lashon HaKodesh* must be the general, but not necessarily exclusive, language used for prayer. However, other commentators provide other reasons to allow an individual certain prayers in Aramaic:

- They permit Aramaic prayers that are only blessings and praises, but do not contain requests.
- They permit Aramaic prayers to be said on Shabbos (when God's Presence manifests).
- They permit Aramaic prayers when praying in *Lashon HaKodesh* would somehow provide incriminating evidence for accusatory angels.

Examples of such prayers include the *Kedusha* in *U'va L'Tzion*, which is not a request; *Yekum Purkan* and *zemiros* (notably *Kah Ribon Olam*), which are said on Shabbos; and *Ha Lachma Anya*, *Kol Chamira*, and the prayer welcoming the *Ushpizin*, which could otherwise be used by prosecuting angels.

Appendix D: Maharal on Aramaic and Lashon HaKodesh

The philosophical and kabbalistic works of Maharal, Rabbi Yehuda Lowe of Prague (1520–1609), created a major impact on Jewish thought throughout the ages. Therefore, we give special attention to his various discourses on the implications and significance of Aramaic and Lashon HaKodesh. Maharal offers several interesting observations regarding Aramaic, and explains matters which are otherwise baffling.

REASON #1: ARAMAIC IS A UNIVERSAL LANGUAGE-THUS EXCLUDING IT FROM THE SEVENTY LANGUAGES

Maharal explains that Adam spoke Aramaic (as we discussed in Chapter 1) because Aramaic is a universal language not associated with any specific nation. Thus, it is appropriate for Adam, the father of all humanity, to speak a language that does not exclude any nation in favor of another. He also writes that all seventy languages are included in Aramaic, just as all nations descend from Adam.[619] This reality is partially reflected in the fact that Aramaic was the *lingua franca* of the ancient world and was spoken by many civilizations therein.

The statue of Maharal, which is currently displayed at the city hall in Prague, Czech Republic (Source: Public domain.)

WHY ARE CERTAIN PRAYERS RECITED IN ARAMAIC?

As we have discussed in Appendix C, two important daily prayers are recited in Aramaic: *Kaddish* and the Aramaic translation of *Kedusha*. These prayers speak of the sanctity of God's Kingship and His everlasting greatness.

Maharal offers his own explanation as to why these specific prayers are recited in Aramaic while the rest of the liturgy is essentially in *Lashon HaKodesh*. He explains that *Lashon HaKodesh* is the language of the Nation of Israel. Thus, it numbers among the seventy languages,[620] which

619 *Chiddushei Aggados* to TB *Sanhedrin* 38b.

620 This contradicts Maharsha's view (TB *Sotah* 36b) that just as Israel is not considered one of the seventy nations, so too *Lashon HaKodesh* is not considered one of the seventy languages. *Tosafos Shantz/Evreux* (TB *Sotah* 36b) write that they are unsure whether *Lashon HaKodesh* is

represent the seventy nations of the world. Aramaic, on the other hand, is not one of the seventy languages. Therefore, as mentioned above, it must be a universal language that is related to all people, as opposed to the language of one specific nation. These prayers, which describe God's all-encompassing sovereignty, are recited in Aramaic—not *Lashon HaKodesh*—because His dominion encompasses the entire universe, not just the Jewish Nation.[621]

REASON #2: ARAMAIC IS NOT CONSIDERED A LANGUAGE

In a separate discussion, Maharal offers another reason why Aramaic is not considered one of the seventy languages. The prophet Isaiah relates that God said, "I will rise up against them—the word of God, Master of legions—and I will discontinue from Babylonia its name and remnant, grandchild and great-grandchild—the word of God."[622] The Talmud tells that Rabbi Yonasan would expound this verse as an introduction to the Book of Esther.[623] The Talmud understood that this verse refers to the Chaldeans (the people of Babylonia) who destroyed the First Temple. Rabbi Yonasan would explain that "its name" refers to their script, "remnant" refers to their language, "grandchild" refers to their monarchy, and "great-grandchild" refers to Vashti—the last scion of the Babylonian royal family who was married to the Persian king Ahasuerus and was executed in the beginning of the Book of Esther. Thus, the Talmud declares that the Chaldeans are a nation that has neither script nor language.[624] However, in actuality the Chaldeans did have a language, for the Chaldeans—who are sometimes called Arameans—spoke Aramaic. Why does the Talmud not reckon with the fact that they spoke Aramaic? Maharal answers that, as we shall explain below, Aramaic is not considered a language.[625]

---

to be included in the seventy languages. *Tosafos HaRosh* (ibid.) and *Piskei HaTosafos* (TB *Sotah* §40) take for granted that it is not included in the seventy languages.

621 *Nesivos Olam*, Path of Worship, Ch. 11.

622 *Isaiah* 14:22.

623 TB *Megillah* 10b.

624 The Talmud elsewhere (TB *Avodah Zarah* 10a) makes a similar comment about the Romans (who destroyed the Second Temple); see the commentators there (especially the uncensored version of Rashi printed in the Oz V'Hadar edition of the Babylonian Talmud).

625 *Tiferes Yisrael*, Ch. 13.

Maharal cites the Talmud that relates that God "regretted" that He created the Chaldeans.[626] Because of this regret, the Chaldeans are considered non-existent, *personae non grata*. If the Chaldeans do not exist, then their language, Aramaic, is to be considered equally non-existent, *lingua non grata*.[627] For this reason, explains Maharal, Aramaic is not counted in the seventy languages.[628]

REASON #3: ARAMAIC WAS NOT BORN FROM THE TOWER OF BABEL

Maharal provides another, more positive, reason that Aramaic cannot be one of the seventy languages. As previously mentioned (in Chapter 2), Assur did not participate in building the Tower of Babel.[629] The nation which spoke Aramaic—the Chaldeans—descended from him, and presumably followed his lead in refusing to participate in the Tower. Obviously, God would not mete out punishment for the Tower to those who did not participate in its building. Given that the seventy languages were formed as punishment for the Tower, and that the Chaldeans did not number among the offenders, it follows that their language—Aramaic—does not rank within the seventy languages. In elaborating upon this idea, Maharal proves Aramaic did not develop as a punishment for the Tower of Babel from the premise that Adam spoke it (as mentioned above).[630]

---

626 TB *Sukkah* 52b.

627 Maharal then notes that his explanation is inconsistent with the words of Ramban in *Parshas Chayei Sarah*, but does not specify what Ramban says, or even to which passage in Ramban he refers. Maharal ostensibly refers to the passage in which Ramban writes (*Genesis* 24:7) that the Chaldeans are descendants of Ham. By equating the Chaldeans with the Arameans, Maharal understood that the Chaldeans were not a Hamitic nation; but rather a Semitic nation descending from Aram the son of Shem (see ibid. 10:22). This issue is at the root of the discussion and, as mentioned in the note above, several other commentators also understood that the Chaldeans and the Arameans are not the same. For more information, see R. C. Klein, "Abraham's Chalden Origins and the Chaldee Language," *Seforim Blog* (December 30, 2014) [http://seforim.blogspot.co.il/2014/12/abrahams-chaldean-origins-and-chaldee.html].

628 *Gevuras Hashem*, Ch. 54; and *Chiddushei Aggados* (to TB *Sotah* 33a).

629 *Gur Aryeh* to *Deuteronomy* 32:23.

630 Maharal does not discuss the status of *Lashon HaKodesh* in this context, i.e., he does not discuss why *Lashon HaKodesh* should be considered from within one of the seventy languages if Adam spoke it and it was not created as a punishment the sinners at Babel.

WHY SHNAYIM MIKRA V'ECHAD TARGUM?

In yet another discussion of languages, Maharal offers an explanation as to why the Talmud assumes that angels do not understand Aramaic.[631] The Talmud (TB *Brachos* 8a) mentions a practice known as *Shnayim Mikra V'Echad Targum*, which is that every male Jew is obligated to maintain his connection to the Jewish community by reading that week's Torah portion twice in the original Hebrew and once in an Aramaic *Targum*.

Maharal sheds light on this obligation based on a statement recorded in the *Pesikta Zutrasa*,[632] which states that the Torah was given three times: once at Mount Sinai, once at the *Ohel Mo'ed* (Tent of the Meeting in the Tabernacle), and once at the Plains of Moab.

As recorded in the Bible itself, Moses "elucidated" the Torah when it was given at the Plains of Moab.[633] Rashi explains that this "elucidation" refers to translating the Torah into seventy languages so that the masses would understand it more easily.[634] Since the Jewish masses were accustomed to speaking in Aramaic, the Torah must have also been translated to Aramaic at the Plains of Moab.[635] The first two times that the Torah was given, it was given only in *Lashon HaKodesh*, but the third time it was given in Aramaic as well.

Therefore, explains Maharal, one is obligated to recite the weekly Torah portion twice in Hebrew and once in Aramaic to mimic the three times that the Torah was given.[636] This explanation states that one must learn the *parsha* twice in *Lashon HaKodesh*, corresponding to the two times

---

631 This issue is discussed in Chapter 8 and in Appendix C.

632 In the beginning of *Leviticus*.

633 *Deuteronomy* 1:5.

634 To ibid.

635 In this explanation, Maharal implies that Aramaic is in fact included in the seventy languages. However, as noted above, Maharal writes elsewhere that Aramaic is not to be reckoned among the seventy languages. Perhaps Maharal understood that, for whatever reason, the Torah was translated into Aramaic despite it not being considered one of the seventy languages.

636 *Nesivos Olam*, Path of Worship, Ch. 13. The same explanation is mentioned by Rabbi Moshe Meth (1541–1606), a slightly younger contemporary of Maharal. He writes (*Mateh Moshe* §464) that he heard that the reason for *Shnayim Mikra V'Echad Targum* is because the Torah was given thrice: at Mount Sinai, at the Tent of the Meeting, and a third time in the Plains of Moab where it was "elucidated clearly."

that the Torah was given exclusively in *Lashon HaKodesh*. Additionally, one must learn it again in Aramaic, since the Torah was also given in many languages, including Aramaic.[637]

ARAMAIC REPRESENTS THE WORLD TO COME

Maharal also writes that the three times that the Torah was given represent the three worlds: This World, the Middle World,[638] and the World to Come. He writes that Hebrew represents the first two worlds, while Aramaic represents the World to Come.

The World to Come is inapplicable to angels, because they do not fulfill commandments or violate prohibitions, and therefore do not receive reward and punishment. Thus, Aramaic, which represents the World to Come, is also irrelevant to angels. Based on this, Maharal explains that angels cannot understand Aramaic because it is inapplicable to them.[639]

The Mishnah in *Avos*[640] records that Ben Bag-Bag said that if one properly delves into the Torah, he will find that it includes everything; and Ben Hay-Hay said that one receives reward according to one's pain in exerting effort for Torah study. These two statements in the Mishnah are written in Aramaic, not in the Mishnah's usual *Lashon HaKodesh*.[641]

Maharal explains that these two statements in specific were written in Aramaic because angels do not understand Aramaic and these two statements apply only to humans and not to angels.[642] He explains that

---

637 However, this explanation fails to address why one must specifically use Aramaic, as opposed to any other language.

638 Maharal himself in *Chiddushei Aggados* to TB *Sotah* 39a explains that the "Middle World" is the world of the celestial bodies, including the sun, moon, planets, stars, and constellations. See also *Rabbeinu Bachaya* (to *Genesis* 1:27 and *Leviticus* 16:4). This concept still requires further explanation to fit this context. I freely admit that I do not understand this at all.

639 *Tiferes Yisrael*, Ch. 13.

640 *Avos* 5:22–23.

641 See also *Avos* 1:13 and 2:6, in which statements from Hillel the Elder are quoted in Aramaic. However, this is probably not significant because Hillel himself was from Babylon (see Rabbi Yechiel Halpern's *Seder HaDoros*, vol. 2, s.v. *Hillel HaZaken*) and naturally spoke Aramaic, while in general the other Tannaic sages mentioned in *Avos* were native to Palestine where *Lashon HaKodesh* was more prominent.

642 This is difficult to understand because most of *Avos* (which deals with moral instruction) and, in fact, most of Mishnayos, are completely irrelevant to angels. In fact, there are other passages

angels do not study Torah and consequently do not receive reward based on the toil of their input. The sole purpose of angels' existence is to serve as emissaries to carry out God's bidding. Thus, they do not experience any pain or distress in exerting their energies for the fulfillment of God's commandments. Since they do not have pain, they cannot receive reward based on their levels of pain and effort.[643]

ANOTHER VIEW: ANGELS ONLY UNDERSTAND LASHON HAKODESH

In another context, Maharal follows the view of those who understand the Talmud to mean that angels *only* understand *Lashon HaKodesh*, not that they understand every language except for Aramaic.[644] Accordingly, he writes that angels only understand *Lashon HaKodesh* because, unlike all other languages, it is not man-made. As mentioned in Chapter 2, all other languages are based on social agreements by groups of people, but *Lashon HaKodesh* was created by God Himself.[645]

APPENDIX SUMMARY

Maharal discusses several fascinating ideas regarding Aramaic. We began with Maharal's assumption that Aramaic is not considered one of the seventy languages and to this Maharal offered three explanations:

- He explains that Aramaic is a universal language, which is not associated with any particular nation. This is the reason that Adam spoke Aramaic and that Aramaic is used for prayers describing God's universal dominion.
- He also explains that the Chaldeans—the nation that spoke Aramaic—is not considered to exist so their language is considered equally non-existent.
- He also explains that the punishment for participating in the

---

in *Avos* that are also seemingly not relevant to angels, and yet they are still in *Lashon HaKodesh*, not Aramaic. This matter requires further explanation.

643 *Derech Chaim* to *Avos* 5:22.

644 This topic was dealt with at great length above in Appendix C "Prayers in Aramaic."

645 See also Maharal's *Chiddushei Aggados* and *Gur Aryeh* to TB *Shabbos* 12b. Rabbi Yosef Engel of Krakow (1858–1920) elaborates on this idea in his work *Gilyonei HaShas* (to TB *Brachos* 21a).

> Tower of Babel was speaking one of the seventy languages. Since the original Chaldeans did not participate in the Tower of Babel, we can conclude that Aramaic is not one of the seventy languages.

Maharal also discusses the ramifications of the fact that the Torah was given three times: twice exclusively in *Lashon HaKodesh*, and once in many languages, including Aramaic. He understands that the obligation to learn *Shnayim Mikra V'Echad Targum* corresponds to this. One must learn the *parsha* twice in *Lashon HaKodesh* and once in Aramaic.

The three times that the Torah was given also correspond to the three worlds, with the third time corresponding to the World to Come. Thus, Aramaic is associated with the World to Come. Since angels neither violate God's will nor exert effort to fulfill it, they are ineligible to receive punishment and reward. Because the World to Come (where reward and punishment are given) is irrelevant to angels, they are unable to understand Aramaic.

POSTSCRIPT

As this work neared completion, I found a letter penned by the fifth Lubavitcher Rebbe, Rabbi Shalom Dov Ber Schneersohn (1860–1920), in which he expresses many of the ideas already discussed in this book.[646]

Rabbi Schneersohn begins by remarking that many people have wondered why there is religious opposition to adopting *Lashon HaKodesh* as the Jewish language. He responds to these questions by explaining that *Lashon HaKodesh* does not belong to any nation—it belongs to the Torah. It is different from all other languages because it is a divine language, not man-made based on social agreements. Hence, Rabbi Schneersohn explains that *Lashon HaKodesh* is reserved only for holy uses, so one should not use *Lashon HaKodesh* for mundane matters—and surely not for forbidden purposes. It is the Torah's language, not our language.

Rabbi Schneersohn mentions that some people base their support of accepting *Lashon HaKodesh* as an everyday language on a historical

646 This letter is printed in Rabbi Yehoshua Mondshein's *Migdal Oz* (Kfar Chabad: Machon Lubavitch, 1980), *Sha'ar HaTorah*, pg. 16.

inaccuracy. They claim that *Lashon HaKodesh* is our historical heritage from the Talmudic sages, who spoke this language, and that we should continue in their path.

He counters that *Lashon HaKodesh* was only used as a spoken language for a brief period of time during the First Temple era, but afterwards it was no longer the exclusive spoken language of the Jews. He notes that the sages of the Mishnah and the Talmud only spoke *Lashon HaKodesh* for ritual purposes, but the language used by the simple-folk and in everyday speech was Aramaic, not *Lashon HaKodesh*. (And, according to some sources that I quoted, even early biblical figures such as Adam and Abraham spoke *Lashon HaKodesh* only for holy purposes and used Aramaic for other uses.)

With a touch of irony, Rabbi Schneersohn comments that even those who have adopted *Lashon HaKodesh* as their spoken language do not refer to the language as such. Instead, they deny the holiness of the language and simply refer to it as *Ivrit* ("Hebrew"), a term used to describe the pre-Sinaitic Jews (the term "Hebrew" is almost always used in the Bible to refer to the Jews before they received the Torah). Afterwards, they are called "Israelites," or "Jews," because the term "Hebrew" implies a Jew on a lower spiritual level, not yet connected to the holiness of the Torah.

In a piece of uncharacteristically harsh criticism, he writes that it is therefore quite appropriate that those Jews with nationalist motivations, as opposed to religious motivations, would call their adaptation of *Lashon HaKodesh* "Hebrew."

Nonetheless, as we have already noted, *Lashon HaKodesh* is certainly a holy language and there is room to view Modern Hebrew as a continuation of that holy language.

Rabbi Moshe Chaim Luzzato (1707–1746) summarizes the values of *Lashon HaKodesh* by grouping them into three categories: historic, spiritual, and aesthetic.[647]

On a historical level, many commentators tout the antiquity of *Lashon HaKodesh* by arguing that it was the only language spoken by man until

---

647 *Lashon Limudim* (Jerusalem: Mossad HaRav Kook, 1945), pgs. 28–31; and *Yalkut Yedios HaEmes* (Tel Aviv, 1966), pgs. 292–297.

the division of languages at the Tower of Babel. Adam, the first man, spoke *Lashon HaKodesh* (even if he also spoke Aramaic and other languages). The language is not limited to any one specific nation because it predates the division of nationalities; it is therefore the quintessential international language (a sort of ancient Esperanto). In fact, the language predates the entire world, just as the Torah predates the creation of the world, because the Torah itself is in *Lashon HaKodesh*. Nonetheless, the Jews became the historic carriers of this language. The language continues to live in the State of Israel, just as it had lived there millennia ago.

Viewed through the lens of spirituality, the holiness of *Lashon HaKodesh* is highly significant because it is the only language whose words intrinsically reflect their meanings. Other languages are simply social agreements to link certain words to certain ideas, but those ideas are not inherently linked to those words. When Adam named the elements of creation, he was able to use his advanced intellect to look into the innate nature of each object and base its name upon that. His mastery over *Lashon HaKodesh* allowed him to easily accomplish this task and discover the names of everything in the world. *Lashon HaKodesh* also has supernatural properties that tie one's ability to master and maintain the language to one's moral and spiritual integrity.

At face value, the simplicity of *Lashon HaKodesh* as a literal language cannot be overstated. The language is sweet and beautiful. It also has the advantage of being concise. That is, one need not sacrifice clarity for brevity. The language is suitable for both flowery poetry and incisive analyses, as well as everything in between.

Do you speak Jewish?

BIOGRAPHICAL INDEX

Tannaic and Amoraic Works | Geonim and Rishonim (until 1492) | Acharonim (until 1939) | Post-Holocaust (from 1939)

TANNAIC AND AMORAIC WORKS

Babylonian Talmud (TB)

Also known as Gemara, this work is a compilation of Amoraic discussions usually centered around explaining the **Mishnah**. Ravina and Rav Ashi originally compiled it, but later authorities until the Geonic period also contributed to its final form. **Rabbi Shlomo ben Yitzchak** (printed on the inner column of the page in standard editions) is the principal commentator of the Gemara, while Tosafos (printed on the page's outer column) is a compendium of in-depth analyses from the Tosafists.

Haggada Shel Pesach: Raavan, Rokeach, Shibolei HaLeket, Abudraham, and Tashbatz

This Tannaic work is customarily recited on the first night of Passover. It recounts the story of the Jews' exodus from Egypt based on Midrashic interpretations. Many Rishonim wrote commentaries to it, which were printed in *Haggadah Shleimah* (Jerusalem, 1967), written by **Rabbi Menachem Mendel Kasher** and edited by **Rabbi Shmuel Ashkenazi**, and *Toras Chaim Haggadah Shel Pesach* (Jerusalem: Mossad HaRav Kook, 1998).

Jerusalem Talmud (JT): *Pnei Moshe*

This work (sometimes called the "Palestinian Talmud" or *Talmud Yerushalmi*) by Amoraic sages was compiled in the Land of Israel and predates the **Babylonian Talmud**. Like its Babylonian counterpart, it seeks to elucidate the **Mishnah**, but tends to be more concise without much back-and-forth discussion. The chief commentaries on it are *Pnei Moshe* and **Rabbi David Frankel's** *Korban HaEida*.

Mechilta, Mechilta D'Rabbi Shimon Ben Yochai

This work is a halachic Midrash that contains the hermeneutical exegeses of various Tannaic sages on the Book of *Exodus*. The standard *Mechilta* is that of Rabbi Yishmael, but in the twentieth century the *Mechilta* of Rabbi Shimon ben Yochai was also discovered and it was later proven that some Rishonim (including **Rabbi Moshe ben Maimon**) may have had access to that work.

Maseches Sofrim

This tractate, sometimes appended to the Babylonian Talmud, was written in Palestine sometime during the Geonic period. It contains many customs and laws (mostly concerning the traditions of reading the Torah) that differed from the prevailing customs and laws in the Jewish communities of Babylon.

Megillas Ta'anis

This was the first written work that the rabbis approved of outside of the Bible. It is a listing of various "happy days" on which the rabbis prohibited fasting and the reasons for those happy occasions. It is ascribed to an early Tanna named Chananya ben Chizkiyahu. A post-script was later added to this treatise that detailed minor fasts and the reasons behind them.

Midrash Aggadah

This Midrash was first printed in Vienna by Rabbi Shlomo Buber (1827–1906) based on a manuscript found in Syria. It is a Midrash (mostly Aggadic) on the books of *Genesis* and *Exodus*.

Midrash Rabbah (Bereishis Rabbah, Vayikra Rabbah, Shir HaShirim Rabbah, Rus Rabbah): Maharzu, Eitz Yosef

Bereishis Rabbah is generally accepted to be the oldest Midrash of the Rabbah series, which encompasses all of the Pentateuch and the Five Scrolls. In the standard edition of *Midrash Rabbah*, several commentaries are printed, most notably *Maharzu* written by Rabbi Zev Wolf Einhorn of Horodna, Poland (d. 1862), and *Anaf Yosef/Eitz Yosef* written by Rabbi Chanoch Zundel of Bialystok (d. 1867).

Midrash Socher Tov

This work is an Aggadic Midrash that contains Tannaic explanations. It exists on *Psalms*, *Proverbs* and the Book of *Samuel*. An early commentary to this Midrash was written by Rabbi Yitzchak Cohen, a son-in-law of **Maharal.**

Midrash Tanchuma

This Midrash on the Pentateuch is ascribed to the Tanna Rabbi Tanchuma and serves as the source for many other Midrashic teachings. Rabbi Chanoch Zundel of Bialystok wrote *Eitz Yosef* as a commentary to this Midrash just as he did for **Midrash Rabbah.**This Midrash should not be confused with **Old Midrash Tanchuma**.

Midrash Yelamdeinu

This early Midrash is quoted by several medieval authorities, but was considered lost for hundreds of years thereafter. The Hungarian/Jerusalemite scholar Rabbi Shlomo Aharon Wertheimer (1866–1935) discovered a manuscript of this Midrash and his grandson published it in a compendium of published manuscripts entitled *Batei Midrashos*.

Mishnah, Mishnayos

This work, a corpus of Tannaic teachings mainly in *Lashon HaKodesh,* was compiled in the third century by Rabbi Yehuda HaNassi (known as Rebbi). This work is the heart of the Oral Torah. The Mishnah is divided into six orders, which are further subdivided into several tractates.

Old Midrash Tanchuma

This Midrash was first published in the nineteenth century by Rabbi S. Buber. The Midrash was known to some Rishonim under a different name: *Midrash Yelamdeinu* but slightly differs from what has been printed under that title.

Pesikta D'Rav Kahane

This Midrash is a collection of homiletic sermons delivered in the late Amoraic to early Geonic period.

Pesikta Rabbasi

This Midrash is a collection of homiletic sermons delivered in the late Amoraic to early Geonic period.

Pirkei D'Rabbi Eliezer

This a Midrashic work of Aggadah arranged not by chapter and verse of the biblical sources, but as its own free–running narration of the Bible's account, with many tangential excursus. It is customarily ascribed to Rabbi Eliezer ben Hyrkanus, but has been proven to have been written later than the Tannaic period. **Rabbi David Luria** authored *Chiddushei HaRadal,* an important commentary to this Midrash.

Sefer HaYashar

This Midrash tells over the history of the Jews from Abraham until Joshua in an embellished story form. The veracity and authority of this Midrash has come under question, yet **Rabbi Yechiel Halpern** deemed this Midrash reliable enough for him to base upon it much of the historical accounts from the Biblical Era in his work *Seder HaDoros*.

Sifrei*: *Sifrei Devei Rav

This work is a halachic Midrash that contains the hermeneutical exegeses of various Tannaic sages on the Books of *Numbers* and *Deuteronomy*. The anonymous opinions expressed in this work are attributed to Rabbi Yehuda in accordance with the stances of his teacher, Rabbi Akiva. **Rabbi Avraham ben David** authored the earliest known commentary to this work. His commentary was first printed in Lakewood in 2009 by Rabbis Ralbag, Sorscher, & Besser. Rabbi David Pardo (1718–1792) authored the commentary *Sifrei Devei Rav* to the *Sifrei*.

Targum Jonathan

This work, erroneously ascribed to Rabbi Yonasan ben Uziel, is a translation of the Pentateuch into Aramaic. From the style of Aramaic used in the translation it seems to have been written in Babylon. Interwoven into the translation are also Midrashic interpretations.

Targum Neofiti

This early *Targum* (sometimes known as *Targum Yerushalmi HaShaleim*) is one of the only extant editions of a Palestinian translation of the Torah into Aramaic. Its style of Aramaic (known as Palestinian or Jerusalemite) differs from the style of Aramaic used by the Babylonian *Targum Onkelos*. It is called *Neofiti* after the *Collegium Ecclesiasticum Adolescentium Neophytorum*, which housed the manuscripts of this *Targum* until it was bought by the Vatican and first published between the years 1968 and 1979.

Targum Onkelos

This work is the most commonly used translation of the Pentateuch into Aramaic. It is ascribed to Onkelos the Convert, a nephew of the Roman Emperor Titus. Onkelos was a student of the Tanna Rabbi Eliezer.

Yalkut Shimoni

This work is a compendium of Midrashic sources on all of Tanach. While it is widely acknowledged to have been assembled sometime during the period of the Rishonim, it is usually given the same credence as other Midrashim because of the fact that it simply quotes earlier sources.

Zohar

This work, which was first published in Spain in the thirteenth century by Rabbi Moshe de-Leon, is ascribed to the Tanna Rabbi Shimon ben Yochai. It is the basic Midrash of Kabbalah and is written in obscure Aramaic. Much about this work's origins and meaning is shrouded in mystery.

GEONIM AND RISHONIM

Akeidas Yitzchak

This homiletic and philosophical work on the Penateuch (broken up into "Gates") was written by Rabbi Yitzchak Arama (1420–1494), a Spanish rabbi and scholar. When the Jews were expelled from Spain in 1492, Rabbi Arama resettled in Naples, Italy, where he died not long after.

Da'as Zekeinim

This work is a compendium of Tosafos on the Pentateuch, mimicking the role of Tosafos on the Talmud. It is printed in the standard *Mikros Gedolos* editions of the Pentateuch.

Donash (920–990)

He was one of the first scholars who explored the rules of Hebrew grammar. He is said to have been born in North Africa, studied under the Geonim of Babylonia, and eventually settled in Spain. Besides his works on grammar, he composed poetry and is famous for writing *Dror Yikra* (customarily sung on Shabbos day).

Hagahos Maimonios

This work was compiled by Rabbi Meir ben Yekusiel HaKohen, a student of **Rabbi Meir of Rothenberg**. It contains the rulings of Ashkenazic authorities and is arranged as a supplement to **Rabbi Moshe ben Maimon's** work.

Menachem ibn Saruk (920–970)

He was a Spanish grammarian famous for having written one of the earliest dictionaries of *Lashon HaKodesh*. He also engaged in a bitter dispute with **Donash** regarding some of the fundamental principles of Hebrew lexicon and grammar.

Midrash Sechel Tov

This work, written in 1139, is a compilation of Midrashic material on the Pentateuch composed by Rabbi Menachem ben Shlomo, a student of Rabbi Toviah ben Eliezer (author of ***Pesikta Zutrasa***). It is unclear where the author lived.

Moshav Zekeinim

This work is an anonymous compendium of Tosafist commentary to the Pentateuch. It was first printed in London by Rabbi S. Sasson in 1959 based on a manuscript found in his library.

Pesikta Zutrasa

This work (which is also called *Midrash Lekach Tov)* was compiled around the late eleventh century–early twelfth century by Rabbi Eliezer ben Tuviah, a German Talmudist and poet.

Pirush HaRokeach

This work was printed based on Oxford Bodleian manuscript 268/1 and is generally assumed to have been written by Rabbi Elazar of Worms (1176–1238), author of *Rokeach HaGadol*. However, others (including Rabbi J. Gellis) attribute the work to Rabbi Eliezer bar Yitzchak HaGadol and/or Rabbi Yehuda ben Klonymos of Speyer.

***Pirush Rabbeinu Efrayim* (1110–1175)**

This commentary to the Pentateuch was written by Rabbeinu Efrayim, a German rabbi from Regensburg. Selections from his commentary to the Pentateuch were first printed by **Rabbi Chaim Yosef David Azulai** in *Nachal Kedumim*. In 1994, his commentary was published in full for the first time by the late Julius Klugmann (1923–2013) from Florida based on a manuscript from Cambridge University.

Rabbeinu Bachaya ben Asher (13th century)

He was a student of **Rabbi Shlomo ben Aderes** who is known for his unique way of blending **Rabbi Moshe ben Nachman**–style Kabbalah with biblical exegesis. His most famous work is his commentary to the Pentateuch, but he also produced several other works including the encyclopedic *Kad HaKemach* and a commentary to tractate *Avos*.

Rabbeinu Chaim Paltiel (13th century)

He was a late thirteenth-century German Tosafist who was a student of **Rabbi Meir of Rothenberg**, thus placing him in the same period as **Rabbi Asher ben Yechiel**. His commentary to the Pentateuch was first discovered and published by I. S. Lange in 1981.

Rabbeinu Chananel (965–1055)

According to tradition, his father Rabbeinu Chushiel was a student of the Geonic Academies of Babylon and was kidnapped by pirates and eventually redeemed by the Jewish community of Kairouan in Tunisia. Thus, Rabbeinu Chananel is an indispensable link in the chain of tradition between the Babylonian Geonim and Europe's Rishonim. He also has the distinction of being the first person to have authored a commentary to the Talmud.

Rabbeinu Gershom Meor HaGolah (960–1028)

He was the father of German Jewry in the early Medieval Period. He famously promulgated several decrees that were essential to Jewish life in his time. Under his leadership, the Jewish community in Mainz, Germany, became a center of Torah rivaling the well-established communities of the Geonim in Babylon.

Rabbeinu Tam (1100–1171)

Rabbi Yaakov ben Meir, known as Rabbeinu Tam, was a grandson of **Rabbi Shlomo ben Yitzchak** (with whom he commonly argues). He is one of the foremost French Tosafists and his halachic opinions are often quoted by other Tosafists (some of which were compiled into *Sefer HaYashar L'Rabbeinu Tam*). His older brother **Rabbi Shlomo ben Meir** was his primary teacher.

Rabbeinu Yonah (1200–1263)

Originally from Girona in Spain, he is famous for authoring the moralistic work *Shaarei Teshuvah*. According to some legends, he authored this work as a means of repenting for his unabashed opposition to **Rabbi Moshe ben Maimon**. Amongst his other works, he also wrote a commentary to the tractate *Avos* and a commentary to TB *Bava Basra* entitled *Aliyos D'Rabbeinu Yonah*. He is often quoted by such Talmudists as **Rabbi Shlomo ben Aderet** and **Rabbi Asher ben Yechiel.**

Rabbi Aharon HaKohen of Lunel (13th century)

He was a late thirteenth-century Provencal scholar who is best known for his work *Orchos Chaim* (which is somehow related to the more popular *Kolbo*). When the Jews were expelled from France in the Great Exile of 1306, he moved to Majorca, a Mediterranean island off the east coast of Spain.

Rabbi Avigdor Kara (d. 1439)

He was originally a judge on the rabbinical court in Regensberg, Germany before he relocated to Prague. In Prague, he served as Rosh Yeshiva as well as a judge. He authored poetry (especially elegies mourning the pogrom in Prague of 1389) and halachik responsa, much of which has only been published recently. He was also known for delving into Kabbalah and had much influence in that field. He was a brother-in-law to Rabbi Yehuda Lowy the Elder, the grandfather of **Maharal**.

Rabbi Avraham ben Ezriel of Bohemia (13th century)

He authored an important work entitled *Arugas HaBosem*, first printed by Mekize Nirdamim in the 1960s. This work takes to offering elucidation and commentary to many of the liturgical poems popular in his time.

Rabbi Avraham de Balmes (1440–1523)

He was an Italian physician, grammarian and translator. He obtained a doctorate in philosophy and medicine from the University of Naples (through special permission from Pope Innocent VIII) and served as the private physician of Cardinal Domenico Grimani for whom he translated several Hebrew books into Latin. His work *Mikneh Avram* is an important one on the grammar of *Lashon HaKodesh*. He was eulogized by **Rabbi Gedaliah ibn Yachya**.

Rabbi Avraham ibn Ezra (1092–1167), Ibn Ezra

He was a Spanish bible commentator, poet, and grammarian. He also wrote works of science and mathematics. His method of bible interpretation followed a literal—rather than Midrashic—methodology and this aroused the ire of **Rabbi Moshe ben Nachman**. He wrote two separate commentaries to the book of Exodus, a "long" one and a "short" one. The "long" one is more common and is printed in the standard *Mikros Gedolos Chumash*, while the "short" one (first printed in Prague in 1840) is printed separately.

Rabbi Avraham Saba (1440–1508)

He was one of the first Spanish scholars to heavily draw from the *Zohar* and other unpublished kabbalistic texts. After the expulsion of the Jews from Spain, he moved to Portugal and eventually to Fez, Morocco. He authored several works including *Tzror HaMor* on the Pentateuch and other works on the Bible, *Avos*, and TB *Brachos*.

Rabbi Avraham Zacuto (1452–1515)

He was a Spanish astronomer and historian. Featured prominently amongst his works is *Sefer Yuchasin*, a historical account of the Jewish people. The crater Zagut on the moon is named after him.

Rabbi Asher ben Yechiel (1250–1328), *Rosh*

Also known as *Rosh*, he was a student of **Rabbi Meir of Rothenberg** whom he succeeded as the foremost authority in Germany. His works include *Piskei HaRosh* (an Alfasi-like halachic code), *Tosafos HaRosh* (a Tosafos-style commentary to the Talmud), commentary to **Mishnayos,** and responsa. He also wrote *Orchos Chaim*, an essay on ethics. There is also a commentary on the Pentateuch erroneously ascribed to him, as well as the forged responsa *Besamim Rosh*.

Rabbi Binyamin of Tudela (1130–1173)

Sometimes known as the "Jewish Marco Polo," he spent the years 1165–1173 traveling around the world and documenting the Jewish- and non-Jewish communities of Europe, Asia, and Africa. He began his journey from Sarragossa in Spain, and then traveled through France, Italy, Greece, Turkey, Syria, Lebanon, Israel, Iraq, Iran, Arabia, Egypt, and North Africa. His records were published under the name *Masaos Rabbi Binyamin*.

Rabbi Chizkiyah ben Manoach (13th century), *Chizkuni*

He was a thirteenth-century French Bible commentator who was largely influenced by **Rabbi Shlomo ben Yitzchak, Rabbi Shlomo ben Meir,** and **Rabbi Yosef Bechor-Schor.** His explanations were quoted and dissected by many later Tosafists in their commentaries to the Pentateuch.

Rabbi David ben Zimra (1479–1573), Radvaz

Known as Radvaz, his family was expelled from Spain in 1492, and resettled in Safed. He then moved to Morocco and then to Egypt where he served on the rabbinical court, eventually becoming the Chief Rabbi of Egypt. There, he founded a prominent yeshiva (**Rabbi Yitzchak Luria** being amongst his more well-known students). In his old age, he relocated to Jerusalem and then to Safed. His thousands of responsa are published under the name responsa *Radvaz* and he also authored several works of Kabbalah.

Rabbi David Kimchi (1160–1235), Radak

He was a Provencal rabbi born to a family of grammarians. He wrote a dictionary of Hebrew known as the *Michlol* and a lexicon known as *Sefer HaShorashim*. He also wrote a commentary to Genesis and much of the Prophets and Hagiography.

Rabbi David ben Avraham (1125–1198), Raavad

He was a Provencal scholar who is known as "Raavad the Objector" because he authored objections to **Rabbi Moshe ben Maimon's** and

Alfasi's halachic works. He also authored commentaries to the halachic Midrashim, *Toras Kohanim* and *Sifrei*, as well as to several Talmudic tractates. Additionally, he wrote several purely halachic works. His responsa are printed under the title *Tamim De'im*.

Rabbi Eliyahu Ashkenazi HaBachur (1469–1549), HaBachur

He was originally German, but spent much of his life in Italy where he took advantage of the intellectual renewal of the Renaissance. He was an expert in Hebrew grammar and even taught Hebrew to Christian enthusiasts. He authored several works on the Hebrew language including *Meturgaman, Sefer HaTishbi, Sefer HaBachur,* and others. He was also known as Elias Levita.

Rabbi Eliyahu ben Binyamin HaLevi (15th century)

He is most famous for his responsa published under the name *Zekan Aharon*. He also served on the rabbinical court of **Rabbi Eliyahu Mizrachi** and was the chief rabbi of Constantinople, Turkey. Rabbi Shlomo of Serilio (*Rash M'Serilio*), who was expelled from Spain in 1492, was one of his students.

Rabbi Eliyahu Mizrachi (1450–1526), Mizrachi

He was of Greek lineage and became the Chief Sephardic Rabbi of Turkey. His most famous work is his supercommentary *Mizrachi* on **Rabbi Shlomo ben Yitzchak's** commentary to the Pentateuch. He also authored responsa published under the titles *Ram* and *Mayim Amukim*. He also composed several books on mathematics and science, as well as a commentary to the *Semag*.

Rabbi Hai Gaon (939–1038)

He was the Rosh Yeshiva ("Gaon") of the Talmudic academy at Pumbeditha (in modern–day Fallujah, Iraq), a position previously held by his father Rabbi Sherira Gaon. He was a very popular leader of the Jewish community both in Babylon and abroad. He penned halachic responsa to questioners from all over the world. He also wrote several legal treatises and poems.

Rabbi Levi ben Gershon (1288–1344), Ralbag/Gersonides

He was a French Jewish philosopher and grandson of **Rabbi Moshe ben Nachman.** In addition to his philosophical works and commentary to Tanach, he also wrote several expositions on mathematics and astrology/astronomy and invented the astrolabe.

Rabbi Meir Abulafia (1170–1244)

He was an early opponent of **Rabbi Moshe ben Maimon's** *Guide for the Perplexed*, but later refused to partake in the campaign against Maimonides. He wrote very detailed commentaries to several portions of the Talmud including TB *Bava Basra*, *Sanhedrin*, and part of *Gittin* (and possibly *Kiddushin*), all published under the title *Yad Ramah.*

Rabbi Meir of Rothenberg (1215–1293)

Known as *Maharam M'Rotenburg* or *Maharam Bar Baruch*, he was a German rabbi who wrote thousands of halachic rulings (printed in several volumes) as well as a work on the Pentateuch and more. He was famously imprisoned by the anti–Semitic government of his time and died in jail. One of his main students was **Rabbi Asher ben Yechiel**, who fled to Spain upon his teacher's death to escape the same fate.

Rabbi Menachem Meiri (1249–1310)

Known simply as Meiri, he was a Spanish rabbi who was a student of the French Narbonne tradition. He authored the voluminous work *Beis HaBechirah* to the Babylonian Talmud, in addition to several other works.

Rabbi Moshe Al–Ashakar (1466–1542)

He was a Spanish rabbi who, after the Jews were expelled from Spain in 1492, lived in several places in North Africa and Greece until he finally came to Cairo, Egypt, in 1522. There, he served on the rabbinic court of **Rabbi David ben Zimra**. He was known as a staunch defender of **Rabbi Moshe ben Maimon's** philosophy and rulings. His numerous halachic responsa were quickly accepted by worldwide Jewry.

Rabbi Moshe ben Maimon (1135–1204), Rambam/Maimonides

He was a Spanish rabbi whose impact on halachah cannot be overstated. His wide spectrum of works include his *Guide for the Perplexed*, which essentially presents Judaism from a philosophical perspective, his commentary to the **Mishnayos**, his code of Jewish Law entitled *Mishnah Torah/Yad HaChazakah* as well as many medical writings and other letters.

Rabbi Moshe ben Nachman (1194–1270), Ramban/Nachmanides

He was a Spanish scholar who authored commentaries on the Torah and Talmud. He was known as a Kabbalist and a philosopher. He famously debated a Jewish apostate who converted to Christianity, and eventually fled Spain for Israel, where he died. He is a student of **Rabbi Yehuda bar Yakar**.

Rabbi Moshe ibn Ezra (1055–1138)

He was a Spanish philosopher, grammarian, and poet. It is said that his poetry had impacted the Arabic world. He was a member of the famous Ibn Ezra family, which also includes **Rabbi Avraham ibn Ezra**.

Rabbi Moshe of Coucy (13th century)

He was a French scholar who studied in Germany under **Rabbi Yehuda HaChasid**. His most famous work is *Sefer Mitzvos Gedolos* (known as *Smag*) in which he listed the 613 commandments. He also authored a commentary to the Pentateuch that is no longer extant but is sometimes quoted by early sources.

Rabbi Nosson of Rome (1035–1106)

He was an Italian scholar responsible for authoring *Sefer Ha'Aruch*, which is the most popular lexicon of rabbinic Hebrew. He served as a transitional figure bridging the Geonic traditions of Babylon with the Rishonim of Europe.

Rabbi Nesanel ben Yishaya (14th century)

He was an early fourteenth-century rabbi who lived in Yemen. His main work, a commentary to the Pentateuch entitled *Meor Ha'Afeila*, was first published by Rabbi Y. Kapach in 1957. It was originally written in mixed Arabic and Hebrew and was translated to pure Hebrew by Kapach.

Rabbi Nissim of Gerona (1315–1376)

Known as the *Ran*, he authored commentaries to the Talmud and Alfasi, as well as responsa. He served as a judge in the rabbinic court at Barcelona. A compilation of homilies known as *Drashos HaRan* is customarily ascribed to him. His method follows that of the school of **Rabbi Shlomo ben Aderes**.

Rabbi Ovadiah of Bartenura (1440–1500), Bartenura

He was an Italian rabbi who eventually moved to Jerusalem and helped strengthen the Jewish community there. He is famous for his Rashi-like commentary to **Mishnayos**, but he also wrote several other works including *Amar Nekeh* (on the Pentateuch) and chronicles of his travels.

Rabbi Perachya ben Nissim (12th–13th century)

He was a brother-in-law to and colleague of Rabbi Avraham, son of **Rabbi Moshe ben Maimon**. He lived in Egypt and authored a commentary to TB *Shabbos*. His commentary is mentioned by several earlier authorities, but was only printed in full by Rabbis A. Shoshana and B. Hirschfeld (Jerusalem–Cleveland: Machon Ofeq, 1998).

Rabbi Ovadiah ben Yaakov Sforno (1475–1550), Sforno

He was an Italian commentator and philosopher. He wrote a commentary on the Pentateuch as well as on other select parts of the Bible. His halachic opinions were eagerly sought out by those of his generation.

Rabbi Sa'adya Gaon (882–942)

Originally from Egypt, he then settled in the Land of Israel before being appointed the Rosh Yeshiva ("Gaon") of the academy at Sura. He also spent time in Baghdad. His works of Jewish philosophy and halachah (some of which were written in Arabic) are very important and studied to this day.

Rabbi Shem Tov ibn Falaquera (1225–1290)

He was a prodigious Spanish philosopher and poet who published many works. One of his very significant works is a commentary to **Rabbi Moshe ben Maimon's** *Guide for the Perplexed.*

Rabbi Shlomo ben Aderes (1235–1310), Rashba

He is the author of an extensive commentary to the Talmud known as *Chiddushei HaRashba* as well as thousands of halachic responsa and other halachic works. He was a student of **Rabbi Moshe ben Nachman** and **Rabbeinu Yonah** and amongst his students are many of the prominent medieval Torah sages, including **Rabbeinu Bachaya**, **Rabbi Yom Tov ben Avraham** and **Rabbi Yehoshua ibn Shuaib**

Rabbi Shlomo ben Yitzchak (1040–1105), Rashi

He is known as the father of all commentators for his clear elucidation of the Bible and the Talmud. He was a French rabbi and was the leading figure of Ashkenazic Jewry during the Crusades. He also wrote other works on Jewish Law including *Issur V'Hetter* and *Sefer HaPardes.*

Rabbi Shlomo ibn Parchon (12th century)

He was a Spanish grammarian who was famous for authoring a lexicon of *Lashon HaKodesh* known as *Machaberes HaAruch.* He considered himself a student of **Rabbi Avraham ibn Ezra, Rabbi Yehuda HaLevi**, and Rabbi Efrayim (a student of Alfasi).

Rabbi Shmuel ben Meir (1085–1158), Rashbam

He was the grandson of **Rabbi Shlomo ben Yitzchak** and followed in Rashi's footsteps. He completed Rashi's commentary to the Talmud (on TB *Bava Basra*) and compiled his own commentary to the Torah and Talmud (especially on *Pesachim*). He is celebrated as one of the leading French Tosafists.

Rabbi Yaakov ben Asher (1270–1340), *Baal HaTurim*

He was a German Talmudist who is famous for his halachic code called the *Arba Turim* on which **Rabbi Yosef Karo** based his *Shulchan Aruch.*

He also wrote *Baal HaTurim*, a short commentary to the Pentateuch expounding the Scriptures using *gematria* and other forms of hermeneutical analyses. He also wrote a longer commentary to the Pentateuch entitled *Pirush HaTur Ha'Aruch*, which quotes many explanations from various Tosafists and especially from **Rabbi Moshe ben Nachman**. He is a son of **Rabbi Asher ben Yechiel**.

Rabbi Yaakov ibn Chaviv (1460–1516)

He is a Spanish scholar who, after the Jews were expelled from Spain in 1492, relocated to Greece. He is famous for authoring *Ein Yaakov,* an anthology of *Aggadic* passages from the Talmud. It sometimes contains variant readings of the Talmud and its chief commentators. The first of many commentaries to *Ein Yaakov* is Ibn Chaviv's own *HaKoseiv*.

Rabbi Yaakov Moelin (1365–1427)

Known as *Maharil,* he is famous for codifying the customs and laws according to the Ashkenazic (German) rite. Many of his rulings were the basis of **Rabbi Moshe Isserles'** final decisions. He is also known for his poetry and the importance he attached to melodies.

Rabbi Yehoshua ibn Shuaib (14th century)

He was a fourteenth-century Spanish rabbi who was a student of **Rabbi Shlomo ben Aderes.** His homilies on the weekly Torah portion are printed under the name *Drashos Ibn Shuaib*.

Rabbi Yehuda bar Yakar (1150–1250)

He was a Spanish rabbi who is best known for being the principal teacher of **Rabbi Moshe ben Nachman**. He authored a commentary to the *Siddur,* which explains various prayers.

Rabbi Yehuda ben Binyamin the Physician (1215–1280)

He belonged to the famous Anavim family of Italy. He is known as the *Rivavan* and authored commentaries to several tractates of the Talmud and to Alfasi.

Rabbi Yehuda HaChasid (1150–1217)

He was the hero of the Chassidei Ashkenaz movement in Germany. His book *Sefer Chassidim* lists many behaviors to achieve piety and stories of pious individuals. Many of his extra-pious behaviors have been accepted into normative halachah.

Rabbi Yehuda HaLevi (1075–1141)

He was a Spanish poet and Jewish philosopher. He yearned throughout his life to live in the Land of Israel and died soon after arriving there. His work *The Kuzari* records a conversation between the King of Khazar and a Jewish scholar concerning Jewish philosophy. Rabbi Yehuda Moscato (1530–1593), an Italian scholar, wrote the popular work *Kol Yehuda*, a commentary to *The Kuzari*.

Rabbi Yehuda ibn Tibbon (1120–1190)

Originally from Spain, he migrated northwards to France to escape persecution from the Almohad Muslim rulers of Spain. He worked as a translator of Arabic works into Hebrew. Amongst his famous works are the Hebrew translations of *Chovos HaLevavos*, **Rabbi Yehuda HaLevi's** *The Kuzari*, and more. His father, Rabbi Moshe ibn Tibbon was the translator of many of **Rabbi Moshe ben Maimon's** works into Hebrew.

Rabbi Yitzchak Abarbanel (1437–1508)

He was a Portuguese Bible commentator and philosopher who worked at the court of King Afonso V of Portugal. After the Jewish Expulsion from Spain, he wrote several treatises to help strengthen the Jewish community's belief in the coming of the Messiah.

Rabbi Yitzchak ben Moshe HaLevi Duran (1350–1415), Efodi

He was a German grammarian who wrote anti-Christian polemics (under the name Profiat Duran). He is known as Efodi because of his work entitled *Ma'aseh Efod* and it is under the name "Efodi" that his commentary to **Rabbi Moshe ben Maimon's** *Guide for the Perplexed* is published.

Rabbi Yitzchak Ohr Zarua of Vienna (1200–1270)

He was one of the most important figures in the history of Ashkenazic

Jewry. His work *Ohr Zarua* is the basis of many rulings in practical halachah. He originally studied in the Great Yeshivas of France and Germany (especially under **Rabbi Yehuda HaChasid** amongst others). One of his foremost students was **Rabbi Meir of Rothenberg**.

Rabbi Yosef Bechor-Schor (12th century)

He was a twelfth-century French Tosafist and poet from Orleans. Amongst his teachers was **Rabbi Shlomo ben Meir** who influenced his literal interpretation of Scripture (as evident from Bechor-Schor's commentary to the Torah). His opinions and explanations on both the Talmud and the Torah are oft-quoted by other Tosafists.

Rabbi Yosef Elbo (1380–1444)

He was a Spanish scholar whose work *Sefer HaIkkarim* is an important work of Jewish dogma. His objective was to list and explain the Jewish articles of belief, as well as to defend Judaism from Christian devices.

Rabbi Yosef ibn Kaspi (1279–1340), Ibn Kaspi

He was a Provencal scholar who excelled in biblical interpretation, philosophy, and grammar. He wrote many works in those fields, but only a few of his works are still extant.

Rabbi Yosef Kara (1065–1135)

He was a French commentator who wrote a commentary to many parts of the Bible. He is associated with the school of Rashi and had a lot of influence over the latter's grandson, **Rabbi Shlomo ben Meir,** as well as over **Rabbi Chizkiyah ben Manoach,** for his preference of literal interpretations over exegetical ones.

Rabbi Yosef Karo (1488–1575)

He is best known for his halachic work *Shulchan Aruch,* which is accepted as the most authoritative work on Jewish Law. He also wrote *Bais Yosef* on the Tur, *Kesef Mishnah* on **Rabbi Moshe ben Maimon's** *Mishnah Torah*, and *Maggid Meisharim*—teachings on the Torah revealed to him by an angel.

Rabbi Yom Tov ben Avraham of Seville (1250–1330), Ritva

He was a leading student of **Rabbi Shlomo ben Aderes** and Rabbeinu Aharon HaLevi. He is famous for his commentary to the Talmud *Chiddushei HaRitva,* but also wrote other commentaries including one on the Haggadah Shel Pesach and *Sefer Zikaron* defending **Rabbi Moshe ben Maimon's** *Guide to the Perplexed* from **Rabbi Moshe ben Nachman's** objections.

Rabbi Zecharia Aghmati (1120–1195)

He was a Moroccan scholar who compiled *Sefer HaNer*, a compendium of Talmudic commentaries to several tractates of the Babylonian Talmud written in Hebrew and Arabic.

Tanya Rabasi

This work is based on *Shibbolei HaLeket* and contains discussions of various laws and customs. The general consensus is that its author was Rabbi Yechiel ben Yekusiel who lived in Rome in the early thirteenth century.

Tosafos HaShaleim

This work is a compendium of various explanations of Tosafists to the Pentateuch, the Five Scrolls, and the Haggadah Shel Pesach. The first volumes were compiled by Rabbi J. Gellis of the Harry Fishel Institute, while later volumes were prepared by that institute following Rabbi Gellis' death. While much of the material in this work is printed in other places, it does utilize several important manuscripts of Tosafists, which have otherwise never been printed.

Yossiphon

This tenth-century Southern Italian work of Jewish history is sometimes mistakenly attributed to the Roman historian Josephus from whose work it heavily draws. This work was widely accepted in Jewish tradition and is quoted by a wide spectrum of commentators.

ACHARONIM

Midrash Pliyah: Niv Sfasaim, Kesones Tashbetz

Midrash Pliyah is a compilation of unsourced, seemingly bizarre Midrashim first printed in Warsaw (1893) with a commentary to the Midrashim entitled *Niv Sfasaim*. Rabbi Shalom Weiss (Chief Rabbi of Ujhel in Hungary before the Holocaust) printed an additional commentary to these Midrashim entitled *Kesones Tashbetz*. Rabbi Weiss survived the horrors of the Holocaust and settled thereafter in New York City.

Mincha Belulah

This work is a compilation of earlier commentaries to the Pentateuch. It was assembled by the Italian Rabbi Avraham Menachem HaKohen Rappaport (1520–1596). He was the forefather of the famous Rappaport family of *Kohanim*.

Rabbi Aharon Marcus (1843–1916)

Originally from Hamburg, Germany, he studied there under Rabbi Baruch Lipschitz (son of **Rabbi Yisrael Lipschitz**) and then attended university in Prague specializing in philosophy, history, and psychology. He was later drawn towards the Hassidic movement and became a close disciple of several leading Hassidic masters in Galicia. He wrote several controversial philological works to reconcile contemporary archeology with Jewish tradition. These works include *Barzilai, Kadmonios,* and *Keses HaSofer*.

Rabbi Alexander Sender Schor (1673–1737)

He is the author of *Simla Chadasha/Tavuos Schor*, the principal halachic work on the laws of ritual slaughtering. He also wrote *Bechor Schor,* a commentary on the Babylonian Talmud. He was a descendant of **Rabbi Yosef Bechor-Schor** and lived in Poland.

Rabbi Avraham the Physician of Portleon/Sha'ar Aryeh (16th century)

He was an Italian rabbi from a family of doctors. His *magnum opus* is called *Shiltei HaGiborim* and includes a vast spectrum of knowledge and information on Torah-related topics as well as gemology, chemistry, physics, medicine, and history. His work was reprinted in 2010 by Machon Yerushalayim.

Rabbi Avraham Yitzchak HaKohen Kook (1865–1935)

He was the son-in-law of **Rabbi Eliyahu David Rabinowitz-Teomim** and served as the Chief Rabbi of Jaffa, eventually becoming the first Ashkenazic Chief Rabbi of the *Rabbanut* of pre–state Palestine. He wrote many works of halachah and Jewish thought and is regarded as the hero of Religious Zionism.

Rabbi Azariah de Rossi (1513–1578)

He was a controversial Italian scholar who applied the scientific method to the study of Torah and rabbinics, as exemplified in his multi-volume work *Meor Einayim*. **Rabbi Yosef Karo** wished to excommunicate him, something which was actually carried out by **Rabbi Moshe Alshich**. **Rabbi Yehuda Lowe of Prague** also strongly disagreed with him, authoring a work against *Meor Einayim*. Nonetheless, he has historically been somewhat accepted by mainstream authorities, including students of those who wished to excommunicate him.

Rabbi Chaim Yosef David Azulai (1724–1806)

Known as *Chida*, he was a Jerusalemite scholar who was sent by the Jerusalem community abroad to collect funds for supporting the community. He spent much of his life abroad in that capacity and spent much time perusing libraries and manuscripts all of which he recorded in his countless works. He engaged in a wide spectrum of Torah literature including halachah, Kabbalah, exegesis, philology, history, and more.

Rabbi David HaLevi Segal (1586–1667)

He was a Polish halachic decider who wrote a widely-accepted commentary to the *Shulchan Aruch* known as *Turei Zahav* (Taz). He also wrote *Divrei David*, a super-commentary to **Rabbi Shlomo ben Yitzchak's** commentary on the Torah.

Rabbi David Frankel (1704–1762)

He was a German Talmudist who was among the first to compose a commentary solely on the Jerusalem Talmud. His commentary is called *Korban HaEida*.

Rabbi David Luria (1798–1855)

Known by his initials *Radal*, he was a Lithuanian rabbi and Rosh Yeshiva and was viewed by many as a successor to **Rabbi Eliyahu Kramer of Vilna**. He was also very involved in communal affairs and even met with Sir Moses Montefiore to help Russian Jewry. Amongst his many works, his glosses to the Babylonian Talmud and *Pirkei D'Rabbi Eliezer* are the most famous.

Rabbi David Menachem Babad of Ternopol (1754–1838)

He was the rabbi of Ternopol in Galicia and was the successor and nephew of the famous Rabbi Yosef Babad, author of the *Minchas Chinuch*. His responsa were printed under the title *Chavatzeles HaSharon*.

Rabbi David Tevel Rubin (1794–1861)

He was one of the foremost students of Rabbi Chaim of Volozhin (1749–1821). He served as the Chief Rabbi of Minsk and produced several works: *Nachlas David* (a popular commentary to several tractates of the Talmud), *Beis David* (responsa and homilies), and *Divrei David* (a less popular commentary to other tracts of the Talmud).

Rabbi Efrayim Zalman Margolis (1762–1828)

He was a rabbi in Brody, Galicia, where he owned a successful bank. He was one of the first to engage in Jewish genealogy, researching the sources of different families. He authored many popular works including responsa *Beis Efrayim*, *Shaare Efrayim*, *Mateh Efrayim,* and others.

Rabbi Elazar Fleckeles (1754–1826)

He is best known for being a student of Rabbi Yechezkel Landau (1713–1793), whom he basically succeeded as Chief Rabbi of Prague. His writings are published in the three-volume responsa *Teshuva*

M'Ahavah. He was known to have a close relationship with the state censor of Prague, a Christian Hebraist named Karl Fischer (1757–1844).

Rabbi Elazar Landau (1778–1831)

He was a grandson of the famed *Noda B'Yehuda* Rabbi Yechezkel Landau (1713–1793) and served as the Rabbi of Brody. His main work is *Yad HaMelech*, excurses on **Rabbi Moshe ben Maimon's** *Mishnah Torah*. His glosses to the Talmud are printed in the standard Vilna Shas.

Rabbi Elazar Strashun (19th century)

He was a cousin to the wife of **Rabbi Shmuel Strashun** and served as the rabbi of Butrimonys in Lithuania. His works are published under the title *Amud Aish*.

Rabbi Eliezer ben Eliyahu Ashkenazi (1515–1585)

He was a rabbi of German lineage whose travels took him to the Rabbinate of Greece, Egypt, Cyprus, Italy, Czech, and Poland. He is best-known for his work *Yosef Lekach*, which is a commentary on the Book of Esther. He also wrote *Ma'aseh Hashem,* which goes into details about various stories in the Torah. This work also contains a section serving as a commentary to the **Haggada Shel Pesach**. He may have also written *Chiddushim Kadmonim* to TB *Kiddushin*.

Rabbi Eliyahu David Rabinowitz-Teomim (1845–1905)

Known by his initials as the *Aderes*, he served as rabbi for several communities in Europe including Mir and Ponovezh. In a tragic twist of fate, he was appointed successor-apparent to the Chief Rabbi of Jerusalem Rabbi Shmuel Salant, but predeceased him. Nonetheless, during his years in Jerusalem he was recognized as a leader of the Old Yishuv. He was the father-in-law of **Rabbi Avraham Yitzchak HaKohen Kook** (1865–1935), the first Chief Rabbi of the *Rabbanut* of pre-state Palestine.

Rabbi Eliyahu HaKohen (1659–1729)

He was a rabbi in Izmir, Turkey, and wrote many works admonishing his readers to adhere to moral values, including *Me'il Tzedaka, Shevet*

Mussar, *Midrash HaIsamari*, and others. He also compiled *Midrash Talpios*, which is an encyclopedia of interesting Torah-related sources and his own comments to those sources.

Rabbi Eliyahu Kramer of Vilna (1720–1797)

He was the foremost leader of Lithuanian Jewry and was an influential authority on halachah, Kabbalah, grammar, mathematics, and other areas of scholarship. He is also known as the Vilna Gaon or by his acronym, the *Gra*.

Rabbi Gedaliah ibn Yachya (1515–1587)

He was an Italian scholar who was exiled and spent much of his life wandering through Italy, Greece, and Egypt especially after the burning of the Talmud in Italy in 1562. He is known for his *Shalsheles HaKabbalah*, which contains a historical account of the Jewish people as well as several essays on various topics.

Rabbi Gershon Shaul Yom Tov Lipman Heller (1578–1654)

He was a principal student of **Rabbi Yehuda Lowe of Prague**, and after having studied in Prague served in the rabbinate of various Jewish communities across Europe. His most well-known commentaries include *Tosafos Yom Tov* to **Mishnayos**, *Divrei Chamudos* and *Ma'adanei HaMelech* to **Rabbi Asher ben Yechiel's** *Piskei HaRosh*, *Tuv Ta'am* to **Rabbeinu Bachaya's** Pentateuchal commentary, *Toras HaAsham* to **Rabbi Moshe Isserles**' *Toras HaChatas*, and many more.

Rabbi Heschel of Krakow (1596–1663)

He succeeded **Rabbi Gershon Shaul Yom Tov Lipman Heller** as Rabbi and Rosh Yeshiva of Krakow. Most of his written works have been lost, but much of his homilies on the *parsha* were preserved through oral tradition and were later compiled under the title *Chanukas HaTorah*. Many of the leading halachic deciders in the generation after him were his students.

Rabbi Meir Leibush ben Yechiel Michel Weiser (1809–1879)

Known by his acronym as the *Malbim*, he is famous for his commentary to the Bible in which he methodologically analyzes the text for variations and expounds upon them. He also wrote several works containing sermons and halachic rulings. He served as the rabbi of various communities throughout Eastern Europe.

Rabbi Meir Simcha HaKohen of Dvinsk (1843–1926)

He was a Lithuanian-born scholar who served as the rabbi of Dvinsk (in Latvia). His two most famous works are his commentary to **Rabbi Moshe ben Maimon** known as *Ohr Somayach* and his commentary to the Pentateuch known as *Meshech Chachmah*. He also wrote novella to the Babylonian and Jerusalem Talmuds, as well as halachic responsa. He died without any surviving offspring.

Rabbi Mordechai Leib Winkler (1845–1932)

He was a student of **Rabbi Moshe Sofer's** son and served as the Chief Rabbi of Madd, Hungary. He authored more than seven volumes of responsa under the title *Levushei Mordechai* and wrote a commentary to TB *Nedarim* under that name. He was also the father-in-law of **Rabbi Yosef Tzvi Dushinsky** of Galanta.

Rabbi Mordechai Yaffe (1530–1612)

Known as *Maharam Yaffe* and *Baal HaLevush*, he was originally from Prague where he established a yeshiva. After the Jews were expelled from Prague in 1561, he moved to Italy and then returned to Eastern Europe to serve as a rabbi of several different communities in Poland. He wrote ten different books, known collectively as the *Levushim*.

Rabbi Moshe Alshich (1508–1593)

Originally born in Turkey, he later moved to Safed where he was a student of **Rabbi Yosef Karo**. He served as a rabbi in Safed and amongst his students is the famous Kabbalist, Rabbi Chaim Vital (1543–1620). He authored commentaries to most of the Bible, which are renowned for their combination of literalist and kabbalistic interpretations.

Rabbi Moshe ben Machir (16th century)

He was a sixteenth-century Kabbalist in Safed and was part of a group of Kabbalists that included **Rabbi Shlomo Alkabetz** and **Rabbi Yitzchak Luria**. His work *Seder HaYom* elucidates Jewish customs and liturgy according to kabbalistic understandings.

Rabbi Moshe Cordovero (1522–1570)

Known as *Ramak*, he was an early Kabbalist in Safed who moved in the same circles as **Rabbi Shlomo Alkabetz** and **Rabbi Yitzchak Luria**. He sought to codify a systematic code of ethics and morals based on Kabbalah, which he did in his most famous work *Tomer Devorah*. He also wrote several other works of Kabbalah, many of which have not yet been published.

Rabbi Moshe Chaim Luzzato (1707–1746)

Sometimes referred to as *Ramchal*, he was an Italian rabbi and playwright who wrote several classic works on Jewish ethics and Kabbalah including *Mesillas Yesharim, Da'as Tevunos,* and *Derech Hashem*. It is reputed that **Rabbi Eliyahu Kramer of Vilna** said that he would have been willing to walk from Vilna to Italy just to see *Ramchal*.

Rabbi Moshe Isserles (1520–1572), Rama

He was the leading codifier of halachah for Ashkenazic Jewry and is known for his glosses to **Rabbi Yosef Karo's** *Shulchan Aruch*. He also wrote *Darkei Moshe* on the Tur, *Toras HaChatas*, and glosses to the *Issur V'Heter*. He also authored glosses to **Rabbi Eliyahu Mizrachi's** commentary to the Pentateuch entitled *Karnei Reim*. His unique blend of Maimonidean philosophy and Kabbalah are exemplified by his works *Toras HaOlah* (on ritual sacrifices) and *Mechir Yayin* (on the Book of *Esther*). His responsa are also a treasure trove of Torah scholarship.

Rabbi Moshe Meth (1541–1606)

He was a Polish rabbi who is known for writing *Ho'il Moshe*, a commentary on **Rabbi Shlomo ben Yitzchak** to the Pentateuch (consisting of two parts: *Be'er HaTorah* and *Be'er Heitiv*). He was one of the foremost students of Rabbi Shlomo Luria (1510–1574), Maharshal, whose halachic teachings were the basis of his work on ritual law, *Mateh Moshe*.

Rabbi Moshe Sofer (1762–1839)

Originally from Frankfurt, Germany, he was a student of the city's two rabbis, Rabbi Nosson Adler and Rabbi Pinchas HaLevi Horowitz. After serving as Rabbi of Mattesdorf, he eventually became the Rabbi of Pressburg/Bratislava where his yeshiva attracted many students and he became the hero of Hungarian Jewry. His novella on the Talmud and a plethora of important halachic responsa were printed under the name *Chasam Sofer*. He also wrote *Toras Moshe* on the Pentateuch.

Rabbi Moshe Yehoshua Leib Diskin (1818–1898)

After serving as the rabbi of various communities in Europe, he eventually settled in Jerusalem where he was greatly venerated. He was known for his sharp intellect in deciphering and answering Talmudic conundrums. He is also known as *Maharil Diskin*.

Rabbi Nachum Eliezer (c. 1660–1764)

He was the rabbi of Adrianpole in Turkey until he relocated to Jerusalem at an advanced age. When in Jerusalem, he was appointed as the *Rishon L'Tzion* (Chief Rabbi of Israel) until his death. He authored *Osiyos Eliezer*, *Midrash Eliezer*, *Chazon Nachum*, and other works.

Rabbi Naftali Tzvi Yehuda Berlin (1817–1893)

Known as *Netziv*, he was a Lithuanian rabbi who served as the Rosh Yeshiva of Volozhin Yeshiva for almost forty years (a position he inherited by virtue of his marriage to a granddaughter of its founder Rabbi Chaim of Volozhin). He wrote many works including *Meromei Sadeh* (on the Babylonian Talmud), *HaEmek Davar* (on the Pentateuch), and more.

Rabbi Raphael Immanuel Chai Ricchi (1688–1743)

He was an Italian Kabbalist and poet who is most known for his work *Mishnas Chassidim*. To sell copies of his books, he traveled to faraway Jewish communities including London, Amsterdam, and several cities in Turkey. He also wrote *Hon Osher*, which is a commentary to **Mishnayos**.

Rabbi Shabsai Bass (1641–1718)

He was a Polish rabbi who was heavily involved in publishing and selling Jewish books. He was most famous for his work *Sifsei Chachamim,* a popular anthology of commentaries to **Rabbi Shlomo ben Yitzchak's** commentary on the Pentateuch. His travels brought him to many communities throughout Germany, Poland, and Holland.

Rabbi Samson Raphael Hirsch (1808–1888)

He was a German rabbi who served on the frontlines in the defense of Orthodoxy from the onslaughts of Reform Judaism. His many works (mostly written in German but subsequently translated into English and Hebrew) contain original and traditional insights into Jewish philosophy, as well as etymologies of Hebrew words.

Rabbi Shimon Betzalel Neuman (1860–1942)

He was the Rabbi of Tarna, Hungary. His work *Peninim Yekarim* is a popular anthology of various explanations to the weekly *parsha* with his own comments to those explanations.

Rabbi Shlomo Alkabetz (1500–1580)

He was one of the leading Kabbalists in Safed during its most active period. His best-known work is the song *Lecha Dodi* which is almost universally sung on Friday nights at the *Kabbolas Shabbos* services. He also wrote *Shoresh Yishai* (on *Ruth*), *Ayeles Ahavim* (on *Song of Songs*), *Bris HaLevi* (on **Haggadah Shel Pesach**), and *Manos HaLevi* (on *Esther*).

Rabbi Shmuel Eidels (1555–1631), Maharsha

He was famous for authoring a two-part commentary to the **Babylonian Talmud**. The first part is a *pilpul*-style analysis of the halachic sections of the Talmud, **Rabbi Shlomo ben Yitzchak,** and Tosafos. The second part consists of explanations and elaborations of Aggadic sections of the Talmud, **Rabbi Shlomo ben Yitzchak**, and Tosafos (and is also printed with **Rabbi Yaakov Ibn Chaviv's** *Ein Yaakov* as well as in the standard editions of the **Babylonian Talmud**).

Rabbi Shmuel HaLevi Segal (1625–1681)

Originally born in Poland, he fled to Germany to escape the Chilmenski massacres and served as rabbi for various communities there. He was a student of **Rabbi David HaLevi Segal** and Rabbi Shabsai Sheftel Horowitz (son of **Rabbi Yishaya HaLevi Horowitz**). He is best known for his *magnum opus, Nachlas Shivah,* a work on the laws of documents.

Rabbi Shmuel Yaffe Ashkenazi (1525–1595)

As a Turkish rabbi, he wrote a multi-volume commentary to **Midrash Rabbah**, arguably the most authoritative commentary to that work. He was a prime student of **Rabbi Shlomo Alkabetz** and served as the rabbi of the Ashkenazic community in Constantinople, Turkey.

Rabbi Shmuel Strashun (1794–1872)

Known as *Rashash*, he was a wealthy philanthropist in Vilna who was also quite a talented Talmudist. He wrote glosses and novella to the **Babylonian Talmud** and **Midrash Rabbah** which are printed in the Vilna edition of those works. Many of his glosses contain textual emendations that better clarify the intent of the Talmud, Midrash, and their commentaries.

Rabbi Shmuel Yehuda Katzenellenbogen (1521–1597)

He was a son of the Italian sage Maharam Padua and served as the rabbi of Venice. He engaged in correspondence with the leading rabbis of his time, including **Rabbi Moshe Isserles** (who was his cousin) and **Rabbi Yosef Karo**. His discourses were published under the misleading name *Drashos Mahari Mintz.*

Rabbi Shalom Dov Ber Schneersohn (1892–1920)

He is known by Lubavitch Chassidim as the "Rebbe the *Rashab*" and served as the fifth Rebbe of Chabad. In addition to having been a prolific writer, he was also responsible for founding the network of Lubavitch yeshivas (*Tomchei Torah*) that continues to operate to this very day.

Rabbi Shalom Mordechai Schwadron (1835–1911)

Known as *Maharsham*, he was not only the rabbi of the town of Berezhany in Galicia, but he was a leading *posek* in his time. He authored many works including several volumes of his responsa *Maharsham* as well as *Da'as Torah*, a commentary to **Rabbi Yosef Karo's** *Shulchan Aruch*.

Rabbi Yaakov Emden (1697–1776)

He was the son of Rabbi Tzvi Ashkenazi, the *Chacham Tzvi*. He wrote many titles (including his famous *Siddur*) and lived in Germany most of his life without accepting any official rabbinic position. He is also known for his dispute with **Rabbi Yehonassan Eyebschitz** concerning Sabbatianism.

Rabbi Yaakov Reischer (1661–1733)

He was an Austrian rabbi who served as rabbi in different communities in Galicia and Germany. He authored several prominent works including the halachic works *Minchas Yaakov, Toras HaShlamim* and *Chok Yaakov*; *Iyun Yaakov* to **Rabbi Yaakov ibn Chaviv's** *Ein Yaakov*, and three volumes of responsa entitled *Shvus Yaakov.*

Rabbi Yaakov Schor of Kitov (1853–1924)

He was a student of **Rabbi Yosef Shaul Nathanson**. For several years, he studied Torah in Karlsruhe at the home of the famed philanthropist Rabbi Shmuel Strauss (founder of "Batei Strauss" in Jerusalem). He was the Rabbi of Kitov and was a prolific writer. He was a descendant of **Rabbi Alexander Sender Schor.**

Rabbi Yaakov Tzvi Meklenburg (1785–1865)

He was a German rabbi who wrote *HaKsav V'HaKabalah* as an effort to bridge the presumed gap between the Written Torah and the Oral Torah by showing how much of the Oral Torah is actually alluded to in the Written Torah. In this, he was at the forefront of the battle against Reform Judaism. He also wrote a commentary on the *Siddur* called *Iyun Tefillah*.

Rabbi Yechiel Halpern (1660–1746)

He was the Rabbi of Minsk who is best known for authoring *Seder*

HaDoros, a classic work of Jewish history. He culled information from many sources including **Sefer HaYashar,** *Sefer HaYuchasin* (written by **Rabbi Abraham Zacuto**), and *Shalsheles HaKabbalah* (written by **Rabbi Gedaliah ibn Yachya**). He wrote other works as well, including the recently published *Sefer Likkutim* and *Sefer HaKlallim*.

Rabbi Yehonassan Eyebschitz (1690–1764)

He was the kabbalistically-inclined Rabbi of Ehu (the "Three Communities": Altona, Hamburg, and Wandsbek in Germany). His many works include original homilies and halachic novellae. He also served as a judge on the rabbinical court in Prague.

Rabbi Yehuda Lowe of Prague (1520–1609), Maharal

He was one of the foremost thinkers of Jewish philosophy and Kabbalah. According to some unconfirmed accounts, he created a *Golem* through Kabbalah who helped defend the Jewish community in Prague. He wrote many works, including *Gur Aryeh* (a supercommentary to **Rabbi Shlomo ben Yitzchak's** commentary on the Pentateuch), *Chiddushei Aggados* (to the **Babylonian Talmud**), and more.

Rabbi Yehuda Roseannes (1657–1727)

He was the *Chacham Bashi* (Chief Rabbi) of the Ottoman Empire in Turkey. He is best known for his work *Mishneh L'Melech,* a commentary to **Rabbi Moshe ben Maimon**. He also wrote *Parshas Derachim,* a compilation of intricate homilies, which also contains his comments to the 613 commandments. His principal student Rabbi Yaakov Culi (1689-1732), author of *Yalkut Meam Loez,* edited and published his teacher's works.

Rabbi Yerucham Levovitz (1873–1936)

He is best known for serving as the *Mashgiach* of the Mir Yeshiva in Poland. His *mussar shmussen* inspired an entire generation of yeshiva students to maintain their upright moral standards. Some of his ideas have been published posthumously in various works including *Da'as Torah*.

Rabbi Yishaya HaLevi Horowitz (1565–1630)

He is known by the acronym of his principal work *Shelah* (*Shnei Luchos HaBris*). Although this work is chiefly kabbalistic in nature, it is also the source of several halachic rulings. As a disciple of the esteemed **Rabbi Moshe Isserles**, he served as the rabbi of Frankfurt, Germany. He is buried in Tiberias near **Rabbi Moshe ben Maimon**.

Rabbi Yisrael Lipschitz (1782–1860)

He was the Rabbi of Danzig, Germany, and wrote the commentary *Tiferes Yisrael* on **Mishnayos**. This work is split into two sections—named after the two pillars of the Holy Temple—*Yachin* and *Boaz*. His nearly scientific methodology has been the subject of controversy by more conservative rabbis.

Rabbi Yisrael Meir Kagan (1838–1933)

He is better known by the title of his work *Chofetz Chaim*, which details the laws of slander. While he wrote many books of halachah and Jewish thought, his most influential book was his *Mishnah Berurah* in which he elucidates **Rabbi Yosef Karo's** *Shulchan Aruch* and which contains his *Biur Halachah* (a commentary that delves into the depths of Jewish ritual law). He also wrote *Likutei Halachos,* which is an Alfasi-style halachic compendium on topics not covered by Alfasi.

Rabbi Yissocher Ber Eilenberg (1550–1623)

He was an Italian rabbi who was a principal student of **Rabbi Mordechai Yaffe**. He wrote *Beer Sheva* as a commentary to tractates of the **Babylonian Talmud** for which the commentaries of the Tosafists did not exist in his time. His responsa are also printed under the name *Beer Sheva*. In addition, he wrote the supercommentary *Tzeidah L'Darech* to **Rabbi Shlomo ben Yitzchak's** commentary on the Pentateuch (usually dealing with **Rabbi Eliyahu Mizrachi's** questions on Rashi).

Rabbi Yitzchak Luria (1534–1572)

He is better known as the *Arizal* and was the progenitor of what is known as a "Lurianic Kabbalah." He lived in Safed where he led a group of Kabbalists. Although he never printed any of his teachings, his principal student, Rabbi Chaim Vital (1543–1620) compiled his teachings and published them.

Rabbi Yosef Chaim of Baghdad (1832–1909)

He was an Iraqi scholar mostly known for his famous halachic work *Ben Ish Chai.* He was the leader of Sephardic Jewry in his time. He also authored *Ben Yehoyada, Benayahu,* (on the Aggadic sections of the Talmud) and *Ben Ish Chayal* (homilies), which contain much kabbalistic and esoteric material.

Rabbi Yosef Chaim Sonnenfeld (1848–1932)

He was the first Chief Rabbi of the *Eidah Chareidis* of Jerusalem during the years of the British occupation of Palestine. Originally from Hungary where he was a student of **Rabbi Moshe Sofer's** son, he served as an assistant to **Rabbi Yehoshua Leib Diskin** in Jerusalem before becoming its Chief Rabbi.

Rabbi Yosef Engel of Krakow (1858–1920)

He was the Chief Rabbi and Rosh Yeshiva in Krakow. He is known for having written many books (although fewer than twenty are still extant). He epitomized the Polish method of *pilpul*, often investigating general issues of Torah scholarship and citing many examples to illustrate his points.

Rabbi Yosef Palagi (1815–1896)

He was the youngest son of Rabbi Chaim Palagi (1788–1869), the Chief Rabbi of Turkey. Although he only wrote a few works, he helped edit and print his father's books.

Rabbi Yosef Shaul Nathanson (1808–1875)

He was a Galician rabbi who served as the Rabbi of Lvov (Lemberg) in Ukraine. He was a prolific writer, authoring tens of works and countless glosses to other works. His most famous work is probably his voluminous responsa *Shoel U'Meishiv.*

Rabbi Yosef Shlomo Delmedigo (1591–1655)

Known as *Yashar M'Kandia*, he was originally from Crete but later relocated to Italy where, *inter alia*, he studied science under Galileo. He wrote several works on medicine and science. His kabbalistic work *Mitzaref L'Chachma* is well-respected and is quoted by many leading authorities.

Rabbi Yoshiyahu Pinto (1565–1648)

He was a Talmudist and Kabbalist in Damascus, although he briefly lived in Safed where he came into contact with the students of **Rabbi Yitzchak Luria**. He is known for his commentary *Pirush HaRif* to **Rabbi Yaakov ibn Chaviv's** *Ein Yaakov*.

Rabbi Zvi Hirsch Chajes (1805–1855)

Known as *Maharatz Chayos*, he was an important Galician Talmudist whose glosses to the Talmud are printed in the standard Vilna Shas. He authored several Polemic works defending the basic tenets of Orthodox Judaism.

POST-HOLOCAUST

Piskei Teshuvos

This popular multi-volume work was written by Rabbi Simcha Benzion Aizik Rabinowitz as a supplementary to the rulings of **Rabbi Yisrael Meir Kagan's** *Mishnah Berurah*. Rabbi Rabinowitz is a Hassidic rabbi in the Ramat Shlomo neighborhood of Jerusalem.

Rabbi Aharon Kotler (1891–1962)

He was a Lithuanian-born rabbi who studied in Slabodka Yeshiva before joining the administration of the Yeshiva in Slutzk. During the Holocaust, he was brought to America where he spearheaded efforts to save other Jews. From 1943, he headed the Yeshiva Beth Medrash Govoha of America in Lakewood, NJ. His lectures, sermons, and halachic rulings have been published under the title *Mishnas Rabbi Aharon*.

Rabbi Aharon Lewin of Reische (1879–1941)

Known as the *Reische Rav*, he was a grandson and student of Rabbi Yitzchak Shmelkes (author of responsa *Beis Yitzchak)*. During World War I, he was appointed as an official advisor to the Emperor of Austria and after the war was elected to the Polish Parliament. He was murdered by the Nazis in 1941.

Rabbi Aharon Roth (1893–1946)

He was the founder of the Hassidic community in Jerusalem which begat the *Toldos Aharon, Toldos Avraham Yitzchak, and Shomrei Emunim* sects. The latter is named after Rabbi Roth's *magnum opus*. His followers are known to be ardently anti-Zionist.

Rabbi Aharon Rother

Rabbi Rother is one of the leading Torah scholars in Bene Barak. He authored the popular multi-volume *Sha'arei Aharon,* a compendium of commentaries and explanations to the Pentateuch, and a multi-volume work on **Rabbi Yosef Karo's** *Shulchan Aruch Orach Chaim* under the same name. Despite his advanced age, he still travels the world promoting his books.

Rabbi Aizik Ausband (1915–2012)

He was one of the original students of the Telz Yeshiva who helped reestablish the Yeshiva in Cleveland, OH, after the Holocaust. He was the son-in-law of the late Rosh Yeshiva of Telz, Rabbi Avraham Yitzchak Bloch (1891–1941), who was murdered in the Holocaust.

Rabbi Akiva Eiger Schlussel (1927–2011)

He was a principal in Emek Hebrew Academy/Teichman Family Torah Center in Los Angeles before starting Pacific Spice Company. He came from the town of Munkatch and brought with him much wisdom from Europe's Hungarian Torah sages.

Rabbi Dr. Akiva Tatz

He is a prominent lecturer and world-renowned expert in Jewish medical ethics. Originally from South Africa, he currently lives in London and is a student of Rabbi Simcha Wasserman (1900–1992).

Rabbi Aryeh Kaplan (1934–1983)

He was an American physicist and rabbi who is celebrated for having brought complicated Torah literature to the English-speaking community. He wrote many scholarly works including *The Living Torah* and several kabbalistic tracts in English.

Rabbi Asher Arieli

He is a senior lecturer at Yeshivas Mir in Jerusalem. His father-in-law was the late Rabbi Nochum Partzovitz (1923–1986), the Rosh Yeshiva in Mir Yeshiva. His lectures are arguably the most popular in the world; over 600 students attend his daily Talmudic lectures.

Rabbi Avraham Yishaya Karelitz (1878–1953), *Chazon Ish*

He was the leading *posek* of his time and author of the originally anonymous work *Chazon Ish* by which he is known. He was the backbone of the Jewish community of Bene Barak. He was famous for his halachic decisions in implementing the agricultural mitzvos.

Rabbi Baruch HaLevi Epstein (1860–1940)

He was the son of the leading *posek* of his time, Rabbi Yechiel Michel Epstein (author of *Aruch HaShulchan)* and was a nephew and student of **Rabbi Naftali Yehuda Tzvi Berlin**, the "Netziv" (Rosh Yeshiva of Volozhin). He was a bookkeeper by profession and bibliophile by hobby. He authored *Torah Temimah* as an encyclopedia of rabbinic teachings on the Pentateuch, *Baruch Sh'Amar* as a commentary to the *Siddur,* and other works.

Rabbi Ben-Zion Meir Chai Uziel (1880–1953)

Born and raised in Jerusalem, he eventually became the Sephardic Chief Rabbi of Jaffa, where he developed a close relationship with his Ashkenazic counterpart **Rabbi Avraham Yitzchak Kook**. In 1939, he became the Sephardic Chief Rabbi of the Mandate of Palestine, a position that he also held in the *Rabbanut* after the creation of the State of Israel in 1948. He authored numerous works including *Mishpatei Uziel*, *Sha'arei Uziel*, *Mikmani Uziel*, and *Hegyonei Uziel*.

Rabbi Binyamin Schmerler (1860–1941)

He was born and died in Bohorodchany, Ukraine, but spent most of his life in Stanislav where he worked on editing and selling Jewish books. He wrote several works of his own including *Ahavas Yehonassan*, an important commentary to *Targum Jonathan*. Several unpublished works of his (including poems) exist in manuscript form.

Rabbi Chaim Aryeh Pam

He serves as the *Mashgiach* overseeing the students of **Rabbi Asher Arieli** in Yeshivas Mir in Jerusalem. He is an American-born grandson of the late Rabbi Avraham Yaakov Pam (1913–2001), Rosh Yeshiva of Mesivta Torah Vodaath. He lives in the Ramat Shlomo neighborhood of Jerusalem with his wife and children.

Rabbi Chaim Shraga Feivel Frank (1908–1973)

He was a nephew of **Rabbi Tzvi Pesach Frank**, the Chief Rabbi of Jerusalem, and served as the rabbi of the Yemin Moshe neighborhood in Jerusalem. He is famous for promoting his particular way of tying the tefillin of the head, as elaborated upon in his works *Tiferes Chaim* and *Nezer Shraga*. He also authored *Toldos Zev*, a three-volume work on Tractate *Shabbos* of the **Babylonian Talmud**.

Rabbi Chananya Jacobson

He is a student of Rabbi Tzvi Kaplan and Edison Yeshiva. He originally hails from Los Angeles, CA, but currently lives in Lakewood, NJ.

Rabbi Efrayim Greenblatt (1932–2014)

He was one of the foremost disciples of **Rabbi Moshe Feinstein** and served for more than half a century as the Rabbi of Memphis, TN. He authored the multi-volume responsa *Rivivos Efrayim*, which contains his own rulings and the rulings of the great sages of our time.

Rabbi Eliyahu Eliezer Dessler (1892–1953)

He was a Lithunanian-born and trained rabbi who studied in the Mussar Yeshiva at Kelm. Before the Holocaust, he moved to England where he tutored students and took the mantle of the Gateshead Kollel. After the Holocaust, he served as the *Mashgiach* of Ponovezh Yeshiva in Bene Barak. He is celebrated as one of the most important thinkers of Jewish philosophy in the last century and his teachings (mostly comprised of letters to his students) on that subject were printed under the name *Michtav M'Eliyahu.*

Rabbi Meir Amsel (1907–2007)

He was the editor of the rabbinic bi-monthly journal *Hamaor* from when he founded it until his death in 2007. His first wife and daughter were killed in the Holocaust and in 1948, he immigrated to America and soon after began publishing his journal. He also wrote several works of his own.

Rabbi Menachem Dov Genack

He is a rabbi in Englewood, NJ, and serves as a Rosh Yeshiva in RIETS and as CEO of the Orthodox Union Kosher Division. He has written several books and many articles on various topics of Torah literature. He is considered one of the foremost students of the late Rabbi Joseph B. Soloveitchik (1903–1993).

Rabbi Menachem Mendel Kasher (1895–1983)

He was a Gerrer Chossid from Warsaw who lived in America and in Israel. He was known for his encyclopedic knowledge of Torah literature, which is evident from his *magnum opus*, *Torah Shleimah,* a 45-volume work on the Torah. He also wrote several other books and treatises and was considered an innovative *posek.*

Rabbi Menashe Klein (1924–2011)

Known as the *Ungvar Rav*, he authored many volumes of responsa and other works mostly published under the title *Mishne Halachos*. He survived the Holocaust and built a strong Hassidic community in New York City and Jerusalem.

Rabbi Meshullam Dovid HaLevi Soloveitchik

A son of **Rabbi Yitzchak Zev HaLevi Soloveitchik**, he is one of the venerated sages of Jerusalem where he heads a yeshiva in the Gush Shmonim neighborhood. He is a scion of the "Brisker" tradition and also serves as the president of the *Eidah Chareidis*. Some of his lectures to the Talmudic Order of *Kodshim* have recently been printed. His older brother was **Rabbi Yosef Dov Soloveitchik**.

Rabbi Mordechai Corcos (1890–1954)

He served as the Chief Rabbi of Marrakech, Morocco, before eventually immigrating to Israel. He authored *Gedulas Mordechai,* which covers many areas of Torah scholarship.

Rabbi Moshe Aryeh Freund (1894–1996)

He was the Rosh Yeshiva in the Romanian town of Satmar before the Holocaust. After his family was murdered at Auschwitz, he relocated to Jerusalem where he led the Satmar community (under the auspices of the Satmar Rebbe, **Rabbi Yoel Teitelbaum**) and in 1979 became the Chief Rabbi of the *Eidah Chareidis* in Jerusalem, a position he held until his death.

Rabbi Moshe Blau (1885–1946)

He was the director of Agudath Israel's operations in Palestine before the creation of the State of Israel. As such, he served as a liaison between the Old Yishuv community and the World Agudath Israel movement. His younger brother was Rabbi Amram Blau (1894–1974), the founder of *Neturei Karta*.

Rabbi Moshe Feinstein (1895–1986)

He was a Russian-born rabbi who served as the rabbi of Luban in Russia before immigrating to America where he lived in Manhattan. He served as the leading *posek* of American Jewry and was its leader in the post-Holocaust years. He wrote several works including *Dibbros Moshe* (much of which is still unpublished) on the **Babylonian Talmud**, *Drash Moshe* (homilies), and *Iggros Moshe* (his volumes of responsa).

Rabbi J. D. Eisenstein (1854–1956)

He was an early defender of Orthodoxy in America and had an encyclopedic knowledge of Torah material. He published several works including *Otzar Midrashim, Otzar Yisrael,*[648] and *Otzar Massaos*. He lived to the ripe age of 102, despite having received a blessing from Sir Moses Montefiore (1784–1885) that he should live to be 120 years old.

Rabbi Reuven Katz (1880–1963)

He studied under several prominent pre-Holocaust figures in Poland and Lithuania where he served as a rabbi and Rosh Yeshiva. He traveled to the USA to raise funds for his yeshiva and ended up staying there for several years before immigrating to Israel to serve as the Chief Rabbi and Rosh Yeshiva of Petach Tikvah, a post which he held until his death. He authored several volumes under the name *Degel Reuven*.

Rabbi Reuven Margolis (1889–1971)

He was a prolific author of many areas of Torah study. His clear, concise, and erudite works earned him the Israel Prize in Rabbinical Literature in 1957. *Margolios HaYam* is his work on the Tractate *Sanhedrin* of the **Babylonian Talmud**.

Rabbi Shamai Ostreicher

He is an American-Israeli rabbi who grew up in Elazar and studied in Ofakim where he developed a special relationship with the town's rabbi, **Rabbi Shimshon Pincus**. He currently delivers lectures on the Prophets and Hagiography at the Mir Yeshiva in Jerusalem. Some of his lectures are published in the various volumes of his work *Machamadeha M'yimei Kedem* on the Bible.

Rabbi Shimshon Pincus (1944–2001)

He was a famous American-born lecturer of Jewish philosophy and

---

648 Some have sought to discredit this work by noting that Jewish apostates contributed to it, however, as Dr. Yaakov Spiegel notes, some of the greatest rabbinic authorities have quoted from *Otzar Yisrael*, thereby lending credence to the work. See Speigel's article in *Yerushaseinu*, vol. 3 (Bene Barak: Machon Moreshes Ashkenaz, 2008), pgs. 304–309.

mussar who lived in Israel. He served as the *Mashgiach* in the yeshiva in Ofakim and eventually became the town's chief rabbi. He was killed along with his wife and one daughter in a tragic car accident at the young age of 56.

Rabbi Shlomo Goren (1917–1994)

He was the first Chief Rabbi of the Military Rabbinate of the Israel Defense Forces and then subsequently served as the Ashkenazic Chief Rabbi of the *Rabbanut* of Israel. He is famous for having blown the *shofar* at the Western Wall following the liberation of East Jerusalem in 1967. He later came under attack by **Rabbi Yosef Shalom Elyashiv** for his permissive ruling in the "Langer case."

Rabbi Shlomo Wolbe (1914–2005)

He was a German-born rabbi who was a leading pioneer of the Mussar Movement in the post-Holocaust era. He studied in the Mir Yeshiva before the war where he was a principal student of **Rabbi Yerucham Levovitz**. His work *Alei Shor* quickly became a classic work of *mussar*.

Rabbi Shlomo Zalman Auerbach (1910–1995)

Born into a family of Jerusalemite rabbis, he was an important figure on his own. He served as one of the leading *poskim* of his time, as well as a Rosh Yeshiva. He was also known for his extreme kindness and acceptance of all Jews. He authored several works of his own including *Meorei Aish* on the halachic status of electricity, *Maadnei Eretz* on agricultural laws, as well as responsa and novella entitled *Minchas Shlomo*. Additionally, other authors quote many of his explanations and rulings which were never published.

Rabbi Shmuel Ashkenazi

He is a well-known Torah scholar, linguist, bibliophile, and collector of Jewish books. He wrote and edited numerous books and articles on various topics. Before his retirement, he worked in the bibliography department of the National Library of Israel. He is an honorary member of the Mekize Nirdamim society.

Rabbi Uri Langner (1896–1971)

He was the Knihynicze Rebbe in Poland before immigrating to the USA in 1924. There, he was the spiritual leader of the *Chesed L'Avrohom* synagogue in Manhattan. He authored many works including his five-volume *Nechmad V'Naim* on the Pentateuch (1934), his three-volume *Ohr HaAggadah* to the Aggadic sections of the **Babylonian Talmud** (1942), and *Ohr HaChagim*, expositions about Jewish holidays (1955).

Rabbi Yaakov Kamenetsky (1891–1986)

He originally studied in the Slabodka Yeshiva in Lithuania and then moved to the USA where he eventually became the Rosh Yeshiva of Mesivta Torah Vodaath in Brooklyn. During his subsequent retirement, he was the driving force behind the Jewish community in Monsey, NY. He is celebrated as one of the senior Rosh Yeshivas of post-Holocaust America as well as one of its leading *poskim*.

Rabbi Tzvi Pesach Frank (1873–1960)

He was a Lithuanian-born rabbi whose family came to Palestine in 1892. In his early 30s, he was appointed a judge to the rabbinical court of **Rabbi Shmuel Salant**, then the Chief Rabbi of Jerusalem. He served in that capacity for almost sixty years, eventually becoming the head of the rabbinical court and Chief Rabbi of Jerusalem. Although he was quite influential in establishing the *Rabbanut* of Palestine/Israel and installing **Rabbi Avraham Yitzchak Kook** as its head, he later distanced himself from that body.

Rabbi Tzvi Yechezkel Michelson (1863–1943)

Born in Lublin, he served as the Rabbi of Plonsk before moving to Warsaw where he served on the rabbinic council. His many works include responsa *Beis Yechezkel, Dagan Shamayim, Pinos HaBayis,* and *Tirosh V'Yitzhar*. He was murdered in Auschwitz by the Nazis at the ripe age of eighty.

Rabbi Yaakov Yehuda Zilberberg/Di Kasif (1914–2003)

He was born in Budapest, Hungary, and studied under the Slovak sages Rabbi Shmuel David Ungar (1885–1945) in Nitra and Rabbi Akiva Sofer

(1878–1959) in Pressburg. After surviving the horrors of the Holocaust, he immigrated to Israel, where he lived in Bene Barak. He wrote several works about *Lashon HaKodesh*.

Rabbi Yisrael Taplin

He is the esteemed author of *Tarich Yisrael,* an intense halachic work concerning the international dateline, and responsa *Orach Yisrael* that deals with intricate halachic matters. He is a student of **Rabbi Aharon Kotler** and continues to live and study in Beth Medrash Govoha (Lakewood, NJ). He also authored *Halichos Yisrael* in which he compiled and explained many rulings and customs of his teacher **Rabbi Yisrael Zev Gustman**.

Rabbi Yisroel Dovid Harfenes

He is a leading *posek* in the Williamsburg neighborhood of Brooklyn, NY, and serves on the court of the Central Rabbinical Congress. He wrote several works of halachah including *Yisroel V'HaZmanim, Nishmas Shabbos,* and more.

Rabbi Yisrael Zev Gustman (1908–1991)

He studied under many of the great Lithuanian Torah scholars before the Holocaust and even sat on the rabbinic court of Rabbi Chaim Ozer Grodzinski (1863–1940). He served as a Rosh Yeshiva in Europe, America, and Israel. His lectures on the Talmud were published under the title *Kuntresei Shiurim*.

Rabbi Yissocher Dov Goldstein (1915–1988)

He was born in Pressburg, Hungary, and studied under many of the leading figures of his time, including **Rabbi Yosef Tzvi Dushinsky** and **Rabbi Avraham Yishaya Karelitz**. He served as a rabbi of Chug Chasam Sofer and Rosh Yeshiva of Shomrei HaChomos in Jerusalem. He spent thirty-three years of his life writing the six volumes of *Likutei Ha'aros,* comments to **Rabbi Moshe Sofer's** responsa, and authored his own responsa published posthumously under the name *Ohel Yissocher.* (He was a first cousin to the author's maternal grandmother, the late Mrs. Rozsi Messinger.)

Rabbi Yitzchak Hutner (1906–1980)

Originally from Warsaw, he studied in Slabodka Yeshiva in Lithuania and joined the Yeshiva's Palestinian branch in Hebron when it was first established. In Palestine, he became a disciple of the Chief Rabbi, **Rabbi Avraham Yitzchak Kook**. Afterwards, he spent several years studying in Berlin and in Jerusalem, before moving to the USA and eventually becoming the Rosh Yeshiva of Yeshivas Rabbeinu Chaim Berlin. His unique style of sermons, which blended philosophy, Kabbalah, and Jewish thought (fashioned after **Rabbi Yehuda Lowe of Prague**), are published under the name *Pachad Yitzchak,* which is also the name of the yeshiva that he founded in Jerusalem in his last years.

Rabbi Yitzchak Zev HaLevi Soloveitchik (1886–1959)

Known as the *Brisker Rav*, he was the successor to his illustrious father, Rabbi Chaim Soloveitchik (1853–1918), who served as a Rosh Yeshiva in Volozhin and then as a Rav and Rosh Yeshiva in the town of Brisk (Brest-Litovsk) in Lithuania. He wrote several works including a commentary to **Rabbi Moshe ben Maimon**, a commentary to the Bible, and a commentary to the Talmudic tractates *Yoma* and *Sukkah*, as well as a commentary to the laws of the Jewish calendar. His lectures on the Talmud (especially the Order of *Kodshim*) have also been published under the name *Chiddushei HaGriz*.

Rabbi Yoel Teitelbaum (1887–1979)

He was the Grand Rabbi of Satmar and the leader of the worldwide Satmar Chassidic community. He was known for his quick wit, incisive halachic decisions, and his extreme devotion. He authored the multi-volume *Divrei Yoel* as well as other works, including an anti-Zionist tract entitled *VaYoel Moshe*.

Rabbi Yosef Dov HaLevi Soloveitchik (1915–1981)

Known as *Rav Berel*, he was the eldest son of **Rabbi Yitzchak Zev HaLevi Soloveitchik** whom he succeeded as Rosh Yeshiva of Yeshivas Brisk in Jerusalem. He was in turn succeeded by his eldest son, Rabbi Avraham Yehoshua HaLevi Soloveitchik. His younger brother **Rabbi**

Meshullam Dovid Soloveitchik also heads a yeshiva that bears the name Brisk.

Rabbi Yosef Greenwald (1903–1984)

Known as the *Pupa Rav*, he was a Rosh Yeshiva in the Romanian town of Satmar until the death of his father, whereupon he inherited the position of rabbi of the Hungarian town of Pupa to which he relocated his yeshiva. After the Holocaust, he was instrumental in helping rebuild the devastated Jewish community, especially in Antwerp, Belgium, and in Brooklyn, NY.

Rabbi Yosef Eliyahu Henkin (1881–1973)

He was a Russian-born rabbi who studied under the greatest of the Lithuanian Torah sages and served as the rabbi of various Russian communities before immigrating to the USA in 1922. In America, he served as the rabbi of a synagogue in Manhattan and as the director of the world-famous *Ezras Torah* charitable organization. He is celebrated as one of the leading *poskim* in America.

Rabbi Yosef Shalom Elyashiv (1910–2012)

He was the son-in-law of Rabbi Aryeh Levin "The Tzadik of Jerusalem" and served as the leading *posek* of his generation. Some of his responsa have been published in *Kovetz Teshuvos,* while his lectures on the Talmud have been published under the name *Haaros.*

Rabbi Yosef Tzvi Dushinsky (1867–1948)

He was originally the Rabbi of Galanta (in Slovakia) and eventually moved to Jerusalem where he succeeded **Rabbi Yosef Chaim Sonnenfeld** as the *Eidah Chareidis*' Chief Rabbi. His many works are published under the name *Maharitz Dushinsky.*

Rabbi Zalman Sorotzkin (1881–1966)

Sometimes known as the *Lutzker Rav*, he was a Lithuanian rabbi who was the son-in-law of the Telzer Rav, Rabbi Eliezer Gordon (1841–1910). He was quite influential and prominent in the Jewish communal organizations of the early twentieth century. His most famous work is *Oznayim LaTorah*, a commentary to the Pentateuch.

Rabbi Zev Gold (1889–1956)

He was a German-born rabbi who studied in some of the most prestigious yeshivas in Lithuania before immigrating to the USA at the age of eighteen to serve as a rabbi. He led several different communities throughout America and served as the president of the Religious Zionist World Mizrachi's branch in America. In 1935, he relocated to Palestine where he worked to help further the Zionist cause and rescue Jews during the Holocaust. He was one of the signatories of Israel's Declaration of Independence.

ADDITIONS AND CORRECTIONS

Which Languages Did Adam Speak? (Page 28)

The Talmud states that Adam spoke Aramaic, but the Midrash says that he spoke *Lashon HaKodesh*. In order to support its assertion that he spoke Aramaic, the Talmud quotes a verse attributed to Adam. However, a reader pointed out that this verse is written mostly in *Lashon HaKodesh*, and only contains one word in Aramaic. The Talmud honed in on that one word to adduce its assertion that Adam spoke Aramaic. Nonetheless, the rest of that verse lends credence to the view that Adam also spoke *Lashon HaKodesh*.

Distancing *Lashon HaKodesh* from Impurity (Page 30, footnote 18)

One should optimally avoid speaking *Lashon HaKodesh* in the presence of impurity (such as idolatry). The Sanzer Rebbe, Rabbi Yekusiel Yehuda Halberstam (1905–1994), suggests that by extension, it is an act of piety for a woman to refrain from speaking *Lashon HaKodesh* during her menses, because then she is ritually impure.[649]

---

649 *Divrei Yatziv* (*Yoreh Deah*, vol. 1 §52:5).

Curtailing the Harmful Influence of Foreign Languages (Page 34)

Rabbi Shmuel Bornstein (1855–1926) offers an interesting Kabbalistic insight as to the relationship between a nation and its language. He writes that a nation's language reflects the essence of that nation. About this, the Rabbis say, "language is the quill of the heart."[650]

Consequently, a nation whose language has certain elements of evil embedded in it will be influenced by their language and become evil themselves. He quotes in the name of Rabbi Yitzchak Meir Alter of Gur (1798–1866) that the French language draws a person towards adultery. He notes that it is well-known that the French are notoriously adulterous, so it is understandable that this is reflected in their language.

On the other hand, the language of the Torah has the ability to convert evil into good. Thus, one who connects to *Lashon HaKodesh* will be able to transform all his evil elements into good qualities. This idea is alluded to in Proverbs, which states "The healing tongue is the Tree of Life [i.e. the Torah]."[651] This means that *Lashon HaKodesh*—the language of the Torah—has the healing property of purifying its speakers from evil.

Rabbi Bornstein explains that this is why Rashi chose to translate many words of *Lashon HaKodesh* into Old French in his commentaries to the Bible and the Talmud. By doing so, he sought to link French with *Lashon HaKodesh*, and thereby "heal" the language to some extent. If not for Rashi's efforts, it is possible that the French language would cause its speakers to be even more deviant than they already are.

Furthermore, Rabbi Bornstein proposes that Moses translated the Torah into seventy languages for a similar reason. Moses foresaw that the Jews were destined to be exiled, where they would be influenced by the languages of the nations of the world. He sought to prevent the damage from spiraling out of control by connecting each of these languages with the Torah in order to minimize their foul influence.[652]

---

650 The earliest source of this dictum is *Chovos HaLevavos* (*Shaar HaBechina*, Ch. 5).

651 *Proverbs* 15:4.

652 *Shem M'Shmuel*, *Parshas Devarim* Year 5789.

Adam Spoke *Lashon HaKodesh* Only on the Sabbath (Page 40)

Rabbi David Kochav (author of *Chumash Mikra Mevuar*) suggested to the author (partially in jest) that perhaps Adam spoke *Lashon HaKodesh* only on the Sabbath, and spoke Aramaic (and other languages) during the rest of the week. See page 132 (and later in this section) for a list of several authorities who encourage speaking *Lashon HaKodesh* specifically on the Sabbath.

Did Baalam Speak *Lashon HaKodesh*? (Page 45)

Rabbi Yaakov Lorberbaum (1760–1832) proposes a distinction between Balaam's prophecies, which were uttered in *Lashon HaKodesh*, and his conversations with Balak which were not held in *Lashon HaKodesh*.[653] This distinction is echoed by Rabbi Naftali Tzvi Yehuda Berlin, who notes that while Balaam's prophecies emanated from his mouth in *Lashon HaKodesh*, his non-prophetic dialogue with Balak took place in the Moabite language.[654]

On the other hand, Rabbi David Luria[655] writes that even Balaam's prophecies were not spoken in *Lashon HaKodesh*. Rabbi Luria supports this by quoting *Pirkei D'Rabbi Eliezer*,[656] which says that after the Jews' miraculous crossing of the Red Sea,[657] Pharaoh sang God's praises in Egyptian.[658] It ascribes the verse "Who is like You, mighty in holiness?"[659] to Pharaoh.

---

653 *Nachalas Yaakov* (*Parshas Balak*).

654 *HaEmek Davar* to *Deuteronomy* 23:12.

655 *Chiddushei HaRadal* to *Pirkei D'Rabbi Eliezer* (ch. 42).

656 *Pirkei D'Rabbi Eliezer* (ch. 42).

657 In this, *Pirkei D'Rabbi Eliezer* is consistent with its view that unlike the rest of the Egyptians present at the Red Sea, Pharaoh survived (see there ch. 43).

658 Rabbi Eliyahu HaKohen explains that the Midrash stresses that Pharaoh sang God's praises in Egyptian—even though he certainly knew *Lashon HaKodesh*—because that was the language is which he had originally sinned against God. During the Exodus story, Pharaoh denied God's dominion over the world by rhetorically asking "Who is God that I should heed to his voice?" (*Exodus* 5:2). Pharaoh later attempted to atone for this sin by rhetorically asking in the same language "Who is like You, mighty in holiness?" Rabbi Eliyahu reasons that Pharaoh must have known a little bit of *Lashon HaKodesh* simply because the Jews had lived under Egyptian sovereignty for so long that they must have had some sort of linguistic influence.

659 *Exodus* 15:11.

Rabbi David Luria explains that this Midrash means that Pharaoh spoke in Egyptian, but when Moses and the Jews later transcribed the Song of the Sea, they translated Pharaoh's words into *Lashon HaKodesh*, the language in which that verse appears in the Torah. Rabbi Luria explains that similarly, Balaam's prophecies were also not originally spoken in *Lashon HaKodesh*, but were translated into that language in the Torah.[660] Thus, Rabbi Luria disagrees with the Midrash that says that Balaam's prophecies were originally said in *Lashon HaKodesh*.

Using a Nation's Language Subjugates One to Their Angel (Page 46, footnote 67)

Targum Jonathan states that as a punishment for the Tower of Babel, God dispatched seventy angels to disseminate the seventy languages. Some commentators explain that each of these seventy angels serves as the patron angel for one of the seventy nations.[661] When one speaks a specific language, he enters a communion with the nation to whom that language belongs; thereby entering the domain of the patron angel of that nation.

Based on this idea, Rabbi Tzvi Elimelech Shapira of Dinov (1783–1841) explains the Jews' linguistic habits in exile. The Jews usually ended up speaking the local languages of whoever was ruling them. However, they were always careful to retain *Lashon HaKodesh*—which they mixed into their speech—so that the patron angels of their rulers would not completely dominate them.

In light of this, Rabbi Shapira laments the efforts of *Maskillic* activists who sought to discourage fellow Jews from speaking any language that contained traces of *Lashon HaKodesh*. He bemoans that in his times the local government decreed that a Jewish couple could not marry unless they demonstrated proficiency in the local gentile language.[662] He explains that

660 Moreover, he explains that the Midrash assumed that there are some words in that verse which show Egyptian influence, allowing for the interpretation that it was originally said in Egyptian.

661 See Ramban to *Numbers* 11:16.

662 Although there is no independent verification for the existence of such a decree, there is evidence of a similar decree. The *Maskillic* activist Herz Homberg (1749–1841) succeeded in convincing the administration of the Austro-Hungarian Empire (which ruled Galicia, where Rabbi Shapira lived) to implement a policy whereby Jewish couples could only apply for civil mar-

the underlying reason for this decree was to prevent parents from transmitting *Lashon HaKodesh* to the next generation. Once the parents gained proficiency in a different language, it would be more likely that they would teach their children that language rather than *Lashon HaKodesh*.[663]

Rabbi Shapira rejects the *Maskillic* campaign for Jews to speak other languages,[664] and encourages his readers to continue speaking the language that their forefathers traditionally spoke in the diaspora—Yiddish—which has many elements of *Lashon HaKodesh* in its makeup.[665]

Abraham Was an Ivri Because He Spoke *Lashon HaKodesh* from Childhood (Page 63)

Rabbi Yechiel Michel Stern suggests that perhaps Abraham was called an *Ivri* precisely because he spoke *Lashon HaKodesh* from such a young age.[666]

Lashon HaKodesh Was Exclusive to Shem, Eber, and Abraham (Page 77)

A Midrashic rendition of the apocryphal work *The Testament of Naftali* echoes *The Kuzari's* assertion that after the Tower of Babel, *Lashon HaKodesh* remained only in the house of Shem, Eber, and their descendant Abraham.[667] Interestingly, this historical account is printed

---

riage if they passed an examination based on Homberg's book *Bene Zion*. This work—filled with *Maskillic* propaganda—was written entirely in German, thus requiring one to be proficient in German before marrying. See R. van Luit, "Homberg, Herz.," YIVO *Encyclopedia of Jews in Eastern Europe* (August 13, 2010) [http://www.yivoencyclopedia.org/article.aspx/Homberg_Herz]. Mark Halpern (a prominent member of the Jewish Genealogical Society) suggested this approach to the author.

663 Rabbi Shapira notes that this phenomenon took place in the time of Ezra, when Jewish men married foreign women, and most of the next generation no longer spoke *Lashon HaKodesh* (see page 106).

664 See *Divrei Yatziv* (Yoreh Deah, vol. 1 §52:1) for discussion regarding a prohibition to speak a "non-Jewish language."

665 *Hosafos Mahartza* to *Sefer Soor MeiRah Va'Aseh Tov* (Jerusalem: *Ohr Torah Munkatch*, 1997), pg. 68.

666 *HaTorah HaTemimah* (Appendices to *Joshua* §18).

667 This Midrash is printed in S. A. Wertheimer (ed.), *Batei Midrashos*, vol. 1 (Jerusalem: Mossad HaRav Kook, 1952), pg. 196 and E. Yassif (ed.), *The Chronicles of Jerahmeel* (Ramat Aviv: Tel Aviv University, 2001), pg. 146.

almost exactly word-for-word in the commentary of the German Tosafist Rabbeinu Yekusiel of Speyer to the laws of Passover.[668]

Modern Hebrew: *Lashon Ivri* or *Lashon HaKodesh*? (Page 81)

The distinction between *Lashon HaKodesh* and *Lashon Ivri* has sometimes been used to deride Modern Hebrew (whether justifiably or not). A story illustrating this point is told about the first Ashkenazi Chief Rabbi of the pre-State *Rabbanut*, Rabbi Avraham Yitzchak HaKohen Kook (1865–1935).

Rabbi Kook was once staying at a hotel in New York when he was approached by a certain Hassidic Grand Rabbi, who insinuated that Rabbi Kook was an extremist in "his adamant demand to speak *Lashon Ivri*." By referring to Modern Hebrew as *Lashon Ivri*, the Grand Rabbi was noting his disapproval of Rabbi Kook's behavior. Rabbi Kook simply shrugged off this criticism and responded, "You mean 'to speak *Lashon HaKodesh*.'" By referring to the language as *Lashon HaKodesh*, Rabbi Kook reaffirmed his belief in Modern Hebrew's religious significance.[669]

Abraham's Healing "Gem" (Page 82)

The Talmud relates that Abraham hung a precious gem from his neck that had the power to heal those who gazed upon on it. After Abraham's death, God transferred that power to the sun itself.[670] Rabbi Shalom Shabazi (1619–1720) explains that this "precious gem" refers to *Lashon HaKodesh*, the language that Abraham used to teach others about the Uniqueness of God. Abraham did so by explaining that God is the supernatural force that causes the sun to rise and set. Upon Abraham's death, no one took his place in spreading God's word to the masses; instead the sun itself served as testimony to God's active role in the world.[671]

---

668 See G. Zinner (ed.), *Sefer Hilchos Pesach M'Rabboseinu HaRishonim* (Jerusalem: Machon Chasam Sofer, 1987), pg. 24.

669 Y. Katan (ed.), *HaMaayan* vol. 54:2 (Jerusalem: Mossad Yitzchak Breuer & Yeshivat Shaalvim, 2014), pg. 48.

670 TB *Bava Basra* 16b.

671 *Chemdas Yamim* (to *Genesis* 24:1).

Defending Rashi (Page 88)

Rashi says that Joseph proved his identity to his brothers by speaking *Lashon HaKodesh*. Ramban objects that this could not serve as proof, for the Canaanites spoke *Lashon HaKodesh*, and the neighboring Egyptians could be expected to do so as well. There are two ways to justify Rashi's view:

Approach #1: Two-Part Proof: Circumcision and *Lashon HaKodesh*

Mizrachi[672] defends Rashi by pointing out that Rashi also says that Joseph showed his brothers that he was circumcised. *Mizrachi* explains that Rashi believes that both of these proofs were required, one without the other would not suffice.

The descendants of Keturah (Abraham's concubine) also practiced circumcision; so circumcision alone could not prove that Joseph was Jacob's son. Similarly Jospeh's use of *Lashon HaKodesh* was also insufficient proof of his identity; since the Canaanites spoke *Lashon HaKodesh*. Therefore, Joseph used both points to prove his identity. His circumcision showed that he was a descendant of Abraham. The fact that he spoke *Lashon HaKodesh*—the language in Canaan—showed that he was not from Keturah's descendants, who lived far to the east of the Holy Land.[673] Maharal also follows this basic approach and argues that Joseph proved his identity via both his circumcision and his use of *Lashon HaKodesh*.[674]

Approach #2: The Canaanites spoke *Lashon Ivri*, not *Lashon HaKodesh*

Rabbi Nosson Nata Shapira (1490–1577)[675] offers another defense of Rashi's explanation. Rashi never wrote that Joseph's translator spoke *Lashon HaKodesh*, he only wrote that the translator spoke *Lashon Ivri*. As discussed at length in Chapter 3, there is a difference between *Lashon HaKodesh* and *Lashon Ivri*.

Rabbi Shapira understands that *Lashon HaKodesh* is a clear and concise strain of *Lashon Ivri*, when the latter is spoken with holiness, purity,

672 To *Genesis* 45:12.

673 See *Genesis* 25:6.

674 *Gur Aryeh* to Genesis 45:12.

675 *Imrei Shefer* to Genesis 45:12.

and great precision. Accordingly, he explains that Ramban is only partially correct in that the Egyptians could be expected to speak *Lashon Ivri*, but not *Lashon HaKodesh*. This is why Joseph's translator could speak *Lashon Ivri* without raising suspicions.[676] Thus, Joseph sought to prove his identity from the fact that he spoke *Lashon HaKodesh*—the strain of *Lashon Ivri* known only by Jacob's family.[677]

---

676 If the Abrahamic family were the sole preservers of the *Lashon HaKodesh*, then why were Joseph's brothers not tipped off to his true identity from the fact that he had a court translator who spoke *Lashon HaKodesh*? In light of the distinction between *Lashon Ivri* and *Lashon HaKodesh* proposed by the commentators (see Chapter 3), Rabbi David Goldberg (*Shiras David* to *Genesis* 45:12) posits that Joseph's translator only spoke *Lashon Ivri*, not *Lashon HaKodesh*. This allowed the translator to speak to Joseph's brothers without arousing their suspicion, because all Canaanites could be expected to speak *Lashon Ivri*. Thus, Rabbi Goldberg essentially offers the same answer as Rabbi Shapira.

Alternatively, one can argue that even if the translator spoke *Lashon HaKodesh*, the brothers might have thought that he was a descendant of Abraham's students, who likely also spoke *Lashon HaKodesh*. Rabbi Solnik (cited below) answers that they thought the translator was a descendant of Dinah, who was sent away from the family. He points to a Midrash (*Bereishis Rabbah* §93:6) that says that in fact, Judah remarked that the translator must have some connection to Jacob's household.

677 Rabbi Yaakov Solnik (*Nachalas Yaakov* to *Genesis* 42:23 and 45:12) initially rejects the differentiation between *Lashon Ivri* and *Lashon HaKodesh*. (He also rejects the view that *Lashon Ivri* means a Mesopotamian language.) He asserts that Rashi believes that *Lashon Ivri* is synonymous with *Lashon HaKodesh*. He supports this from the fact that Rashi states that Joseph's translator spoke Egyptian and *Lashon Ivri*, and then immediately identifies the translator as Joseph's son Manasseh. According to Rabbi Solnik, this juxtaposition shows that Rashi believes that identifying the translator as Manasseh was necessitated by the fact that he spoke *Lashon Ivri*. Since in Rashi's opinion only Jacob and his family understood *Lashon HaKodesh*, the fact that the translator spoke *Lashon Ivri* proved that he must have been from that family—thereby solidifying his identification as Manasseh.

Rabbi Solnik also rejects Ramban's assertion that *Lashon HaKodesh* was the language spoken by the Canaanites, and that therefore Egyptian royalty could also be expected to speak that language. He argues that if this was true, why do we find that Pharaoh did not understand *Lashon HaKodesh* (see Chapter 4)? He fails to account for the possibility that Divine intervention prevented Pharaoh from learning the language which he otherwise should be expected to know. He also argues that according to Ramban, Joseph's brothers should not have spoken *Lashon HaKodesh* amongst themselves, because they would have suspected that the viceroy could understand what they were saying, even though he employed a translator (similar to Rabbi Genack's comment on page 89, footnote 195).

Rabbi Solnik delivers his final blow to Ramban's explanation by writing that he finds Ramban's entire premise troubling. He notes that just as each of the seventy gentile nations possesses one of the seventy languages; the Jews—who transcend the seventy nations—possess *Lashon HaKodesh* as their special language. (Rabbi Solnik does not view *Lashon HaKodesh* as one of the seventy languages, see page 235, footnote 620). Thus, he cannot accept that any other na-

Did Moses Speak Egyptian? (Page 95, footnote 219)

Some commentators explain that Moses was reluctant to interact with Pharaoh because he had forgotten how to speak Egyptian. However, we see that he spoke to Jethro's daughters in Egyptian. Rabbi Moshe Sofer resolves this contradiction by explaining that Moses did not literally mean that he could not speak Egyptian. Rather, he meant that since he had not spoken before the king for over seventy years, he was unfit to serve as God's emissary to the Egyptian king. However, Rabbi Sofer explains that in truth, this actually made Moses more fitting to serve as God's emissary, because he was not accustomed to speaking in the Egyptians' depraved manner.[678]

Did Pharaoh speak Latin? (Page 96)

In discussing the meaning of the word *mann*, Abarbanel[679] clearly writes that the Roman language (Latin) did not yet exist at the time of the Jews' exodus from Egypt.

The Jews in Egypt Spoke a Jewish Dialect of Egyptian (Page 98)

Rabbi David Baharan (1866–1946) points out that the Midrash does not explicitly state that the Jews in Egypt spoke *Lashon HaKodesh*. The Midrash speaks in negative terms ("they did not replace their language"); as opposed to in positive terms ("they spoke *Lashon HaKodesh*"). This implies that while the Jews did not actually speak *Lashon HaKodesh* in Egypt, they also did not totally replace it with Egyptian. Instead, Rabbi Baharan proposes that they spoke a distinctively Jewish dialect of Egyptian. This accounts for the Midrash saying that the Jews did not adopt Egyptian, but not explicitly stating that they spoke *Lashon HaKodesh*.[680]

---

tion would speak the Jews' special language. Despite initially expressing skepticism as to the distinction between *Lashon Ivri* and *Lashon HaKodesh* offered by *Mizrachi* and Rabbi Shapira; Rabbi Solnik ultimately endorses their view. On a historical level, it is interesting to note that Rabbi Shapira taught Rabbi Solnik's father.

678 *Drashos Chasam Sofer*, vol. 2, pgs. 676–677.

679 To *Exodus* 16:15.

680 Y. Goldberg & N. Silman (eds.), *Orach David* (Jerusalem, 2011), pg. 257.

The Jews in Egypt Spoke Egyptian in a Holy Fashion (Page 99)

Rabbi Kalonymus Kalman Epstein of Krakow (1751–1823) also rejects a literal understanding of the Midrashim which say that the Jews in Egypt did not depart from speaking *Lashon HaKodesh*. He reasons that the Jews must have spoken another language, for the gentiles among whom they lived did not understand *Lashon HaKodesh*.

He explains that "maintaining *Lashon HaKodesh*" means not defiling one's mouth by eating forbidden foods, and not tainting one's tongue by speaking falsehoods, slander, and mocking words. When a person refrains from these wrongdoings, his mouth and tongue retain a certain level of holiness. This is what is meant by saying that they "maintained *Lashon HaKodesh*;" which literally means that they maintained a holy tongue. Thus, even if one does not actually speak the language *Lashon HaKodesh*, he can still be said to be preserving *Lashon HaKodesh*. Accordingly, he argues that the Jews in Egypt actually spoke Egyptian; but maintained the degree of holiness required to qualify as speaking "*Lashon HaKodesh*."[681]

Use of the Term "Ivri" (Page 103, footnote 231)

Rabbi Yaakov Kamenetsky notes that it is evident from the Bible that the term "Hebrew" (*Ivri*) was used to refer to a group of people from the time of Abraham and Joseph. He explains that it is likely that this term was used when referring to anyone who was a follower of the faith of Abraham, regardless of their ethnicity or nationality. He further argues that since the term *Ivri* was used to refer collectively to individuals who came from different backgrounds and were only united by their faith—not by any familial or geographical affiliation—the term *Ivri* evolved into referring to any person who was wandering, homeless, or not permanently domiciled.

This explanation accounts for all of the times that the Bible uses the term *Ivri*. A Jewish male bondsman is called an *eved Ivri* (עבד עברי, *Ivri* slave) because he does not own property,[682] and is therefore like a wanderer. Moreover, Rabbi Kamenetsky explains that the Philistines called

681 *Maor VaShomesh* (*Rimzei Pesach, Avadim Hayyenu*).

682 See TB *Kiddushin* 20a which says that as long as a destitute person owns a house, he cannot sell himself as a slave.

the Jews *Ivrim* as a means of taunting them; as if to say that they have no claim to the Land of Israel and are therefore like wandering nomads.

Similarly, when the sailors on the boat asked Jonah for his nationality, he identified himself as an *Ivri*. Jonah was from the northern Kingdom of Israel, and had left his home on a festival pilgrimage to Jerusalem (in the southern Kingdom of Judah), and then traveled directly to the port of Jaffa (where he boarded the boat). Because Jonah had come to Jaffa from Jerusalem, rather than from his home, he was like a wanderer.[683] Thus, the term *Ivri* was a fitting description for him at that time.

King Josiah the Torah Scholar (Page 105)

During the end of the First Temple Era, the Kohen Gadol found a Torah scroll, which was brought to King Josiah. Efodi understands that King Josiah was not proficient in *Lashon HaKodesh*, and was therefore unable to read the Torah scroll.

However, a reader noted that this seem to be at odds with a Talmudic passage describing the righteousness of King Josiah. The Talmud[684] says that King Josiah used his personal funds to reimburse the litigants in all of the court cases upon which he had presided from the age of eight (when he began his reign) until eighteen. Rashi explains that when the Kohen Gadol found the Torah scroll, Josiah delved into the Torah and began to analyze the Torah and its laws. Josiah concluded that he may have made mistakes in some of his rulings, so he personally compensated all the litigants with whom he had previously been involved.

The reader justifiably reasoned that if Josiah was able to so thoroughly examine the Torah, he was most likely familiar with *Lashon HaKodesh*. While this is not a direct contradiction to Efodi's understanding, it certain raises an important point.

Only the Children Forgot *Lashon HaKodesh* (Page 106)

While several sources cite the verse in Nehemiah about the Jews speaking Ashdodite to prove that the Jews returning from the

683 *Emes L'Yaakov* to *Genesis* 40:15.

684 TB *Shabbos* 56b.

Babylonian exile had forgotten *Lashon HaKodesh*, a closer examination of that verse reveals just the opposite. Nehemiah explains that many of the returnees married foreign women, so their children ended up speaking foreign "Ashdodite" languages. A reader pointed out that Nehemiah only laments the language used by the *children* of the returnees. Nehemiah complains that half of the younger generation no longer speaks *Lashon HaKodesh*. This implies, by omission, that the adults did speak *Lashon HaKodesh*.

Rebuke That Was Doomed to Fail (Page 109)

There is a difference of opinion as to whether the Jews replaced *Lashon HaKodesh* with Aramaic only after the destruction of the First Temple, or whether this occurred in the years before the destruction. The Talmud[685] relates that prosecuting angels argued that the Elders were responsible for the destruction of the First Temple because they did not protest against the sins of the masses. These sins caused the Temple's destruction. The Talmud clarifies that in actuality even had they protested, the masses would not have heeded rebuke. Nonetheless, the Elders did not know this, and therefore they should have reprimanded them.

Rabbi Moshe Sofer explains[686] why rebuke would have been ineffective: When one preaches in a language other than *Lashon HaKodesh*, he "dresses the Torah in sackcloth and ashes."[687] Thus, even if the message and intention of the speaker is good, his words will never enter the hearts of his listeners. Rabbi Sofer maintains that the Jews began to speak Aramaic instead of *Lashon HaKodesh* from the time that Aramean and Assyrian influences permeated the Jewish community—long before the destruction of the First Temple. Accordingly, when the Elders offered words of rebuke to their sinning brethren, they did so in Aramaic, not in *Lashon HaKodesh*. Therefore, their rebuke would automatically fall on deaf ears. Thus,

---

685 TB *Shabbos* 55a.

686 *Toras Moshe* to *Numbers* 6:23.

687 In his ethical will, Rabbi Sofer warns his followers not to preach in the language of the gentiles, see *Tzavaas Moshe* (Jerusalem, 1924), pg. 4a. Rabbi Akiva Yosef Schlesinger (1837–1922), in his commentary *Lev HaIvri* to Rabbi Sofer's ethical will, discusses this at great length. See also *Piskei Chasam Sofer* (Bene Barak, 2000), pgs. 1–2, where he writes that this prohibition is not so clear-cut, and has exceptions. This crusade against rabbis preaching in gentile languages began as a way of resisting the changes which the *Haskalah* wished to impose on the Jewish community.

the Talmud considers the Elders to not have rebuked the sinners of their generation.[688] For this, those Elders are considered guilty.

The Jews only forgot *Lashon HaKodesh* so quickly once in exile because they had already begun to forsake the language when they still lived in the Land of Israel. Once they left the Holy Land, their connection to the Holy Language was so utterly severed that they quickly forgot it.[689]

More Proponents of Speaking *Lashon HaKodesh* (Page 132)

Rabbi Yisroel of Shklov (1770–1839) was one of the foremost students of Rabbi Eliyahu Kramer of Vilna; and served as the leader of the Ashkenazi settlement in Safed and subsequently in Jerusalem. He was said to only speak *Lashon HaKodesh* on the Sabbath.[690] In fact, according to one source,[691] Rabbi Kramer himself also spoke *Lashon HaKodesh*; although his actions are viewed as atypical, and not to be taken as a precedent for the masses.

Nonetheless, Rabbi Yisrael Meir Kagan writes[692] that on the Sabbath "men of deeds" are careful to only speak *Lashon HaKodesh* (in order to distance themselves from idle chatter). By mentioning this in his halachik work, it seems that Rabbi Kagan endorses such an approach for the masses, and not just for the elite.

Can *Lashon HaKodesh* Truly Be "Secularized"? (Page 138)

Some have claimed that Modern Hebrew was deliberately designed in a way that strips *Lashon HaKodesh* of its religious associations. Dr. Gershon Scholem (1897–1982), the man who brought the study of Kabbalah to the academic world, believes that such an endeavor is doomed to fail. He explains his view in a letter written to Dr. Franz Rosenzweig (dated December 26, 1926):

---

688 Rabbi Sofer notes that even though the wording of the Talmud implies that the Elders literally did not offer rebuke, this is only because the Talmud was quoting what the prosecuting angels claimed. The truth is that the Elders did offer rebuke, but since it was given in Aramaic, a language which the angels do not understand, the angels did not realize it.

689 See responsa *Divrei Yatziv* (*Yoreh Deah*, vol. 1 §52:3) who reconciles this explanation with Rabbi Sofer's other explanation that the Rabbis purposely had the Jews in exile stop speaking the language to avoid speaking *Lashon HaKodesh* in the proximity of idols.

690 See A. Lunz (ed.), *Pe'as HaShulchan* (Jerusalem: Seforim Pardes, 1959), pg. 5.

691 See responsa *Divrei Yatziv* (*Yoreh Deah* vol. 1 §52:6, §53:1).

692 *Mishnah Berurah*, *Orach Chaim* §307:5.

> What will be the result of updating the Hebrew language? Is not the Hebrew language, which we have planted among our children, an abyss that must open up? People here do not know the meaning of what they have done. They think they have turned Hebrew into a secular language and that they have removed its apocalyptic sting, but it is not so: the secularization of the language is merely emptied words. We live with this language as on the edge of an abyss. The language is composed of names, the power of the language is hidden within the names, its abyss is sealed therein. After invoking the ancient names day after day we shall no longer be able to hold off their power. God cannot remain silent in a language in which He has been evoked thousands of times to return to our life.[693]

Thus, Scholem also recognizes the supernatural properties of *Lashon HaKodesh*, and warns his secular colleagues that they cannot expect to use this holy language in a secular way without it eventually reawakening their Jewish spirituality.

Same Words, New Meanings (Page 138, footnote 349)

Modern Hebrew sometimes changes the meaning of *Lashon HaKodesh* words. For example, the word *hartza'ah* (הרצאה) means "appeasement" in *Lashon HaKodesh* (usually in the context of ritual sacrifices, which serve as an "appeasement" for those who offer them). In Modern Hebrew it has been redefined to mean "lecture." Another example is the word *ba'ayah* (בעיה) which means "problem" in Modern Hebrew. This word is derived from the Aramaic word בעיא, which means "question".[694]

---

693 G. Scholem, "Thoughts About Our Language (1926)," *On the Possibility of Jewish Mysticism in Our time and Other Essays* (Philadelphia: The Jewish Publication Society, 1997), pg. 27.

694 The א at the end of the Aramaic word was Hebraized into a ה in accordance with a grammatical rule codified by *Shulchan Aruch* (*Even HaEzer* §129:34) who writes that names ending with the same sound are spelled differently in Aramaic than in *Lashon HaKodesh*, for the former ends words with an א while the latter, with a ה.

Is Yiddish the Holy Language? (Page 142)

Rabbi David Cohen (Rav of Gvul Yaabetz) authored a work entitled *Yiddish HaSafa HaKedoshah*, which pinpoints the sources of various Yiddish words and phrases in Biblical and rabbinic literature.

Does the Bible Use Foreign Words? (Page 169)

We presented various views regarding whether the Bible uses words in languages other than *Lashon HaKodesh*. Some commentators say that it does, while others say that it does not. A reader suggested harmonizing the two views by differentiating between the Pentateuch and the Prophets/Hagiography. The reader argued that seemingly foreign words in the Pentateuch are actually from *Lashon HaKodesh* (but their meanings have been lost and only rediscovered through usage in other languages); while foreign words in the other books of the Bible do, in fact, come from other languages.

The reasoning behind this approach lies in a fundamental difference between the Pentateuch and the Prophets/Hagiography. The choice of words in the text of the Prophets is determined by the prophet/writer, albeit influenced by prophecy/divine inspiration. On the other hand, the text of the Pentateuch was determined by God Himself. God dictated the text to Moses, who recorded it exactly, devoid of his own influence. Thus, the words of the Pentateuch must be *Lashon HaKodesh*; which is not necessarily true of the other books of the Bible.

Is "Pardes" Persian? (Page 171)

Academic scholars believe the word *pardes* to be of Greek or Persian origin. However, Rabbi David Luria suggests a Semitic origin for the word in his glosses to *Pirkei D'Rabbi Eliezer* (Ch. 42). He notes that in the Bible[695] the word *pardes* means an orchard containing various species. Accordingly, he suggest that the word *pardes* is related to the Hebrew word *parud* (פרוד), which means "separate," denoting the separation between different types of trees planted in an orchard.

---

695 See *Ecclesiastes* 2:5. (Although we claimed that the word *pardes* appears in the Bible only once (in Song of Songs), several readers have noted that it also makes an appearance in the plural form in there.)

Sources for the Explanations in the Composite Words Chart (Page 172)

Due to technical difficulties, the sources for the explanations given in the chart were not printed. The etymologies of the Hebrew words *pilegesh*, *androginus*,[696] and *Cartigni* are given by Rabbi Yaakov Emden in his work *Migdal Oz* (*Beis Middos*, *Aliyas HaLashon*). The explanation of the word *vayehi* is presented by Rabbi Shlomo Alkabetz (1500–1580) in the beginning of his commentary to the book of Ruth, *Shoresh Yishai*. The explanation of the word *terumah* is presented by Maimonides (in his commentary to the *Mishnah Terumah* 4:3), Bechor-Schor (to *Deuteronomy* 18:4), *Pirush HaRokeach* (to *Exodus* 25:2), and others.

The Palmyrene Script of Aramaic (Page 191)

The script portrayed has been identified by academia as the one used to write the dialect of Aramaic that existed in the Syrian city Tadmur (known by the Romans as Palmyra) and the surrounding area. Rabbi Avraham the Physician also describes this alphabet (as printed by the de Bry brothers, see page 190) and assumes that it is, in fact, the *Ivri* script.[697] In light of the similarities between *Lashon HaKodesh* and Aramaic, it is quite understandable that one could misidentify the Palmyrene script of Aramaic as the ancient *Ivri* script of *Lashon HaKodesh*.

Why Must the Scroll of Esther Be Written in Ashuri? (Page 194)

There are different opinions regarding which scripts the Jews used for *Lashon HaKodesh*. Many believe that the Jews used *Ivri* script and switched to *Ashuri* when Ezra led the exiled Jews of Babylon back to Israel.

A reader pointed out the following question: The Mishnah[698] rules that one can only fulfill his obligation to read the Scroll of Esther on Purim if the scroll was written in *Ashuri* script. The Talmud[699] derives this law from the fact that the Scroll states that the Jews accepted the

---

696 Nonetheless, *HaBachur* (in *Sefer HaTishbi*, also quoted by *Tosafos Yom Tov* to *Yevamos* 8:6) writes that *androginus* is Greek, not Hebrew.

697 *Shiltei Hagiborim, Ma'amar HaLashon* (Machon Yerushalayim: Jerusalem, 2010), pgs. 574–575.

698 *Megillah* 2:2.

699 TB *Megillah* 19a.

laws of Purim "as they are written and in their times."[700] However, the Scroll of Esther was originally written in *Ivri* script, not *Ashuri* script; since it was written during the Babylonian exile! Therefore, one would assume that one could fulfill his obligation with a Scroll of Esther written in *Ivri* script. Furthermore, how can the Talmud use this verse to support the assertion that one must use a Scroll written in *Ashuri*?

Rabbi Meir Simcha HaKohen of Dvinsk answers this question by examining the words of the verse that the Talmud quotes. If one was obligated to read a Scroll written in the script that was used for the original Scroll, then the Talmud should have simply said to use a Scroll "as they are written." However, the Talmud also quoted the rest of the verse "and in their times." This implies that the verse should be understood to mean "as they are written [according to the script used] in their times." "Their" refers not to the Jews who wrote the original Scroll, but to the Jews in each generation. This means that the Scroll must be written in whatever script the Jews of that generation use. In the time of the Mishnah the Jews used *Ashuri* script, so the Scroll had to be written in Ashuri.[701]

Archeological Artifacts Showing Use of Ivri (Page 201, footnote 520)

There are three views in the Talmud as to which script was originally used to write Torah scrolls. Rabbi Yose believes that *Ivri* was always used until Ezra switched to *Ashuri*. Some archeological artifacts contain *Ivri*, but these artifacts probably originate from the post-Ezra era. Thus, they have no bearing on the discussion of which script was used before Ezra's times.

The earliest known fragments of a Biblical passage are the silver scrolls found at Ketef Hinnom (located in Jerusalem, southwest of the Old City), which date to the First Temple period (i.e., pre-Ezra). These scrolls contain the passages of the Priestly Blessings (Numbers 6:24–25) written in *Ivri* script. This seems to prove Rabbi Yose's view that Torah

700 *Esther* 9:27.

701 *Meshech Chachmah* (to *Esther* 9:27).

scrolls were originally written *Ivri*. Nonetheless, even these scrolls do not conclusively validate Rabbi Yose's view, since they were not written as Torah scrolls—they were likely special amulets used to grant blessings to their holders. The only piece of evidence that could irrefutably resolve this discussion would be a Torah scroll from the First Temple period belonging to the mainstream Jewish community.

Alternate Definitions of "Ivri" and "Ashuri" (Page 207)

The eminent philologist Dr. Naftali Herz Torczyner (1886–1973), known as Tur-Sinai, offers a completely different spin on the discussion regarding use of *Ivri* and *Ashuri*. He arrogantly rejects the view of all the commentaries who assume that the Tannaic and Amoraic passages in question discuss the script used for writing *Lashon HaKodesh*. Instead, he dissects the rabbinic sources to cobble together a new explanation.[702]

He explains that the terms *Ksav Ivri* and *Ksav Ashuri* refer not to different *scripts*, but to different *Scriptures*. He argues that at the end of the Babylonian exile, there were two versions of the Hebrew Bible: Ezra's edition of the Bible, which the Jews in Babylon kept (known as *Ashuri*); and another edition that was preserved by the Israelites and Judeans who remained in the Holy Land, as well as by the Samaritans (known as *Ivri*).

He argues that the Talmudic passages in question were simply relaying a tradition that when Ezra led the returning Jews from Babylon, his community rejected *Ivri*, i.e. the Samaritan version of the Bible, (which

---

702 Tur-Sinai rejects the consensus understanding because he finds it difficult to reconcile archeological findings—which prove that the Jews used *Ivri* script well into the Tanaaic period—with the Tanaaic opinions in the Talmud that the Jews always used *Ashuri* script. Furthermore, he asks: How can some sages assert that the Jews never used *Ivri* script, if even during the lifetimes of those sages (or their teachers), *Ivri* script was still in use? Furthermore, Tur-Sinai questions why it is appropriate to name the earlier script "*Ivri*," as if it was something unique to the Jews. After all, the Paleo-Hebrew script essentially mimics the Phoenician script, which was commonly used by many different nations in the ancient Middle East.

Tur-Sinai's first question ignores the many commentators who explain that the entire Talmudic discussion of *Ivri* vs. *Ashuri* is limited to which script was used in Torah Scrolls; for it is an undeniable fact that the Jews used *Ivri* script for other purposes. Tur-Sinai's second objection raises an interesting point, but hardly disproves the consensus understanding.

was viewed as corrupt). Instead, they advocated universal adoption of the *Ashuri* version which Ezra himself had brought to the Holy Land. According to Tur-Sinai, this is the sole meaning of the passages under discussion.[703] Although this is a novel theory, it is incompatible with the traditional view.

Forbidding Prayer in Foreign Languages (Page 225)

Rabbi Elazar Fleckles, in his capacity as a judge on the rabbinic court of Prague, was among the signatories of a declaration which states that it is forbidden to deviate from the established customs of praying in *Lashon HaKodesh* and switch to a different language. Their declaration further asserts that those reformists who seek to do so are lacking in their religious beliefs, and that their entire objective is to give themselves a reputation amongst the nations of being more enlightened than the traditional Jews. The rabbinic court of Prague concludes that these reformers' actions "are neither Hebrew nor Christian."[704]

Rabbi Moshe Sofer writes that while one can technically fulfill his obligation of praying in any language, optimally one should pray in *Lashon HaKodesh*. Furthermore, he notes that only individuals may pray in a language other than *Lashon HaKodesh*, and only occasionally; but to pray thusly frequently or in a *minyan* with a cantor is completely forbidden. He proves this by simply noting that the Men of the Great Assembly instituted the exact *Lashon HaKodesh* liturgical text. If it is permissible to pray in any language, then the Men of the Great Assembly should not have instituted prayer in *Lashon HaKodesh*—especially in a generation wherein half the Jews only spoke Ashdodite, and not *Lashon HaKodesh*.

He then refutes a common argument of those who wished to institute prayer outside of *Lashon HaKodesh*. They claim that since the ignorant masses are no longer proficient in *Lashon HaKodesh*, it is worthwhile to institute that they pray in whatever language they feel more comfortable.

---

703 *Ksav HaTorah* (Jerusalem, 1943), pgs. 3–34.

704 *Eleh Divrei HaBris* (Altona, 1819), pg. 17. This work was published by the rabbinic court of Hamburg in response to the efforts of the early Reformists to introduce changes to synagogue rituals, including changing the language of prayer from *Lashon HaKodesh*. It contains letters from the leading halachik authorities of its time who condemned these efforts.

However, Rabbi Sofer asserts that it is more worthwhile to institute that the ignorant masses learn *Lashon HaKodesh* in order to use it for prayer, than to allow them to pray in whatever language they want.

He notes that the prevailing etiquette in royal courts is that a foreign guest who wishes to address the king must do so in the king's language, even if the king understands the guest's language. A king's honor demands that those who speak to him must speak in his language. Similarly, the honor of God demands that those who speak to Him must speak in His language—*Lashon HaKodesh*—even though He understands all languages.[705] The same sentiment is expressed by Rabbi Sofer's two leading colleagues: his father-in-law Rabbi Akiva Eiger (1761–1837)[706] and Rabbi Yaakov Lorberbaum of Lissa (1760–1832).[707]

Why Does the Passover Haggadah Use Aramaic? (Page 230)

Rabbi Eliezer Ashkenazi explains that the *Ha Lachma Anya* section of the Passover Seder was instituted after the destruction of the Second Temple. It serves as a means of mourning the Temple's destruction and the exile, and evoking the Jewish yearning for its restoration.[708] Similarly, Rabbi Moshe Sofer writes that the poem which concludes the Passover *Seder*, *Chad Gadya* (חד גדיא, one kid) also serves as a means of mourning the destruction of the Temple and the exile. The kid mentioned repeatedly in that poem alludes to the young lamb customarily offered as the Paschal sacrifice.[709] These two explanations can be combined with the Talmudic assertion that Aramaic is a language especially appropriate for elegies.[710] These two passages—which mourn the exile and destruction of the Second Temple—were understandably penned in Aramaic, because that is the language of mourning.

Which Language Do Demons Speak? (Page 230)

Rabbi Moshe ben Machir explains why the nullification of leavened

---

705 *Eleh Divrei HaBris* (Altona, 1819), pgs. 10–11.
706 *Eleh Divrei HaBris* (Altona, 1819), pgs. 27–28.
707 *Eleh Divrei HaBris* (Altona, 1819), pg. 81.
708 *Ma'ase Hashem* (Warsaw, 1833), 22b–23a.
709 *Haggadah Shel Pesach Im Pirush Chasam Sofer* (Jerusalem: Machon Chasam Sofer, 2004), pg. 269.
710 See pages 31; 182.

bread is recited in Aramaic. His explanation is built on the assumption that just as angels do not understand Aramaic, demons also do not understand the language (see page 232).

When Rabbi Shlomo Zalman of Liadi (1745–1812) discusses the nullification of the leavened breads, he writes that he purposely omits Rabbi Machir's explanation. According to Rabbi Shlomo Zalman, the contrary is true: while Aramaic is not understood by angels, it is the main language of demons. He proves this from the *Zohar*,[711] which says that *Kaddish* (recited in Aramaic) is said in the language of the "other side" (*lishna d'sitra achra*, לישנא דסיטרא אחרא). This means that Aramaic is associated with the "other side"—the netherworld of the demons. However, the position that the demons speak Aramaic is contradicted by a slew of commentators who explain the Passover night invitation was instituted in Aramaic so that the demons would be unable to understand it.[712]

By disagreeing with the basis of Rabbi Moshe ben Machir's explanation, Rabbi Shlomo Zalman is forced to offer a different reason as to why the nullification was instituted in Aramaic. He explains that this nullification is a legal declaration which can only be enacted by someone who understands its meaning. The declaration was instituted in Aramaic since at that time Aramaic was the language understood by the masses. Consequently, Rabbi Shlomo Zalman rules that one who does not speak Aramaic should be taught the text of the nullification in a language which he does understand.[713]

Language of Liturgical Formulas (Page 231)

A reader asked why the formulas for *Eruv Tavshilin*[714] and *Eruv*

---

711 *Terumah* 129a.

712 See Rabbi Chaim Rapaport in *Haggadah Shel Pesach, Aleh Zayis* (Lakewood: Machon Aleh Zayis, 2015) pgs. 191–208 who offers a comprehensive survey of all the early commentators who offered this explanation and variations on it. He then defends Rabbi Shlomo Zalman of Liadi's assertion by arguing that his explanation was in accordance with the *Zohar*; while the other commentators offered their view before the *Zohar* was "discovered" (or quoted sources from before the *Zohar* was discovered).

713 *Shulchan Aruch HaRav, Kuntres Acharon* (*Orach Chaim* §434:4).

714 *Shulchan Aruch, Orach Chaim* §527:12.

Chatzeros[715] are customarily recited in Aramaic, while the formula for *Eruv Techumim*[716] is customarily recited in *Lashon HaKodesh*.

Rabbi Menachem Mendel Bramson answers that *Eruv Tavshilin* and *Eruv Chatzeros* create exemptions to rabbinic laws, while *Eruv Techumim* creates an exemption of a biblical law. He makes two assumptions: that angels might prosecute Jews for not adhering to biblical laws, but will not do so for rabbinic laws; and that angels do not understand Aramaic.

There is no need for the angels to understand the meanings of the *Eruv Tavshilin* and *Eruv Chatzeros* formulas because the angels will not prosecute the Jews for violating the rabbinic laws to which these formulas create exemptions. On the other hand, *Eruv Techumim* is related to biblical law. If the angels did not understood this formula, they would prosecute the Jews under the mistaken impression that the Jews disobeyed a biblical injunction, which was in actuality addressed by the *Eruv Techumim*. Therefore, the *Eruv Techumim* formula is recited in *Lashon HaKodesh* to allow the angels to understand it.[717]

Man's Advantages Over Angels (Page 232)

Rabbi Naftali Hertz Ginzburg explains that God created humans and angels in such a way that each has an advantage over the other, thereby eliminating the possibility that one should be jealous of the other.[718]

Man has a special advantage over angels in that when praising God, man has permission to say His name after only two words; while angels may only mention God's name after reciting three words.[719] Angels possess the advantage of being free from the temptations of the Evil Inclination; unlike man who must constantly battle it in order to remain free from sin.

According to Kabbalah, the act of destroying and nullifying the leavened breads before Passover also destroys and nullifies each person's Evil Inclination, which is metaphorically called a leavening agent.

---

715 *Shulchan Aruch, Orach Chaim* §366:15.

716 *Shulchan Aruch, Orach Chaim* §415:4.

717 *Toras Menachem* (Warsaw, 1907), pgs. 425–426.

718 See pages 34–35 for an explanation of how man is similar to both animals and angels.

719 See *Sifrei* to *Deuteronomy* 32:3.

When the Jews recite the nullification formula before Passover, they rid themselves of the Evil Inclination, thus neutralizing the angels' advantage over humankind. If the angels see that mankind has more advantages than they do, they would likely become jealous and prosecute the Jews. In order to avoid this outcome, the Jews recite the nullification formula in Aramaic, so that the angels will not realize what has been said.[720]

The Seventy Languages and Wax on a Torah Scroll (Page 235, footnote 620)

Although the discussion regarding whether *Lashon HaKodesh* is considered one of the seventy languages seems merely theoretical, it may bear practical halachik ramifications. Rabbi Yehuda Leib Sirkis (1652–1733) discusses whether wax that fell on some words within a Torah scroll would render the scroll invalid or not. He explains that at the root of the question is whether or not words coated with a layer of wax are considered erased.

To answer this, he cites the opinion of Rabbi Yehuda[721] who believed that when the Jews wrote the Torah on boulders in seventy languages, they first wrote the Torah and then coated the boulders with a layer of plaster.[722] This raises a serious question: It is forbidden to erase God's name. If so, how could they coat the words of the Torah (including God's name) with plaster, if doing so would overlay the writing of the Torah in seventy languages, which would thereby erase God's name multiple times?

In order to avoid this question, Rabbi Sirkis suggests that coating writing in plaster is not considered erasing. By extension, words covered by wax are also not considered erased. This means that wax which falls upon on a Torah scroll would not invalidate it.

Nonetheless, there is a complicating factor: The ruling that a Torah scroll is not invalidated by wax is predicated on the assumption that erasing God's name in one of the seventy languages is forbidden. However, this is not necessarily a given because some leading authorities rule that

720 *Naftali Seva Ratzon* (Fürth, 1705), pgs. 2a–2b.

721 TB *Sotah* 35b.

722 See *Deuteronomy* 27:1–28.

the prohibition of erasing God's name only applies to His name as written in *Lashon HaKodesh*.[723] According to those authorities, the proof that Rabbi Sirkis offered to his case is moot because it was predicated on the assumption that the seventy languages include *Lashon HaKodesh*.

However, afterwards Rabbi Sikris mentions the opinion of Maharsha who wrote that *Lashon HaKodesh* is not included in the seventy languages. According to him, there is nothing wrong with Rabbi Yehuda saying that they first wrote the Torah in seventy languages and then plastered it because there is no issue of erasing the name of God because those seventy languages exclude *Lashon HaKodesh*. If so, then there is no proof as to the law in the case of wax on a Torah Scroll from the case of the boulders, and it is possible that coating letters with plaster or wax is, in fact, considered erasing those letters.[724] Thus, the issue of whether or not *Lashon HaKodesh* is included in the seventy languages may create a difference in the law of wax that falls on words of a Torah Scroll.[725]

ADDITIONS TO BIOGRAPHICAL INDEX

Rabbi Akiva Eiger (1761–1837)

Renowned for his intellectual prowess in Talmudic analysis, he is celebrated as the paragon of in-depth study. He authored many works, including *Tosafos Rabbi Akiva* to the Mishnah, volumes of responsa, and novella and glosses to the Talmud and Shulchan Aruch. He was the Rabbi of Posen in Prussia, and was instrumental in Orthodoxy's early fights against reformists. He was also the father-in-law of his slightly younger contemporary, Rabbi Moshe Sofer.

---

723 See *Sifsei Kohen* to *Shulchan Aruch, Yoreh Deah* §179:11. Cf. *Magen Avraham* (*Orach Chaim*, §334:17).

724 *Livyas Chein* (*Parshas Ki Savo*), quoted by Rabbi Akiva Eiger in his responsa, *Tinyana* §15.

725 However, see *Targum Jonathan* (to *Deuteronomy* 27:8) who writes that the boulders had the *Lashon HaKodesh* text of the Torah, which was then translated into seventy languages. He clearly understood that *Lashon HaKodesh* is not included in the seventy languages, yet also explains that the boulders had the Torah written upon them in *Lashon HaKodesh*. According to *Targum Jonathan*, one sees from Rabbi Yehuda that coating with plaster/wax is not considered erasing; even without assuming that *Lashon HaKodesh* is one of the seventy languages. See also responsa *Dovev Meisharim* (vol. 1, §114) by Rabbi Dov Ber Wiedenfeld (1881–1965).

Rabbi Akiva Yosef Schlesinger (1837–1922)

He was a Hungarian scholar whose father was a student of Rabbi Moshe Sofer, and who himself studied under Rabbi Sofer's son. Although he authored many works and responsa, his most famous work is *Lev HaIvri*, a commentary to Rabbi Moshe Sofer's ethical will. He later relocated to Jerusalem, where he was an important community leader.

Rabbi David Baharan (1866–1946)

He was a great-grandson of Rabbi Hillel Rivlin (the founder of the non-Hassidic Ashkenaz community in Jerusalem). He was born and raised in Jerusalem, where he later served as a rabbi. He studied under many of the leading scholars in Jerusalem, and married the daughter of Rabbi Akiva Yosef Schlesinger. He reputedly studied Torah daily from midnight until the next day's night prayers, and is famous for being pious in his actions and meticulous in his observance.

Rabbi David Cohen

Rabbi Cohen is the Rav of Gvul Yaabetz in Brooklyn, NY. He authored over fifty works on various topics, and continues to spread Torah.

Rabbi David Goldberg

Rabbi Aharon David Goldberg is one of the Roshei Yeshiva of Yeshivas Telz in Clevland, OH; and the son-in-law of the late Rabbi Aizik Ausband. He authored several volumes of *Avodas David* to the Talmud, and *Shiras David* to the Siddur and Pentateuch; as well as commentaries to classic works of Mussar.

Rabbi Nosson Nata Shapira (1490–1577)

He was the chief rabbi at Horodna, Poland. He authored several works including *Mevo Shearim* (a commentary to *Sha'arei Dura*), *Imrei Shefer* (a supercommentary to Rashi on the Pentateuch), and *Chiddushei Maharan Shapira* on the Tur (and possibly Alfasi). He also served as the namesake for his more well-known grandson, Rabbi Nosson Nata Shapira (1584–1633), author of *Megaleh Amukos*.

Rabbi Kalonymus Kalman Epstein of Krakow (1751–1823)

He was one of the most important Hassidic masters, and is celebrated as a foremost student of Rabbi Elimelech Weissbloom of Lezhensk (known by the title of his work Noam Elimelech). The latter sent him to preach in Krakow, despite the strong opposition to Chassidus in that city. His teachings and writings were published posthumously under the title *Maor VaShomesh*.

Rabbi Shalom Shabazi (1619–1720)

He was a Yemenite scholar and poet. His most famous work is *Chemdas Yamim*, a commentary to the Pentateuch. This impressive work—which draws from hundreds of earlier Kabbalistic, Midrashic, and textual commentaries to the Pentateuch—was completed before he reached the age of thirty. In addition to his poems and his Pentateuchal commentary, he also authored a treatise on astrology.

Rabbi Shlomo Zalman of Liadi (1745–1812)

He was the founding Rebbe of the Chabad/Lubavitch Chassidus. He is known by his initials as the *Graz*; or as the *Baal HaTanya* after his masterpiece work of Hassidic philosophy. Additionally, he wrote an important halachik work entitled *Shulchan Aruch HaRav*; as well as his own edition of the siddur, according to the rite of Rabbi Yitzchak Luria.

Rabbi Shmuel Bornstein (1855–1926)

Known as the Sochatchover Rebbe, he was the son of Rabbi Avraham Bornstein (author of *Avnei Nezer*) and grandson of the Kotzker Rebbe. His work *Shem M'Shmuel* on the Pentateuch and festivals is a masterpiece of Hassidic thought and interpretation. He is revered by Hassidim and non-Hassidim alike.

Rabbi Tzvi Elimelech Shapira of Dinov (1783–1841)

He was a renowned Hassidic master, Kabbalist, and Talmudist who served as the Rabbi of several communities (notably Dinov in Galicia and Munkatch in Hungary). He is most famous for his work *Bnei Yissaschar* (sermons arranged calendrically); but he also authored *Igra D'Kallah* (a commentary to the Pentateuch) and tens of other works on the Pentateuch, Talmud, Zohar, and more. He was a great-nephew and student of his namesake Rabbi Elimelech of Lezhensk (1717–1787).

Rabbi Yaakov Solnik (16th century)

He was the chief rabbi of the Polish city Pidhaitsi. He is known for his work *Nachlas Yaakov*, a supercommentary to Rashi's commentary on the Pentateuch. His father, Rabbi Binyamin Aharon Solnik (1550–1619), author of responsa *Masas Binyamin*, was a student of the leading scholars of his time including Rabbi Moshe Isserles, Rabbi Shlomo Luria (1510–1574), and Rabbi Nosson Nata Shapira.

Rabbi Yaakov Lorberbaum of Lissa (1760–1832)

Known as the *Nesivos* after his major work *Nesivos HaMishpat* (to *Shulchan Aruch, Choshen Mishpat*), he was an important halachik decider and commentator. He served as the Chief Rabbi of Lissa in Poland, and worked tirelessly with his two contemporaries, Rabbi Akiva Eiger and Rabbi Moshe Sofer in battling the efforts of the Maskillim. He wrote many important works, including *Chavos Da'as* (to *Shulchan Aruch, Yoreh Deah*), *Mekor Chaim* (on the laws of Passover), other halachik works, and commentaries on the Talmud and Bible.

Rabbi Yechiel Michel Stern

He is the chief rabbi of the Ezras Torah neighborhood in Jerusalem, and has authored close to 100 Torah works, including the multi-volume *Otzar HaYideos*. He is the son of the American-born mashgiach of Kaminetz Yeshiva, Rabbi Moshe Aharon Stern (1926–1998).

Rabbi Yehuda Leib Sirkis (1652–1733)

He was a great-grandson of Rabbi Yoel Sirkis (known as *Bach* after his work *Bais Chadash* to the Tur), and served as the Rabbi of the Polish town Sokal. He published his work *Livyas Chein*—detailed expositions related to the weekly parasha—along with his son's work *Ohr Yekaros* on the parasha. Rabbi Akiva Eiger admired his work and frequently referred to it.

Rabbi Yekusiel Yehuda Halberstam (1905–1994)

As a scion of the esteemed Halberstam Hassidic dynasty, he served as the Rabbi of the Transylvanian capital, Klausenberg, from the age of twenty-two. He miraculously withstood the trials of the Holocaust, and eventually re-established his Hassidic community in Union City, NJ and in Kiryat Sanz in Netanya. He authored several volumes of responsa under the title *Divrei Yatziv*, and homilies under the title *Shefa Chaim*.

Rabbi Yisroel of Shklov (1770–1839)

He was a student of Rabbi Eliyahu Kramer of Vilna, and even edited and published the latter's *Biur HaGra* to *Shulchan Aruch, Orach Chaim*. He was instrumental in leading the group of Rabbi Kramer's students to the Holy Land; and authored the work *Pe'as HaShulchan* to better clarify the halachos associated with agriculture in the Holy Land. He is best known for his work *Taklin Chaditin*, a commentary to tractate *Shekalim* of the Jerusalem Talmud.

Rabbi Yitzchak Meir Alter of Gur (1798–1866)

Known as the *Chiddushei HaRim*, he lived in Poland and was the first Gerrer Rebbe. He was well versed in Talmudic studies, and authored both halachik and Talmudic works under the title *Chiddushei HaRim*. Roughly a century after his death, his Hassidic-style discourses on the Pentateuch were compiled and also printed under that name.

We would like to thank the following people for their contributions in helping finance this book. Without the efforts of these individuals and their families, the publication of this book would not be possible.

Patrons

Anonymous

Mr. & Mrs. David Ash

Mr. & Mrs. Michael Klein

Mr. & Mrs. Max Steg

Mr. & Mrs. Sol Teichman

Mr. & Mrs. Barry Weiss

Benefactors

Dr. & Mrs. David Boxstein

Dr. & Mrs. Martin Kay

Mr. Avi Klein

Mr. & Mrs. Yossi Klein

Mr. & Mrs. Yosef Y. Manela

Mr. & Mrs. Frank Menlo

Mr. & Mrs. Shlomo Yehuda Rechnitz

Donors

Altberg Family

Mr. Leslie Barany

Mrs. Pearl Barany

Mr. Joel Berman

Mr. & Mrs. Leslie Blau

Rabbi & Mrs. Zvi Block

Mr. Gerald Blume

Mr. & Mrs. Steve Darrison

Rabbi & Mrs. Dovid Edelstein

Rabbi & Mrs. Aharon Dov Friedman

Mr. & Mrs. Eli Gabay

Rabbi & Mrs. Doron Jacobius

Rabbi & Mrs. Avrohom Low

Mr. & Mrs. Rob Kershberg (לע"נ בתי' בת יוסף)

In memory of Ozer & Chaya Klara Kesel and Yehudit Kesel

Mrs. Rozsi Klein

Mr. Yerucham Shimon Klein

Rabbi & Mrs. Yanky Lunger

Mr. & Mrs. Steve Mazlin

Ms. Tova (Frances) Quintanilla

Dr. & Mrs. Paul Rabin

Mr. & Mrs. Shlomo Rackliff

Mr. & Mrs. Adam Rich

Mrs. Shoshana Rosenblatt

Mr. Ralph Rubenstein

Mr. Howard Schreiman

Dr. & Mrs. David Stoll

Mr. & Mrs. Beni Warshawsky

Supporters

Mr. & Mrs. Daniel Bayar

Mrs. Judy Bayar

Mr. & Mrs. Lazar Berger

Mr. & Mrs. Moshe Chopp

Mr. & Mrs. Brian Dror

Mr. & Mrs. Josh Goodman

Mr. & Mrs. Ron Heckman

Mr. & Mrs. Yisroel Hertz

Mr. & Mrs. Lionell Levy

Mr. & Mrs. Yisrael Mehdizadeh

Mr. & Mrs. Greg Meyer

Mr. Josh Okhovat

Mr. Yehoshua Siskin

Dr. & Mrs. Jeff Ungar

We thank them for their generosity and pray that HaShem will grant them the ability to continue contributing to the dissemination and support of Torah throughout the world for many years to come.

ABOUT THE AUTHOR

Rabbi Reuven Chaim Klein is a native of Valley Village, CA. He graduated Emek Hebrew Academy and Yeshiva Gedolah of Los Angeles before going to study at the famed Mir Yeshiva in Jerusalem and in Beth Medrash Govoha of America in Lakewood, NJ. He received rabbinic ordination from some of the leading authorities in Jerusalem, including Rabbi Moshe Sternbuch, Rabbi Zalman Nechemiah Goldberg, and Rabbi Yosef Yitzchak Lerner.

His writings have been published in several prestigious journals, including *Jewish Bible Quarterly* (Jerusalem), *Kovetz Hamaor* (New York), *Kovetz Kol HaTorah* (London), and *Kovetz Iyun HaParsha* (Jerusalem) among others.

He is currently a fellow at the Kollel of Yeshivas Mir in Jerusalem and lives with his wife and children in Beitar Illit, Israel.

The author can be reached via email at: historyofhebrew@gmail.com

ABOUT MOSAICA PRESS

Mosaica Press is an independent publisher of Jewish books. Our authors include some of the most profound, interesting, and entertaining thinkers and writers in the Jewish community today. There is a great demand for high-quality Jewish works dealing with issues of the day — and Mosaica Press is helping fill that need. Our books are available around the world. Please visit us at www.mosaicapress.com or contact us at info@mosaicapress.com. We will be glad to hear from you.

MOSAICA PRESS